WILLIAM MORRIS'S UTOPIA OF STRANGERS

VICTORIAN MEDIEVALISM
AND THE IDEAL OF HOSPITALITY

It is commonly claimed that William Morris's notion of the good or ideal society is uniquely tolerant. This book asks whether Victorian medievalism offered Morris the resources to develop an alternative conception based around the nineteenth-century preoccupation with the idea of welcome and the complex significance of hospitality. A range of artistic and intellectual contexts is surveyed, from early Victorian paternalism and neo-feudalism to socialism and the Arts and Crafts Movement, taking in fields as diverse as literature, architecture, anthropology, political theory, law, art history and translation. Together with an examination of the sources and legacy of Morris's work, the book offers a detailed analysis of his various projects.

Dr MARCUS WAITHE lectures in Victorian Literature at the University of Sheffield.

ENGLISH ASSOCIATION STUDIES

ISSN 1750–3892

Series Editor
Norman Vance

The English Association was founded in 1906 to further knowledge, understanding and enjoyment of the English language and its literatures. English Association Studies, inaugurated to mark the centenary, seeks to advance these aims by publishing distinctive original research in the various areas and periods of English studies.

Proposals for the series are welcomed, and should be sent in the first instance to the Chief Executive of the Association, the series editor, or the publisher, at the addresses below.

Helen Lucas, The English Association, University of Leicester, Leicester LE1 7RH

Professor Norman Vance, Department of English, University of Sussex, Brighton BN1 9QN

Boydell & Brewer Limited, PO Box 9, Woodbridge, Suffolk, IP12 3DF

WILLIAM MORRIS'S
UTOPIA OF STRANGERS

VICTORIAN MEDIEVALISM
AND THE IDEAL OF HOSPITALITY

Marcus Waithe

D. S. BREWER

First published 2006
D. S. Brewer, Cambridge

ISBN 1 84384 088 X

D. S. Brewer is an imprint of Boydell & Brewer Ltd
PO Box 9, Woodbridge, Suffolk IP12 3DF, UK
and of Boydell & Brewer Inc,
668 Mt Hope Avenue, Rochester, NY 14620, USA
website: www.boydellandbrewer.com

A CIP catalogue record for this book is available
from the British Library

This publication is printed on acid-free paper

Printed in Great Britain by
MPG Books Ltd, Bodmin, Cornwall

CONTENTS

ILLUSTRATIONS

The author and publishers are grateful to the institutions mentioned above for
permission to reproduce these images. Every effort has been made to trace the
copyright holders; apologies are offered for any omission in this regard, and the
publishers will be pleased to add any necessary acknowledgement in subsequent
editions.

ACKNOWLEDGEMENTS

I wish to acknowledge the moral support, professional advice and careful scrutiny of those who have read and discussed my work over the last five years. Particular thanks are due to Clive Wilmer, Tony Pinkney, Stefan Collini, Georgina Evans, Jane Partner, Michael Hurley, John Batchelor and Norman Vance, all of whom have seen and commented on this project at various stages of development.

Thanks are also due to those friends in Leigh-on-Sea, Leeds, Cambridge, London, and now Sheffield, who have offered companionship and support during the writing of this book.

I am especially grateful to my parents for their unfailing generosity and support.

Notes

All Bible quotations are taken from The Holy Bible, King James Version (Cambridge: Cambridge University Press, [n.d.]).

INTRODUCTION

The manner in which a household receives its guests – the unexpected as well as the expected – can tell us a great deal. Most obviously, it reveals the extent to which the community in question measures up to certain culturally-prescribed standards. It also demonstrates something more fundamental. Policies governing the reception of outsiders tend to reflect social needs. They indicate, in particular, the degree to which one feels obliged to maintain relations with the outside world. A generous display of hospitality may express many things. Kindness, munificence, indebtedness, and ambition are all associated qualities; but at its most basic level, an emphasis on the reception of strangers implies recognition of, and interest in, an extramural realm.

A rude, ungenerous, reception usually indicates contrary impulses. It might suggest proud independence, a rejection of what is unknown and unnecessary. Yet such behaviour is not merely expressive of contempt for what seems alien. Nor is it sufficient simply to blame malice or bad breeding. Such a response may actually reflect a neutral perception that solutions to internal problems are not to be found in other places. This need not indicate greater devotion to the cause of self-interest. That, after all, could be furthered through commerce with strangers. The question is not, then, one of *bad* manners, but of an alternative set of manners, manners orientated towards a different social policy.

The same distinction between outward- and inward-looking societies may be applied to the analysis of utopias. Whimsical fictions, political manifestos, and materially realized communities, are all amenable to these categories. In the Western tradition, states that place a premium on isolation and inwardness are often said to be founded upon the Spartan model of social arrest described first by Plutarch,[1] and later adapted by Plato.[2] Equating perfection with stasis, and movement with decadence, such societies seek to police their borders. They are suspicious of strangers. As emissaries of the unknown, strangers disrupt settled social structures. They foment change. The stranger who arrives at the gates of utopia is seen as posing a threat to the harmony achieved therein.

The most prominent attack on this tradition was launched by Karl Popper in the 1940s.[3] His influential book, *The Open Society and its Enemies*, risks exaggeration in seeking to present Plato, and 'utopianism' generally, as straightforward precursors to fascism. But Popper was right in certain respects. His work remains valuable today because it identifies a tendency among the vast majority of architectural, conjectural, and literary utopias to favour an ideal condition of stasis.

---

1   'Lycurgus', in Plutarch, *Plutarch's Lives*, trans. by Bernadotte Perrin, 11 vols (London: William Heinemann, 1959), I, pp. 204–303.
2   Plato, *The Republic*, trans. by Paul Shorey, 2 vols (London: William Heinemann, 1963).
3   K. R. Popper, *The Open Society and its Enemies*, 2 vols (London: Routledge, 1945).

This condition, he observes, implies successful exclusion of the outside world and all its miserable contents. Few Western utopias operate entirely beyond this tradition. From Thomas More,[4] to Henry Thoreau,[5] to Edward Bellamy,[6] the common inheritance has been decidedly classical. The emphasis has fallen on perfectionism, on order, on social unity and splendid isolation.

It is especially interesting, in the light of this observation, to consider apparent exceptions to the rule. Many surveys of utopianism have sought to identify William Morris's *News from Nowhere* (1890) as a clear and unmistakable departure from the logic of the closed society; one, moreover, that was conceived long before 'Socialism in One Country' and Nazism succeeded in discrediting totalitarian and autarkical regimes as humane paths to happiness.[7] Through the eyes of his fictional visitor, William Guest, Morris describes a London of the future. Some familiar landmarks remain, among them the Palace of Westminster and the National Gallery; but in most respects London has been transformed beyond all recognition. Historical forces, in combination with a native love of beauty, have turned Nowhere into something resembling an earthly paradise.[8] This study is not concerned exclusively with the reception of Morris's utopian vision. In accounting for the political and social significance of Victorian medievalism, it is necessary to survey a wider perspective. However there is much to be gained, as will become clear, from treating Morris as a central exemplar. Historically and professionally expansive in scope, his legacy provides the scholar with an opportunity to analyse the particular without losing conceptual or historical breadth.

Contributing to a collection of essays, published to commemorate the centenary year of Morris's death, Ady Mineo offers a typical formulation of the view that Morris's ideal world is in some way unique: 'by comparison with the classic utopias', it is argued, '*News from Nowhere* is a constructive utopia where change and growth are paramount in the narrative strategies of the text'.[9] Krishan Kumar, one of Britain's foremost historians of utopian thought, grounds remarks made in 1993 on a similar acceptance of Morris's special place in history. Reflecting on the 'ferment of change in Eastern Europe', and on the collapse of confidence in 'the whole concept of socialism and, with it, of utopia', he suggests that 'it may well be [. . .] a socialist utopia like Morris's that can restore some faith in the great utopia of modern times'.[10] Many other critics have endorsed this emphasis on Nowhere's openness. Stephen Coleman, for instance, argues that Morris's 'affirmation of the freedom of individuals to think or behave differently from those around them places Nowhere in a tradition of libertarianism from which most utopias must be

4   Thomas More, *Utopia* in *The Yale Edition of the Complete Works of St Thomas More*, ed. by Edward Surtz and J. H. Hexter, 14 vols (New Haven: Yale University Press, 1965), IV.

5   Henry David Thoreau, *Walden: or Life in the Woods* (Boston, Mass.: Ticknor and Fields, 1854).

6   Edward Bellamy, *Looking Backward 2000 to 1887* (Boston, Mass.: Ticknor & Company, 1888).

7   William Morris, *News from Nowhere*, in *The Collected Works of William Morris*, ed. by May Morris, 24 vols (London: Longmans Green and Company, 1910–15), XVI, pp. 1–211.

8   'Nowhere' henceforth designates the utopian world depicted in *News from Nowhere*.

9   Ady Mineo, 'Beyond the Law of the Father: The "New Woman" in *News from Nowhere*', in *William Morris: Centenary Essays*, ed. by Peter Faulkner and Peter Preston (Exeter: University of Exeter Press, 1999), pp. 200–6 (p. 200).

10   Krishan Kumar, 'News from Nowhere: The Renewal of Utopia', *History of Political Thought*, XIV (Spring, 1993), 1, 133–43 (p. 143).

excluded'.[11] Distancing Morris's vision from fascist and Stalinist totalitarianism, and from the dystopian logic of Orwell,[12] Huxley[13] and Zamyatin,[14] he approves Morris's attempt to depict a community of 'free, friendly, non-aggressive beings' who are yet 'unmistakably human'.[15] Norman Kelvin suggests, in a similar spirit, that 'Morris's will is aimed at imagining small social groups living in implausible harmony internally and with each other but with no external control'.[16]

It would be inaccurate to assert that Morris was uninfluenced by the Platonic tradition, or that he was individually responsible for redeeming the utopian form. He was not the first to combine political dreaming with open-endedness, the indeterminate and the ludic. After all, a similar spirit of playfulness pervades the otherwise orderly *Utopia* of Thomas More. In More's work, narrative authority is similarly removed from the authorial voice, and it is not clear how seriously one is supposed to take the social arrangements described. Yet the arguments set out in the preceding paragraph are not entirely unreasonable. In being only 'some chapters from a Utopian romance', *News from Nowhere* is hybrid in form and modest in scope. It invites participation, and frustrates formal closure, in such a way as to leave its readers considerable interpretative leeway. The work's *dramatis personae* include 'grumblers' and 'obstinate refusers'. These characters are allowed to articulate dissent. They express powerful arguments that run counter to communal objectives, whilst enjoying the cheerful tolerance of contented neighbours. The book even contains an account of a murder, committed in unfortunate and impassioned circumstances. Thus it is not hard to build a case for Morris having achieved something different, something peculiar. His contribution to utopian literature is distinguished by an apparent willingness to entertain conflict. He allows the imperfect to intrude upon and unsettle the perfect with startling regularity. He demonstrates an unflagging taste for the disruptive, a consistent unwillingness, in the words of C. S. Lewis, to institute 'world-without-end fidelities'.[17]

Assuming that this exceptionist account of Morris's contribution is partially justified, it remains true that little effort has been made to account for his apparent departure from the tradition of the closed society. Critics have rarely investigated the intellectual influences Morris drew upon to achieve his 'tolerant' idealism. I aim to explore the development and character of Morris's 'utopia of strangers', to identify its roots and to determine the extent of its capacity for accommodating difference.[18] I shall do so, principally, by considering the importance of Morris's medievalism. Far from representing a quaint prelude to the mature political conviction of his socialist years, Morris's medievalism formed an

---

11 Stephen Coleman, 'How Matters are Managed: Human Nature and Nowhere', in *William Morris & News from Nowhere: A Vision for Our Time*, ed. by Stephen Coleman and Paddy O'Sullivan (Bideford, Devon: Green Books, 1990), pp. 75–89 (p. 88).

12 George Orwell, *Nineteen Eighty-Four* (London: Secker and Warburg, 1949).

13 Aldous Huxley, *Brave New World* (London: Chatto & Windus, 1932).

14 Yevgeny Zamyatin, *We*, trans. by Clarence Brown (Harmondsworth: Penguin Books, 1993).

15 Coleman, 'How Matters are Managed: Human Nature and Nowhere', p. 89.

16 Norman Kelvin, Introduction, *The Collected Letters of William Morris*, ed. by Norman Kelvin, 4 vols (Princeton: Princeton University Press, 1984–96), II, pp. xix–xxxiv (p. xxxii).

17 C. S. Lewis, 'William Morris', in *Rehabilitations and Other Essays* (Oxford: Oxford University Press, 1939), p. 42.

18 Here, and in my title, I borrow from Julia Kristeva's conceptualization of hospitality as 'l'utopie d'étrangers', in *Étrangers à nous-mêmes* (Paris: Gallimard, 1988), pp. 22–3.

integral part of his peculiar brand of socialism. As my title implies, this book grants special attention to one particular feature of this revivalism, namely Morris's enduring preoccupation with the archaic ideal of unconditional or idealized hospitality. The medieval practices of dispensing alms to the poor, of offering hospitality in the great hall and accommodating the leper in the lazar house, have received little attention from scholars examining the sources of Morris's political vision. And yet the inclusive social model such gestures evoke would seem an obvious inspiration for the apparent departure from vulgar perfectionism. One advantage of focusing on medievalist hospitality is that it elucidates the ethnological nature of the utopian encounter between *here* and *there*. It also supplies a useful means of bridging the gap between the largely historicist and biographical focus of Morris scholarship, and the more conceptual approach employed by critics working in the field of utopian studies.[19]

Studying the evolving representation of hospitality in Morris's writings has one further advantage. It steers attention towards an interior ideal of greater relevance to the early Morris than the classical utopia. Medievalism, far more than dreams of the ideal city, filled his thoughts in these years. As stated, it would be a misinterpretation to conclude that Morris's pattern of mind first became political on accepting socialism in 1883. In this respect, my approach encourages a movement away from the dichotomy suggested by E. P. Thompson's 'romantic to revolutionary' thesis.[20] The following investigation operates on the premise that it is not possible to explain the openness, the emphasis on growth, which critics like Coleman and Mineo praise, without giving serious attention to the debt Morris owed to medievalist predecessors like Cobbett and Ruskin, the non-Marxist sources of that concern with alienation which characterized his outlook long before he made an official commitment to socialism.

The scope of this book is not confined to the particulars of Morris's critical reception as a utopist. Identifying the importance of medievalist hospitality in the work of one Victorian artist, writer and thinker presents an obvious opportunity to consider the wider set of concerns and influences in which his work is enmeshed. Here one finds a similar and surprising lack of any comprehensive account. Since the early 1970s, successive critics have sought to describe and decode the Victorian ideology of domesticity. Beginning with such ground-breaking studies of etiquette as Leonore Davidoff's *The Best Circles*,[21] this interpretative project has since been extended through the work of Nancy Armstrong,[22] Mary Poovey,[23] Elizabeth Langland[24] and George K.

[19] Works employing this latter approach include: A. L. Morton, *The English Utopia* (London: Lawrence & Wishart, 1952); Marie Louise Berneri, *Journey through Utopia* (London: Freedom Press, 1982); Krishan Kumar, *Utopia and Anti-Utopia in Modern Times* (Oxford: Basil Blackwell, 1987); and Michael Wilding, *Political Fictions* (London: Routledge & Kegan Paul, 1980).

[20] E. P. Thompson, *William Morris: Romantic to Revolutionary*, 2nd edn (London: Merlin Press, 1976).

[21] Leonore Davidoff, *The Best Circles: Society Etiquette and the Season* (London: Croom Helm, 1973).

[22] Nancy Armstrong, *Desire and Domestic Fiction: A Political History of the Novel* (New York: Oxford University Press, 1987).

[23] Mary Poovey, *Uneven Developments: The Ideological Work of Gender in Mid-Victorian England* (London: Virago Press, 1989).

[24] Elizabeth Langland, *Nobody's Angels: Middle-Class Women and Domestic Ideology in Victorian Culture* (Ithaca: Cornell University Press, 1995).

Behlmer.[25] Their largely feminist accounts of the household realm have achieved a great deal in refining understanding of the public–private divide as it developed in nineteenth-century Britain. Despite the existence of so many thorough and insightful studies, certain important lines of inquiry remain unexplored. Most surprising is the absence of any sustained analysis of hospitality, both as a concept and as a Victorian ideal. With the notable exception of Peter Mandler, historians of the nineteenth-century household have made only limited reference to the construction of this important domestic virtue.[26]

It is also surprising that scholars of the Gothic Revival have not paid more attention to the movement's recurrent emphasis on the idea of welcome. The links between socialism and radicalized medievalism – of the kind pioneered first by William Cobbett, and then by Morris – are well documented. And it is not difficult to see how a preoccupation with sociability and social codes formed a bridge between these two positions. It is, then, hard to understand why no attempt has been made to explore or to account for the equalitarian strand emerging from the paternalism of antique hospitality. Critics and historians working in the field of utopian studies have been comparably slow in recognizing this Victorian enthusiasm as the possible germ of an alternative utopian tradition, one that seems to place a premium on openness, tolerance and pluralism. Understandably, Mandler's largely historicist approach finds little place for existing anthropological and philosophical statements on the subject.[27]

There are many reasons why one might want to qualify and complicate this basic linkage of personal and political tolerance with the ideal of a warm welcome. Hospitality does not dispense with the uneven power relations that separate hosts from guests: it merely softens and sublimates them. And it is no coincidence that formalistic and hierarchical societies are often those placing most emphasis on the value of hospitality. This admittedly important consideration does not disqualify the basic premise and investigative aim of this book. For it is precisely the *impractical*, indeed the *fanciful*, application of this theme in nineteenth-century literature, architecture and historiography that is to be explored. Morris's approach is particularly revealing. In the course of a long career, his invocation of hospitality was developed across different media, different artistic movements and different political loyalties. He represents the

---

25 George K. Behlmer, *Friends of the Family: The English House and Its Guardians, 1850–1940* (Stanford, California: Stanford University Press, 1998).

26 Peter Mandler, *The Fall and Rise of the Stately Home* (New Haven and London: Yale University Press, 1997).

27 Of these, the following deserve particular attention: Immanuel Kant's advocacy of cosmopolitanism (an extramural and universal right to hospitality) in *Perpetual Peace*, trans. by Helen O'Brien (London: Sweet & Maxwell, 1927); Julian Pitt-Rivers's identification of the stranger as a figure whose innate hostility is laid in abeyance, rather than extinguished, during the hospitality ritual: see Julian Pitt-Rivers, 'The Stranger, the Guest and the Hostile Host. Introduction to the Study of the Laws of Hospitality', in *Contributions to Mediterranean Sociology: Mediterranean Rural Communities and Social Change*, ed. by J. G. Peristiany (Paris: Mouton & Co., 1968), pp. 13–30 (p. 18); and Jacques Derrida's work on the antinomy of hospitality, the conflict between hospitality's operation as an informal code, and the accompanying requirement that law be dispensed with, that the guest be offered the freedom of the house: see Jacques Derrida and Anne Dufourmantelle, *Of Hospitality*, trans. by Rachel Bowlby (Stanford: Stanford University Press, 2002).

bridge between an earlier medievalism – with roots variously in Romantic radicalism, Tory Radicalism and Gothicism – and that later preference for vernacular forms favoured by more pragmatic medievalists. Of this last group, the Arts and Crafts pioneers, the planners of garden suburbs, and Back-to-the-Land campaigners are among the most notable.

My first chapter explores the ideal of unconditional hospitality in the literature and culture of nineteenth-century medievalism. Commencing with an account of biblical, Homeric and medieval hospitality, it examines the roots of the Romantic and Victorian fascination with the idea of welcome. This involves a careful effort to distinguish the different political and religious agendas motivating allusion to the 'laws of hospitality', or 'old English hospitality'. Although the chapter includes reference to a wide range of writers and artists, from William Dyce, to Thomas Carlyle, to Benjamin Disraeli, my treatment consists of three discrete sections. The first examines sceptical representations of hospitality with particular reference to the social order; the second investigates the lament for 'old English hospitality' expressed in the works of William Cobbett and A. W. Pugin; and the final section concentrates on John Ruskin's vision of the perfect village inn, a commodious and welcoming institution unpolluted by the monetary or managerial excesses of the Victorian hospitality industry.

Morris confronted a basic conflict between the available artistic responses to alienation in the 1860s and 1870s. In these years, his work stages a dialogue between escapism or separatism and a form of communality that both pre-dates and anticipates his conversion to Marxian socialism. I argue in Chapter 2 that this openness is partly expressed through commitment to the principle of unconditional, or idealized, hospitality. The aim is to determine whether a preoccupation with the theme of welcome, as it emerges in the design of Philip Webb's Red House, in the activities of Morris, Marshall, Faulkner & Company, and in the poems of *The Earthly Paradise* (1868–70), countered Morris's early drift towards isolationism; or whether, in fact, the attempt to install a vision of wanderers and pilgrims in place of the commercial world was itself an inward-looking gesture.

Chapter 3 explores Morris's activities in the ostensibly dissimilar areas of travel, translation and architectural preservation. These ventures exhibit in common several core preoccupations, and they facilitate Morris's encounters with a variety of imagined pasts. They provide him with opportunities to stage an escape from his own culture, to play the role of the stranger in utopia. The chapter is concerned, accordingly, with attempts to 'visit' difference. It also examines the problems that arise when, in a general sense, he attempts to *translate* these emblems of alternative society, to make them useful and accessible to his own culture. The chapter considers two kinds of utopia, then: a medieval or heroic past, which serves as a source of instructive contrast; and a reformed, hospitable present capable of tolerating in its midst such buildings, texts and places as testify to alternative ways of life. As before, the questions addressed relate to the difficulty of achieving a redemptive openness. My estimation of Morris's achievement in pursuing this elusive condition will depend, therefore, upon his success in 'entertaining' or 'translating' what is past, what is foreign.

In the last two decades of his life, Morris returned to writing prose fiction. His work from this period can be divided into three categories: the first containing the

Teutonic romances, *The House of the Wolfings* (1888)[28] and *The Roots of the Mountains* (1889);[29] the second, his political romances (of which *News from Nowhere* and *A Dream of John Ball* (1886–87) are examples);[30] and the third, those works published during the 1890s that seem to be pure fantasy (for example, *The Well at the World's End* (1896)).[31] My fourth chapter engages primarily with Morris's portrayal of inclusive societies in the first two categories of prose romance. Referring in detail to contemporary historiographic accounts of primitive German societies, the first section explores Morris's fictional evocation of communistic households. It addresses the central paradox that hospitality is portrayed at once as the defining virtue of these societies, and as the root of their decline. The second section investigates a similar idea, this time as it concerns Morris's treatment of a different communal institution, the medieval guild. The final section examines Morris's formal utopia, *News from Nowhere*. It sets critical assertions of Morris's pluralism in the context of the collapse of Soviet communism, of the subsequent history of utopian studies, and of Marcel Mauss's theory of generosity and the gift.[32]

My final chapter investigates the legacy of Morris's 'hospitable socialism', and gauges its success in offering an alternative resource for utopists wishing to draw on a tolerant or open tradition of the ideal society. It begins by considering the influence of *News from Nowhere*'s hospitable utopianism on H. G. Wells's *A Modern Utopia*, as well as upon other utopists writing at the end of the nineteenth century and the beginning of the twentieth.[33] The second section assesses the influence of the medievalist veneration of hospitality on the architecture and planning of English Garden Suburbs and Garden Cities. The book concludes with a discussion of the extent to which the medievalist ideal of unconditional hospitality, and the Morrisian interpretation of it, offered an alternative to the values of control, enclosure and exclusivity associated with the classical utopia, and with modern totalitarian thought.

28 Morris, *A Tale of the House of the Wolfings and All the Kindreds of the Mark*, in *Collected Works*, XIV, pp. 1–208.
29 Morris, *The Roots of the Mountains*, in *Collected Works*, XV.
30 Morris, *A Dream of John Ball*, in *Collected Works*, XVI, pp. 215–88.
31 Morris, *The Well at the World's End*, in *Collected Works*, XVII–XIX.
32 Marcel Mauss, *The Gift*, trans. by W. D. Halls (London: Routledge, 1990).
33 H. G. Wells, *A Modern Utopia* (London: Chapman & Hall, 1905).

Chapter 1

WANDERERS ENTERTAINED:
IDEALIZED HOSPITALITY IN THE LITERATURE
OF NINETEENTH-CENTURY MEDIEVALISM

Introduction

In the summer of 1849, the Royal Commission supervising the decoration of the new Palace of Westminster rejected a preliminary design for the central compartment of the Queen's Robing Room. The work in question was entitled *Piety: The Departure of the Knights of the Round Table on the Quest for the Holy Grail.* It has been argued by Joanna Banham and Jennifer Harris that this subject was not considered suitable for the adornment of a legislative building.[1] 'The incident', they suggest, 'appeared too pessimistic and demoralising' (p. 156); indeed 'its attention to Queen Guinevere, whose infidelity opened the way to corruption in the court' made it 'doubly inappropriate'. William Dyce, the author of the rejected design, responded to this rebuff by completing a new painting. This time, he offered a subject calculated both to satisfy the original remit – to produce a general depiction of Arthur and his knights – and the need to supply a more convincing symbol of good government. The accepted replacement was entitled *Hospitality: The Admission of Sir Tristram to the Fellowship of the Round Table* (begun c. 1848; incomplete in 1864). Ostensibly, this represented a less troubling subject. Standing on a raised platform, at the end of a crowded hall, King Arthur confers the privileges of his order on an honoured guest. A display of social unity and benevolent rule is thus combined with a solemn recognition of individual merit. Yet as a eulogy to the social benefits of hospitality, it could itself be regarded as an unfortunate choice. Tristram, after all, was an adulterer, a knight whose pursuit of love had once before brought him into conflict with royal authority.

The performance of hospitality was seen by many Victorians as suggestive of *order*, a notion convenient in its concise evocation of prudent and benevolent government, whether of a household or a realm. On a wider historical level, hospitality frequently commands a different resonance. This is especially so where pre-Romantic literature is concerned. The tension between Arthur's act of integration, and the reputation of Malory's Tristram – a knight who has 'ado in many

[1] Joanna Banham and Jennifer Harris, eds, *William Morris and the Middle Ages: A Collection of Essays, Together with a Catalogue of Works Exhibited at the Whitworth Art Gallery, 28 September–8 December 1984* (Manchester: Manchester University Press, 1984), p. 156.

1

countries' – indicates that the admission of a guest is as likely to announce the unleashing of internal disorder as the domestication or taming of external forces.[2] Portrayals of guests as anarchic figures abound in Western literature. The most obvious site and source of this theme is the Trojan War, an event precipitated by that most famous infringement of the laws of hospitality, Paris's seduction and abduction of Helen, his host's wife. Sophocles' rendering of the Oedipus myth is also of pivotal importance.[3] His tragic hero is characterized as an eternal stranger: in him are embodied the two archetypal functions of the guest. He exhibits the potentially redemptive role of the stranger by answering the riddle of the Sphinx, but he also kills his father on the road to Thebes. In so doing, he demonstrates the disruptive, revolutionary, aspects of strangerhood.

Similar anxieties assume importance in the various theoretical analyses of hospitality devised more recently by anthropologists, literary critics and historians. The first phase of this discussion sketches the sceptical tradition upon which such work is based, and indicates what influence its literary manifestations had upon Morris and his predecessors. Although this inquiry illuminates similar preoccupations as they affect other Victorian representations of hospitality, its primary function is contrastive. To appreciate the distinctiveness of the comparatively optimistic, nineteenth-century treatments of hospitality that form the focus of Part II and Part III, one must first recognize the existence of a powerful counter-tradition, which associates hospitality not with resolution but with the entertainment of disruptive and disorderly forces.

The Stranger at the Gate: Hospitality and the Social Order in Western Literature and Culture

What, then, are the modern sources for this sceptical reading of relations between hosts and guests? Is it legitimate to speak of a literary tradition whose implied position is one of hostility towards outsiders? And if so, what influence has it had upon the apparently distinct, comparatively optimistic, approach of Victorian medievalism? These and related questions are addressed in what follows.

In the medieval tradition, the fabliau is the form best known for depicting the dangers associated with admitting strangers. Chaucer's 'The Miller's Tale'[4] and 'The Shipman's Tale'[5] both feature hosts who are cuckolded. 'The Reeve's Tale' is especially extreme in this respect. Its protagonist is a Miller who grants 'herberwe' to a pair of scholars he has cheated.[6] He wakes the next morning to discover they have taken revenge by sleeping with his wife and his daughter. The Cook, in the Prologue to his tale, extracts a moral from the story germane to these concerns:

---

[2] Thomas Malory, *Works*, ed. by Eugène Vinaver (London: Oxford University Press, 1971), X, 6, p. 352.

[3] Sophocles, *Oedipus the King*, in *Sophocles*, trans. by F. Storr, 2 vols (London: William Heinemann, 1962), I, pp. 1–139.

[4] Geoffrey Chaucer, 'The Miller's Tale', in *The Riverside Chaucer*, ed. by Larry D. Benson, 3rd edn (Oxford: Oxford University Press, 1987), pp. 68–77.

[5] Geoffrey Chaucer, 'The Shipman's Tale', in *The Riverside Chaucer*, pp. 203–8.

[6] Geoffrey Chaucer, 'The Reeve's Tale', in *The Riverside Chaucer*, pp. 78–84 (p. 81).

This millere hadde a sharp conclusion
Upon his argument of herbergage!
Wel seyde Salomon in his langage,
'Ne bryng nat every man into thyn hous,'
For herberwynge by nyghte is perilous.
Wel oghte a man avysed for to be
Whom that he broghte into his pryvetee.[7]

The Cook's recourse to biblical authority is indicative less of confidence in his assertions than of the need to justify an argument that runs so obviously counter to the word and spirit of Christian teaching. It is nevertheless apparent that he draws on a recognizable and established point of view: that hospitality is both perilous and a cause of grief to those who incautiously admit strangers.

The plays of Shakespeare also stand out as developed and nuanced studies on this theme. When Macbeth murders Duncan, he does not simply break the law or the bonds of loyalty that tie him to the monarch.[8] He also commits a grave offence against the laws of hospitality. In his capacity as a host, Macbeth should protect Duncan. He 'should against his murderer shut the door' (I.vii.15). Later in the play, the appearance of Banquo's spirit at the feast table serves as a literal reminder of the apparent etymological connection between the words, *guest* and *ghost*, of the danger that sanctioned outsiders may mutate to become intruders.[9] *King Lear* (1605–06) is also preoccupied with the usurpation of roles within a household.[10] Lear's mistake is to resign control of his kingdom in such a way as also to resign his role as host.[11] Goneril and Regan choose not to tolerate the pranks and clownish games of his retinue. The spirit of lordly entertainment is banished, and Lear, reduced from host to guest to outcast, is left to enact parodies of entertainment in the inhospitable eye of the storm. Of all Shakespeare's plays, *The Winter's Tale* (1610–11) is the most directly concerned with such issues.[12] It introduces the theme of sexual usurpation, and specifically adultery. When Leontes comes to suspect his Bohemian guest, Polixenes, of conducting an affair with his wife, he is driven mad by jealousy. He attempts to poison Polixenes, thus becoming a transgressive host at the thought of harbouring an ungrateful, deceitful guest. The work begins, however, with conspicuous play on another motif, relying upon the unstable distinction between hospitality and imprisonment. Hermione, anxious that Polixenes should not return to Bohemia prematurely, jests, 'Will you go yet?/ Force me to keep you as a prisoner' (I.ii.50–1). 'How say you?' (I.ii.53), she adds,

7 Geoffrey Chaucer, 'The Cook's Prologue', in *The Riverside Chaucer*, pp. 84–5 (p. 84).
8 William Shakespeare, *The Tragedy of Macbeth*, ed. by Nicholas Brooke (Oxford: Oxford University Press, 1990).
9 While their semantic kinship may be more fanciful than real, the *OED* shows that *guest* and *ghost* are derived, respectively, from *gast-s* (Goth.) and *gást* (OE).
10 William Shakespeare, *The Tragedy of King Lear*, ed. by Jay L. Halio (Cambridge: Cambridge University Press, 1992).
11 In *The Needs of Strangers* (London: Chatto & Windus, 1984), Michael Ignatieff offers a different, but nonetheless pertinent, perspective on the play. Noting that 'Lear learns too late that it is power and violence that rule the heath, not obligation' (p. 53), he argues that the play 'is a tragedy of need' (p. 50).
12 William Shakespeare, *The Winter's Tale*, ed. by Stephen Orgel (Oxford: Oxford University Press, 1996).

'My prisoner or my guest?' (I.ii.54). Polixenes replies, assuring her that he prefers the role of guest. Hermione concludes this passage of cheerful manipulation with the words, 'Not your jailer, then,/ But your kind hostess' (I.ii.58–9).

Alongside canonical evocations of this theme, one must consider more recent treatments. Two seminal medievalist works demand particular attention, Wolfgang von Goethe's history play, *Götz von Berlichingen* (1773),[13] and Walter Scott's popular novel, *Ivanhoe*.[14] These literary productions are to a certain extent distinct from the texts already discussed, in that they evoke both the tendencies identified thus far, the sceptical and the idealized. The ambivalence that sets Morris's own medievalism apart from that of his immediate predecessors may be traced to this combination of attitudes. On a general level, it announces the continued existence of a competing, sceptical, tradition within those founding texts of Victorian medievalism ordinarily associated with the romance of entertainment and welcome.

Goethe was responsible for the first and arguably most important Romantic exploration of hospitality. *Götz von Berlichingen* has been identified by Nick Shrimpton as an early example of 'a particular kind of medievalist literature', in which 'the competitive individualism of modern life' is 'disadvantageously compared with the hierarchical social system of the Middle Ages'.[15] The story concerns a German nobleman whose way of life seems tragically at odds with the tide of European history. As the play develops, he mounts a last stand against the forces of Renaissance legalism and centralization threatening his feudal liberties.[16] The action of the play begins when Götz captures and brings back to his castle an old enemy, named Weislingen. Instead of torturing or incarcerating Weislingen, Götz treats him as a guest: 'Come, sit down', he urges, 'think yourself at home! Consider you are once more the guest of Goetz'.[17] This policy of openness, however ill-advised, effects a change of heart in Weislingen. Encouraged at first merely to play the role of a friend, he eventually becomes one, led on to greater intimacy by the romantic allure of Götz's daughter. Weislingen responds as one would expect of any guest in utopia: he recognizes the superior attractions of his host's domain, and promptly changes his allegiance. Yet Weislingen's loyalties, both amorous and political, revert as soon as he is again exposed to the commercial and legal forces ascendant in the wider world. Götz's welcome, so effective in converting an enemy, in forging political and marital alliances in the feudal situation, is thereby invalidated. What was once a source of strength, a projection of *largesse* and hence power, is transformed into a point of weakness. In this way,

---

13 Johann Wolfgang von Goethe, *Götz von Berlichingen with the Iron Hand*, in *Goethe's Plays*, trans. by Charles E. Passage (London: Ernest Benn, 1980), pp. 89–218.

14 Walter Scott, *Ivanhoe*, 3 vols (Edinburgh: Archibald Constable and Co., 1820).

15 Nick Shrimpton, ' "Rust and Dust": Ruskin's Pivotal Work', in *New Approaches to Ruskin*, ed. by Robert Hewison (London: Routledge & Kegan Paul, 1981), pp. 51–67 (p. 52).

16 This account of Goethe's play builds on Clive Wilmer's unpublished lecture, 'Ruskin, Morris and Medievalism' (Mikimoto Memorial Ruskin Lecture, Lancaster University, 1996). Wilmer writes that 'one can see the seeds in it both of *Ivanhoe* and of subsequent versions of the legend of Robin Hood' (p. 20). He adds that it is also 'the picture of the Middle Ages that lies behind much of Morris's Socialist writing' (p. 20).

17 These lines are taken from Walter Scott's translation, *Goetz of Berlichingen, with the Iron Hand: A Tragedy* (London: J. Bell, 1799), p. 32.

Goethe associates feudalism with hospitality, with loyalty, and, ultimately, with a tragic vulnerability.

Walter Scott, who was responsible for the first English translation of Goethe's play, produced his own evocation of antique hospitality in *Ivanhoe*. Here the civilization under threat is not German feudalism, but rather the world of the Anglo-Saxon hall. It is primarily through a difference in attitudes towards entertainment that Scott distinguishes the increasingly second-class band of Saxons from their Norman rulers. This is nowhere more apparent than at the beginning of the novel, when two Norman nobles find themselves benighted in unfamiliar country. Caught in the open on a cold night, the men are left with no other option than to crave shelter at a Saxon hall. This unusual occurrence provides their host, Cedric of Rotherwood, with an opportunity to explain the laws of his house:

> Normans both; – but Norman or Saxon, the hospitality of Rotherwood must not be impeached; they are welcome, since they have chosen to halt – more welcome would they have been to have ridden further on their way – But it were unworthy to murmur for a night's lodging and a night's food; in the quality of guests at least, even Normans must suppress their insolence.[18]

As in *Götz von Berlichingen*, much emphasis is placed on the exemplary generosity of an offer to accommodate a sworn enemy, and, similarly, on the host's assumption (ill-advised, but ultimately rewarded) that hospitality will automatically inspire mannerly conduct in his guest. While *Ivanhoe*'s message with respect to the admission of guests is for the most part optimistic, Scott sometimes sounds a darker note. He, like Morris after him, was aware that vulnerability and the threat of extinction were intrinsically bound up with the forms of antique and archaic welcome he wished to celebrate. Cedric's generosity, this is to say, is presented as a laudable social instinct; but at the same time one sees it revealed as an outmoded and potentially self-defeating manoeuvre.

Having established the strength of this sceptical literary tradition, it is helpful to explore more recent analyses of the guest–host relationship. The most influential investigation of Western hospitality rituals is conducted by Julian Pitt-Rivers in his seminal article, 'The Stranger, the Guest and the Hostile Host. Introduction to the Study of the Laws of Hospitality' (1968).[19] Pitt-Rivers's central contention is that 'the stranger is always potentially hostile', a figure who 'derives his danger, like his sacredness, from his membership of the "extra-ordinary" world'. If his danger is to be avoided, he must 'be socialised': the stranger must become a guest. This 'implies a transformation from hostile stranger, *hostis*, into guest, *hospes* [. . .] from one whose hostile intentions are assumed to one whose hostility is laid in abeyance'. Traditional rituals of disarming, bathing, gift-exchange and feasting would serve within such a scheme of reception to neutralize the threat posed by an individual from beyond the social order. Pitt-Rivers suggests that, to fulfil his role, a guest 'must at least understand the conventions which relate to hospitality and which define the behaviour expected of him'. Hence 'the distinction which

18 Scott, *Ivanhoe*, I, p. 59.
19 Pitt-Rivers, 'The Stranger, the Guest and the Hostile Host', pp. 13–30.

the Greeks made between *Xenoi*, strangers who were nevertheless Greeks and *Barbaroi*, outlandish foreigners who spoke another language'.

Two main arguments emerge from Pitt-Rivers's article. First, hospitality constitutes a response to a hostile presence; and second, it imposes an informal code of conduct on host and guest alike:

> The law of hospitality is founded upon ambivalence. It imposes order through an appeal to the sacred, makes the unknown knowable, and replaces conflict by reciprocal honour. It does not eliminate the conflict altogether but places it in abeyance and prohibits its expression.

While Pitt-Rivers draws his conclusions from data collected in the field and from Harry L. Levy's 'The Odyssean Suitors and the Host-Guest Relationship', his references to the original ambivalence of the Latin root-word, *hostis*, indicate the partial dependence of his thesis on the history of the word's meaning, on the fact that, at different times, it has connoted both *guest* and *enemy*.[20] This willingness to discuss the relationship between hospitality and social forms in etymological terms is also a feature of Emile Benveniste's work. In his *Indo-European Language and Society* (1969; tr. 1973), Chapter Five ('The Slave and the Stranger') and Chapter Seven ('Hospitality') set out the complex history of the Latin words, *hostis* (meaning 'guest', then a 'stranger' enjoying equal rights as Roman citizens, then 'enemy'), *hospes* (meaning 'guest') and *potis* (from the Greek, *pótis* and *despótēs*, meaning the master or chief representative of a family). These terms were subsequently combined to form the English, *hospitality*. The Latin, *peregrinus* ('stranger'), the Greek, *xénos* ('guest', or friendly 'stranger') and the Gothic, *gasts* ('guests') are also analysed.[21] After some examination of Persian sources, Benveniste concludes that while 'far removed from one another', these words come back to the same problem: 'that of institutions of welcoming and reciprocity, thanks to which the men of a given people find hospitality in another, and whereby societies enter into alliances and exchanges'.

Matilda Tomaryn Bruckner's *Narrative Invention in Twelfth-Century French Romance: The Convention of Hospitality (1160–1200)* operates on a typological rather than a philological premise. She notes that hospitality, 'like the Gothic cathedral [. . .] has its repertoire of forms, its distinct parts forming a variety of patterns'.[22] She relates it to 'the highest virtues of courtly society [. . .] *corteisie* and *franchise*':

> as such it [hospitality] confers or confirms status, sorts out the deserving from the undeserving, opens or closes the door to adventure.

Particular attention should be paid to her assertion that 'in general, love has a more troubling effect on the development of Hospitality than Combat'. Of similar

---

[20] Harry L. Levy, 'The Odyssean Suitors and the Host-Guest Relationship', *Transactions and Proceedings of the American Philological Association*, 94 (1963), 145–53.

[21] Emile Benveniste, *Indo-European Language and Society*, trans. by Elizabeth Palmer (London: Faber and Faber, 1973), pp. 71, 83.

[22] Matilda Tomaryn Bruckner, *Narrative Invention in Twelfth-Century French Romance: The Convention of Hospitality (1160–1200)* (Lexington, Kentucky: French Forum Publishers, 1980), pp. 11–12, 117, 144, 154.

significance is her exploration of its equivocal social function: 'Hospitality', she states, 'often leads the way to battle or mops up the results'. This identification of hospitality with conflict *and* order is a familiar one, but Bruckner's designation of love as a related theatre of conflict, which disrupts rather than feeds the smooth performance of convention, is useful in so far as it introduces the theme of adultery, a subject that Tony Tanner explores comprehensively in his book, *Adultery in the Novel*.[23]

In his opening chapter, 'The Stranger in the House', Tanner draws on the insights of Pitt-Rivers, of Meyer Fortes (whose essay, 'Strangers' is heavily reliant on Pitt-Rivers's analysis)[24] and of Benveniste to produce a reading of the primary myths of adultery and disruption in the Western tradition. The abduction of Helen by Paris, the doomed marriage of Jason and Medea, the adulterous union of Tristram and Iseult, of Lancelot and Guinevere, and the plays by Shakespeare already mentioned, are all discussed in the light of his conviction that adultery signifies an archetypal violation of the laws of hospitality. Of particular interest is his reading of Malory's *Le Morte D'Arthur* (posth., 1485).[25] Starting from the premise that bonds of trust are the structural units that hold a feudal society together, he discusses adultery's *social* ramifications:

> The breaking of one bond (by adultery) portends the dissolution of all bonds. From then on, everything in Arthur's kingdom does, indeed, fall apart. Individual transgression leads ultimately to social disintegration.[26]

In common with other accounts, Tanner's analysis places considerable emphasis on the general instability threatened by seemingly limited domestic transactions.

By granting special attention to the significance of adultery in a medieval and Arthurian context, Tanner provides a convenient opportunity to move from sceptical theories of hospitality to an analysis of Morris's contribution. His treatment of adultery in *The Defence of Guenevere and Other Poems* (1858) (and, less overtly, in his easel painting, *La Belle Iseult* (1858)) has a clear bearing on these concerns.[27] It uncovers, at an early stage, a conflict at the heart of his medievalism, between respect for the law-governed, ordered society of Arthur's Round Table, and sympathy for those who inadvertently bring about its downfall. Any simple characterization of Morris's mature utopianism as 'tolerant' or 'open' is thereby challenged. In 'The Defence of Guenevere', the title-poem of this collection, the guest-stranger, the agent of adultery, assumes the role of a deliverer. Guenevere recalls how 'it chanced upon a day that Launcelot came/ To dwell at Arthur's

23   Tony Tanner, *Adultery in the Novel: Contract and Transgression* (Baltimore, Maryland: Johns Hopkins University Press, 1979).
24   Meyer Fortes, 'Strangers', in *Studies in African Social Anthropology*, ed. by Meyer Fortes and Sheila Patterson (London: Academic Press, 1975), pp. 226–53.
25   Malory, *Works*, X.
26   Tanner, *Adultery in the Novel*, p. 37.
27   Morris depicted unhappy love-triangles in *La Belle Iseult*, 1858–59 (oil on canvas, Tate Britain, London); and in his Oxford Union mural, *How Sir Palomydes Loved La Belle Iseult with Exceeding Great Love Out of Measure, and How She Loved Not Him Again but Rather Sir Tristram*, 1857 (tempera on whitewashed brick wall). Although his interest in the *necessarily* adulterous nature of 'courtly love' predated his marriage, Jane Morris's affair with Dante Gabriel Rossetti, and Morris's decision to tolerate it, become increasingly pertinent to evocations of this theme.

court'.[28] She describes the effect of his presence in a language that suggests the breaking of bonds: she is cut loose in 'a cool sea on a summer day'; she feels 'far off from any ships'. Guenevere, of course, is still technically guilty. The sympathetic platform provided for her 'defence' does not alter its wider, social significance. Her liaison with Arthur's most trusted knight is never dissociated in this work from the ensuing outbreak of civil disorder. What then distinguishes this handling of Guenevere and Launcelot's adulterous act from other contemporaneous treatments is not a lack of concern for the fact of betrayal, or for its harmful consequences. Morris's Arthur, like Tennyson's, could with some justice proclaim, 'my house hath been my doom';[29] and Launcelot, as characterized by Guenevere in 'King Arthur's Tomb' (she calls him a 'crooked sword'),[30] retains his Judas-like status as the knight at the table who betrays his lord. What sets Morris's version apart is the implicit suggestion that transgression, if not excusable, may at least be understood.

Morris continued to explore themes of usurpation and generosity betrayed in his unfinished cycle, *Scenes from the Fall of Troy*.[31] Particular emphasis is placed in this work on the domestic disorder that characterizes the war's causes and effects. At an important juncture, Priam defiantly describes the displacements of natural succession suffered by the Greek enemy at home and abroad:

> [. . .] their white wives left behind
> Are childless these nine years, or take new lords
> And bear another breed of hostile sons.
> The houses they all loved, far off in Greece,
> Are painted fresh by men they knew not of.

Morris's Talthybius reminds us that Priam's city is also sheltering a guest whose allegiances are uncertain: 'Yet deadly shall Queen Helen be to you', he warns. *The Earthly Paradise* includes several stories that revolve around comparable events.[32] In Morris's version of the Perseus legend, 'The Doom of King Acrisius', Perseus gives the 'fatal gift' of Medusa's head to his domineering host, and later, as a 'stranger' at the games of Teutamias, accidentally kills his grandfather, Acrisius.[33] 'The Son of Crœsus',[34] a story derived from Herodotus's *Histories*,[35] follows a similar pattern. King Crœsus of Lydia generously takes in Adrastus, a 'luckless stranger' who has 'kindred blood' on his hands.[36] Crœsus ritually purifies Adrastus and welcomes him into the bosom of his household. When a wild boar lays waste the countryside, Crœsus enlists his help to act as a bodyguard for his

---

[28] Morris, *The Defence of Guenevere and Other Poems*, in *Collected Works*, I, pp. 1–145 (p. 3).

[29] Alfred Tennyson, 'The Passing of Arthur', *Idylls of the King* in *The Poems of Tennyson*, ed. by Christopher Ricks, 3 vols (London: Longman, 1987), III, 547–61 (p. 553).

[30] Morris, *The Defence of Guenevere*, p. 22.

[31] Morris, *Scenes from the Fall of Troy*, in *Collected Works*, XXIV, pp. 3–51.

[32] Morris, *The Earthly Paradise* in *Collected Works*, III–VI. Subsequent notes refer to the numbering of this edition, not to the poem's original volume divisions.

[33] Morris, 'The Doom of King Acrisius', *The Earthly Paradise*, III, pp. 171–238 (p. 230).

[34] Morris, 'The Son of Crœsus', *The Earthly Paradise*, IV, pp. 145–58.

[35] Herodotus, *Herodotus*, trans. by A. D. Godley, 4 vols (London: William Heinemann, 1966), I, pp. 34–1.

[36] Morris, 'The Son of Crœsus', pp. 148–9.

son, Atys. The consequences of this action combine the redemptive promise of hospitality with its attendant dangers: Adrastus aims his spear at the boar but misses and fatally wounds Atys. The prophecy that Crœsus's son would die by a wound from an iron spearhead is in this way fulfilled.

Such themes are also prominent in *The Story of Grettir the Strong* (1869), a translation that features as its eponymous hero the most notorious guest of Icelandic legend, an outlaw capable of redeeming and destroying a household;[37] it is also central to *The Tale of Beowulf Sometime King of the Folk of the Weder Geats* (1895), in which Grendel, the 'grim guest', haunts Heorot after nightfall.[38] Even in his original works, Morris accords this subject considerable attention. *The Sundering Flood* (1897) contains a chapter entitled 'Surley John Brings a Guest to Wethermel', in which the goodman's willingness to provide 'every comer' with 'Meat and drink and an ingle in the hall' is exploited by the imperious Hardcastle, who seizes control of the household by force.[39]

Considerable evidence exists, first, to support the existence of a tradition of literature that emphasizes the dangers associated with the admission of guests, and second, to indicate Morris's sensitivity to it through translation and through thematic engagement with similar concerns. What distinguishes Morris's rendering of this tradition is the implication that the transgressions of guests, while undoubtedly destructive, may yet qualify for sympathy. Such a textual devolution of power is best understood in relation to the influence on Morris of Ruskin's theory of Gothic architecture. Ruskin praised the Gothic as an architecture that 'confesses its imperfection', an architecture that does not attain to the finish characteristic of modern work.[40] To apply this celebration of human fallibility to the subject of sexual relations means going beyond what Ruskin would have countenanced: he made a strict distinction between a 'healthy' and a 'diseased love of change'. But any reader of *The Defence of Guenevere and Other Poems* must be struck by the frequency with which the 'freedom of hand and mind' Morris associated with medieval conditions comes into conflict in this work with the greater 'co-operative harmony',[41] with what Ruskin (and, in theory, Morris) saw as its enabling context. In his unusual rendering of the adultery theme, I locate at its formative stage Morris's engagement with a particular kind of tolerance. This tolerance is best understood as a hospitality at once idealized and sensitive to the risks incurred through its extension.

Morris's peculiar willingness to invest conflict with redemptive qualities is accorded further attention in Chapter Four. This attitude towards disorder is thereby identified as a crucial, not to say functional, aspect of his utopianism. For the moment, the roots of a parallel, and superficially contrary, concern are placed

---

37 Morris, *The Story of Grettir the Strong*, in *Collected Works*, VII, pp. 1–279.
38 Morris, *The Tale of Beowulf Sometime King of the Folk of the Weder Geats*, trans. by William Morris and A. J. Wyatt, in *Collected Works*, X, pp. 173–284 (p. 182).
39 Morris, *The Sundering Flood*, in *Collected Works*, XXI, p. 56.
40 John Ruskin, 'The Nature of Gothic', *The Stones of Venice*, in *The Library Edition of the Works of John Ruskin*, ed. by E.T. Cook and Alexander Wedderburn, 39 vols (London: George Allen, 1903–12), X, pp. 180–269 (p. 190).
41 Morris, 'Gothic Architecture', in *William Morris: Artist Writer Socialist*, ed. by May Morris, 2 vols (Oxford: Basil Blackwell, 1936), I, pp. 266–86 (p. 276).

in the foreground: the sentimental confidence in the benefits of 'guesting' that was a distinctive feature both of Morris's approach, and of those who influenced him.[42]

Pugin, Cobbett and 'Old English Hospitality'

The idealized, or Romantic, hospitality to which this book accords primary focus is rooted just as deeply in Western culture as is the popular suspicion of outsiders already documented. In the Homeric world, responsibility for the protection of strangers was deemed so important that it was assigned to Zeus.[43] The Christian Bible, the principal source of Western conceptions of hospitality, also associates guests with God. In the Old Testament, this relationship springs from the Judaic emphasis on exile. Jehovah declares in Genesis 17:8, 'I will give unto thee, and to thy seed after thee, the land wherein thou art a stranger, all the land of Canaan, for an everlasting possession.' From this promise issues an ethics of hospitality that ascribes sacred significance to the stranger, and favours an attitude of respectful welcome towards all who do not belong. Thus Exodus 22:21 counsels, 'thou shalt neither vex a stranger, nor oppress him: for ye were strangers in the land of Egypt.'

Hospitality also has a practical bearing on relations between God and man. In the Bible, discreet liaison between the divine and human realms is often achieved, as in the Greek myths, through the visitation of intermediary spirits or angels. Since these emissaries often arrive in disguise, it is of great importance that all strangers are given a fair hearing. Thus in the New Testament, Hebrews 13:2 enjoins, 'be not forgetful to entertain strangers: for thereby some have entertained angels unawares' (an allusion, perhaps, to the hospitality Abraham showed to the three strangers at Mamre in Genesis 18, and which Lot subsequently offered to the angels at the gate of Sodom in Genesis 19:1–16). As the famous words from Matthew 25:35 imply, the kind of welcome Jesus received in the houses of ordinary people proved an effective test of their spiritual receptivity: 'I was an hungred, and ye gave me meat: I was thirsty, and ye gave me drink: I was a stranger, and ye took me in'. Indeed, it was in recognition of Christ's original status as a guest that hospitality was included in the Rule of St Benedict as a basic virtue of monastic life.[44] The related activity of feasting is also of paramount importance within Christian traditions. Jesus's ministry begins when as a wedding guest he turns water into wine; it culminates in the symbolic breaking of

---

42 In his translation of the *Odyssey*, Morris attaches a verbal function to the word, *guest*: ' "There are stranger guests come hither, Menelaus God-bred king,/ [. . .] What say'st thou then? Their horses swift-footed shall we loose,/ Or speed them on to another who to guest them may be fain?" ', *The Odyssey of Homer Done into English Verse*, in *Collected Works*, XIII, p. 42. In this, he follows George Chapman, whose translation includes the lines, 'And tell me, best of Princes, who he was/ That guested here so late?' (1.627), *The Odyssey* in *Chapman's Homer*, ed. by Allardyce Nicoll, 2nd edn, 2 vols (Princeton, N. J.: Princeton University Press, 1967), II, pp. 11–469.

43 The classical model of hospitality became more important to Morris in later years. In his translation of the *Odyssey*, Nausicaa reminds her handmaids that 'from Zeus come guestfolk all' (XIII, p. 86).

44 David Parry, *Households of God: The Rule of St Benedict with Explanations for Monks and Lay-people Today* (London: Darton, Longman & Todd, 1980), pp. 140–3.

bread at the Last Supper. In food, in wine, in hospitality, the divine and the human find both temporary meeting-place and the promise of permanent union.

The theme of hospitality first surfaces in a form directly relevant to Victorian medievalism in the early Romantic period. The poetry of Wordsworth[45] and Coleridge[46] is notable for exhibiting an intense interest in the figure of the stranger or wanderer. The roots of this tradition – based on the biblical story of Cain and Abel and on the medieval legend of the Wandering Jew – run far back into the past. Its influence is most marked in the early modern period. A series of texts, composed during the sixteenth and seventeenth centuries, present various states of exile in a metaphysical light. The world, and by extension the body, are compared to mere stopping places, or hostelries, for the soul. This analogy is typically applied as a means of encouraging meditation upon transience. Notable examples include John Donne's reference to 'this soul's second inn',[47] Sir Walter Ralegh's characterization, in 'The Lie', of the soul as 'the boddies guest',[48] and Thomas Browne's even less optimistic preference for the figure of a hospital in speaking of the world as 'a place, not to live, but to die in'.[49]

In 'XVI Persuasion', a poem included in Wordsworth's *Ecclesiastical Sonnets* (1822), this tradition is applied in a modern context to a more literal scenario, involving the warm reception of an unbidden guest on a cold winter's night.[50] Reflecting on the soul's brief time 'in the Body lodged, her warm abode', the speaker looks to the predicament of man, a creature who in life would seem to move from the cold to the warm, and then back into the cold: 'This mystery if the Stranger can reveal,/ His be a welcome cordially bestowed!' A similar analogy is deployed by Wordsworth in his 'Song: For the Wandering Jew'.[51] The eponymous and legendary figure is compared implicitly by the authorial persona to 'the Wanderer in my soul'. Unlike the Alpine Chamois, he has no 'home to enter/ In some nook of chosen ground' and, unlike the Sea-horse, requires a 'domestic cave'. It is apparent, nevertheless, that most Romantic poems present the wanderer simply as the fortunate beneficiary of that 'domestic power' whose purpose it is the poet's to eulogize. John Scott's 'Ode XVIII. To Hospitality' is one such work. Here, 'The traveller, doubtful of his way,/ Upon the pathless forest wild' seeks and finds 'the festive bower' and shares 'the free repast'.[52] 'The Convent of the Great St.

45 William Wordsworth, 'The Ruined Cottage', in *The Poetical Works of William Wordsworth*, ed. by E. de Selincourt and Helen Darbishire, 5 vols (Oxford: Clarendon Press, 1972), V, pp. 379–404.
46 Samuel Taylor Coleridge, 'The Rime of the Ancient Mariner' in *The Collected Works of Samuel Taylor Coleridge*, ed. by J. C. C. Mays, 16 vols (Princeton, N.J.: Princeton University Press, 2001), 16, 1.1, pp. 365–419.
47 John Donne, 'The Progress of the Soul', in *The Poems of John Donne*, ed. by Herbert J. C. Grierson, 2 vols (Oxford: Oxford University Press, 1966), 1, pp. 295–316 (p. 301).
48 Sir Walter Ralegh, 'The Lie', in *The Poems of Walter Ralegh: A Historical Edition*, ed. by Michael Ruddick (Tempe, Arizona: Renaissance English Text Society, 1999), pp. 30–3 (p. 30).
49 Thomas Browne, *Religio Medici*, in *The Works of Sir Thomas Browne*, ed. by Geoffrey Keynes, 4 vols (London: Faber & Faber, 1978), pp. 11–93 (p. 87).
50 William Wordsworth, 'Part 1: XVI Persuasion', *Ecclesiastical Sonnets*, in *The Poetical Works of William Wordsworth*, 4 vols (Oxford: Clarendon Press, 1946), pp. 341–416 (p. 349).
51 William Wordsworth, 'Song: For the Wandering Jew', *Poems of the Fancy*, in *The Poetical Works of William Wordsworth*, pp. 124–205 (p. 159).
52 John Scott, 'Ode XVIII. To Hospitality', *The Poetical Works of John Scott Esq.* (London: J. Buckland, 1782), pp. 214–17.

Bernard', a poem by William Sotheby, is similar, extolling a famous mountain resting place as the 'Temple of hallow'd hospitality!'.[53] Within the walls of the convent one finds 'The pilgrim's and lost wanderer's sole retreat'.

Odes to hospitality continue to appear well into the second half of the nineteenth century. They are characterized by an insistent interest in exemplary personal conduct, especially as manifested in the manners of the host. Scott's early poetic works often present generous hospitality as a chivalric ideal. This stanza, from his long poem, *Marmion* (1808), is particularly illustrative, offering a formulaic and ritualistic portrait of social cohesion:

> Lord Marmion's bugles blew to horse:
> Then came the stirrup-cup in course:
> Between the Baron and his host,
> No point of courtesy was lost.[54]

The conventional nature of the encounter is important in this case. But, for Scott, hospitality serves as far more than an analogy for successful prosecution of the game of courtesy. This is especially apparent in the celebratory, yet wistful, preface to his edition of *Götz von Berlichingen*. Here, Scott expresses sympathy for what he takes to be Goethe's message. Without downplaying the 'obvious mischiefs' attending medieval life, he is at pains to stress that 'Men daily exposed to danger, and living by the constant exertion of courage, acquired the virtues as well as the vices of a savage state'.[55] Indeed, Scott reflects, such a state of society was also 'frequently the means of calling into exercise the highest heroic virtues'. It is not surprising that domestic generosity features prominently among the virtues invoked. Scott admits that 'the fortress of a German knight was the dread of the wealthy merchant and abbot', but is also at pains to suggest that it was equally 'the ready and hospitable refuge of the weary pilgrim and oppressed peasant'. As noted, Götz soon discovers that a domestic strategy distinguished as virtuous and politic in the feudal situation represents an Achilles heel in the new commercial era. In the words of Goethe's doomed hero, 'The age of frankness and freedom is past'. It is nonetheless apparent that Scott saw something serviceable in the notion of a savage, yet essentially kindly, approach to the welcoming of outsiders.

It is helpful to revisit the set-piece reception scene included in the second chapter of *Ivanhoe*. As in Goethe's play, there is no attempt to suppress the vulnerability that characterizes the welcome Cedric of Rotherwood offers to his Norman guests. Cedric's references to 'wily strollers' who 'devise to cheat us into hospitality' is a reminder that the gesture is not only grudging, but more a duty or obligation than a gift.[56] Scott nevertheless provides the reader with several opportunities to regard Cedric's conduct in a different light. Later the same evening, the porter's page informs Cedric that there is 'a stranger at the gate, imploring admittance and hospitality'. Cedric replies, 'Admit him, [. . .] be he who or what he may'. On

53 William Sotheby, 'The Convent of the Great St. Bernard', *Italy and Other Poems* (London: John Murray, 1828), p. 197.
54 Walter Scott, *Marmion*, XXXI, in *The Poetic Works of Walter Scott . . . Complete in One Volume* (Edinburgh: Robert Cadell, 1841), pp. 76–143 (p. 86).
55 Scott, Preface, *Goetz of Berlichingen, with the Iron Hand: A Tragedy*, pp. vii, viii.
56 Scott, *Ivanhoe*, I, pp. 62, 79, 82, 84, 85.

learning that the stranger is a Jew, he answers the objections of his Norman guests with the words, 'my hospitality must not be bounded by your dislikes'. As it turns out, this gesture is hardly an unqualified welcome. For the 'reception of this person in the hall of Cedric the Saxon, was such as might have satisfied the most prejudiced enemy of the tribes of Israel'. Whilst making the lamentable coldness of Isaac's reception absolutely patent, Scott keeps open the ideal, if not the practice, of a less discriminating and more humane welcome:

> Probably the same motives which induced Cedric to open his hall to this son of a rejected people would have made him insist on his attendants receiving Isaac with more courtesy.

Unfortunately, Cedric is more interested in his discussion 'on the breed and character of his favourite hounds' than in the lot of his poor guest. What counts for the purposes of this discussion is the narrator's reference to a hospitable ideal, rather than its actual fulfilment. For this offer of shelter to a religious outsider is distinguished and significant in so far as it introduces tolerance to the circle of values surrounding the literary representation of hospitality. On the level of narrative commentary, tolerance is supplemented by a principle defined less negatively: a recognition of common humanity that pays no heed to religious or political differences.

In Scott's work, the formulaic play of convention and courtesy gives way to politically charged reflections on the virtues of an unconditional welcome. Other writers, roughly contemporary with Scott, go even further along this path. They offer laments for a perceived decline of manners, for the passing of a golden age identified sometimes with the Middle Ages, and sometimes with the Olden Time (a vague designation implying a less religiously controversial affiliation with the Tudor period). This regretful, yet fascinated, concern for the passing of a festive era begins in the 1780s with the politicized nostalgia of William Blake's 'An Island in the Moon':

> Thus sitting at the table wide the Mayor & Alderman
> Were fit to give law to the city each eat as much as ten
> The hungry poor enterd the hall to eat good beef & ale
> Good English hospitality O then it did not fail.[57]

The social ideal of 'Good English hospitality', combined with free access to the bounty of traditional English agriculture, articulated for Blake a national fall from grace. Like the Romantic interest in the 'wanderer' or 'wayfarer', this theme represents more a revival than an innovation. Laments for the suppression of public charity recur in literature after the English Reformation. And even earlier, in William Langland's *Piers Plowman* (posth., 1550), one reads that in former times great prelates, Bishops and Archbishops kept company with Charity, while nowadays 'Avarice hath almaries and yren-bounden cofres'.[58]

As the century progressed, it became increasingly common for pro-Catholic

---

57 William Blake, 'An Island in the Moon', in *William Blake's Writings*, ed. by G. E. Bentley, Jr, 2 vols (Oxford: Clarendon Press, 1978), pp. 875–900 (pp. 893–4).
58 William Langland, *The Vision of Piers Plowman* (London: J. M. Dent, 1995), Passus XIV, 247.

writers to associate the destruction of the medieval church, and the Elizabethan poor laws, with a decline in 'Good English hospitality'. This tendency is even discernible in the work of writers who did not support the cause of Catholic emancipation. Among such was Robert Southey, whose poem 'Hospitality' couples reference to the 'iron rod' of 'High Reformation' with a prediction that 'Hospitality will feel the wound!'[59] A strong current of opinion inclined towards the traditional Protestant reading of the past. Earlier in the century, Henry Hallam's *View of the State of Europe during the Middle Ages* (1818) sought to remind readers of 'the general corruption' of the monasteries, of their 'whole scheme of hypocritical austerities' and 'their extreme licentiousness'.[60] A year later, John Keats visited the hospital of St Cross at Winchester, and wrote in a letter that it is 'a very interesting old place, both for its gothic tower and alms-square and for the appropriation of its rich rents to a relation of the Bishop of Winchester'.[61] The ambivalence that characterizes this entry – admiration of fine medieval architecture coupled with distaste for accompanying institutional corruption – never really goes away. Later in the century, reports that the Earl of Guildford had defrauded charitable work at the same hospital of more than £10,000 inspired Anthony Trollope, in his novel *The Warden* (1855), to draw comparisons between the unreformed institutions of past and present.[62]

Southey's poem demonstrates that the tide of opinion was turning in favour of a more sympathetic interest in the charitable institutions of medieval England. Scott was in this respect a pioneer, but he would not go so far in his medievalism as his successors. He never jettisoned his confidence in the merits of enlightened modernity. The past might be treated as a source of romance, a reserve of manners and ideals to which all might profitably aspire, but there is rarely any suggestion that the old ways are entirely superior to the new. The roots of what Thomas Carlyle called 'Götzism'[63] – a kind of protest writing that employed Goethe's strategy of forcing antithetical social structures into telling encounters – lay elsewhere, most notably in the work of A. W. Pugin, the early Victorian architect and polemicist whose strident Catholicism laid the foundations for a series of politically charged comparisons between the past and the present. Pugin's famous condemnation of classical and industrial architecture in *Contrasts* (1836) represents an early example of the approach to which Carlyle's term alludes.[64] In addition to a long essay on the failings of neo-classical urban and industrial archi- tecture, the work comprises a set of provocative drawings that expose recent edifices to the 'shame' of comparison with their medieval counterparts. This will-

59   Robert Southey, 'Hospitality', in *The Poetical Works of Robert Southey* (Paris: A. and W. Galignani, 1829), p. 706.
60   Henry Hallam, *View of the State of Europe during the Middle Ages*, 3 vols (London: John Murray, 1853), 3, p. 303.
61   John Keats, 'To the George Keatses', 21 September 1819, *The Letters of John Keats*, 2 vols, ed. by Hyder Edward Rollins (Cambridge, Mass.: Harvard University Press, 1980), 2, pp. 208–12 (p. 209).
62   Anthony Trollope, *The Warden* (Oxford: Oxford University Press, 1990).
63   Thomas Carlyle, 'Sir Walter Scott', in *The Works of Thomas Carlyle* ('Centenary Edition'), ed. by H. D. Traill, 30 vols (London: Chapman and Hall, 1896–1901), XXIX, pp. 22–87 (p. 58).
64   A. Welby Pugin, *Contrasts; or, A Parallel Between the Noble Edifices of the Middle Ages, and Corre- sponding Buildings of the Present Day; Shewing the Present Decay of Taste*, 2nd edn (London: Charles Dolman, 1841).

ingness to elevate the past above the present, to treat it as an authority capable of guiding present practice, operates on the level both of individual buildings and institutions, and of whole cities. Thus the reader is asked on one page to compare the merits of modern and ancient college gateways, and on another to see the 'decline' evidenced by two pictures of the same town, one set in 1440, the other in 1840.

What bearing might Pugin's critique of modern architecture have on this developing treatment of idealized hospitality? It is important, first of all, to appreciate that he did not confine his appraisal of architecture to the aesthetic sphere. Architecture for Pugin, like Ruskin after him, was indicative of a whole way of life. In the lineaments of a new building he believed one could read the virtues as well as the crimes of an entire society. In religious and charitable institutions, it was by extension possible to draw far-reaching conclusions concerning the effects and historical logic of the English Reformation. Commenting on the degradation of cathedral buildings since the sixteenth century, Pugin lays particular emphasis on the Protestant clergy's destructive departure from a collegiate manner of life:

> All the ancient characteristic features have been totally changed, for after the clergy had left off ecclesiastical discipline for ease and comfort; exchanged old hospitality for formal visiting; and, indeed, become laymen in every other respect but in that of their income and title, they found the old buildings but ill suited to their altered style of living.[65]

In the appendix to *Contrasts*, Pugin compares medieval institutions that received strangers to their modern equivalents. His illustration of a medieval inn features a large, welcoming doorway, which puts its terraced Georgian namesake to shame; and his rendering of an 'Antient Poor Hoyse' combines depictions of monastic discipline with scenes of refreshment and charity. The building is surrounded by gardens and has a large open court. In this, it differs markedly from the closed structure of the Benthamite institution pictured above it. Pugin provides a more comprehensive account of the relationship between society, architecture and hospitality in *The True Principles of Pointed or Christian Architecture*. Here he contrasts modern architecture, including Gothic Revival buildings like Fonthill, with the 'old English Catholic mansions' of the Middle Ages, whose 'porter's lodging', 'entrance porch', 'capacious chimney' and 'guest chambers' presented 'a standing illustration of good old English hospitality'.[66] More importantly, he notes that 'our ancestors did not confine their guests, as at present, to a few fashionables'. At festivals, friends and tenants would assemble in their 'capacious halls', while 'humbler guests partook of their share of bounty dealt to them by the hand of the almoner beneath the groined entrance of the gate-house'. Catholic England, Pugin concludes, 'was merry England'; and its 'architecture was in keeping with the faith and manners of the times, – at once strong and hospitable'.

Pugin's reference to 'merry England' illuminates the main point of convergence between his religiously partisan appraisal of medieval architecture and the less

---

65 Pugin, *Contrasts*, p. 45.
66 A. Welby Pugin, *The True Principles of Pointed or Christian Architecture: Set Forth in Two Lectures Delivered at St. Marie's, Oscott* (London: John Weale, 1841), pp. 50–1.

refined, populist lament for a past age of rural plenty and aristocratic *largesse* that took hold during the first half of the nineteenth century. The fiercest advocate of this vision of the past was William Cobbett. Despite humble origins, Cobbett began life as a rural traditionalist and Tory. This same devotion to a certain idea of England compelled him to turn Radical pamphleteer on discovering that all was not well in the kingdom. The Tory patriot in him, the lover of king and country, recoiled in horror on discovering the extent of the corruption and 'borough-mongering' endemic to Britain's electoral system. Cobbett nurtured dislike for many facets of modern life, but he did not equate opposition to taxation, to big cities, and to landlordism, with anti-progressive tendencies. He felt sufficiently close to the rural culture of eighteenth-century England to believe that any departure from its simple and honest ways might conceivably be reversed. This, after all, was the world of his boyhood. It was a simplification of the true picture, and as such a utopian ploy, a benchmark against which to measure the failings of the present. Cobbett called out for reform, but always he had at the back of his mind a return to the rural bliss of eighteenth-century England, a place where agricultural plenty might be shared out equally in the form of roast beef and good English ale. He nevertheless remains a pioneer, as one of the first writers who brought a nostalgic reading of the Middle Ages into direct, polemical confrontation with contemporary modes of existence.

It is through Cobbett that this sympathetic reading of the past departs from a merely wistful appreciation of bygone days, and becomes a serious comment on contemporary living standards. In *A History of the Protestant 'Reformation'* (1824–26), he, like Pugin, condemns the dissolution of the monasteries[67] and the subsequent substitution of '*legal pauperism*' for '*Catholic charity*'. The work offers a strange and skewed history, even when viewed as a corrective or alternative account. What Cobbett's record of the period lacks in historical accuracy, it makes up for in fearless polemic and willingness to question the usual hagiography. He draws particular attention to the disjunction between the myth and the reality of Elizabeth I's rule, while restating his continuous interest in the destruction of social ease and plenty:

> when '*good* Queen Bess' had put the finishing hand to the plundering of the Church and poor, once-happy and free and hospitable England became a den of famishing robbers and slaves.

In a later work, *Rural Rides* (1830), Cobbett continues to record the deterioration of country living standards.[68] This intriguing travelogue encompasses a striking range of tone. It contains much that is humorous and light-hearted. Elsewhere, the author's pen draws attention to a trail of agricultural destitution, wreaked for the most part by parasitical landlordism. As a portrait of the landscape and its inhabitants, *Rural Rides* is sadly at odds with Cobbett's idealized vision of the fourteenth-century hall. This common space, once a place where lord and serf

---

67 William Cobbett, *A History of the Protestant "Reformation," in England and Ireland, Showing How that Event Has Impoverished and Degraded the Main Body of the People in those Countries* (London: John Dean, 1825), XI, 330, 332.

68 William Cobbett, *Rural Rides*, 2 vols (London: J. M. Dent & Sons, 1941), vol. 1, p. 266.

might dine together, had long been converted to other uses. Cobbett's memory of its eighteenth-century equivalent, the open and convivial farmhouse, encourages him to question the inevitability of change:

> Why do not farmers now *feed* and *lodge* their work-people, as they did formerly? [. . .] All the world knows that a number of people, boarded in the same house, and at the same table, can, with as good food, be boarded much cheaper.

The 'old English hospitality' that Cobbett held so dear had succumbed to cynical profiteering and social atomism. It is striking, nonetheless, that he continues to offer arguments in its defence based on practical advantage and economy. He refuses to accept the utilitarian monopoly on such concerns.

As the country's economic condition worsens in the late 1830s, and the 1840s, there is a corresponding growth in the number of works invoking a nostalgic reading of the past. Many relied upon myths of rural plenty and harmony far more conservative than those championed by Cobbett. The paintings, poems, novels and pamphlets in question engaged with one myth in particular, namely that romantic and non-specific era known as 'Merry England'. In 1993, Ronald Hutton published *The Rise and Fall of Merry England*.[69] Hutton's inquiry focuses on the demise of England's traditional machinery of ritual and festival which attended the passing of the Middle Ages. In historical terms he uses the phrase much as the Victorians used it, whilst abstaining from its exemplary connotations. *Merry England* now serves more commonly as a label for a particular romantic reading of the past. One of the more useful and extended discussions applying this latter sense appears in Peter Mandler's book, *The Fall and Rise of the Stately Home* (1997). Mandler focuses on an adaptation of the notion 'in what the early Victorians came to think of as "the Olden Time", broadly the period between medieval rudeness and aristocratic over-refinement, the time of the Tudors and Early Stuarts':[70]

> The Olden Time had put firmly behind it the crudity and barbarity of the Middle Ages, but it had not yet embraced the exclusiveness of fashion and taste. Aristocratic display in the Olden Time served communal purposes: public rituals, like the great royal peregrinations, seasonal rituals like Maying and the Yuletide, and especially the daily responsibility of hospitality. Great men kept open house for dependents and strangers alike, thus continuing to discharge the charitable functions of the Catholic Church dissolved by the Reformation.

Mandler's conception of the Olden Time is that of an idyllic and non-specific period, which somehow combines the virtues of medieval communal rites with modern liberalism. His emphasis on the 'daily responsibility of hospitality' is particularly telling, in that it offers a succinct expression of two otherwise divergent social models.

The most important catalyst for the popularity of the Merry England myth,

---

69 Ronald Hutton, *The Rise and Fall of Merry England: The Ritual Year 1400–1700* (Oxford: Oxford University Press, 1993).
70 Mandler, *The Fall and Rise of the Stately Home*, pp. 31, 33.

and by extension, for the construction of an idyllic and hospitable Middle Ages, was the introduction in 1834 of the new Poor Law. Replacing the relatively generous and expensive Speenhamland system of wage subsidy, it withdrew relief from the able bodied, who were henceforth obliged to regard the workhouse as a last resort. This attempt to promote the virtues of work, and effectively legislate against public charity, reflected the orthodox thinking of the time. The Act nevertheless provoked a backlash. For those like Pugin, the medieval systems of poor relief – whether involving the giving of alms or the running of monastic guesthouses – represented the most compelling alternative to modern approaches. For others, the 'folk memory' of a time when the wealthy took care of the poor formed a more appealing and less controversial alternative.

The Merry England myth also appears in the writings of Lord John Manners, a prominent member of the Young England parliamentary group. His collection, *England's Trust and other Poems* is notable for its homage to the lost festive calendar.[71] Manners characterizes medieval survivals as instances of 'good old English ways'. In so doing, he shows how antiquarian pastimes might serve to support rather than threaten national identity. His pamphlet, 'A Plea for National Holy-days', undertakes a far more direct and political appraisal of the situation. The chief enemy emerging from this piece is that 'utilitarian selfishness' which, it is claimed, banished 'unproductive amusements from the land'.[72] Shocked by the excesses of imperial adventure, foreign investment, and modern production, Manners argues defiantly that 'any one conversant with history, or who has lived in those parts of England – the lakes, for instance – where old customs and the old character still linger, must confess that the "all work and no play" system, which is defended as adapted to the English character, and the modern and unchristian bars which now separate wealth from poverty, have their source elsewhere than in the English national character'. His aim, whilst eminently impracticable from a modern point of view, is that Merry England should once again 'merit her epithet'. The rash schemes of socialism and Chartism are therefore considered to be unnecessary: for 'there is no need for striking out a new path' when 'the old one, that leads over the village green to the church door is patent'. It is important to appreciate the central role that hospitality plays in this conception of Merry England. Not merely a pleasing domestic virtue, the fellow feeling integral to this account of the past is presented as a solution to very modern social problems. In reference to the nation's cathedral cities, Manners asks whether 'the poor, and the needy, and the friendless throng into those glorious buildings, which the piety of our ancestors raised for them, to bear their part in thanking the Lord of Hosts for his later mercies'? The problem posited lies not for him in the essential adequacy of antique arrangements, but in the consequences of several centuries' neglect. If given the chance, Manners implies, a medieval cathedral can function just as well now as it did when first constructed.

Manners was not alone in drawing parallels between current social conditions, and the plentiful days of Merry England. In the 1840s there were compelling

[71] The poem 'Christmas' is a particularly good example: 'With morris dance, and carol-song,/ And quaint old mystery,/ Memorials of a holy day/ Were mingled in their glee', *England's Trust and other Poems* (London: J. G. F. & J. Rivington, 1841), pp. 95–7 (p. 96).
[72] John Manners, 'A Plea for National Holy-days' (London, 1843), pp. 4, 5, 14, 15, 25.

economic reasons for the attractiveness of such myths. For those unwilling to advocate more radical solutions to the devastating decline in trade, generous hospitality, based on a nostalgic, rural model, seemed as good a tonic as any for social division. Indeed, conditions of economic depression, of retrenchment in the country at large, engendered among some a spirit of defiant feasting. The extravagant pageantry of the Eglinton Tournament (1839) exemplifies such challenges to the austere public mood, endorsed as it had been by Queen Victoria's 'penny coronation'. In *The Illustrated London News*, engraved depictions of maypoles and rustic ceremonies appeared.[73] A supplement to the same paper, from 1848, emphasises the virtues of a universal welcome:

> the Hospitality of the Hall at this festive season is not only a romantic fiction, but an historical fact. All were welcome.[74]

In 1849, *The Illustrated London News* carried the story of the recent revival of traditional 'Christmas gambols' at the Manchester Mechanics Institute, a highlight of which was 'The Procession of the Wassail Bowl'. This last event included mummers, minstrels and a yule log processional. Depictions of medieval hospitality appeared in Daniel Maclise's paintings, *Merry Christmas in the Baron's Hall* (1838) and *Robin Hood and his Merry Men Entertaining Richard the Lionheart in Sherwood Forest* (1839). John Rogers Herbert's *The Monastery in the Fourteenth Century: Boarhunters Refreshed at St Augustine's Monastery, Canterbury* (1840) and George Cattermole's *Wanderers Entertained or Old English Hospitality* (1839) also treated the theme. Similar scenes emerged in the literature of the period. Edward Bulwer-Lytton's *The Last of the Barons* (1843) evoked the old 'greensward, before the village (now foul and reeking with the squalid population [. . .])' where 'were assembled youth and age'.[75] Such eulogies to festivity and coherent community often culminated in celebrations of hospitality. Charles Mackay's poem, 'Hospitality', is typical in this respect.[76] Accepting that his medieval forebears had 'errors great', he asserts that 'They made the poor their welcome guests –/ They hush'd the widow's moan'. This message is developed especially clearly across the following stanzas:

> Then glow'd the fire upon the hearth
>   In many an ancient hall;
> The tables shook – the platters smoked –
>   The poor were welcome all.
>
> The ancient Virtue is not dead,
>   And long may it endure;
> May wealth in England never fail,
>   Nor pity for the poor.

---

73 'Spring in the Olden Time. – The Maypole', *Illustrated London News*, 27 May 1843, p. 367.

74 John A. Heraud, 'Christmas Eve, and Welcome to Old Friends', Supplement to *Illustrated London News*, 23 December 1848, p. 411.

75 Edward Bulwer-Lytton, *The Last of the Barons* (London: George Routledge and Sons, 1875), p. 260.

76 Charles Mackay, 'Hospitality', *The Collected Songs of Charles Mackay* (London: G. Routledge & Co., 1859), pp. 72–3.

[...]
    We'll imitate our sires –
    We'll spread the board – we'll feed the poor –
    We'll light the cottage fires.

Thus Mackay's nostalgic glance back to 'the fire upon the hearth' in an 'ancient hall' leads to a general recommendation of revivalist imitation.

Like most sites of social yearning, or loss, the myth of 'Merry England' had a strong political dimension. Whether express or implied, it facilitated severe comment on contemporary customs, living conditions and laws. It is nevertheless meaningful to distinguish between material of the kind treated above and the conscious politicization of medievalism favoured by those more forthright Victorian commentators who built upon popular attachment to these romantic myths. In the hands of such writers, expressions of hospitality ordinarily suggestive of pleasing social graces become symbolical of an alternative social structure.

Apart from Cobbett and Pugin, one further figure qualifies for attention: the popular sage and prophet, Thomas Carlyle. Carlyle's *Past and Present* (1843) owes a great deal to the strategy of historical contrast established by Pugin. It also concentrates on the alternative attitude to household management, to economy, evoked by medieval institutions. In this case, he was concerned with the example of the well-run monastery. Set within that context, the benefits of hospitality were evidently of interest to Carlyle. They emerge most clearly in his commentary on the journey from Durham undertaken by Jocelin, the chronicler upon whose account of medieval times his reflections are based:

> 'the dark night caught me at Risby, and I had to beg lodging there. I went to Dominus Norman's, and he gave me a flat refusal. Going then to Dominus Willelm's, and begging hospitality, I was by him honourably received. The twenty shillings therefore of *mercy*, I, without mercy, will extract from Dominus Norman; to Dominus Willelm, on the other hand, I, with thanks, will wholly remit the said sum.' Men know not always to whom they refuse lodgings; men have lodged Angels unawares![77]

Yet hospitality for Carlyle represents more than a laudable principle of action. Only if it is combined with strong leadership, with an acknowledgement of the right and duty of the host to control his household, can it play a role in returning a habitation to the status of a home. As the actions of Abbot Samson indicate, its precepts may demand an expulsion of 'parasites' – in this case, money-lending Jews – from the monastic household. If effective household management requires firm leadership, it may also imply an oppressive paternalism and a ruthless suppression of perceived offences against the laws of hospitality, their primary tenet being that a guest should on no account become a parasite. Carlyle, it seems, does not insist on unconditional hospitality. The idea of home was important to him, but he evidently saw a threat to domestic unity in unwary forms of openness.

For a more accepting politicization of medievalism, one must revisit the work of John Manners, and the One Nation Conservatism of Benjamin Disraeli and his

---

[77] Thomas Carlyle, *Past and Present*, in *Works*, X, p. 95.

Young England circle. As with Cobbett, conservative politics act here in support of a radical agenda, at least on a rhetorical level. In the novels of Disraeli, the unifying influence of aristocratic largesse is a recurrent theme. *Sybil* is particularly concerned with the demise of rural 'comfort'.[78] The novel contains several passages that contrast the lack of community characteristic of modern society with the attractions of a medieval abbey:

> here might still be traced [. . .] the capacious hospital, a name that did not then denote the dwelling of disease, but a place where all the rights of hospitality were practised; where the traveller from the proud baron to the lonely pilgrim asked the shelter and the succour that never were denied, and at whose gate, called the Portal of the Poor, the peasants on the Abbey lands, if in want, might appeal each morn and night for raiment and for food.

Disraeli's *Coningsby* explored similar themes.[79] The Duke of Beaumanoir is presented as the perfect landlord and the perfect host. 'He was', we are informed, 'munificent, tender and bounteous to the poor, and loved a flowing hospitality.'

Disraeli was not alone in exhibiting sympathetic interest in monasticism. It would be a simplification to characterize the Oxford Movement as the religious wing of medievalism, but that nevertheless was its broad cultural effect. The enthusiasm for religious communities shared by Newman, Keble, and Pusey especially, encouraged renewed interest in the advantages of a simple, clearly defined, and pious existence. Thus the removed, but not necessarily *unsociable*, life of the monk came to serve as a model for a new generation of artists and thinkers. The Pre-Raphaelites' bid to form an artistic brotherhood in 1848 was of particular importance. This project shared important features with the earlier experiment of the Nazarenes, a quasi-religious order that sought to return art to the workshop practice of the medieval guilds. Like them, the Pre-Raphaelites combined religious primitivism with artistic primitivism and sensitivity to social issues. The legacy of these investigations is obvious in the early writings of Morris's Oxford 'Set'. The 'Set' published a successor to the Pre-Raphaelite *Germ*, a periodical called *The Oxford and Cambridge Magazine*. One article in particular, entitled 'Oxford', elucidates the attractiveness of medieval communities to artistic young men of the time.[80] Although the following lines are rather austere and Carlylean, they express romantic interest in the monastic life:

> Again, what was a mediaeval college? Let the modern reader, if he can, conceive a monastery, a college, and an alms-house united into a single building, and governed by fixed laws, the bounty providing thin diet, shelter, and perhaps a yearly present of coarse clothing; the head a real *ruler*, the fellows obedient students, with suffrages on important occasions; all of them poor monks, who have renounced the world, and chosen Oxford for their recess.

---

78 Benjamin Disraeli, *Sybil; or, The Two Nations*, 3 vols (London: Henry Colburn, 1845), I, pp. 129–30, 140.
79 Benjamin Disraeli, *Coningsby; or, The New Generation*, 3 vols (London: Henry Colburn, 1844), I, p. 177.
80 'Oxford', *The Oxford and Cambridge Magazine* (April, 1856), 234–57.

The Pre-Raphaelite experiment was short-lived, and indeed dubious in its cohesiveness. Nevertheless, one readily sees in the art and literature of the Victorian period the legacy of its stress on brotherhood, on community and on primitivism.

One product of the movement, William Holman Hunt's painting *The Light of the World* (1854), treats a subject of particular relevance to the ideas under discussion. The figure of Christ stands at the centre of Hunt's canvas. He holds up a lantern in the dark of the night. The heavy symbolism of this gesture is supported by these familiar words, which are inscribed on the frame: 'Behold, I stand at the door, and knock: if any man hear my voice, and open the door, I will come into him, and will sup with him, and he with me.' There is no handle on the door. According to orthodox interpretation, the handle is to be found on the inside. Christ, it follows, will only enter on receiving invitation, a suggestion that returns us helpfully to the ethical, the religious and the mystical significance of hospitality.

Hosts and Hospitallers: John Ruskin's Notion of a Village Inn

Of all the medievalist writers and thinkers mentioned thus far, John Ruskin was the most rigorous and thoughtful in theorizing the individual and social benefits accruing to generous hospitality. This section serves partly as a prelude to the next chapter, which considers Morris's treatment of hospitality in various social and artistic contexts. The following analysis also represents in its own right a concerted, and thus far unprecedented, attempt to investigate the recurrence of this medievalist theme in Ruskin's critical and imaginative corpus.

On first approaching this subject, it is helpful to consider in what respects Morris's 'master'[81] borrowed from the traditional, literary, and religious conventions so far discussed. It is notable, for instance, that the thematic and metaphoric interest in transience favoured by sixteenth- and seventeenth-century writers is present also in Ruskin's work. His treatment of this theme is couched in comparable allusions to the customary and mystic significance of receiving strangers. Like Thomas Browne, Ruskin compares the world to a kind of hotel, or 'hospital' in the archaic sense:

> we look upon the world too much as our own, too much as if we had possessed it and should possess it for ever, and forget that it is a mere hostelry, of which we occupy the apartments for a time, which others better than we have sojourned in before.[82]

Ruskin invokes the claims of previous generations in support of his campaign against the hubris of architectural 'restoration'. The parallel is also significant on a number of other levels. The first thing one should observe is that it relies upon a distinctly medieval conception of ownership. Not simply a meditation upon transience, the world-as-hostel metaphor has a direct bearing upon social and

---

[81] In 'How I Became a Socialist' (1894), Morris recalls that, of all those 'in open rebellion against [. . .] Whiggery', Ruskin was his 'master' (in *Collected Works*, XXIII, pp. 277–81 (p. 279)).

[82] John Ruskin, *Modern Painters*, in *Works*, III, p. 203.

economic questions. The system of feudalism paid deference to the implications of human frailty and fragility. No man could *own* land as such. The relativity of title that persists in English land law to this day derives from the perception that it would be nonsensical to speak of absolute ownership in relation to a commodity as fixed and permanent as land. Thus the king's subjects were granted something less than ownership in return for their loyalty: strictly speaking, they were given estates in land. It followed that the possessor of an estate sufficient to occupy land was known as a tenant, in the older sense of someone who *holds*. Thus Ruskin's liking for the notion of a life lived on an ownerless earth in which, at least metaphysically, every person is as homeless as the next, fits very neatly with his interest in the social ramifications of an age of faith.

Ruskin's commitment to the preservation of ancient buildings owes something to the same medieval doctrine of tenure. Although this subject will be dealt with at more length in Chapter Three, it is helpful to remember the precise terms in which Ruskin condemned the harmful effects of architectural 'restoration' at Oxford and Venice. Relics of past ages were not owned exclusively by their current inhabitants and users. They were better considered the 'property' of the people who built them, and of the people who would use them in the future. For him, such trans-historical assets resisted ownership in the conventional sense. They were not appropriate surfaces upon which to prosecute either grand plans for change or schemes for enhancing present convenience. Ruskin's most vigorous articulation of this idea appears in *The Seven Lamps of Architecture* (1849):

> it is again no question of expediency or feeling whether we shall preserve the buildings of past times or not. *We have no right whatever to touch them.* They are not ours. They belong partly to those who built them, and partly to all the generations of mankind who are to follow us.[83]

Thus a mystical emphasis on transience, combined with medievalist interest in prior social forms and systems of ownership, leads relatively quickly into distinctively Ruskinian territory.

Before addressing Ruskin's more substantive and individual applications of hospitality as a medieval ideal, it is worth granting further attention to his figurative or rhetorical reliance upon it. On one level, he merely draws upon the common stock of poetic devices to enhance communication of his point. On another, the choice of metaphor is far from accidental or merely instrumental, in that it gestures towards larger themes and deeper concerns. In the fourth volume of *Modern Painters* (1856), for instance, Ruskin seeks to consolidate the reader's understanding of how great artists ought to marshal their material and, in a wider sense, behave:

> A great artist is just like a wise and hospitable man with a small house: the large companies of truths, like guests, are waiting his invitation; he wisely chooses from among this crowd the guests who will be happiest with each other, making those whom he receives thoroughly comfortable, and kindly remembering even those whom he excludes; while the foolish host, trying to receive all, leaves a large part of

---

83 John Ruskin, *The Seven Lamps of Architecture*, in *Works*, VIII, p. 245.

his company on the staircase, without even knowing who is there, and destroys, by inconsistent fellowship, the pleasure of those who gain entrance.[84]

While this passage serves the ostensible function of recommending a judicious and selective approach to composition, the extent to which the analogy is allowed to crowd out the primary message is remarkable. As the parable of goodly entertainment moves to the fore, an otherwise technical lesson assumes moral significance. The various concepts and types invoked – among them, the 'wise and hospitable man', the importance of comfort and kindness, the anti-types of 'the foolish host' and of 'inconsistent fellowship' – stick in the mind far more readily than the message they purport to exemplify.

The parabolic quality of this passage is also a feature of Ruskin's comparatively explicit and direct treatments of hospitality. This tendency to ascend from the domestic, the mundane, and the particular, to the level of law and morality, derives for the most part from maternal schooling in the culture and language of the Bible. Moral fables concerning hospitality were also a feature of the Romantic texts that Ruskin and his followers consumed voraciously in their adolescence. A particular favourite of Morris's Oxford 'Set' was Frederic La Motte Fouqué's romance, *Sintram and his Companions* (1815). In this work, a father and son, named Gotthard and Rudlieb, are said to have been 'dashed by a raging winter-storm against the Norwegian shores'.[85] Seeing the form of a 'mighty knight's castle' nearby, they go 'to request assistance and refreshment, as is customary and seemly amongst Christian people'. At their entrance, events take an unpleasant turn. The courtyard suddenly fills 'with armed men, all turning their sharp, steel-pointed lances against the helpless strangers'. Just as their doom seems certain, they are delivered by 'an angelically beautiful woman'. The narrator of the tale is drawn finally to reflect on 'what heathen could be so devilish, as to offer to a shipwrecked claimant of his protection death instead of refreshment and aid?' Events such as these, incorporating the arrival of unannounced strangers, and an abuse of the laws of hospitality, rely on motifs that are widespread in the literature of the period.

Ruskin's earliest work partakes in this Romantic fascination at the same time as it reflects the non-conformist Christian morality of his childhood. This is particularly true of his moral fable, *The King of the Golden River* (written 1841; published 1850).[86] Gluck, the unhappy victim of his brothers' avarice and bullying, is told on no account to admit strangers to the family cottage. One day, while he is alone, he hears somebody knocking at the door. This pivotal moment is depicted by Richard Doyle on the frontispiece to subsequent versions of the tale. A terrified Gluck peers anxiously from a window at the outlandish stranger who is waiting on the step. Despite his brothers' warning, he opens the door, and allows the man imploring admittance to stand by the fire. Later in the story, it transpires that Gluck's guest is a powerful supernatural being. He rewards Gluck for his hospitality and takes vengeance on the brothers' selfishness in a fashion brutally remi-

---

[84] Ruskin, *Modern Painters*, in *Works*, VI, p. 63.
[85] Frederic La Motte Fouqué, *Sintram and his Companions: A Romance*, trans. by J. C. Hane (London: C. and J. Ollier, 1820), p. 76.
[86] Ruskin, *The King of the Golden River*, in *Works*, I, pp. 305–54.

niscent of the retributive justice meted out in the Grimm fairytales. Ruskin's decision to yoke this folk tradition, of nasty ends for the unregenerate, to the largely biblical form of the hospitality fable, powerfully conveys his early conviction that the provision of generous entertainment was a moral imperative. What complicates that message, at least in the eyes of readers unaccustomed to the absolutist forms of punishment favoured by Romantic collectors of 'traditional' tales, is that any customary understanding that a host should be generous, selfless, and unwilling to discriminate, conflicts with the implication that death awaits those who choose not to open their doors. This is a problem common to much Christian morality. Couched as it is in the language of generosity, it simultaneously demonstrates that alternative behaviour is not an option for any rational person concerned for the safety of their soul. The long span of life prior to judgement tends to obscure this difficulty, but in *The King of the Golden River* the verdict is more immediate and thus more susceptible to criticism. Such problems may be ascribed to Ruskin's primary purpose, which was the composition of an entertaining, as well as thrilling, tale. The brutal ending is part of its functionality, as well as a reflection of the story's origin. Ruskin had been challenged by his future wife, the twelve-year old Effie Gray, to accomplish 'the least likely task for him to fulfil'.[87] He responded by writing a fairy tale designed to delight and to provoke.

Ruskin was better known for writing instructive, rather than overtly 'entertaining', works, so it is unsurprising that treatments of this subject become more subtle and less extreme in later years. Nor is it surprising that he sought to integrate it conceptually with his lifelong focus on the perceptual, and the social, significance of *seeing*. In his 1854 pamphlet, 'The Opening of the Crystal Palace' he crosses a scene of jovial good times and hearty feasting with stark reference to the realities of life beyond.[88] The device is to a large extent Dickensian, but the author adds distinctively Ruskinian touches:

we never thoroughly feel the evils which are not actually set before our eyes. If, suddenly, in the midst of the enjoyments of the palate and lightnesses of heart of a London dinner-party, the walls of the chamber were parted, and through their gap, the nearest human beings who were famishing, and in misery, were borne into the midst of the company – feasting and fancy-free – if, pale with sickness, horrible in destitution, broken by despair, body by body, they were laid upon the soft carpet, one beside the chair of every guest, would only the crumbs of the dainties be cast to them – would only a passing glance, a passing thought be vouchsafed to them? Yet the actual facts, the real relations of each Dives and Lazarus, are not altered by the intervention of the house wall between the table and the sick-bed – by the few feet of ground (how few!) which are indeed all that separate the merriment from the misery.

This passage juxtaposes a conventional, politically undemanding form of sociability – the London dinner-party where all are 'feasting and fancy-free' – and a more radical interpretation of hospitable duties. The latter viewpoint implies a determi-

87   W. G. Collingwood, *The Life of John Ruskin*, 7th edn (London: Methuen, 1911), p. 69.
88   John Ruskin, 'The Opening of the Crystal Palace', in *Works*, XII, pp. 415–32.

nation to disregard walls altogether, to abolish the convenient blindnesses that foster and preserve the comfort of those inside and the discomfort of the unfortunate beyond. Ruskin's reliance on the motif of sight represents an obvious point of convergence between the aesthetic theories propounded in *Modern Painters* regarding the importance of close observation – of not missing things in the way that an untrained, idle eye will tend to – and the prophetic and redemptive significance of the 'true' vision underpinning Ruskin's later socio-political writings.

It would nevertheless be a mistake to conclude that Ruskin always subjected conviviality and merriment, on a popular sentimental model, to the kind of unflinching critique mounted in 'The Opening of the Crystal Palace'. Victorian fascination with the practice of entertainment, so clearly evidenced in the many domestic conduct books of the time,[89] is traceable partly to Dickens. One episode in *Pickwick Papers* (1836) opens with a typical linguistic play on this theme:

> 'Welcome,' said their hospitable host, throwing it open and stepping forward to announce them, 'Welcome, gentlemen, to Manor Farm'.[90]

This nostalgic approach is accompanied by extensions of the Romantic interest in the figure of the wanderer, and by the long-standing notion that the art of hospitality had fallen into sad decline. William Watt's 'Hospitality: An Evening Scene' (1845) is a good example. It commences with the lines, 'Welcome, wand'rer! old and poor,/ Here to pass the night secure', and moves to conclusion with the exclamation, 'So stay, old stranger, for thy weal,/ Thou'lt share our fire, our bed, our meal'.[91] Henry Wadsworth Longfellow's prelude from *Tales of a Wayside Inn* (1863) advances the antique hospitality thesis already discussed:

> As ancient is this hostelry
> As any in the land may be,
> Built in the old Colonial day,
> When men lived in a grander way,
> With ampler hospitality.[92]

Even at the beginning of the twentieth century, similar refrains were commonplace. Marie Corelli's article in *The Bystander*, 'The Decay of Hospitality',[93] is notable, as is the obvious pleasure James Joyce takes in satirising nostalgia for old Ireland's famed hospitality, in his short story, 'The Dead'.[94] Most cases can be explained as a reaction to the perceived spread of utilitarianism into the 'sacred'

[89] See, for example, Mrs Isabella Beeton, *The Book of Household Management; Comprising Information for the Mistress . . . Also, Sanitary, Medical, & Legal Memoranda; with a History of the Origin, Properties, and Uses of all Things Connected with Home Life and Comfort* (London: S.O. Beeton, 1861).
[90] Charles Dickens, *The Posthumous Papers of the Pickwick Club* (London: Chapman and Hall, 1837), p. 50.
[91] William Watt, 'Hospitality: An Evening Scene', *Poems, on Sacred and Other Subjects; and Songs, Humorous and Sentimental*, 3rd edn (Glasgow: William Eadie & Co, 1860), p. 280.
[92] Henry Wadsworth Longfellow, *Tales of a Wayside Inn* (London: Routledge, Warne, and Routledge, 1864), p. 1.
[93] Marie Corelli, 'The Decay of Hospitality', *The Bystander*, 29 June 1904, pp. 203–5.
[94] James Joyce, *Dubliners* (Oxford: Oxford University Press, 2001); see also, Mary Power, 'A Note on Hospitality and "The Dead"', *James Joyce Quarterly*, 13, Fall 1975, 1, p. 109.

areas of home life and public lodging. It is in this context that Ruskin depends upon and promulgates the Victorian strain of affection for Longfellow's 'ampler hospitality'.[95]

To justify this proposition, it is necessary to revisit the fourth volume of *Modern Painters*. In the section entitled 'The Mountain Glory', Ruskin refers to the 'special greatness' of the Swiss character. The peculiar virtues bred by Alpine life were being undermined, he suggests, by an 'influx of English wealth, gradually connecting all industry with the wants and ways of strangers [. . .] thus resolving the ancient consistency and pastoral simplicity of the mountain life into the two irregular trades of innkeeper and mendicant'.[96] Condemnation of these social types may at first seem at odds with Ruskin's medievalism. He appears conscious of the difficulty himself, and provides a gloss for the word 'innkeeper'. In the process, he offers a sustained critique of the creeping utilitarianism and commercialism attending the 'influx of foreigners into Switzerland':

> Not the old hospitable innkeeper, who honoured his guests, and was honoured by them, than whom I do not know a more useful or worthy character; but the modern innkeeper, proprietor of a building in the shape of a factory, making up three hundred beds; who necessarily regards his guests in the light of Numbers 1, 2, 3–300, and is too often felt or apprehended by them only as a presiding influence of extortion.

Ruskin thus considers the unfavourable contrast between the 'old hospitable innkeeper' and the 'modern innkeeper'. The former embodies the practical virtues of a 'better time', when the currency in question was honour rather than paper money. The latter is the representative of an 'irregular trade'. In distinguishing the two kinds of host, Ruskin stresses the notion of *usefulness* as well as *worthiness*, in the hope perhaps that this will counter the utilitarian monopoly on economy and practicality in the popular mind. He then moves to condemn the depersonalising effects of commercial hospitality, the mechanisms for accommodating large numbers of people in an age of vastly increased travel and tourism.

A passage in Letter 44 of *Fors Clavigera* elucidates Ruskin's vision of what constitutes exemplary hospitality still further. Here he quotes a passage from Lockhart's *Life of Scott*,[97] in which the lack of any 'inn' or '*public house of any kind*' in a 'whole valley' provides a context for the observation that 'travellers passed from the shepherd's hut to the minister's manse, and again from the cheerful hospitality of the manse to the rough and jolly welcome of the homestead'.[98] As discussed in Chapter Three, Morris discovered similar practices in Iceland, and incorporated them into the form of communism he developed the decade after his visits to that country. In common with Morris, Ruskin was impressed by the kind of 'absolute' economy described by Lockhart. This was based not upon a one-sided imposition of cost, but upon the knowledge that 'the host only gave what he in his turn received, when he also travelled'. The suggestion of a fully

---

95   Longfellow, *Tales of a Wayside Inn*, p. 1.
96   Ruskin, *Modern Painters*, in *Works*, VI, p. 455.
97   John Gibson Lockhart, *Memoirs of the Life of Sir W. Scott*, 10 vols (Edinburgh: 1839).
98   John Ruskin, 'Letter 44', August 1874, *Fors Clavigera*, in *Works*, XXVIII, pp. 125–40 (p. 130).

social economy, with costs and benefits distributed on a public rather than individual basis, is the subject of discussion in later chapters, as is the concluding observation that 'Every man thus carried his home with him'. It may at first seem strange that Ruskin praised the inn as an institution at all, given his primary interest in domestic generosity. He explains his position as follows:

> This absolute economy, of course, could only exist when travelling was so rare that patriarchal hospitality could still be trusted for its lodging. But the hospitality of the inn need not be less considerate or true because the inn's master lives in his occupation. Even in these days, I have had no more true or kind friend than the now dead Mrs. Eisenkraemer of the *old* Union Inn at Chamouni; and an innkeeper's daughter in the Oberland taught me that it was still possible for a Swiss girl to be refined, imaginative, and pure-hearted, though she waited on her father's guests, and though these guests were often vulgar and insolent English travellers.

The inn succeeds in exhibiting the old virtues, notwithstanding the fact that it is the decline in 'patriarchal hospitality' that Ruskin most regrets. Mrs Eisenkraemer's friendship is symbolic of a non-commercial bond, now passed out of the world, but not so distant that Ruskin cannot invoke its memory and significance. And the manners of the innkeeper's daughter in the Oberland are suggestive of what survives, in the more isolated regions of Europe, despite the best efforts of 'vulgar and insolent English travellers'. Ruskin restates this principle in Letter 69 of *Fors*, quoting the words of a correspondent, who noted that 'wherever I left the beaten track of tourists, and the further I left it, so did the friendliness of my entertainers increase'.[99] Ruskin was drawing in large part upon personal experience of inns not simply as an adult, travelling across Europe in search of endangered architecture, but also as a child in the company of his parents on their continental and Highland tours. Tim Hilton offers an insightful commentary on the love of inns Ruskin inherited from his businessman father. He also indicates that this same affection for traditional accommodation caused Ruskin to set up house at the Crown and Thistle Inn, Abingdon, when lecturing at Oxford:

> Like John James Ruskin before him he [Ruskin] was a connoisseur of inns, hotels, *auberges* and other resting places, both British and European. John James would never spend a night in another person's house, and in 1848 had declared that he had not done so for thirty years. [. . .] *Fors* resembles Scott's novels, with their peerless descriptions of hostelries and of the proud, combative and garrulous men to whom they gave hospitality. Nobody can tell a person what not to write from an inn. A guest there is his own master. When Ruskin chose to live at the Crown and Thistle at the beginning of his professorship he was not being eccentric. [. . .] Ruskin could leave the dining table when he wished.[100]

It is striking that Hilton ascribes to Ruskin motives that conflict with his declared preference for 'patriarchal hospitality'. He does, after all, imply that Ruskin

---

99   John Ruskin, 'Letter 69', September 1876, *Fors Clavigera*, in *Works*, XXVIII, pp. 687–701 (p. 690).
100 Tim Hilton, *John Ruskin: The Later Years* (New Haven and London: Yale University Press, 2000), pp. 264–5.

preferred being left to his own devices, having the freedom to come and go as he wished. The advantages of a relatively impersonal experience include a degree of autonomy and independence from kindly disturbance. A guest is not 'his own master' unless he is paying. This hardly accords with the spirit of 'Old English Hospitality'. And yet the very fact that Ruskin found the environment of an old inn so congenial is evidence enough that his evaluation of traditional hospitality extended beyond merely theoretic appreciation.

Before examining Ruskin's most developed, and indeed, utopian accounts of what hospitality should and could be, it is necessary to consider the philosophy of the house, home and household expounded by him. This in itself involved an attempt to anatomize the modern dwelling, along with its many faults, before postulating a semi-archaic remedy along utopian lines. Ruskin was not alone in considering how the modern house might be redesigned with a view to the social effects of redistributing space. In *Walden*, Henry Thoreau outlines a 'dream of a larger and more populous house, standing in a golden age, of enduring materials, and without gingerbread work, which shall still consist of only one room, a vast, rude, substantial, primitive hall'.[101] At this 'cavernous house', the 'traveller may wash, and eat, and converse'. Thoreau's text includes a passage criticizing modern manners, which would perhaps have appealed to Ruskin:

> Nowadays the host does not admit you to *his* hearth, but has got the mason to build one for yourself somewhere in his alley, and hospitality is the art of *keeping* you at the greatest distance. There is as much secrecy about the cooking as if he had a design to poison you. [. . .]
>
> It would seem as if the very language of our parlors would lose all its nerve and degenerate into *parlaver* wholly, our lives pass at such remoteness from its symbols, and its metaphors and tropes are necessarily so far fetched, through slides and dumb-waiters, as it were; in other words, the parlor is so far from the kitchen and workshop. The dinner even is only the parable of a dinner, commonly.

Concern for the hearth is a feature also of Ruskin's thought on the nature of a successful household and of a fitting home. In *Sesame and Lilies* (1865), he famously described home as 'the place of Peace; the shelter, not only from all injury, but from all terror, doubt, and division':[102]

> In so far as it is not this, it is not home; so far as the anxieties of the outer life penetrate into it, and the inconsistently-minded, unknown, unloved, or hostile society of the outer world is allowed by either husband or wife to cross the threshold, it ceases to be home; it is then only a part of that outer world which you have roofed over, and lighted fire in.

The focus on retreat and comfort in this passage is slightly at odds with the emphasis on hospitality already discussed, especially when considered in the light of the lessons on *seeing* delivered in 'The Opening of the Crystal Palace'.[103] All the

---

101   Thoreau, *Walden*, pp. 161, 162.
102   John Ruskin, *Sesame and Lilies*, in *Works*, XVIII, pp. 1–187 (p. 122).
103   Ruskin, 'The Opening of the Crystal Palace', p. 430.

same, it is apparent that Ruskin wished to see a rehabilitation of home and hearth, partly because they represented a means of civilizing and domesticating the outside world. The best expression of this idea – this ideal traffic between hearth and world – comes in Ruskin's preface to *Unto this Last* (1862). Here, he substitutes for the term *economy* the compound word 'House-law' (a literal translation of the Greek root-word, *oikonomia*).[104] By this, Ruskin implies that the wider economy is actually akin to the domestic realm; that it is ideally governed by the same sense of justice that underwrites paternal responsibility and co-operation in a household.

Both Ruskin's account of 'patriarchal hospitality', and of 'house-law', posit a fundamental link between the domestic realm and a wider economy or society now sadly fallen into desuetude. It follows that hospitality, and the available scope for its renewal, became for him a powerful form of utopian speculation, a means of challenging wilful blindness to poverty, utilitarianism, individualism, even the modern division between the public and the private realms. The powers of renewal that Ruskin invests in the idea of archaic or medieval hospitality are nowhere more apparent than in Letter 36 of *Fors Claveriga*:

> if we duly recognise the laws of God about meats and drinks, there will for every labourer and traveller be such chancing upon meat and drink and other entertainment as shall be sacredly pleasant to him. And there cannot indeed be at present imagined a more sacred function for young Christian men than that of hosts or hospitallers, supplying, to due needs, and with proper maintenance of their own lives, wholesome food and drink to all men: so that as, at least, always at one end of a village there may be a holy church and vicar, so at the other end of the village there may be a holy tavern and tapster, ministering to the good creatures of God, so that they may be sanctified by the Word of God and His Providence.[105]

Just as the virtues of the domestic realm should be spread widely, so Ruskin implies that the mission of Christian youth is as fittingly expressed in the guest house as in the village church. Thus the boundaries that separate the secular and the sacred are challenged, and a symmetry and co-equality of function emerge between the components of village life. Later, in Letter 93, Ruskin builds on this idea, acknowledging its whimsical, utopian character, but also presenting it as a serious proposition:

> Think [. . .] what roadside-inns might be kept by a true Gaius and Gaia! You have perhaps held it – in far back *Fors* – one of my wildest sayings, that every village should have, as a Holy Church at one end, a Holy Tavern at the other! I will better the saying now by adding – 'they may be side by side, if you will.' And then you will have entered into another mystery of monastic life, as you shall see by the plan given of a Cistercian Monastery in the second forthcoming number of *Valle Crucis* – where, appointed in its due place with the Church, the Scriptorium and the school, is the Hospitium for entertaining strangers unawares. And why not awares also? Judge what the delight of travelling would be, for nice travellers (read the word 'nice' in any sense you will) – if at every village there were a Blue Boar, or a Green Dragon,

---

104 John Ruskin, Preface, *Unto this Last*, in *Works*, XVII, pp. 17–23 (p. 19).
105 John Ruskin, 'Letter 36: "Traveller's Rest"', *Fors Clavigera*, in *Works*, XXVII, pp. 668–76 (pp. 671–2).

or Silver Swan – with Mark Tapley of the Dragon for Ostler – and Boots of the Swan
for Boots – and Mrs. Lupin or Mrs. Lirriper for Hostess – only trained at Girton in
all that becomes a Hostess in the nineteenth century![106]

Here Ruskin conflates several versions of archaic hospitality – Roman, rustic and
monastic – such as to reiterate the integrationist view outlined in Letter 36.[107] He
also incorporates reference to the famous Dickensian hostelries in *Great Expectations* (1860–61), *Martin Chuzzlewit* (1843–44), and to their famous guardians.
These details invest Ruskin's vision of a perfect village, blessed by a Holy Church
and Holy Tavern, with that composite quality typical of imagined communities.

Ruskin was influenced by a diverse set of literary and cultural sources, each
conducive to close engagement with the moral, social and architectural mechanisms governing the reception of strangers. The influence of mystical treatments
of the theme of transience, the Romantic preoccupation with wanderers, Christian morality tales and fables, even the Dickensian penchant for festivity and
family celebration, are all of relevance. Closer to home, there are the views of John
James Ruskin on the merits of old fashioned wayside entertainment, and the
experiences of Ruskin himself on his travels in Switzerland and Scotland.
Although Ruskin was reliant on the language of hospitality as a mode of explica-
tion, in the way he was reliant on many biblical subjects, it served more than an
analogical purpose in his writings. The duties of a host represented an ethical
touchstone, a code of conduct devoid of financial or utilitarian imperatives, which
guided him towards an alternative conception of 'house-law' or economics. In
determining the literary precedents for Morris's vision of a utopian 'guest-house'
in *News from Nowhere*, one must take into account the biblically resonant
prescription of his 'master',[108] Ruskin's counsel that every village should include a
'Holy Tavern' in addition to the customary 'Holy Church'.

Conclusions

Many nineteenth-century writers and artists celebrated the virtues of a warm
welcome and the folkloric benefits of the feasting hall. A select few remained
attuned to the dangers of hospitality, exploring the anarchic significance of the
guest as a literary type. Morris's peculiar brand of utopianism paid considerable
heed to this notion, particularly where the accommodation and management of
dissent was concerned. Earlier writers, Goethe and Scott most prominently,
combined this sceptical tradition with evocation of an optimistic, idealized hospitality. The latter notion possesses neither unitary cultural meaning nor a fixed
political complexion. It emerges in the nostalgic radicalism of Blake and Cobbett
and in the Catholic polemics of Pugin. It informs the Romantic preoccupation
with outsiders and wanderers, but also the home worship of Dickens and the periodical press. Its folkloric associations were attractive to those wishing to transcend
the austerity and depression of the 1840s, and its organic communality and

---

106 John Ruskin, 'Letter 93', Christmas 1883, *Fors Clavigera*, in *Works*, XXIX, pp. 466–77 (pp. 474–5).
107 Ruskin, 'Letter 36', *Fors*, p. 671.
108 Morris, 'How I Became a Socialist', p. 279.

hierarchy rendered it a useful tool in the hands of political writers like Manners and Disraeli. Many of these strands – the romantic, the Tory, and the utopian – combine in the work of John Ruskin. Ruskin influenced not just Morris, but a range of social thinkers, from Edward Carpenter to Tolstoy and Gandhi. With this in mind, it is easier to appreciate the critical significance of his emphasis on the utopian household, and on the external reverberations of sound husbandry and generous domestic economy.

Chapter 2

BEFORE 'THE DAYS WHEN HOSPITALITY HAD TO BE BOUGHT AND SOLD': IDEALIZED HOSPITALITY AND AESTHETIC SEPARATISM IN MORRIS'S WORK OF THE 1860S AND 1870S*

Introduction

Chapter 1 examined the medievalist idealization of hospitality evoked by a range of Romantic and Victorian writers. The use to which Morris put this complex and politically diverse legacy in formulating his own 'utopia of strangers' forms the focus of what follows. The decision to accord Morris a central position is justified on two grounds. First, his works form an effective bridge between Cobbett's old English hospitality and late-nineteenth-century socialism. His importance is ensured, in addition, by consistent sensitivity to the political ramifications of hospitality in a utopian setting.

Readers approaching the previous chapter with a strong sense of Morris as a practitioner of aestheticism would be entitled to question the compatibility of the Ruskinian ethic of openness, tentatively posited, with the premium placed on inwardness and high art values popularly associated with Pre-Raphaelitism. There is, admittedly, a certain amount to be said in support of such observations. Morris's artistic allegiances may seem far removed from aesthetic isolationism of the kind associated with James Whistler or Oscar Wilde. This impression appears especially warranted when one considers that he took Ruskin as his 'master',[1] a figure whose reputation evokes the questing spirit of the socially concerned Victorian, the communal ethic of guild socialism and a notorious legal stand-off with the new aestheticism (the Ruskin *v.* Whistler Trial of 1878). Yet one should not lose sight of Morris's familiarity and sympathy with the other side of the question. Early friendship and collaboration with Dante Gabriel Rossetti had ensured that he became acquainted with aestheticism at a formative stage in his career.[2]

Even after becoming a socialist, Morris retained an awareness that certain

---

*   *News from Nowhere*, p. 185
[1]   Morris, 'How I Became a Socialist', p. 279.
[2]   While Rossetti was by no means an unqualified aesthete (there was a strand of Christian Socialism in Pre-Raphaelite thinking), Morris came later to see his influence as a distraction from Ruskin's assertion of a link between art and politics (identifying it as 'the maundering side of medievalism', 'To Andreas Scheu', 15 September 1883, in *Collected Letters*, II, pp. 225–31 (p. 229)).

things might not be achieved in the public arena. 'Art for Art's Sake', it is true, became anathema to him. As a theory of the aesthetic, or an artistic ideal, it was everything he held in contempt. But aesthetic separatism as a way of working, as a determination to resist the encroachments of 'shoddy' commercial manufacture, remained an essential feature of his artistic practice.[3] Like those he later criticized for attempting to 'cultivate art intellectually', Morris was in this respect 'living in an enemy's country'.[4] Though certain that art was essentially the property of all, he recognized that under prevailing conditions, artists who relinquished control of their work did so at the risk of accepting externally imposed standards. Morris was torn between two opposing responses to this problem: either he would establish a closed society of artists, and thus protect what might at least be achieved in isolation; or he would attempt to reform the wider world, leading 'Crusade and Holy Warfare against the age'.[5]

It was in the early decades of his career, in the 1860s and 1870s, that Morris first confronted the conflict between available artistic responses to alienation. In these years, his work stages a dialogue between escapism, or separatism, and a form of communality that both pre-dates and anticipates his conversion to Marxian socialism: an openness expressed through commitment to an unconditional, or an idealized, hospitality. This chapter asks whether a preoccupation with the theme of welcome, as it emerges in the design of Red House and in the poems of *The Earthly Paradise*, countered Morris's early drift towards isolationism; or whether, in fact, medievalist hospitality itself suggested a fanciful substitution, an attempt to install in place of the commercial world a vision of wanderers and pilgrims roaming abroad, a receptiveness necessarily selective, because anachronistic, and so not wholly applicable to the problems of the age.

The Pilgrim's Rest: Privacy, Property and the Structures of Welcome at William Morris's Red House[6]

In 1859, work began on the construction of Morris's first family home: a kind of domestic paradise situated in the Kent countryside near Bexleyheath. It is a familiar story that Morris, Philip Webb (Red House's architect), and Charles Faulkner first discussed the idea of building Red House while on a boating holiday in France. It is also well known that recent inheritance of a sizable personal fortune enabled Morris to prosecute these ambitious plans; and that the Burne-Jones family had intended eventually to occupy an extension to the building. A considerable amount has been written about the house itself, and about the lives of the Morrises during their five-year period of residence. But few critics have attempted a broader, conceptual investigation of the building, or

3 Morris, 'How We Live and How We Might Live', in *Collected Works*, XXIII, pp. 3–27 (p. 9).
4 Morris, 'The Beauty of Life', in *Collected Works*, XXII, pp. 51–80 (p. 56).
5 From a letter sent by Edward Burne-Jones to 'a school fellow still in Birmingham' on 1 May 1853, quoted in J. W. Mackail, *The Life of William Morris*, 2 vols (London: Longmans, Green, and Co., 1899), I, p. 63.
6 A version of this section was previously published as an article, under the title, 'The Stranger at the Gate: Privacy, Property, and the Structures of Welcome at William Morris's Red House', *Victorian Studies*, 46 (Summer 2004), 4, 567–95.

submitted to sustained critical analysis the two features of the house frequently ascribed to the influence of the Gothic Revival: its idyllic privacy and its warmth of hospitality.[7]

This is particularly regrettable, as the structural characteristics of Red House evoke not only the ideals of its architect and owner, but also the link between medievalism and embryonic socialism, between paternalism and equalitarian inclusiveness. It would be some time before Morris became actively involved in socialist politics, but the house he built as a young man bears witness to the beginnings of a cultural shift. In material form, Red House evokes a mid-way point between those largely conservative myths of sociability and festivity popularized during the economically depressed 1840s, and the less hierarchical forms of welcome and seclusion that came to the fore later in the century, with the Arts and Crafts Movement and guild socialism.

In the past, discussion of Red House has been confined largely to scrutiny of its contentious status as a landmark in the history of design. Even today, its significance is too often assessed solely in relation to criteria of architectural originality, criteria that did not cease to be applied when Sir Hugh Casson,[8] Mark Girouard[9] and Paul Thompson[10] began to challenge Nikolaus Pevsner's view that the house's design was revolutionary,[11] that it represented a germ or source of the modern movement. In the wake of this factual corrective, critics have been slow in substituting alternative evaluative techniques for the old emphasis on originality. In consequence, the building is still sometimes dismissed merely because it is architecturally derivative. Fiona MacCarthy, in her recent biography of Morris, goes further than most in extending the discussion beyond these concerns. Describing Red House as 'a deeply symbolic building', she poeticizes Morris's commission in a way that successfully restores the building's integrity.[12] She emphasizes its 'monastic quality' and its 'apartness', arguing that 'Red House is symbolic as an act of separation, the retreat from and defiance of the world'. This, in itself, is nothing new, but MacCarthy complicates her account with the assertion that 'it is

---

7   Fiona MacCarthy writes that the door to Red House is 'set in a deep porch, giving a sense of monumental welcome' (caption III to Red House illustrations, *William Morris: A Life for Our Time* (London: Faber and Faber, 1994)). These 'architectural surroundings', she adds, 'established the young Morris in his persona of the genial host'. In her biography of Philip Webb, Sheila Kirk describes Red House as 'warm and welcoming on the outside, informal and spacious within' (p. 35), *Philip Webb: Pioneer of Arts & Crafts Architecture* (Chichester, West Sussex: Wiley-Academy, 2005).

8   Sir Hugh Casson, 'Red House: The Home of William Morris', *The Listener*, 1 October 1953, pp. 536–7 (p. 536).

9   Mark Girouard, 'Red House, Bexleyheath, Kent', *Country Life*, 16 June 1960, pp. 1382–5 (p. 1383).

10 Paul Thompson, *The Work of William Morris* (London: Heinemann, 1967), p. 13.

11 In *Pioneers of the Modern Movement: From William Morris to Walter Gropius* (London: Faber and Faber, 1936), Pevsner presented Red House as a landmark in the development of modern architecture; he restated his case in *The Sources of Modern Architecture and Design* (London: Thames and Hudson, 1968), arguing that Red House was 'an exception in its own day and more prophetic of the coming twentieth century than anything in the field of domestic design in any country for thirty years to come' (p. 23); Pevsner's views accord with Lawrence Weaver's earlier assertion that 'every brick of it [Red House] is a word in the history of modern architecture', *Small Country Houses of To-Day* (Woodbridge, Suffolk: Baron Publishing, 1983), p. 180; and with Hermann Muthesius's similar identification of the building as a major turning point, *The English House*, trans. by Janet Seligman (London: Crosby Lockwood Staples, 1979), p. 17.

12 MacCarthy, *William Morris*, p. 156.

also the place the knights ride out from', 'the departure point for the crusade against the age'. By this she implies that Red House's 'apartness' is not total; the house must remain in dialogue with the world it rejects in order to effect change.

Within the limits of a biography, it is understandable that MacCarthy does not develop the suggestion of contradiction implicit in her reference to a *retreat* and a *crusade*. It is the main business of this section to make good this omission. I begin by considering the extent to which utopian separatism and hospitality inform the construction and design of Red House. I then demonstrate the sense in which these values are limited in their realization, and potentially contradictory in their conjunction. As will become clear, the latter is especially the case where the medievalism facilitating the conceptual unity of openness and withdrawal is disrupted by the exigencies of modern economic life.[13]

The idea of founding a new household, of beginning again, was the subject of two poems by Tennyson no doubt familiar to Morris: *The Princess* (1847)[14] and 'The Palace of Art'.[15] Yet in one important respect, these works do not serve as blueprints for the construction of Red House. Neither the plans for an all-female college in *The Princess*, nor the concept of a 'lordly pleasure-house' outlined in 'The Palace of Art', are presented as adequate solutions to the problem of alienation. Morris's reference, in 1864, to the eventual failure of his plan to live in a 'palace of Art' indicates that he and Burne-Jones once invested some hope in the viability of this castle in the air, in the possibility of an aesthetic separatism untroubled by Tennysonian assertions of the reality principle.[16] In a letter to Cormell Price, dated July 1856, Morris declared that he felt unable to put right the 'muddle' suggested by 'politico-social subjects'.[17] It makes sense that he should have responded to this declared incapacity by resorting to a sphere that *did* concern him directly. In a household, at least, things might realistically be set in order. But Morris was not content with the power to effect change offered by mere control of an interior space. He opted instead to start completely from scratch. Rather than buy an existing property, he had one built to his own specifications. As his biographer J. W. Mackail put it, Morris wished to construct 'a house after his own fancy', a place 'in which life and its central purposes need not be thwarted by any baseness or ugliness of immediate surroundings'.[18]

One important feature of Morris's audacious attempt to secure Red House from 'any baseness or ugliness' was the philosophy of reinvention that underpinned its ongoing decoration. Mackail states that 'Only in a few isolated cases – such as Persian carpets, and blue china or delft for vessels of household use – was there anything then to be bought ready-made that Morris could be content with in his own house'. Only close companions were entrusted to create the furniture. Red House's separatist credentials were also enhanced by the fact that its architect was a friend of Morris's, that, by employing a member of his own social circle, he

13   The conceptual unity of openness and withdrawal finds exemplification in the monastic ideal of a life spent in retreat, which is yet sociable and receptive to the stranger at the gate.

14   Alfred Tennyson, *The Princess*, in *The Poems of Tennyson*, II, pp. 185–296.

15   Alfred Tennyson, 'The Palace of Art', in *The Poems of Tennyson*, I, pp. 436–56 (p. 438).

16   Morris, 'To Edward Burne-Jones', [November 1864], in *Collected Letters*, I pp. 38–9 (p. 38).

17   Morris, 'To Cormell Price', July 1856, in *Collected Letters*, I, pp. 28–9 (p. 28).

18   J. W. Mackail, *The Life of William Morris*, 2 vols (London: Longmans, Green, and Co., 1899), I, pp. 137, 139, 142–3.

was able to bypass the market for house design. Indeed, few residences of Red House's size were architect-designed in the 1850s. Most borrowed their features from the available pattern books. In this respect, also, Morris was expressing autonomy, his power, as a man of wealth, to opt out of established procedures where they seemed degrading or conducive to ugliness.

Morris conducted the revivalism so often identified as a feature of Red House in a similar spirit of self-determination. This attitude is expressed succinctly in the motto he embroidered onto the pre-Red House hanging, '*If I Can*'.[19] Clearly influenced by the results his recent employer, G. E. Street, had achieved (with Agnes Blencowe) in recommencing the production of ecclesiastical embroidery, Morris's domestic variant on this work expresses a belief that the arts of the past might be resuscitated. The spirit of autonomy resides here not so much in the attempt to revive extinct crafts as in the lack of reverence shown towards the ideal of historical veracity: Red House, though built, according to Morris, in a thirteenth-century style, is not dogmatically historical.[20] It instead exudes confidence that the best art of several periods might be combined to form a pleasing whole. Hence one finds quarries of domestic stained glass, typical of fifteenth-century dwellings, in the ground-floor gallery of this 'thirteenth-century' house. Indeed, the building shuns the strict imitation of classical styles, Palladian or Greek, in favour of a freer revivalism, a revivalism not bound by rules or orders. Much later in life, Morris argued in his lecture, 'Gothic Architecture' (1889), that the Gothic was potentially a modern architectural style.[21] It was, he claimed, far better fitted to the present day than classical architecture, because of its adaptability. As an 'Organic architecture', open to a variety of uses and amenable to extension as needs changed, it was the only style he thought suitable for use in the future. Webb later rose to this challenge at Standen (1892–94), a residence in Sussex he built in an adapted vernacular style. Applying principles of organic design to the needs of the estate, rather than attempting the recreation of an 'authentic' country-house style, he even managed to incorporate into the plan a number of pre-existing vernacular buildings. At Red House, Webb is already utilizing Gothic principles to achieve a design autonomy in sympathy with tradition.

Implicit in the decorative technique of fresco, which Morris and his friends applied at Red House (as they had done already at the Oxford Union, in 1857), was a belief in the value of transforming one's immediate environment. Hanging brass rubbings from his bedroom walls at Oxford, and then joining Burne-Jones in the manufacture of suitable furniture for their rooms at Red Lion Square, Morris clearly had great confidence in the transfiguring power of decoration. Reflecting this preoccupation were the plans made for an entire mural scheme at Red House. It was to be ambitious in scope, and would eventually have changed the whole mood of the interior.

Another form of ornamentation involved the pricking of holes in wet ceiling plaster. Once the surface had dried, these marks enabled easy application of

19 *If I Can* hanging, 1856–7, Society of Antiquaries of London, Kelmscott Manor.
20 Of Red House, William Bell Scott recalls, 'It was designed by Morris in what he called the style of the thirteenth century', *Autobiographical Notes of the Life of William Bell Scott*, 2 vols (London: James R. Osgood, McIlvaine & Co, 1892), II, p. 61.
21 Morris, 'Gothic Architecture', pp. 268, 273.

painted repeat-patterns. With its emphasis on the possibility of redecoration, the technique also gestured toward the importance of continually renewing one's environment, of taking an active part in its refashioning. It is significant that Rossetti's paintings on the doors of the drawing-room settle are aestheticist in theme, evoking an abandonment of the world, and of worldly concerns, in favour of a high ideal. The *Salutation of Beatrice* panels (including *Dantis Amor*) (1860) allude to the idea that paradise might be attained through love (another separatist ideal at odds with economic claims).[22] Burne-Jones's *The Wedding Procession of Sir Degrevaunt* (1860) also sets the tone, a vision of sociability depicting likenesses of Morris and Jane in the roles of king and queen.[23] It presents a striking alternative to Tennyson's dark vision of a king reigning 'apart'.[24] These decorative schemes also enabled the group of friends to enshrine their particular ideals as household gods. In the window inserts now in the ground-floor gallery, Love and Fate are depicted as presiding deities. The various mottoes painted in and around the house also had the effect of reflecting and reinforcing the group's defining principles on an environmental level, insisting that each and every surface declared positive affiliation to their shared aims.

The principles applied by Webb in his design of Red House were consistent with the teachings of Pugin, who insisted that the decoration of an object should always be in harmony with its function.[25] Red House has no façade as conventionally understood. Instead of concealing its fabric of support, interior beams and brick arches are flaunted as decorative features. The beautiful and the useful are in this way reconciled. Ceilings that make concessions, and occasionally succumb fully, to the shape of the roof express this principle. The exposed cross-bracing specified by Webb in his plans for the wooden gates make a point of structural frankness.[26] The undisguised joints on the underside of the main staircase and the exuberant decoration of wrought-iron strap hinges also adhere to this philosophy. Even the bricks laid in the dining-room fireplace appear to mimic the movement of rising smoke. In this way, they suggest a sympathy between the materiality of the chimney and its final use.

Beyond the emphasis on honesty of design, there is evidence of an attempt to incorporate Ruskin's Gothic virtue of 'imperfection'.[27] Deliberate exposure of saw marks, and fabled willingness to allow the bricklayer creativity in his work on the fireplace, do not exactly render this architect-designed house an example of folk art. But such measures might at least indicate an attempt to accommodate Ruskin's model of unalienated labour within the overall scheme. Even from a

22 Dante Gabriel Rossetti, *Dantis Amor*, from *The Salutation of Beatrice on Earth and in Eden*, 1860, oil on panel, Tate Britain, London.
23 Edward Burne-Jones, *The Wedding Procession of Sir Degrevaunt*, 1860, The National Trust, Red House, Bexleyheath, Kent.
24 Tennyson, 'The Palace of Art', p. 438.
25 In *The True Principles of Pointed or Christian Architecture*, Pugin stated that 'The two great rules for design are these: *1st, that there should be no features about a building which are not necessary for convenience, construction, or propriety; 2nd, that all ornament should consist of enrichment of the essential construction of the building*' (p. 1).
26 In his plans, Webb also indicates that the woodwork on the gates (Webb E.63–1916 DD22), and on the well (Webb E.64–1916 DD22), should be left with the 'saw marks' still visible, Print Room, Victoria and Albert Museum.
27 Ruskin, 'The Nature of Gothic', *The Stones of Venice*, p. 234.

distance, the building appears to express this aim. Edward Hollamby has noted a remarkable 'freedom of fenestration'[28] in the house's design, a feature conceivably symbolic of Webb's attempt to unite modern architectural aesthetics with Ruskin's emphasis on 'Changefulness',[29] on a 'confession of Imperfection'. It also suggests adherence to Ruskin's call in *The Stones of Venice* (1851–53) for the positioning of windows to be determined by interior needs rather than by the demands of exterior symmetry.[30]

Red House's symbolic claim to 'apartness' is strengthened by its evocation of the kind of seclusion and privacy that Ruskin identified as a feature of fifteenth-century landscapes. In *Modern Painters* (1843–60), he explains the link between fortifications and paradise:

> the trouble and ceaseless warfare of the times [. . .] rendered security one of the first elements of pleasantness [. . .] making it impossible for any artist to conceive Paradise but as surrounded by a moat, or to distinguish the road to it better than by its narrow wicket gate, and watchful porter.[31]

Red House seems indebted to this account of fortification. The effect of the huge wall that surrounds the property, like the walls enclosing the medieval gardens Morris admired in illuminated manuscripts, is to domesticate, as well as to protect, what lies within.[32] Privacy of this kind represents less a seizure of access rights to a given stretch of land, than the staking of a human claim to a garden amidst the wilderness. The grounds of Red House have been identified as the first attempt to revive the layout of the medieval plot garden, where hedges and wattle fences create a network of enclosures. Later in his career, in a lecture entitled 'Making the Best of it' (in or before 1879), Morris expressed his views on gardening.[33] On the evidence of the original garden at Red House, his opinions in these matters had changed little since the early 1860s:

> It should be well fenced from the outside world. It should by no means imitate either the wilfulness or the wildness of Nature, but should look like a thing never to be seen except near a house. It should, in fact, look like a part of the house.

Just as the garden may be taken as a symbol of joyful isolation, so the plan of the building harnesses a more positive conception of enclosure. Built in an 'L'-shape,

---

28 Edward Hollamby, 'Philip Webb Red House Bexleyheath, Kent 1859', in *Arts and Crafts Houses I*, ed. by Beth Dunlop (London: Phaidon, [n.d.]).

29 Ruskin, 'The Nature of Gothic', *The Stones of Venice*, pp. 184, 214.

30 Ruskin observes that 'it is one of the chief virtues of the Gothic builders, that they never suffered ideas of outside symmetries and consistencies to interfere with the real use and value of what they did. If they wanted a window, they opened one; a room, they added one; a buttress, they built one; utterly regardless of any established conventionalities of external appearance, knowing (as indeed it always happened) that such daring interruptions of the formal plan would rather give additional interest to its symmetry than injure it', 'The Nature of Gothic', *The Stones of Venice*, p. 212.

31 Ruskin, *Modern Painters*, in *Works*, V, p. 260.

32 Jan Marsh, in her recent study, *William Morris & Red House* (National Trust Books, 2005), is unusual in finding Red House 'neither curious nor welcoming' (p. 22), stressing the 'excluding wall and gate' (she admits that the 'well-garden' 'feels more hospitable' (p. 23)). Her remarks are justified as applied to the house's *approach*, but they nevertheless reflect a failure to appreciate that medievalist privacy and hospitality are mutually dependent.

33 Morris, 'Making the Best of It', in *Collected Works*, XXII, pp. 81–118 (p. 91).

Red House was designed to allow for easy extension. In 1864, Webb conceived a new wing, which was intended to make room for workshops, and to accommodate the Burne-Jones family. It was never built, apparently because the house's situation and conditions no longer seemed suitable for Georgiana Burne-Jones, who was in delicate health due to scarlet fever and the related death of a child.

Had it been realized, the proposed extension would have produced the effect of a cloister based on the well-side corridor. Though the resulting court would have been open to the south, the suggestion of self-sufficiency must nevertheless have been heightened, with the structure of the well now dominating all views from that side of the house. Obviously designed to enhance this effect is the oriel window included in Webb's design for the additional wing, a feature that produces a formalized view of the newly enclosed space. As in an Oxford college, one effect of the proposed quadrangular structure would have been to stress the fellowship of those inhabiting the building. Along the inner walls, all eyes would necessarily be focused on the central symbol of sustenance, the well. In such a *paradisus claustralis*, the forms of fortification are transformed into a celebration of independence, a refuge from the commercially interconnected world beyond.

Though the pursuit of domestication and seclusion need not preclude a communal life, there is, nevertheless, a tension apparent between the two ideals that inspired the construction of Red House: the inwardness encouraged by the Rossettian brand of Pre-Raphaelitism and the ideal of brotherhood celebrated by the Oxford 'Set'. Morris did not accept that 'home' had to mean isolation, but it is apparent from the design of Red House – which steers a middle course between the removed communality of a monastery and the less radical isolation of the conventional middle-class dwelling – that the danger of it becoming anti-social was to him a real concern. The pursuit of aesthetic separatism, he recognized, could end in a sterile solipsism. In his letter to Cormell Price (quoted earlier), Morris reflects, 'I was slipping off into a kind of small (very small) Palace of Art'.[34] 'Ned and I', he adds, 'are going to live together'. Moving in with one of his friends (here he refers to the rooms at Red Lion Square) may have struck Morris as a way of avoiding this unhappy fate.

There is, moreover, much in Webb's original plans to suggest an attempt to solve the problems Tennyson's poem had associated with palaces of art. It is important to understand that medieval aristocratic households were, as social units, far more open than the average nineteenth-century villa.[35] Blood relatives, domestics and young noblemen from other families often lived under one roof as a complete community. The design of Red House would seem to suggest cognizance of this distinction. In fact, there are several indications that Webb and Morris sought consciously to break up the closed inner circle of the Victorian family. The attempt is reminiscent of the church built by G. E. Street at Boyn Hill, in Maidenhead, Berkshire (1854–57). Here a place of worship is set amidst a

---

34 Morris, 'To Cormell Price', July 1856, pp. 28–9.
35 Lawrence Stone writes that 'The most striking characteristic of the late medieval and early sixteenth-century family, at all social levels, was the degree to which it was open to external influences, a porosity that is in contrast to the more sealed off and private nuclear family type that was to develop in the seventeenth and eighteenth centuries', *The Family, Sex and Marriage in England 1500–1800* (London: Weidenfeld and Nicolson, 1977), p. 85.

complex of related buildings, including a school, a vicarage, two clergy houses and an almshouse. Boyn Hill typifies Street's efforts to found structurally coherent neo-medieval communities. As pupils of Street, it is hard to imagine that Webb and Morris were not influenced by his pursuit of functional integration.

As Mark Girouard remarks, this effort was chiefly characterized by an unconventional distribution of working spaces:

> The original kitchen is down a passage a short way from the dining-room and has a capacious window looking west on to the garden, a friendly feature typical of the Red House; at the time it was built servants were usually hidden in the basement or a concealed wing.[36]

The features of the building already discussed (such as the number of windows looking onto the well-court, and the proposed cloister) that evoke the architecture and life of a monastic foundation, are, moreover, suggestive of equality, rather than hierarchy. They ensure that no individual member of the household enjoys a privileged view or an immaculate vista. The suggestion of communality is also enhanced by the attempts Morris and Burne-Jones made to combine in Red House the functions of family home and workshop. This aspiration clearly invokes the medieval willingness to combine places of work with places of leisure.

Unlike the planned workers' villages executed by Robert Owen at New Lanark (1800–25), and Sir Titus Salt at Saltaire (1851–76), the design of Red House encourages a combination of work and play under one roof. The studio in which Morris worked is placed in close proximity to the drawing-room. As the plans for the foundation of a design company became more serious, he even proposed to establish a manufactory in an extension to the building. These measures suggest that Morris did not anticipate a form of work undertaken in accordance with Ruskinian principles – that is, an unalienating work incorporating the 'freedom of thought'[37] characteristic of that 'life and liberty' supposedly enjoyed by the medieval workman – posing any threat to the tranquillity of home life. In an important sense, then, Morris's conception of privacy, or retreat, was distinct from the more widespread conception of ideal home life. That, after all, implied complete removal of work from the domestic setting, with such activities as needlework and music pursued in a determinedly amateurish fashion. Although it would be inaccurate to treat Red House as a building reviving the 'general absence of functionally differentiated space' that Lewis Mumford identifies as a defining feature of medieval dwellings, there is much, in the probable co-operation of architect and client, and in the shared effort to decorate the interior, that suggests an attempt at combining privacy with community, and work with pleasure.[38]

The most obvious sense in which the house remains outward-looking despite its seclusion is through visible quotation of an idea already treated at some length: the obligation to provide hospitality that was written into the statutes of most medieval institutions.[39] In his lecture, 'Ruskin, Morris and Medievalism', Clive

---

36 Girouard, 'Red House, Bexleyheath, Kent', p. 1384.
37 Ruskin, 'The Nature of Gothic', *The Stones of Venice*, pp. 193, 194.
38 Lewis Mumford, *The City in History* (Harmondsworth: Penguin Books, 1966), p. 330.
39 See, for example, The Rule of St Benedict, *Households of God: The Rule of St Benedict with Explanations for Monks and Lay-people Today* (pp. 140–3).

Figure 1. Porch and door of Red House, designed by Philip Webb

Wilmer observes that Red House, though in 'some ways withdrawn and secluded', 'seems in others to reach out into the surrounding countryside [. . .] with a medieval offer of hospitality'.[40] More 'important to it than any actual building', he suggests, 'is Cedric the Saxon's Rotherwood in Scott's *Ivanhoe*, a hall that welcomes all travellers, peasant or nobleman, Norman, Saxon or Jew'. This short passage is the only searching analysis of Red House's evocation of hospitality thus far published. As such, it forms a startingpoint.

To what degree does the structure of Red House enshrine this ideal of openness? Markers of Morris and Webb's desire to frustrate the growth of an 'unhealthy' inwardness are most obvious at the building's points of access. At the main entrance, the visitor discovers a generous porch set within a pronounced Gothic arch [figure 1]. Flanking the front door are two wooden benches, which run along the sides of the porch. It has been argued by Jacques Migeon[41] that Ruskin's call for houses to be built with Gothic porches, 'walled in on both sides',[42] was carried out to the letter at Red House. Ruskin explains his liking for the porch as follows:

> Under that, you can put down your umbrella at your leisure, and, if you will, stop a moment to talk with your friend as you give him the parting shake of the hand. And if now and then a wayfarer found a moment's rest on a stone seat on each side of it, I believe you would find the insides of your houses not one whit the less comfortable.

40 Wilmer, 'Ruskin, Morris and Medievalism', pp. 8, 9.
41 Jacques Migeon, 'Red House and Ruskin', *Journal of the William Morris Society*, III (Spring, 1977), 3, 30–2.
42 John Ruskin, *Lectures on Architecture and Painting*, in *Works*, XII, pp. 3–133 (p. 49).

Figure 2. View of the well and Pilgrim's Rest porch at Red House

Whether or not Morris really hoped to find 'wayfarers' lodging themselves on these benches will never be known, but it is striking just how closely Webb has followed Ruskin's advice. The porch at Red House really does seem to offer the newcomer a welcoming and social space. Set deeply into the building, it seems affiliated to the house's inner world. Yet, as a porch, it remains open to the air, and fully accessible from the outside.

The charitable medievalism Ruskin identified as a principle of good architecture (and by extension, of a just society) is also in evidence at the more secluded well side of the house. Here, a secondary porch, known as the Pilgrim's Rest, leads into the ground-floor gallery [figure 2]. The name is an allusion to the proximity of the medieval route to Canterbury. Mackail suggests that Morris 'may have pleased himself with the notion of living close to the track of the Canterbury pilgrims, the *vena porta* of mediæval England'[43] and Morris's first biographer, Aymer Vallance, includes in his description of Red House a detailed account written by an early visitor, who recollects that 'Upon entering the porch, the hall appeared to one accustomed to the narrow ugliness of the usual middle-class dwelling of those days as being grand and severely simple'.[44] As he moves into the building, he notices 'a fireplace' which 'gave a hospitable look to the hall place'. Commenting, similarly, on the well, and on Webb's decision to emphasize its 'protecting roof rather than the well-head itself', Lawrence Weaver once remarked that the encircling bench 'reminds us of the immemorial usage of wells as

---

43 Mackail, *The Life of William Morris*, I, p. 141.
44 Aymer Vallance, *The Life and Work of William Morris* (London: George Bell & Sons, 1897), p. 49.

resting-places'.[45] Even the 'L'-shaped plan of the building seems to offer welcome on a structural level. If pilgrims are expected, however fancifully, to take rest at the side porch, it is possible to imagine the half-courtyard formed by the two wings of the house offering a kind of embrace to the wary stranger. This motif is repeated in the Garden City architecture of Letchworth, where 'L'-shaped blocks combine at least a semblance of openness with a protective enclosure of surrounding space. (See, for example, the house at Letchworth named 'Melverley' (1910), built by Underwood and Kent). Also of relevance is the roof of Red House, which Edward Hollamby has described as 'barn-like'.[46] Ruskin argues that a 'dwelling-house' should always have a conspicuous roof.[47] He justifies this assertion through reference to the design of the traditional English cottage: it has a 'thick impenetrable coverlid of close thatch', in which 'its whole heart and hospitality are concentrated'. The steep, gabled roof of Red House would seem to reflect the importance Ruskin attaches here to the symbolism of shelter.

Related to the idea of hospitality is the similarly medievalist preoccupation with entertainment and merriment. Georgiana Burne-Jones's recollections in *Memorials of Edward Burne-Jones*[48] and the material compiled by Mackail indicate that Morris was a liberal host. It is clear that he did not maintain the elaborate gradations of privacy used within conventional middle-class homes to sort guests according to their status.[49] Indeed, Mackail writes that 'as soon as the Morrises moved into it [Red House] at the close of the wet summer of 1860, open house was kept for all their friends'.[50] Morris, as Burne-Jones's depiction of him in the Sir Degrevaunt murals would seem to suggest, approached the job of entertaining in the spirit of a medieval king anxious that festivals should be observed; and he was not overly concerned if these celebrations became riotous. Philip Webb's addition of a minstrels' gallery to the drawing-room settle was designed with a view to holding Christmas concerts, and is typical of Morris's attitude in its encouragement of festive cheer. Mackail records the memories of one frequent guest at the house who emphasizes the feeling of co-ownership encouraged by Morris's hospitality: 'we seemed to be coming home just as much as when we returned to our own rooms. No protestations – only certainty of contentment in each other's society'.

---

45 Lawrence Weaver, *Small Country Houses of To-Day* (Woodbridge, Suffolk: Baron Publishing, 1983), p. 184.
46 Hollamby, 'Philip Webb Red House Bexleyheath, Kent 1859'.
47 Ruskin, *Lectures on Architecture and Painting*, pp. 33, 34.
48 Georgiana Burne-Jones, *Memorials of Edward Burne-Jones*, 2 vols (London: Macmillan and Co., 1904), pp. 208–12.
49 John Marshall and Ian Willox point out, in *The Victorian House*, that 'the Victorians expressed the gradations of status with meticulous care. Guests were admitted to the best room – the parlour; this would contain the most expensive and expansive furnishings in the house, probably arranged around a marble fireplace. As you moved away from this room towards the back and the top of the house you would notice not only the furnishings and appointments shrinking and cheapening but also fixtures such as the skirting boards, plaster cornices and fireplaces. The marble fireplace would become a slate fireplace, then be reduced further to a cast iron one, until its final manifestation in the servant's room at the very top of the house – a mean little thing with a plain wood surround, designed to burn as little coal as possible', *The Victorian House* (London: Sidgwick & Jackson, 1989), p. 60.
50 Mackail, *The Life of William Morris*, I, pp. 159, 160.

Yet the house is not only accommodating in the welcome it extends to its visitors. It also seems to express, as Morris's comments on gardens would suggest, a harmonious and interdependent relationship between its interior and the surrounding area. (It is significant that Webb, in his plan for the house's east elevation, indicated in pencil which flowers – roses, white jasmine and passion flower – would be planted against the exterior walls).[51] There is here a deliberate attempt to evoke the old, manorial role of the big house, especially its dependency on, and responsibility for, the upkeep of the demesne. Though Red House was never really more than a country villa, the Disraelian emphasis on *land* (as opposed to *capital*), on fixity and responsibility, rather than commercial free flow, seems to have been an influence. (Morris never considered himself to be a Tory, even a radical one, but his sympathetic interest in feudalism does share something with the conservative thinking of the time.) It is also significant that Webb planned the house in such a way as to limit the number of orchard trees felled. Mackail's remark that 'apples fell in at the windows as they stood open on hot autumn nights'[52] only confirms Edward Hollamby's impression that 'Red House and its garden were designed as one', that 'there is a special harmony between the house – solid and romantic – and its setting'.[53] Indeed the window seat in the oriel and the ceiling lights in the study structurally enshrine a free passage of light and sight between the house's interior and its wider environment. Even the particular features of the Kent countryside seem to have suited Morris's determination not to create a beautiful prison, a 'small (very small) Palace of Art'.[54] Mackail notes that Morris did not feel comfortable in the 'normal English landscape' of undulating hills, because he felt it enclosed and imprisoning.[55] He preferred instead the open and fertile country that he saw in Essex, Kent and the Upper Thames.

The pragmatism that characterized Webb's design-practice also acts to qualify the force of Red House's 'apartness'. The potential for change he built into it from the very beginning, through the construction of an incomplete court, and even the ongoing nature of its decoration, reinforce the point that the achievement of perfection or fixity were not Morris's objectives. Even the policy of reinvention, of not tolerating the shoddy goods attainable on the open market, did not prohibit recognition and use of products commercially available where they *were* of the required standard. Stylistically, also, the house borrows features from periods other than the Middle Ages. Pevsner notes that Webb 'even admitted the sash-windows of William and Mary and Queen Anne without ever being afraid of clashes between the various styles to which he went for inspiration'.[56] In this, he follows Weaver, who remarked in 1911, that 'Few men would have dared at that date [1859] to mix sliding sashes with pointed door-heads – the useful with the ecclesiastical; but here it is, and how remarkable it looks!'[57] These remarks reflect an earlier lack of attention to antecedents in existing buildings by William

---

51 Webb E.61–1916 DD22.
52 Mackail, *The Life of William Morris*, I, p. 144.
53 Hollamby, 'Philip Webb Red House Bexleyheath, Kent 1859'.
54 Morris, 'To Cormell Price', July 1856, pp. 28–9.
55 Mackail, *The Life of William Morris*, I, p. 140.
56 Nikolaus Pevsner, *Pioneers of Modern Design: From William Morris to Walter Gropius*, 2nd edn (Harmondsworth: Penguin Books, 1960), p. 58.
57 Weaver, *Small Country Houses of To-Day*, p. 183.

Butterfield (such as the parsonage at All Saints, Margaret Street, London (1849–59)). But the emphasis on architectural pragmatism holds true. The sashes and the pointed arches of the brick surrounds find common ground in this structure. The Gothic features are not obtrusive, and the window frames work without being entirely square.

Returning to Fiona MacCarthy's assertion that Red House 'is symbolic as an act of separation', I wish to suggest that, whatever attempts Morris may have made to create and justify this complex mixture of privacy and openness in medievalist terms, these efforts were never likely to be unproblematic.[58] A great deal has been written about the subsequent encroachment of suburbia on Morris's medievalist idyll.[59] But it is important to remember that the house was located in that vicinity for the same reason that the area was developed. Morris chose the site because the London and Greenwich railway had recently been extended to form the North Kent Line. Even before the Firm was launched, he clearly felt the need to keep open lines of communication with London. He was not, after all, the local squire. The locality was convenient and to his taste, not the ancient seat of his family.

Indeed the Morrises were not noble at all. The money used to build Red House was new money, wealth generated in the industrial economy. This by no means disqualifies Morris's good intentions. But it must nevertheless feed into any evaluation of his medievalist separatism. Later in life, he reflected on the unrealistic hopes cherished by the architects of the mid-century Gothic Revival:

> The enthusiasm of the Gothic revivalists died out when they were confronted by the fact that they form part of a society which will not and cannot have a living style, because it is an economical necessity for its existence that the ordinary everyday work of its population shall be mechanical drudgery.[60]

Although informed by a later adherence to Marxism, these comments assume acceptance of the basic unity between aesthetic and social realms that Pugin had argued for in *True Principles*.[61] It is an insight that casts doubt on the feasibility of Morris's first and only architectural commission, for it was the same condition of interdependence that threatened to undermine the seclusion so carefully cultivated at Red House. Indeed, there is no more fitting symbol of the inconsistencies that troubled Morris's early medievalism than his decision to locate the building close to a railway station. It reflects a hopeful, but ultimately disappointed, expectation that self-enclosed idylls and the commercial world might successfully coexist.

It is not necessary to believe Red House an entirely original, or, in its day, influential building to think it significant. Yet any understanding of its 'apartness' is

---

58   MacCarthy, *William Morris*, p. 156.
59   See, for example: Weaver, *Small Country Houses of To-Day*, p. 180; Casson, 'Red House: The Home of William Morris', p. 156.
60   Morris, 'The Revival of Architecture', in *Collected Works*, XXII, pp. 318–30 (p. 330).
61   In *The True Principles of Pointed or Christian Architecture*, Pugin explained that 'Catholic England was merry England, at least for the humbler classes; and the architecture was in keeping with the faith and manners of the times, – at once strong and hospitable' (p. 61). In his lecture 'Traffic', Ruskin made explicit what he had already implied in *The Stones of Venice*, that 'All good architecture is the expression of national life and character; and it is produced by a prevalent and eager national taste, or desire for beauty', *Works*, XVIII, pp. 433–58 (p. 434).

inevitably affected by the extent of Webb's indebtedness to architectural precedent. Mark Girouard has pointed out that the idea of carrying the first-floor
ceilings up to the roof to give them extra height had been adopted before by Pugin
in his Bishop's House at Birmingham (1840),[62] and that 'Pretty well everything
about Red House – the grouping of high red roofs, the red brick, the brick Gothic
arches, the lantern of the staircase roof, even the sash windows [. . .] could be
paralleled in work by Butterfield or Street existing before Red House was started'.
Paul Thompson observes that 'Webb's notebooks from this period contain several
sketches of buildings by Butterfield'.[63] This secular example of Gothic style, they
claim, had its precedents in the village schools and parsonages built by Butterfield
in the early 1850s. Even the style of Red House, many critics have observed,
contains a hint of the conventional French Gothic that was popular at the time.[64]
In drawing attention to such precedents, I do not wish to suggest that the case
made here is especially novel: these remarks do in fact reflect fifty years of revi-
sionist criticism by architectural historians. As long ago as 1935, W. R. Lethaby
noted that 'Butterfield had made good use of brick before this time'.[65] It is nevertheless important to restate these arguments in order to understand the limits
inherent to Morris's act of withdrawal.

Had Morris's vision of medieval seclusion really been achieved, he would, in
any case, have been confronted by those problems that always dog bids to evade
the world. The young man who wrote 'Golden Wings' (the poem, rather than the
story) knew that happiness can degenerate into *ennui* under conditions of sheltered monotony.[66] Indeed, Hugh Casson, in his article for *The Listener*, suspects
that this was a very real problem:

> How *jolly* they all were, with their bear-fights and nicknames and practical jokes,
> their bellowing laughter and laborious puns! Was it all perhaps some curious
> instinctive revolt from the utopian dream-world of Arthurian legend in which they
> lived?[67]

John Ball's revolt, after all, was against feudalism, not capitalism, and Morris does
not seem to have been unaware that fortifications were as likely to create a sense of
imprisonment as they were to foster idyllic conditions.

Another metaphor of frustrated separatism has informed the debate over the
success of Red House. Mark Girouard summarizes the question as follows:

> The drawing-room [. . .] is lit mainly from the north, with a small oriel window on
> the west for the evening sun; this alignment has come in for a good deal of criticism,
> but the reason probably was that it was planned to be a room of great splendour, full

---

62 Girouard, 'Red House, Bexleyheath, Kent', pp. 1383, 1384.
63 Thompson, *The Work of William Morris*, p. 13; W. R. Lethaby's biography, *Philip Webb and his
    Work* (London: Oxford University Press, 1935) contains the earliest reference to this fact.
64 Weaver, *Small Country Houses of To-Day*, p. 180; Casson, 'Red House: The Home of William
    Morris', p. 536.
65 Lethaby, *Philip Webb and his Work*, p. 27.
66 In 'Golden Wings' (*Collected Works*, I, pp. 116–23), Fair Jehane du Castel beau lives in a 'happy
    poplar land' (p. 116). These idyllic surroundings become oppressive because her lover stays away, a
    figure who seems to represent the outside world.
67 Casson, 'Red House: The Home of William Morris', p. 537.

of fresco, painting and embroidery, and it was wished to keep these from the sun. Generally speaking, Morris (and the Victorians as a whole) did not have our enthusiasm for the sun; at the Red House the sunny side of the house facing south and east is filled almost entirely with passages, which is very odd planning indeed by modern notions. Even Morris and his friends noticed that the house was bitterly cold in winter.[68]

If the measures Webb took to protect the house's contents from the sun were signs of a desire to achieve 'apartness', so the chill that they inadvertently produced, and that contributed to the house's unsuitability as a residence for anyone not in robust health, may be regarded as an indication that the outside world had not been successfully shut out. It also suggests that the house did not achieve a perfectly harmonious relationship with its surroundings. Even Mackail admits that Red House had 'certain disadvantages'. It was 'very cold in winter', and, significantly, in so far as the strategy of romantic isolationism is concerned, 'it was not well situated for medical or other aid on emergencies'.[69] The orientation, which Girouard ascribes to attempts at preservation of the projected mural schemes,[70] meant that the heat of the sun was concentrated on the kitchen just at that time when food was being prepared.[71] Whether considered as design faults, or as symptoms of Morris's unconventional priorities, these observations reiterate the point that Red House did not grow up from the Kentish soil. It was designed instead by a fallible individual who, unlike the Ruskinian workman, enjoyed less than perfect knowledge of the locality, having first seen the site and planned the building in dry conditions.[72] This leads to one further point. Morris was eventually forced to respond to these problems, and to the trouble of commuting into London, by selling, in 1865, and moving back to the metropolis. Even if the original intention had been to operate in splendid isolation (and there is little evidence that it had been), this decision serves to confirm his final acceptance that outside concerns could not be ignored with impunity.

It is equally possible to question the oppositional significance that certain critics attach to Morris's 'act of separation'. It has been accepted for some time that Red House was in certain respects a 'cockney villa' of the kind its owner vehemently disparaged in later life.[73] Far from reviving the living conditions of the medieval house – which consisted of a single hall, perhaps with a screens passage – Red House is a two-storey, Victorian house with the usual reliance on differentiated space. The 'friendly' features Girouard discerns in Webb's distribution of the functional interior, the proximity for instance of the kitchen to the dining-room, do not go as far as to reproduce the layout of a medieval hall. Red House, even in its unrealized, extended form, did not propose anything more than a bourgeois communality based around the lives of two nuclear families. As Peter Davey notes,

68 Girouard, 'Red House, Bexleyheath, Kent', p. 1384.
69 Mackail, *The Life of William Morris*, I, p. 163.
70 Girouard, 'Red House, Bexleyheath, Kent', p. 1384.
71 Weaver, *Small Country Houses of To-Day*, pp. 182–3; Peter Davey, *Arts and Crafts Architecture*, p. 40.
72 Mackail, *The Life of William Morris*, I, p. 163.
73 William Guest, who occasionally plays the role of Morris's proxy in *News from Nowhere*, notes with approval 'the absence of cockney villas' (p. 159) in Nowhere.

the functions of each room were clearly determined in the design. Indeed the effect of Webb's 'chain-like plan',[74] together with the 'corridor down the side which connected all the rooms', was to obviate 'the need for walking through one room to get to another, common in medieval planning, but potentially embarrassing for nineteenth-century Britons'.

Again, Morris might conceivably be praised for a brave accommodation of his servants on the same floor as the master bedroom. But to modern eyes the maids' dormitory, with its slender partitions, seems cramped and the height of the window a mean denial of views of the garden. The back staircase was essentially an access route for servants and as such another concession to the orthodox domestic layout. Even the country houses of the eighteenth century would have supported a less private living environment, with servants liable to interrupt proceedings without warning. In many ways, Red House does depart from the home-as-sanctuary model of Victorian living. But it must be acknowledged, as many critics have argued before, that Morris's choice of the home as a suitable place in which to resist the commercial world was a typical middle-class strategy.[75] He had responded to the prospect of marriage by securing the seat of privacy then considered a requirement of family life. He may have clothed his betrothal to Jane in the colours of a mystic marriage, but the household he founded was in certain respects a realization of the mid-century family ideal, a modern house located at a respectable distance from the city smog.

Red House combines a dream of separatism with a medievalist offer of hospitality, of domestic fellowship. It evokes Morris's compromise between a desire to remain open to the stranger at the gate, and a wish to assert the alternative value of retreat. But it inherits the problems associated with the pursuit of these ideals, and the conflicts that emerge between them in a nineteenth-century setting. Where Morris achieved seclusion, he also relied on a system of private property; where he practised hospitality, the recipients were for the most part his friends, there being few pilgrims passing through Upton to Canterbury in the 1860s. If Morris defied the age by asserting a power of separatism and a modification of existing boundaries between the public and the private, it is also important to appreciate just how closely such aspirations were shadowed by the defining virtues of bourgeois home-life, by a continued attachment to privacy and to property.

It would nevertheless be unfair to treat Red House as yet another *nouveau riche* villa. It has been my aim to demonstrate how the invocation of a supposedly medieval outlook – architecturally and linguistically – served to establish an exemplary, rather than a strictly practical, 'solution' to the problem of alienation in an industrial society. The utility of archaism lay for Ruskin, and for Morris, in

74 Peter Davey, *Arts and Crafts Architecture: The Search for Earthly Paradise* (London: The Architectural Press, 1980), pp. 30–2.

75 Ruskin's much later remarks in *Sesame and Lilies* are pertinent here, as they reveal a less hospitable premise for home-worship: 'This is the true nature of home – it is the place of Peace; the shelter, not only from all injury, but from all terror, doubt, and division [. . .] so far as the anxieties of the outer life penetrate into it, and the inconsistently-minded, unknown, unloved, or hostile society of the outer world is allowed by either husband or wife to cross the threshold, it ceases to be home; it is then only a part of that outer world which you have roofed over, and lighted fire in', *Works*, XVIII, pp. 4–187 (p. 122).

the evocation of a previous semantic context, one established according to a different way of viewing the world. Ruskin's use of the word *wayfarer* (as opposed to *vagrant* or *tramp*) may be seen accordingly as a deliberate, rather than naïve, attempt to restore an 'obsolete' representation of the poor.

This strategy was not immune to the difficulties imposed by the revivalist's captivity within the present. It was a problem affecting the whole range of Ruskin's etymologically-dependent displacements of modern usage. In Victorian England, after all, the poor were more likely to be seen as parasites than honoured as virtuous mendicants. The disjunction between the archaic ideal and the realities of nineteenth-century poverty nevertheless discloses the intentionally and necessarily impractical nature of Red House's symbolism of openness. It reveals the deliberately fanciful, or utopian, basis for Morris's attempt to reconcile idyllic seclusion with a generous extension of hospitality. Viewed in this way, a lack of practicality, realism, or even originality, cease to represent adequate grounds for dismissing the artistic and historical significance of this intriguing building.

The Symbolism of the Great Hall: Morris, Marshall, Faulkner & Company in Cambridge

The decoration of Red House prompted two realizations of far-reaching importance. Morris and his friends recognized the inadequacy of most existing products and materials for achieving their aims. They also obtained a clear sense of the role collaboration and group effort had to play in overcoming such difficulties. These lessons inspired the establishment of Morris, Marshall, Faulkner & Company, a firm of decorators and fine craftsmen who achieved a great deal in the areas of stained glass, furniture reform, wallpaper design, weaving and tapestry.

As the Tractarian penchant for ritual and Gothic architecture spread beyond the Church, and began to influence secular institutions, Morris, Marshall, Faulkner & Company found opportunities to diversify. From beginnings in ecclesiastical furnishings, they began to produce decorative schemes for the kind of communal spaces celebrated by Cobbett, Disraeli and Ruskin. The commissions for work at Queens' College hall, Cambridge, in 1861, and at the South Kensington Museum (now the Victoria and Albert Museum), between 1866 and 1869, should be considered in this light. Taking as their subject matter the evocation and encouragement of sociability, these were, of all the Firm's undertakings, the most obviously indebted to the experience gained at Red House.

The following discussion is concerned principally with the paradox of openness and exclusivity suggested by the Firm's decoration of a Cambridge college hall. The South Kensington Museum commission was less troubled by such questions, however. The new museum was founded as an attempt to rejuvenate the standard of British industrial design and to foster better public knowledge of art. In its public character, it served an exemplary as well as an educational function. All aspects of the building, and not just the contents or exhibits, were recruited to serve that objective. The Museum authorities decided to commission a dining and reception area that would evoke the artistic ideals the institution was founded to promote. Needing more than a utilitarian provision of facilities, they appointed

Figure 3. The Green Dining Room, 1866–69, decorated by Morris, Marshall, Faulkner & Company for the South Kensington Museum (now Victoria and Albert Museum)

Morris, Marshall, Faulkner & Company to create a sociable and inspiring place that would befit the rationale underpinning the larger enterprise.

The new space became known as the Green Dining Room [figure 3]. Although lacking the lighter touch of later work, it represents one of the first interiors cast in the Aesthetic style. The Museum was happy with the effect created, and it was popular with visitors to the building. The dining-room, and the Museum itself, were emblematic of a new conception of the public space. No longer the exclusive possession of monarchs and wealthy families, art was beginning to assume a public role as an object of contemplation and edification for all. Putting art treasures in the public sphere, as Ruskin had argued in 'The Opening of the Crystal Palace', constituted a vital qualification of the antiquary's walled-in privacy, and a powerful metaphor for the sharing of wealth.[76] Morris profited from these changes, notwithstanding his intuitive aversion to museums. The Green Dining Room[77] was one of the few opportunities he enjoyed, across his career, to create

76 Ruskin, 'The Opening of the Crystal Palace', p. 430.
77 It is noted by Lethaby that the 'green dining-room at South Kensington Museum was wholly Webb's work, except for the Burne-Jones figures in the glass and panelling', *Philip Webb and his Work*, p. 44. This was also true of Red House, as Jan Marsh emphasizes ('Although it's sometimes said that William Morris built Red House, he was not its architect [. . .] he contributed to the design by discussing specifications [. . .] but all the architecture was Webb's', *William Morris & Red*

and practise an 'art for the people'.[78] Such considerations are in a sense anachronistic, as Morris did not become uncomfortable with the idea of 'ministering to the swinish luxury of the rich' until he developed socialist convictions in the early 1880s.[79] It remains the case that he received his first opportunity to fashion a public space at South Kensington in 1866, an experience that may have served later to inspire related reflections on the nature of communal arrangements.

Proceeding to the more representative venture, at Queens' College, one finds reliance on the politically less progressive motif of the medieval great hall. This constitutes the architectural equivalent of the 'old English hospitality' discussed at length in Chapter One. The antiquity of the interior rules out any question of Morris imposing this layout on the commission. The medieval hall, after all, was there already. However, the manner of decoration did serve to enhance and to invoke the hall's significance as a folkloric temple to the rites of hospitality and to the festive calendar.

The detail of this decorative scheme should be viewed in the context of the fascination with the great hall and its symbolism that arose in the early decades of the nineteenth century. Beginning with the 'wedding cake' Gothic of the Georgian period, the structure of the medieval hall had long been in a process of abortive revival. In *The Victorian Country House*, Mark Girouard documents the 'first full-blown revived medieval great halls'.[80] They included Pugin's Alton Towers in Staffordshire and Bayons Manor in Lincolnshire, both erected in 1836. Although the fashion had largely passed by the time Webb was designing Red House, Girouard notes that '[George Gilbert] Scott in his *Secular and Domestic Architecture* (1857) gives a good Puginesque puff to the great hall as a vehicle for "that broader hospitality which belongs especially to the great landlord"'. Interest in the 'Olden Time', around the 1830s and 1840s, also prompted painterly evocations of this comfortably indeterminate period of social cohesion. Daniel Maclise's *Merry Christmas in the Baron's Hall* (1838) [figure 4] represents a particularly striking example. There is an attempt in this composition to imbue the great hall with significance as a site of communion between the various orders of society. The lord presides from the dais, surrounded by his immediate family and friends. Further forward, are depicted musicians, players, and a jester. They entertain the common people, eating and frolicking on either side. The scene suggests revelry, but not misrule. Hierarchy remains visible. It is an implicit message of this work that the order portrayed is more benign precisely for being visible and complete in its extension. Jill Franklin, in her study of the English country house, makes an observation that serves very well as a commentary on Maclise's painting. For those, she writes, 'living through the social unrest of the 1830s and 1840s the vision of the medieval lord exercising benevolent rule over his docile peasantry

House, p. 33). However, the question of authorship is here less important than the nexus of influence and ideas within which these projects were executed.

78 Morris later articulated this ambition in 'The Art of the People', in *Collected Works*, XXII, pp. 28–50 (p. 39).
79 Morris is said to have uttered the complaint that 'I spend my life ministering to the swinish luxury of the rich' while supervising work at the house of the Northern industrialist, Sir Lowthian Bell (Lethaby, *Philip Webb and his Work*, pp. 94–5).
80 Mark Girouard, *The Victorian Country House*, rev. edn (New Haven: Yale University Press, 1979), pp. 44, 46.

Figure 4. Daniel Maclise, *Merry Christmas in the Baron's Hall*, 1838

and all carousing in harmony under one roof, must have had a special appeal'.[81] At the universities, the revival of the great hall found a particularly apt home. Routine gatherings of scholars and students were more suited to the setting than the occasional private amusements of the aristocracy. The hall of King's College Cambridge (1828) is a particularly early and striking example of the 'Tudor' variation on the theme. Stained glass windows, a minstrels' gallery, and a screens passage all allude to a structural form closely tied to the machinery of archaic festivity.

Given the close association of social life and architecture depicted in *Merry Christmas in the Baron's Hall*, it is hard to escape the implication that the design of interior space determines as well as reflects the order of society. Whether the reintroduction of the great hall succeeded in reorientating social relations, in the way that modern theorists of space have sometimes argued architecture may do, is another question.[82] Revivalism in its simplest form nevertheless rested upon such an assumption. Joseph Nash, in his *Mansions of England in the Olden Time* (1839), provides a lively picture of what some architects, notably A. W. Pugin, hoped to achieve by resurrecting the quadrangular structure and grand layout of medieval buildings:

> the artist's object has been to present them in a new and attractive light; not as many of them now appear, gloomy, desolate, and neglected, but furnished with the rude comfort of the early times of 'merry England' [. . .] enlivened with the presence of their inmates and guests, enjoying the recreations and pastimes, or celebrating the festivals, of our ancestors. Thus, not only the domestic architecture of past ages, but the costumes and habits of England in the 'olden time', are brought before the eye.[83]

81 Jill Franklin, *The Gentleman's Country House and Its Plan, 1835–1914* (London: Routledge, 1981), p. 68.
82 Henri Lefebvre, *The Production of Space*, trans. by Donald Nicholson-Smith (Oxford: Blackwell, 1991).
83 Joseph Nash, *The Mansions of England in the Olden Time* (London: Thomas Mclean, 1849), pp. 1–2.

It was the hope of some architects that the 'habits of England in the "olden time"' might undergo mysterious resurrection by means of an architectural revival. This hope proved groundless, as Morris himself remarked later in life, on writing his essay, 'The Revival of Architecture'.[84] A more recent view of the situation is provided by Peter Mandler in *The Fall and Rise of the Stately Home*:

> Only those elements of the Olden Time that were also found in the Gothic lingered. A curious example is the recurrence of the great hall in purpose-built Victorian country houses. Gothicists felt that the heyday of the great hall had been in their beloved fourteenth century, not later. They urged great halls upon their patrons on stylistic, symbolic and even functional grounds, though only the most utopian – Pugin – imagined that the latter-day aristocracy were genuinely interested in reviving Old English Hospitality. The result was that a few dozen great halls were built in the 1840s and 1850s, which never had any real use at all and soon degenerated into over-large billiards rooms or were used for coat and gun storage.
>
> The bathetic fate of the great hall is nicely symbolic of the aristocracy's true feeling for the Olden Time. They were often cheerfully willing to go along with their architects' enthusiasms or with currents in popular taste, but they rarely took them to their hearts.[85]

Mandler's analysis would imply that the cause of revival was hopeless. In a sense, it probably was. One could offer the explanation given by Morris, regarding the impossibility of acting in isolation from the values of the surrounding society. One could rely on Mandler's observation, that there was a lack of will in the face of the general inconvenience presented by antique and obsolete structures. It is, nevertheless, worth assessing the scope for success enjoyed by the Firm. A great deal more was at stake than the obvious consideration that there was little prospect of Queens' College hall being converted into a billiard room.

In what respects did the Firm's work at Queens' evoke the 'habits of England in "the Olden time"'? How did the forms of decoration introduced to the interior enhance the hall's function as a sociable space? At the heart of the decorative scheme is G. F. Bodley's fireplace [figure 5], an object of attention and a source of warmth. Above this symbolically resonant structure, a tile series was installed by the Firm. It evokes the established medieval subject of *The Labours of the Months*. Various figures are depicted, all involved in different agricultural occupations. Each activity represents a new phase of the year, a distinct seasonal imperative. The tile scheme thereby suggests the union of the calendar with the various modes of work, as well as with time and place. A medieval version of this subject, such as that surviving at the parish church of Easby in North Yorkshire, carries a straightforward message. It represents the rhythms of earthly existence, and gratitude for a successful harvest. In a late-nineteenth-century context, its significance must be quite otherwise. It implicitly invokes the contrast between the life of the city dweller, removed from the land and its seasonal rituals, and an integrated vision of the past. The emphasis on the traditional calendar not only naturalizes the occupations of man, but focuses attention on the festive year, and the role of

---

84 Morris, 'The Revival of Architecture'.
85 Mandler, *The Fall and Rise of the Stately Home*, p. 66.

Figure 5. *The Labours of the Months* fireplace tiles, 1864, designed by Morris, Marshall, Faulkner & Company for the Old Hall, Queens' College, Cambridge

the hall in marking its stages. In its traditional guise, the hall would have been a location for feasting, and for revelry. The introduction of medievalist subject matter may have enhanced its capacity for performing this role, and may have counteracted the sophistication of previous classicizing additions, but one should never discount the role played by the *contrast* between medieval and modern in emphasizing the reasons for *revival*, the idea that there was something lacking in present conditions.

It is also important to register the special significance of the college model in the collective imagination of the Oxford 'Set' (several of whom became partners in the Firm). The earliest statement of this fascination appears in the essay quoted earlier from the pages of *The Oxford and Cambridge Magazine*, in which a 'mediaeval college' is compared to 'a monastery, a college, and an alms-house united into a single building, and governed by fixed laws'. The aesthetic inclinations expressed here were not Morris's own. His sympathy for the Carlylean emphasis on strong government by a 'real ruler' did not endure after the publication of his earliest short stories. Nevertheless, this account of an institution possessed of spiritual, educational, and charitable functions is crucial to understanding the broad appeal of the Oxford and Cambridge college. At Queens', Morris transferred a privately conceived style of decoration to the environment most fitted to receive it in the outside world, a still functioning community of 'workers' whose physical context materialized their social relations.

Unlike the country house commissions discussed by Mandler, the medieval nature of Queens' College protected the Firm from the need to compromise. Practical convenience was not dictated by modern social relations. The college hall, this is to say, worked in the way that it always had done. Fundamentally, it survived as a shared dining facility, serving the needs of a scholarly community. What role did hospitality – unconditional or otherwise – play in the Firm's interpretation of medieval customs and social space? At Queens', this recurrent aesthetic ideal did not translate into anything more than a thematic emphasis. Meeting the needs of private clients precluded the incorporation of a more radical openness. Irrespective of intent, the Firm could hardly have overturned the exclusivity of university elites merely by installing a decorative scheme. By the nineteenth century, Cambridge colleges were closed spaces, inhabited mainly by the sons of wealthy men. There was no question of welcoming poor townspeople into their fortified courts and halls on a routine basis. One need look no further than Thomas Hardy's 1895 novel, *Jude the Obscure*, to appreciate the meaning and the persistence of this exclusion.[86]

It should also be remembered that the medieval hall incorporated a hierarchical plan, with the lord or fellows presiding from the dais. The presence of that layout would have reduced the scope for an openness or sociability superior to that offered by modern institutions. This limitation is not wholly attributable to the commercial constraints under which the Firm operated. It is not fundamental

---

[86] Hardy's hero, Jude Fawley, is a self-taught labourer whose efforts in Ancient Greek meet with no approval from the college authorities at Christminster (Hardy's name for Oxford). Their refusal to grant Jude the university admission he desires symbolizes the insufficiency of ambition not supported by financial means; Thomas Hardy, *Jude the Obscure* (London: Osgood, McIlvaine, 1896).

to the nature of universities in the Victorian period. Nor, indeed, does it reflect Morris's intentions at this point in his life. It stems, instead, from the nature of medievalist hospitality. This form of sociability, as will be explored, relies upon a measure of exclusivity. The pleasure of festivity and community derives in part from the sensation of keeping the world out. The hospitable qualities of a college hall in the 1860s are in this respect no different from those of its medieval predecessor. They rely upon its fortified quality, its power to draw clear lines between the assembled company and the people who have not been admitted.

A 'secure and sacred house of Beauty'?[87] – Hospitality and Aesthetic Separatism in *The Life and Death of Jason, The Earthly Paradise* and *Love is Enough*

Two architectural evocations of idealized hospitality have been considered thus far. From the family home as artists' workshop or 'pilgrim's rest', to the festive interior of a Cambridge great hall, Morris and his medievalizing contemporaries resorted to spatial effects in seeking to alter customary relations between the inside and the outside, between a host and his guest. The object of attention in this final section is not architecture, but poetry. The aim is to interrogate the play of equivalent social and political gestures in the aesthetic theories, and modes of reception, dramatized by the long poems Morris wrote in the 1860s. Special attention is granted to the dialectic of inwardness and openness running through the greatest achievement of these years, the six-volume poetic tale cycle Morris entitled *The Earthly Paradise*.[88]

Ever since the publication of Jessie Kocmanová's 'Some Remarks on E. P. Thompson's Opinion of the Poetry of William Morris',[89] a growing number of critics have sought to challenge Thompson's negative assessment of *The Earthly Paradise*.[90] Dismissing it as a 'poetry of despair', Thompson complained that in pursuit of refuge, escape, and the attractions of pure mood, the work shunned engagement with the problems of the age. Florence Boos has been at the forefront of efforts to overturn this verdict, arguing that the poem's prolonged neglect – largely ascribable to the intolerance of narrative poetry and archaic language engendered by Symbolism and the New Criticism – should not deter critics from reassessing a work that in its own time enjoyed extraordinary popularity. In *The Design of William Morris' The Earthly Paradise*, she argues that it 'was *not* [. . .] an escapist work, but one of the major achievements of Morris' life [. . .] and an attempt to find historical meaning in literature of grief, shared memory, and renewal'.[91] In a later article, she complains that 'every hostile critic since the work

87 Oscar Wilde, 'English Renaissance of Art', in *Aristotle at Afternoon Tea: The Rare Oscar Wilde*, ed. by John Wyse Jackson (London: Fourth Estate, 1991), pp. 3–28 (p. 13).
88 Morris, *The Earthly Paradise*, in *Collected Works*, III–VI.
89 Jessie Kocmanová, 'Some Remarks on E. P. Thompson's Opinion of the Poetry of William Morris', *Philologica Pragensia*, III (1960), 3, 168–78.
90 E. P. Thompson, *William Morris*, pp. 110–50 (p. 121).
91 Florence Saunders Boos, *The Design of William Morris' The Earthly Paradise* (Lewison/Queenston/ Lampeter: The Edwin Mellen Press, 1990), p. 5.

appeared has cited the singer's ironic claim to be an "idle singer of an empty day" with credulous asperity'.[92] The Apology, she adds, 'is a consciously ironic, even severe commentary on the nature of literary composition, and not a naive disclaimer of serious purpose'.

These otherwise conflicting critical responses to *The Earthly Paradise* find common ground in their objection to the 'escapism' many of the original press reviews discovered and applauded in the poem.[93] Even the critics who dispute the assertion that escapism was what Morris either intended or achieved are at one with Thompson in placing a high value on openness and the importance of engagement. What they dispute is not the inadvisability of evading the claims of 'reality' but whether indeed Morris ever attempted to do so. Yet there would seem to be a limit to what critics like Boos can achieve in claiming that *The Earthly Paradise* is not an escapist work. While there is much evidence, in the poem taken as a whole, to suggest complication and qualification of the idle singer's expressed intention, one should not for that reason ignore the thematic importance of the escapist agenda he articulates.[94] Critically naïve as it would be simply to identify this figure with Morris the author, the disenfranchised singer still serves to provoke reflection upon the relationship between art and reality. While it would be wise to exercise caution in trusting Morris's confession of inadequacy regarding the 'muddle' suggested by 'politico-social subjects' (especially considering its status as an isolated, private communication, evidently written in an exasperated frame of mind), it would be equally imprudent to ignore it altogether. Even as a consciously parodic echo of youthful despair, the Apology asks readers to entertain the idea of aesthetic separatism, to consider the advantages of a regrettable but necessary break with the world's 'heavy trouble'.

Locating this tendency within what Morris 'rightly or wrongly saw as Rossetti's province', Clive Wilmer has sought to distinguish the first stage of Morris's career – during which Rossetti's influence over him was at its strongest – from the second, when a Ruskinian insistence on 'the connections between art and society' assumed dominance (he reminds us that Morris had been interested in Ruskin since his undergraduate days, but had subsequently been distracted by the aesthetic side of Pre-Raphaelitism).[95] Wilmer's article provides a useful framework within which Morris's career may be understood. In the process, it supplies grounds for questioning Boos's sceptical reading of the singer's sincerity and significance. Whilst making it clear that Ruskin's influence over Morris declined during the period of close association with Rossetti, Wilmer resists the institution of too rigid a division between these two phases, indicating that the power of Ruskin's message at no point completely fell away; that it remained 'the hidden current of his life'.

As a supplementary proposition, I would argue that the 'inwardness' associated with Rossetti was not rejected altogether when Morris became actively involved in

---

92 Florence Boos, 'Victorian Response to *Earthly Paradise* Tales', *Journal of the William Morris Society*, V (Winter, 1983–84), 4, 16–29 (p. 22).

93 See, for example, the unsigned review in the *Spectator*, 12 March 1870, 332–4.

94 Morris, The Apology, *The Earthly Paradise*, in *Collected Works*, III, pp. 1–2 (p. 1).

95 Clive Wilmer, 'Maundering Medievalism: Dante Gabriel Rossetti and William Morris's Poetry', *P.N. Review*, 29 (January–February, 2003), 3, 69–73 (p. 70).

political parties and pressure groups. The same tension between the urge to escape and the desire to reform, discernible at Red House, is also present in *The Earthly Paradise*, as it would be later in his socialist utopia, *News from Nowhere*. This work was billed, after all, as an 'Epoch of Rest'.[96] In order to understand why Morris retained aspects of this aesthetic separatism in his later years, one must appreciate that it continued to serve a politically functional purpose after it had ceased to embody an artistic ideal. The following discussion is concerned, accordingly, with articulations of escapism that express a utopian exclusion of negativity. It also seeks to determine the extent to which this tendency is qualified by a parallel commitment to openness and social engagement. I shall investigate the latter by giving further attention to Morris's representation of hospitality. What light, I will ask, does the continual revisiting of this theme, whether in the Prologue or in such stories as 'The Doom of King Acrisius'[97] and 'The Son of Crœsus',[98] shed on the poem's disputed endorsement of separatism? How might an examination of a transitional text like *The Earthly Paradise* – which bridges the two phases outlined by Wilmer – explain Morris's divided allegiances, his lifelong hesitation between the aesthetic isolationism of Rossetti and the confrontational questing of Ruskin, between the virtues of refuge and intervention?

Coined by Benjamin Constant in his *Journal intime* (1887–89),[99] the term *L'art pour l'art* had been in circulation as a concept since the beginning of the nineteenth century. Despite his later remarks in 'The Art of the People' (1879), in which he attacked artists who 'guard carefully every approach to their palace of art', Morris's involvement in its rise to prominence as a 'school of art' was not limited to his association with Rossetti.[100] An early adherence to Keats's famous equation of truth and beauty underlay much of his youthful confidence in the feasibility of a life dedicated to art.[101] Moreover, Morris had been friendly with Swinburne – whose *Poems and Ballads* (1866) is often regarded as the first literary symptom of Art for Art's sake – since the Oxford Union mural days.[102] Although his admiration for Ruskin and for the Pre-Raphaelites meant that he never

---

96 Morris, *News from Nowhere*, p. 1. Here I correct the typographic error that appears on the title-page of the text as printed in the *Collected Works*. It reads, 'An Epoch of Unrest', p. 1.

97 Morris, 'The Doom of King Acrisius', *The Earthly Paradise*, III, pp. 171–238.

98 Morris, 'The Son of Crœsus', *The Earthly Paradise*, IV, pp. 145–59.

99 Benjamin Constant wrote, 'J'ai une conversation avec Robinson, élève de Schelling. Son travail sur l'*Esthétique* de Kant a des idées très énergique. L'art pour l'art, sans but, car tout but dénature l'art' (*Journal intime*, in *Journal intime précédé du cahier rouge et d'Adolphe* (Monaco: Éditions du Roucher, 1945), 10 February 1804, pp. 153–437 (p. 159)); in the preface to *Mademoiselle de Maupin* (trans. by Joanna Richardson (Harmondsworth: Penguin Books, 1981)), Théophile Gautier advocated the divorce of art from morality; in *Notes Nouvelles sur Edgar Poe* (1857), Charles Baudelaire argued that 'Poetry cannot, except at the price of death or decay, assume the mantle of science or morality; the pursuit of truth is not its aim, it has nothing outside itself' ('Further Notes on Edgar Poe', in *Selected Writings on Art and Artists*, trans. by P. E. Charvet (Cambridge: Cambridge University Press, 1981), pp. 188–208 (p. 204)).

100 Morris, 'The Art of the People', p. 39.

101 John Keats's 'Ode on a Grecian Urn' ends with the words 'Beauty is truth, truth beauty, – that is all/ Ye know on earth, and all ye need to know', in *The Poetical Works of John Keats*, ed. by H. W. Garrod, 2nd edn (Oxford: Clarendon Press, 1958), pp. 260–2 (p. 262).

102 Algernon Charles Swinburne, *Poems and Ballads*, in *The Complete Works of Algernon Charles Swinburne*, ed. by Sir Edmund Gosse and Thomas James Wise, 20 vols (London: William Heinemann, 1925–27), I, pp. 135–364.

publicly repudiated – in a way Swinburne did – the idea that art might have a moral content, it is clear that many saw in his poetry a confirmation of the aestheticist position.[103] Building on Arnold's defensive isolation of criticism from 'political, practical considerations',[104] it was Walter Pater who used a review of the *Earthly Paradise* (which, in its subsequent incarnation as the conclusion to Pater's *The Renaissance* (1873), became in effect the manifesto of English aestheticism) to test his conviction that the only defence against death lay in expanding the 'interval'.[105] For him, the sensory 'pulsations' produced by 'art and song', 'the poetic passion, the desire of beauty', and 'the love of art for art's sake' were best fitted to this purpose.

While it would be a mistake to equate Morris's artistic principles with those informing the Aesthetic Movement, it is notable that even in its later phase Morris's name was often invoked by its adherents. In the 'English Renaissance of Art' (1882), Wilde had argued, 'Art never harms itself by keeping aloof from the social problems of the day: rather, by so doing, it more completely realizes for us that which we desire'.[106] Relying heavily on Morris's dictum, '*Have nothing in your houses that you do not know to be useful, or believe to be beautiful*',[107] he insists that, 'the true artist will admit nothing that is harsh or disturbing, nothing that gives pain, nothing that is debatable, nothing about which men argue'.[108] This statement provides a useful summary of the aestheticist position as one might extract it crudely from the idle singer's Apology. It is useful because it harnesses the same domestic metaphor that Morris employed to advance an opposing view in 'The Art of the People' (quoted above).[109] The apparent inconsistency reflects the differences between the older Morris and the aestheticist Wilde, but it also has to do with a conflict already current within the youthful Morris: that between the Rossettian ideal of a palace of art and the sheltered haven of the Ruskinian household. Both offered sanctuary, both were predicated upon the need for refuge, but the latter demanded a maintenance of intercourse between the interior and the outside world. The former did not. The following discussion begins by paying attention to aspects of Morris's poetry that reflect the less Ruskinian side of the argument, those that support the aestheticist dream of absolute separation established in England even before the French influence takes hold.[110]

In what sense, then, is *The Earthly Paradise* suggestive of aestheticism as a mode of escape? The first stanza begins on a negative note. It introduces the 'poet',

103 Swinburne attacked the moral theory of art in 'Charles Baudelaire: Les Fleurs du Mal', *Spectator*, 6 September 1862, pp. 998–1000 (p. 998).
104 Matthew Arnold, 'The Function of Criticism at the Present Time', in *The Complete Prose Works of Matthew Arnold*, ed. by R. H. Super, 11 vols (Ann Arbor: University of Michigan Press, 1962), III, pp. 258–85 (p. 270).
105 [Walter Pater], 'Poems by William Morris', *Westminster Review*, XXXIV (October, 1868), 300–312 (p. 312).
106 Oscar Wilde, 'English Renaissance of Art', in *Aristotle at Afternoon Tea: The Rare Oscar Wilde*, ed. by John Wyse Jackson (London: Fourth Estate, 1991), pp. 3–28 (p. 12).
107 Morris, 'The Beauty of Life', p. 76.
108 Wilde, 'English Renaissance of Art', p. 13.
109 Morris, 'The Art of the People', p. 39.
110 Note that it is only with the Ruskin *v.* Whistler trial that art theories derived respectively from Carlyle and Poe become publicly polarized, and it becomes possible to draw a line between Ruskin and such former disciples of his as Wilde.

a figure defining himself solely in terms of personal incapacity. He is the 'idle singer of an empty day' and, as such, works neither in the manual nor the professional sense. This may seem like a Bohemian pose, but these stanzas are still apologetic.[111] The singer does not denigrate the active life (spent slaying 'ravening monsters'). He simply craves exemption from a task unfitted to him. It is the suggestion that a poet has no role beyond the provision of entertainment or hopeless consolation – that song has no social ramifications, no part in setting the 'crooked straight' – that has provoked most indignation among critics. At the time of its first publication, the figure of the idle singer was most probably interpreted as a rejoinder to Carlyle's celebration of the *vates* in 'The Hero as Poet' (1841).[112] But the reluctance of the singer to make claims, to tell a tale in any way 'importunate' is not simply a timid rejection of Poe's reviled 'heresy of *The Didactic*'.[113] It is also an admission of failure. The singer's escapism is in no way militant; it does not constitute an artistic manifesto. The mere fact that the life spurned by the poet is rendered symbolically, in the language of romance, as the good fight of the monster-slaying hero, implies that such acts do not possess incontestable reality. In this way, even the Carlylean and Ruskinian paths of protest are encompassed within the singer's palace of art. The object the hero strives for is displaced accordingly, made to seem an intangible and 'shadowy isle of bliss'.[114]

Yet the realm of art, passively accepted as an alternative rather than as an antidote, is still granted special status, a quality of exemption. The lines, to 'sing of names rememberèd,/ Because they, living not, can ne'er be dead' suggest the transcendence of temporal constraint. In the penultimate stanza of the Apology, a wizard at Christmas time conjures the appearance of spring, summer and autumn through different windows of a palace. In the midst of a season representing both the consummation of the calendar and a festive suspension of time, this illusion provides a foretaste of the utopian situation in which the variety of the year might be appreciated without subjugation to its temporal scheme, and represents the most positive emblem of the singer's art yet offered. It asserts the possibility of independence from external hardship, given acceptance of enchantment, and realization that the opposed categories of the real and the imaginary collapse into one another as soon as one entertains the idea of earthly amelioration. It is with this condition that the singer identifies his 'Earthly Paradise', and it is with 'those who in the sleepy region stay' that he wishes to lull his readers into fellowship.

The tentative, apologetic message of the 'idle singer' then gives way to the forthright separatism of the Wanderers' Prologue. Rolf, who has been set dreaming of the 'ancient faith' of the North, rejects both Christianity and the 'scanty' land that is his home.[115] When it succumbs to a ravaging pestilence, he and a band of seekers talk of finding the earthly paradise they have heard described by a Swabian priest. In a passage that echoes the point in Giovanni

111 Morris, The Apology, *The Earthly Paradise*, III.
112 Thomas Carlyle, 'The Hero as Poet', in *Heroes, Hero-Worship and the Heroic in History*, in *Works*, V, pp. 78–114 (p. 81).
113 Edgar Allan Poe, 'The Poetic Principle', in *The Works of Edgar Allan Poe*, 10 vols (New York: Funk & Wagnalls, 1904), pp. 22–52 (p. 28).
114 Morris, The Apology, *The Earthly Paradise*, III, pp. 1, 2.
115 Morris, The Prologue, *The Earthly Paradise*, III, p. 6.

Boccaccio's *The Decameron* (c. 1351) when the young people decide to leave the city,[116] Nicholas finally asks, 'How long shall we/ Abide here, looking forth into the sea/ Expecting when our turn shall come to die?'[117] As in *The Decameron*, their decision to depart is partly legitimized by the antisocial behaviour of those who remain. Nicholas urges caution as they leave, because the 'pestilence/ Makes all men hard and cruel'. For a while, the Wanderers seem confident that they will be able to give 'warring lands a full wide berth'. This aspiration is destined to suffer disappointment, but on the level of the work as a whole the 'idle singer' succeeds in producing a poem devoid of further references to the 'six counties overhung with smoke', which the Prologue, and the aestheticist verses headed 'L'envoi', encourage readers to forget:

> [. . .] if indeed
> In some old garden thou and I have wrought,
> And made fresh flowers spring up from hoarded seed,
> And fragrance of old days and deeds have brought
> Back to folk weary; and all was not for nought.[118]

The desire here is to defy seasonal change, to suspend the cruel cycle of the year and fashion a self-sufficient alternative. As an attempt to bypass nature, it anticipates the cult of artifice symbolized later in the century by the hothouse flowers of Decadence. Of course the poems of *The Earthly Paradise* do internalize the gloomy transition from spring, to summer, to winter. They contain 'warring lands' and acts of violence aplenty. But being merely 'fragrance of old days and deeds', these troubles are kept at one remove from the immediate experience of the 'idle singer', and from the concerns of his readership.

Like Boccaccio, Morris uses a framing narrative as the pretext for a regular exchange of stories. On a thematic level, the storytelling of the Wanderers and Elders seems designed to test the efficacy of art in offering insulation from change and death. By distracting, consoling, and inviting thoughts of different climes, the tales bring to their audience discernible relief from the sad contemplation recorded in the accompanying lyrics. This motif is familiar from the hugely popular *Arabian Nights' Entertainments*, which was translated into English by Edward Lane between 1838 and 1840. The premise of this story-cycle involves the clever Scheherazade saving her life, and effectively suspending the flow of time, by telling tales to her murderous husband.[119] The application of an equivalent strategy in *The Earthly Paradise* seems not to achieve a wholesale cancellation of destiny. However, there is clearly an expectation that 'the beating of the sudden rain' on the windowpane will for a time be drowned out.[120] After 'The Love of Alcestis',[121] for instance, one learns that the audience 'in despite of death,/ With sweet content [. . .] drew their breath'.

---

[116] Giovanni Boccaccio, *The Decameron*, trans. by Guido Waldman (Oxford: Oxford University Press, 1993), p. 17–18.

[117] Morris, The Prologue, *The Earthly Paradise*, III, pp. 3, 9, 10, 14.

[118] Morris, 'L'envoi', *The Earthly Paradise*, VI, p. 333.

[119] *The Arabian Nights' Entertainments*, trans. by Edward William Lane, 3 vols (London: John Murray, 1859).

[120] Morris, *The Earthly Paradise*, III, p. 84.

[121] Morris, 'The Love of Alcestis', *The Earthly Paradise*, IV, pp. 89–125.

The traditional relationship between storytelling and the defiance of mortality is explored also in relation to the Paterian idea of filling the interval, maximising the yield of passing time by packing it with aesthetic content. If narrative cannot actually break the flow of time, the 'land's chief priest' reflects, it may at least enhance the good times, or 'crown our joyance', and, in the bad, produce pleasing contrast between the storytellers' existence and the life of those 'hurled/ By the hard hands of fate and destiny'.[122] The tales thus grant their audience a glimpse of a world free of earthly contingency, one ''neath another law'.[123] They may even serve as a talking cure. Before setting out to relate the story of the Wanderers' failed quest, Rolf asserts that 'grief once told brings somewhat back of peace'.[124] For the participants, this exchange of stories would appear to have a social function not accounted for by Thompson.

Morris's poems of this period also gesture towards the possibility of separatism through frequent allusion to the idea of earthly paradise. Rarely resulting from reform or heroic deliverance of the old country, the good life lies more often over the sea, in a region remote and impenetrable. It is a place one must journey towards at the risk of losing what little one possesses. *The Life and Death of Jason* (1867), a poem Morris originally intended for *The Earthly Paradise*, is no exception in its preoccupation with this elusive goal.[125] Like 'Frank's Sealed Letter', this work is, on the whole, hostile to the idea that amnesia might bring about happiness.[126] There are, nevertheless, passages in which it is represented more favourably. One such is the description of the gardens of the Hesperides. The daughters of Hesperus continue to find that 'rest is sweet',[127] and when Jason is made King of Iolchos, it is revealed, approvingly, that the Queen 'and all these folk' had 'forgotten pain', that to them 'Death and Fear' had become 'idle words'. *The Earthly Paradise*, itself, begins with this famous repeated imperative:

> Forget six counties overhung with smoke,
> Forget the snorting steam and piston stroke,
> Forget the spreading of the hideous town.[128]

This is not the only point at which pure escape is represented in positive terms. In 'Ogier the Dane', when the hero has reached Avallon he lives in 'sweet forgetfulness/ Of all the troubles that did once oppress'.[129] As is suggested by the title that Morris originally gave to the Prologue ('The Fools' Paradise'), *The Earthly Paradise* is as much concerned with sham paradises as with authentic ones.[130] The 'nameless city in a distant sea' that the Wanderers eventually reach is a version of utopia, if one strangely lacking in vitality.[131] This identity is conferred in part by the island's status as a language enclave, a place where 'the ancient tongue' of the

---

122 Morris, The Prologue, *The Earthly Paradise*, III, p. 84.
123 Morris, *The Earthly Paradise*, III, p. 239.
124 Morris, The Prologue, *The Earthly Paradise*, III, p. 5.
125 Morris, *The Life and Death of Jason*, in *Collected Works*, II.
126 Morris, 'Frank's Sealed Letter', in *Collected Works*, I, pp. 309–25.
127 Morris, *The Life and Death of Jason*, pp. 210, 258.
128 Morris, The Prologue, *The Earthly Paradise*, III, p. 3.
129 Morris, 'Ogier the Dane', *The Earthly Paradise*, IV, pp. 210–55 (pp. 233–4).
130 Morris, 'The Fools' Paradise', *The Earthly Paradise*, III, p. xiij.
131 Morris, The Prologue, *The Earthly Paradise*, III, pp. 3, 5, 7, 13.

'Ionian race' remains in use. The Prologue is replete with references to the many paradise myths of Greek, Northern and Oriental tradition. They include Asgard (the Norse home of the gods), an 'Earthly Paradise' sighted by 'an English knight', Leif Ericsson's 'Greenland' (see the Vineland Sagas) and the 'Spice-trees' of an eastern garden where the seasons are softened by a gentle year.[132] Many of the lands mentioned exist according to the premise that the world at large is shut out.

The story material assembled within *The Earthly Paradise* is itself distant and displaced. The claims of contemporary London are dismissed at the beginning of the Prologue, neutralized by the invocation of a different context, a peaceful vision of Chaucer's city that forms an effective buffer between the world of the Wanderers and that of the Victorian readership. The mythological subject matter confers on the tales a referred and unshackled quality, intensified by their location beyond at least three levels of narrative displacement (even more in those tales that utilize the narrative device of the dreamer). The city of the Elders is 'nameless' and is 'White as the changing walls of faërie'.[133] Such details seem designed to preserve the independent integrity of the story material, to hedge it off from sources of contamination.

The separatist ideal existing in parallel with paradise is clearly that of love. Jason's affection for Medea seems for a time to take precedence over that other 'precious burden', the Golden Fleece, which he plans to return to Greece.[134] Love operates here, as in his other works, according to its own laws, laws not necessarily conducive to good government. This idea is the subject of *Love is Enough*, a verse drama Morris published in 1872.[135] The play derives its dramatic energy from the tension between King Pharamond's new calling as a lover, enthralled to the purposes of Love, and his governmental responsibilities. Pharamond is finally set free to pursue a life of love infused with a suggestion of spiritual transcendence. Here 'the House of Love' represents a viable alternative to the secular realm, a mystical kingdom in which Pharamond will have his seat.

In an unsigned review of *The Earthly Paradise*, published in *Temple Bar*, Alfred Austin responded to this rhetoric of escape by complaining that Morris had 'given the go-by to his age', that he had 'evaded the very conditions on which alone the production of great poetry is possible'.[136] Austin's objections to *The Earthly Paradise*'s lack of 'co-operation' were echoed in the twentieth century by critics who saw in it the relaxation of a prior commitment to dramatizing the 'dangers of the escape into romance'.[137] Discussing the fruitful dialectic of romance and modernity in Morris's earlier work, David Riede has written:

> These conflicting impulses, intertwined and simultaneous within the text, provided the vitality of Morris's best early work, as of Keats's romances, but Morris was ultimately satisfied, appeased, within the 'autonomous domain of literature', and his later poetry consequently suffers from a certain sterility.

---

132 In a letter to Oscar Fay Adams, Morris reveals that Sir John Mandeville was the English knight of whom he was thinking, 'after 17 June, 1887', in *Collected Letters*, II, p. 671.
133 Morris, The Prologue, *The Earthly Paradise*, III, p. 3.
134 Morris, *The Life and Death of Jason*, p. 136.
135 Morris, *Love is Enough*, in *Collected Works*, IX, pp. 3–89.
136 [Alfred Austin], 'The Poetry of the Period. Mr. Matthew Arnold. Mr. Morris', *Temple Bar*, XXVII (November 1869), 35–51 (p. 51).
137 David G. Riede, 'Morris, Modernism, and Romance', *ELH*, 51 (1984), 1, 85–106 (p. 88).

There is, I have argued, a distinct sense in which Morris's poetry rejects the need for 'co-operation' as defined by Austin.[138] Yet even in *The Earthly Paradise*, isolationism – aesthetic, Romantic, or otherwise – is not always presented as sustainable, or even desirable. Reluctant sympathy for the utopian dimension of the aestheticist claim to independence exists in critical tension with a Ruskinian belief in the value of fellowship and the communally redemptive nature of the quest, a task that cannot be performed by excluding pain, negativity and other factors hostile to the ego, or by refusing responsibility for what occurs in a world designated unpoetic. As his early review of Browning's *Men and Women* (1855) demonstrates (especially the commentary on 'Cleon'), Morris was aware from the very beginning of his career that an 'intense appreciation of beauty' could yet be 'intensely selfish', that a solipsism enlisted in the service of art was neither morally justifiable, nor effective as a strategy for the furtherance of its ends.[139]

The conventional reading of aestheticism as a yearning for the apolitical is immediately problematized when one examines what actually is at stake in the Prologue. The singer's invitation, it is important to remember, is issued to the reader. It is hard, for this reason, to conclude that straightforward solipsism is being recommended, or that art is being presented as an alternative to sociability. The tone, instead, is hospitable. We are encouraged to pass through a crowded square, to 'push the brazen door' inside the porch of a 'pillared council-house', and thus to witness an exchange of stories.[140] Indeed, it is possible to argue that the theme of the whole poem is the infinite receptivity of narrative, the link between sociability and the transmission of a de-individualized, common stock of story matter.[141] The tale-telling scenario allows Morris to stress the removed sociability achieved by the Wanderers and the Elders. At the same time, it momentarily admits the questing world, on the imaginative level of narrative. This is the very context that resting and feasting would otherwise serve to deny. The aestheticism evoked in the process need not be construed as hostile to openness or pluralism. Pater, for one, valued *The Earthly Paradise* because it served as the ground upon which 'two worlds of sentiment are confronted', the classical and the medieval.[142] In *The Renaissance*, he developed this idea, arguing that 'in the *House Beautiful* the saints too have their place', that in 'the enchanted region of the Renaissance' there are 'no fixed parties, no exclusions'.[143] Pater's remarks reflect a personal agenda distinct from Morris's, but *The Earthly Paradise*'s hospitable approach to the selection of story-material – combining tales of classical, Oriental, Norse and medieval origin – does ensure a diversity internal to the 'unity

---

138 [Austin], 'The Poetry of the Period', p. 51.
139 Morris, ' "Men and Women" by Robert Browning', in *Collected Works*, I, pp. 326–48 (p. 326).
140 Morris, Prologue, *The Earthly Paradise*, III, p. 4.
141 Laying less stress on hospitality than on participation, Clive Wilmer has argued that what the Wanderers find in poetry is 'not simply a *paradis artificiel*' ('The Names of the Roses: Modernity and Archaism in William Morris's *The Earthly Paradise*', *Times Literary Supplement*, 6 June 2003, pp. 3–4 (p. 3)); it depends instead upon 'an experience of life' (pp. 3–4) renewed by the formation of 'a new relationship' (p. 4), that 'between the reader and the writer or, in terms of Morris's fable, between the narrator and his audience'.
142 [Pater], 'Poems by William Morris', p. 309.
143 Walter Pater, *The Renaissance*, in *The Works of Walter Pater*, 8 vols (London: Macmillan and Co., 1900), I, pp. 26–7.

of culture' created on the page.[144] In the manner of an anthologist, he achieves a suggestion both of difference and reconciliation.

Furthermore, the poem is not built solely on a narrative of abandonment or exodus. It is also concerned with the reception offered to a group of Wanderers appearing on an unknown shore. From the very beginning, the welcome they receive is warm and respectful:

> Speak out and fear not; if ye need a place
> Wherein to pass the end of life away,
> That shall ye gain from us from this same day,
> Unless the enemies of God ye are.[145]

The Wanderers' final destination is not a closed society. Its inhabitants make no attempt to police their shoreline or to withhold permission for the newcomers to settle. Rolf recalls with gratitude, how, on first landing, they were treated 'like brothers for ten days'. Their health recovers, and their thirst for 'friendly words' is satisfied. The warmth of the welcome depicted in the published version of the Wanderers' Prologue is of particular significance because it is far less pronounced in Morris's earlier attempt at the subject.[146] Comparison of the two versions reveals marked differences in his treatment of the encounter between the Wanderers and their hosts. Florence Boos, in her article, 'The Evolution of "The Wanderers' Prologue"', has detailed many points of divergence, and highlighted Morris's original indebtedness to Coleridge's 'The Rime of the Ancient Mariner'.[147] In the first version, she observes, the mariners (a group of piratic adventurers) 'are much more truculent' and even threaten ' "The People of the Shore" [. . .] in almost ludicrous contrast to the Wanderers' and Elders' mutuality and kindred feeling'.

These differences are significant because they show Morris consciously enshrining a positive example of hospitable behaviour in the framing narrative. He made a decision, it seems, to discard Coleridge's model of an 'ancient Mariner' (who 'inhospitably killeth the pious bird of good omen').[148] Elsewhere in the published version, a warm welcome is used as a marker of a good society. The framing narrative Morris devised for 'The Land East of the Sun and West of the Moon' conjures a scene of courtly hospitality through Gregory the Star-gazer's dream.[149] It is Christmas time in the great hall of King Magnus. Outside, the snow is drifting and the wind howling. All of a sudden, a shout is heard from the porch; the outer door opens to reveal a stranger. The king responds with generosity and

144 Pater, *The Renaissance*, p. 27.
145 Morris, The Prologue, *The Earthly Paradise*, III, p. 5.
146 This earlier version was published as 'The Wanderers' in May Morris's introduction to volume XXIV of *The Collected Works*, pp. 87–170.
147 Florence S. Boos, 'The Evolution of the "The Wanderers' Prologue"', *Papers on Language and Literature*, 20 (1984), 4, 397–417 (p. 398).
148 Coleridge, 'The Rime of the Ancient Mariner' in *The Collected Works of Samuel Taylor Coleridge*, 16, 1.1, pp. 365–419 (p. 379).
149 Morris, 'The Land East of the Sun and West of the Moon', *The Earthly Paradise*, V, pp. 24–120. Morris based this tale on Benjamin Thorpe's 'The Beautiful Palace East of the Sun and North of the Earth', *Yule-tide Stories: A Collection of Scandinavian and North German Popular Tales and Traditions, from the Swedish, Danish, and German* (London: Henry G. Bohn, 1853), pp. 158–68.

courtesy, and receives in turn the conventional reward for hospitality: 'News from over sea/ Of Mary and the Trinity', and a story. Once again, art and narrative depend as much upon a trade in stories as upon the more exclusionary suspension of worldly affairs within the four walls of the festive hall.

The link between narrative and hospitality is particularly obvious in 'The Lovers of Gudrun', Morris's reworking of *Laxdæla Saga*.[150] The decision to anglicize the Icelandic name 'Gest', to produce 'Guest', serves to emphasize the link between this character's role as a prophet or interpreter of dreams, and his status as an honoured outsider. Responsible, paradoxically, for revealing fate *and* precipitating its unfolding (as a story-teller and story-maker), Guest is both foreign to the household and party to its innermost secrets. Gudrun, standing near the 'guest-worn threshold-stone' of Bathstead, beckons him in; and, in so doing, welcomes in her fate:

> 'Be welcome here, O Guest the Wise!' she said,
> 'My father honours me so much that I
> Am bid to pray thee not to pass us by,
> But bide here for a while.'

On one level, these observations are unremarkable: Morris's source materials, many of them heroic legends and medieval romances, would inevitably make allusion to the central oppositions of heroic culture, between inside and outside, the human and the divine, a gift and a debt. Where the tales bear the imprint of his particular, as opposed to inadvertent or translated, interest in hospitality – as where he uses the English, 'Guest', for 'Gest' – these episodes have a different significance, indicating a concern to qualify the celebration of inwardness suggested by the Apology.

The high value attached to openness is reinforced by the recurrent appearance in Morris's work of the false paradise motif, of a place apparently devoted to pleasure and comfort, but in practice conducive to *ennui*. This is a problem to which the propagandists of Art for Art's Sake were not blind. The famous remark attributed to Théophile Gautier – 'plutôt la barbarie que l'ennui!' – was echoed in Pater's conviction that man's lamentable departure from the Hellenic idea of unity had in a sense been necessary.[151] The most direct treatment of this theme occurs in *The Life and Death of Jason*, when the Sirens describe the charms of existence in a 'changeless land', a land 'roofed over by the changeless sea'.[152] Their bowers are 'thornless'; and the seasons have been shut out. Orpheus's response constitutes a direct and powerful repudiation of the separatist utopia, and a reassertion of a Ruskinian commitment to the quest: to 'toil rather, suffer and be free'. Achieving exemption from pain or misfortune is equivalent to dying, in Morris's imaginative world, and it is for this reason that no wholesome shelter is available beneath the 'undying trees' of the Hesperides, and that Pelias's undoing stems from his unreasonable wish to be immortal. Closed societies of this kind are often presented in negative terms for the simple reason that they reject heroic values.

---

150   Morris, 'The Lovers of Gudrun', *The Earthly Paradise*, V, pp. 251–395.
151   Pater, *The Renaissance*, pp. 222–3.
152   Morris, *The Life and Death of Jason*, pp. 95, 199, 209.

The limit imposed by the exclusion of strangers on a society's capacity for change (and thus adventure) is one aspect of this negative status; another is the failure to perpetuate the circulation of gifts so crucial in forging external alliances, and in securing honour. In *The Life and Death of Jason*, King Æetes epitomizes the type of the deceitful and self-serving host. Yet even while he lays plans to kill his guests and steal their treasures, he feels the need to mimic the role of the generous host, to refute any suggestion 'that King Æetes fearing guests doth dwell'.

It is nevertheless possible to argue that hospitality itself is a separatist ideal. As a concept, it is definitively housebound; as a festive principle, it celebrates the privilege of being on the inside. The Elders' offer of refuge represents rest to the Wanderers, an opportunity to give up the quest and bury their pains. In the tales, banqueting, which is an important component of heroic hospitality, is often presented as an opportunity to forget. In the midst of winter, just before the tale of 'Bellerophon in Lycia',[153] the old men stay by the fire and 'shut out the memory of the cloud-drowned sun'. By questioning the symbolism of openness originally attached to Morris's representation of hospitality, one may even doubt the cultural diversity evoked by the tales' sources. Pater's remarks on the confrontation of 'two worlds of sentiment' might be construed equally as a dream of unity. *The Earthly Paradise*, as a project, betrays a similar desire to demonstrate the unity of beautiful things at their root, to bring together 'whatsoever things are comely'.[154] Even where Morris conjures a scene of trade, of apparent cultural and commercial interchange (as at the beginning of the Prologue), differences in collision are softened into a medievalist unity. Ships bearing 'Levantine staves', 'pointed jars that Greek hands toiled to fill', 'spice', 'Florence gold cloth', 'Ypres napery', 'cloth of Bruges' and 'hogsheads of Guienne' pass through the harbour not as harbingers of nineteenth-century mercantile culture, but as cargoes equally sympathetic to the attention of Chaucer's pen.[155] And yet the mere fact that death is such a brooding presence in this work indicates that the aestheticist agenda of reconciled diversity is not altogether triumphant. In a displaced form, anxiety emerges concerning the persistence of underlying reality. This is the plane of existence whose exigencies the tales sublimate as themes, tokens of an organicist aesthetics hostile to intrusion. The accompanying lyrics manifest this tendency in their recurrent stress on mortality, a source of despair not productive in itself, but crucial in problematizing the singer's separatist call to forget. In this way, Morris deliberately leaves his work open to an intrusive form of memory.

In *The Earthly Paradise*, the language of separatism occupies the foreground, causing the memory of industrial Britain to be suppressed. The poem's escapist strategies are qualified by an equally medievalist commitment to representing openness and generosity in positive terms. This countervailing insistence on engagement has the effect of qualifying the poem's celebration of inwardness. It thus witnesses Morris's movement towards a different kind of medievalism. As a literary production, *The Earthly Paradise* offered the opportunity to assert on the page a more convincing illusion of independence from exterior reality than was

153   Morris, 'Bellerophon in Lycia', *The Earthly Paradise*, in *Collected Works*, VI, pp. 176–277.
154   Pater, *The Renaissance*, p. 27.
155   Morris, The Prologue, *The Earthly Paradise*, III, p. 3.

possible at Red House. However, the fact that Morris permits the intrusion of the mortality theme should not be ignored. The Wanderers, it seems, have spread a kind of disease among their hosts, a disease that finds its most obvious expression in the lonely melancholy of the lyrics. In this sense, the mode of retreat is deliberately undercut, exposed to a demonstration of its limitations. Still, the poem does not support a wholesale rejection of the separatist urge. As a purely pragmatic device, assertions of independence remain useful as the only means by which art can be produced in a hostile context. The qualification and violation of inwardness staged in *The Earthly Paradise* might be viewed locally as a symptom of Morris's struggle to move beyond Rossetti's aestheticism. More generally, it provides the groundwork for an unstable truce between the functional aspects of separatism and the more hospitable aspirations of utopian endeavour.

Conclusions

The idea of hospitality usefully encapsulates Morris's compromise between receptivity and confidence in the utility of retreat or inwardness. The invocation of a 'medieval' outlook in the fields of architecture and literature served to establish an exemplary approach to the problems of poverty and alienation for an age bereft of equivalent models. Ruskin's use of the word *wayfarer* might be seen, accordingly, as a deliberate, rather than naïve, attempt to restore an 'obsolete' representation of the poor. The disjunction between the archaic ideal and the realities of nineteenth-century poverty discloses in this way the intentionally and necessarily impractical nature of Red House's symbolism of openness. Where commercial commissions like the work undertaken at Queens' College Cambridge are concerned, practical constraints and an existing institutional structure limit the scope for revivalism. Other factors are of relevance, however. Had Morris's idealized medievalism been given full licence, the scope for openness would still have been limited. This is because hospitality also implies limits, a contained form of fellowship and festivity.

Medievalist hospitality was itself a separatist ideal. It relied upon the availability of a certain kind of guest. On this level, the openness of hospitality and the inwardness of romance approach reconciliation. Just as Red House is at once surrounded by a high wall and structurally receptive to the stranger, so the Wanderers in *The Earthly Paradise* are seekers who have rejected community in favour of a high ideal, and participants in a cycle of feasting and storytelling. This strategy was not immune to the difficulties imposed by the continuance in the wider world of a hostile social context. At Red House, one finds only interdependence behind the symbolism of autonomy, a fact demonstrated powerfully by Morris's eventual return to London following the founding of the Firm. If these limitations were a corollary of the project's utopian nature, and if medievalist hospitality was conditioned by a dependence on anachronism wedded to its exemplary function, it is also possible to see Morris learning from this problem, and in the process developing a more sophisticated utopianism. By this, I mean that he began to accommodate the distinction between the form of a utopian statement (removed, self-contained) and its content (in Morris's case, open and engaged – in short, hospitable). Theoretically, at least, these categories did not need to come into conflict, being attitudes adapted to different challenges. Friction between them only arose when hospitality ceased to function exclusively as utopian content and became an actual proposition, the application of an unconditional welcome to an unwelcoming age. At such times, the mode of retreat, even in its pragmatic, protective form, is displaced, and one witnesses an exemplary but potentially self-defeating attempt to humanize a hostile world.

Chapter 3

ENTERTAINING THE PAST: PROBLEMS IN TOURISM, TRANSLATION AND PRESERVATION

Introduction

In her preface to the second edition of *Darwin's Plots*, Gillian Beer writes that *The Origin of Species* (1859) 'can be seen either as providing a grounding vocabulary for colonialism, or [. . .] as resisting "intrusion" and idealising the closed environment of island spaces'.[1] During the 1870s, Morris showed a comparably ambiguous interest in a different kind of 'closed environment': his activities in this period manifest a fascination with the remote setting of the medieval past. He, like Darwin, exhibits both a desire to publicize the appeal of this 'island space' – to present it as a source of reform or artistic inspiration – and an urge to protect it as a delicate ideal, a rare and endangered habitat. In this respect, Morris was faced with a familiar epistemological problem. He wanted to access the 'past'. This might mean visiting a 'backward' civilization, translating a textual artefact, or merely entering an ancient building. But he wanted to do so without compromising its integrity, without polluting it with a sensibility hostile to its organizing principles.

Morris continually wrestles with this problem in his lectures on art. There are occasions, as in 'The Lesser Arts' (1877), when he shows great confidence in the possibility of drawing innocently on the resources of previous eras.[2] Those, he claims, 'who have diligently followed the delightful study of these arts are able as if through windows to look upon the life of the past'. In the same lecture, he contextualizes this impulse in a way that complicates matters. His own interests, he admits, build upon wider changes in historiography; they benefit from the acquirement of a 'new sense', an historicism that combines thirst to know the 'reality' of distant times with new respect for the ineluctable divide between past and present. It is this reference to a new appreciation of the past's impenetrability that makes Morris's window metaphor unconvincing. As he came to associate the arts of the present with a systemic malaise, with a wider 'sickness of civilization', he was increasingly afraid that the irreplaceable remnants of past cultures would be contaminated.[3] Hence he advises the students of the Birmingham Society of

---

[1] Gillian Beer, *Darwin's Plots*, 2nd edn (Cambridge: Cambridge University Press, 2000), p. xxi.
[2] Morris, 'The Lesser Arts', in *Collected Works*, XXII, pp. 3–27 (p. 7).
[3] Morris, 'The Art of the People', p. 36.

Arts and School of Design to study antiquity, 'not steal it'.[4] Apart from condemning imitation as a hopeless endeavour, this statement issues the warning that it is possible to do violence to the past. It was in recognition of this danger that Morris bemoaned the effect Western commerce was having on the arts of the East. An otherwise salutary upsurge of interest in Indian craftwork, he complained, was 'destroying the very sources of that education' which it was his purpose to promote.[5] Morris's attitude to the past therefore involved a delicate balancing act: the past was to be used, but not stolen; studied, but not imitated; preserved, but certainly not 'restored'.

Critics interested in the cultural phenomenon of nostalgia typically fail to appreciate the subtle distinctions that complicate Morris's position. The 'sentimentalizing regard for the past', which David Lowenthal associates with Arts and Crafts revivalism, was in Morris's case the expression of a preference for a different political order, not simply a vague and abstract longing for past times.[6] Lowenthal is justified in asserting that 'Ruskin and Morris condemned restoration as a fraudulent modern contrivance', but not in presenting their position as one opposed to his own view that the past's strangeness is 'domesticated by our own preservation of its vestiges'. For this, surely, was exactly their point. Ruskin and Morris placed far more emphasis on the fallaciousness of restoration as a principle, as an attitude to the past, than on the feasibility of preservation. It was simply that the latter option, in all its imperfection, seemed to them the least damaging of the two.

The following discussions treat Morris's activities in the ostensibly dissimilar areas of travel, translation and architectural preservation. These ventures exhibit in common several core preoccupations. Most obviously, they facilitate Morris's encounters with a variety of imagined pasts. They provide him with opportunities to stage an escape from his own culture, to play the role of the stranger in utopia. The chapter is concerned, accordingly, with his attempts to 'visit' difference. But it also examines the problems that arise when, in a general sense, he attempts to *translate* these emblems of alternative society, to make them useful and accessible to his own culture. There are, then, two kinds of utopia: a medieval or heroic past that serves as a source of instructive contrast; and a reformed, hospitable present capable of tolerating in its midst such buildings, texts and places as testify to alternative ways of life. As before, the questions addressed relate to the difficulty of achieving a redemptive openness, what might in this case be considered a socio-temporal pluralism. Any estimation of Morris's achievement in pursuing this elusive condition must therefore depend upon his success in 'entertaining' or 'translating' what is past, what is foreign.

---

4   Morris, 'The Art of the People', p. 28.
5   In the 'Manifesto of the S. P. A. B.', Morris identified a similar correlation between *interest* and destruction: 'We think that those last fifty years of knowledge and attention have done more for their destruction [ancient buildings] than all the foregoing centuries of revolution, violence, and contempt', in *Collected Letters*, I, pp. 359–60 (p. 359).
6   David Lowenthal, *The Past is a Foreign Country* (Cambridge: Cambridge University Press, 1985), pp. xvii, xxi, 411.

'Where nature is so rugged, and man so kind and hospitable':[7]
Tourism in an 'Isle of Refuge'[8]

Like most expressions of primitivism, Morris's dismay at the commercialization of Indian carpet weaving merely reverses the flow of the colonial exchange: instead of civilizing, he suggests, the British were destroying the sources of authentic craftwork, spreading the contagion of a modernity inimical to the arts upon whose health 'true' civilization depended. As a result, a source of 'education' – the kind of education the South Kensington Museum had been established to promote – was in danger of becoming extinct. Morris's comments also invert the terms of L. P. Hartley's famous assertion that 'the past is a foreign country'.[9] Where his references to India are concerned, it is the foreign country, not the past, that contains vestiges of pre-capitalist civilization and serves as a symbol of former times. In an early essay, written for the *Oxford and Cambridge Magazine*, Morris had claimed that he was able to see 'some little of mediaeval times' through the tombs inside Amiens cathedral.[10] Such a convergence of past and present becomes possible for him because, like most Victorians, he viewed development in temporal as well as economic terms. Certain nations or regions were seen to lag behind others, retarded, for whatever reason, at an earlier stage of civilization. This section explores Morris's most intense experience of a place combining geographical isolation with the markers of historical remoteness.

In 1871 and 1873, Morris visited Iceland, a country that for him came to represent the last refuge of an otherwise dead culture.[11] In a lecture given on the subject in 1887, 'The Early Literature of the North – Iceland', he described the island as a 'casket' that had 'preserved the records of the traditions and religion of the Gothic tribes'.[12] It is this identification of Iceland as an enclave or time capsule that makes Morris's journals so interesting in the context of this inquiry. Icelandic society appealed to him because the people were 'kind, hospitable, and honest', and because they had 'no class degradation'; but these markers of sociability were also the products of a wider isolation from the rest of Western Europe. Though by no means the first Englishman to visit the country, Morris was among those bringing that isolation to an end. In this capacity, he was able to enjoy the country as an 'Isle of Refuge', a place of precious exemption. And yet, as the following analysis should serve to demonstrate, he was also conscious of a certain complicity in the process of opening it up.

Morris's Iceland journals cannot be understood fully unless seen as a response

---

7   Morris, 'To the Editor of *The Pall Mall Gazette*', 13 December [1890], in *Collected Letters*, III, p. 242.

8   Morris, 'The Early Literature of the North – Iceland', in *The Unpublished Lectures of William Morris*, ed. by Eugene D. LeMire (Detroit: Wayne State University Press, 1969), pp. 179–98 (p. 181).

9   L. P. Hartley, *The Go-Between* (London: Hamish Hamilton, 1953), p. xvi.

10 Morris, 'The Churches of North France: Shadows of Amiens', in *Collected Works*, I, pp. 349–66 (p. 349).

11 Morris was accompanied on this first journey by Charles Faulkner (an Oxford friend), Eiríkr Magnússon (his friend and tutor of Icelandic) and W. H. Evans (usually described as a country sports enthusiast).

12 Morris, 'The Early Literature of the North – Iceland', p. 181.

to the works produced by previous visitors to the country, many of which he had read.[13] Only by taking account of what other travellers thought of Morris's unconventional utopia in the north can one appreciate why he felt it necessary to emphasize certain things, and to omit mention of others. The wider difficulties entailed by his pilgrimage also need to be considered. Morris wanted to pay homage to the home of the sagas, and he was interested in a nation that could be described as 'a mere drop of water in the commercial ocean', but he never felt able to transcend his position as a tourist, and as such, his status as an agent of commerce.[14] In short, this section must be concerned with the politics of Morris's role as a traveller; and, more particularly, with that self-conception which stems from his sensitivity to Iceland's 'backwardness': his sense of being a guest in another time.

E. J. Oswald, a subsequent visitor to the island, provided a brief summary of Iceland's attractions in her 1882 book, *By Fell and Fjord*: 'Every year', she explains, 'a few people go [. . .] to Iceland for their summer holidays; they are generally drawn there by one of three attractions – the fishing, the geology, or the old literature'.[15] Morris was a devoted angler, and his journals take a keen interest in the geological life of the island, but his visit to Iceland was primarily a literary pilgrimage. He had begun his study of the sagas in 1869. By the time of his first visit, he, and his Icelandic friend, Eiríkr Magnússon, had translated *Gunnlaugs Saga*, *Grettis Saga*, *Laxdæla Saga* and *Eyrbyggja Saga*. Critics commonly attach great weight to Morris's subsequent assessment of this experience, stressing in particular his recollection that it was 'a good corrective to the maundering side of mediaevalism'.[16] With these remarks apparently in mind, Mackail linked the growth of his interest in the North to 'the final extinction of Rossetti's influence over him as an artist'.[17] This argument has its weaknesses. Morris did not abandon the dreamy, listless qualities of late-Romantic poetry immediately upon translating the sagas, nor, indeed, upon visiting Iceland. The publication of *Love is Enough* in 1872 testifies to this fact: the play sympathetically treats the maundering predilections of a king no longer interested in kingship. The world of the sagas nevertheless impressed Morris in ways that influenced the development of his politics. He admired the passionate reserve of the typical saga-hero, and may even have found comfort in the sagas' stoical world view at a time when his marriage was failing. His interest in the country, it is important to emphasize, went beyond literary hero worship. 'Much would be lost,' Carlyle suggested in

13 References in the first Iceland journal indicate that, in preparation for his voyage, Morris had read Sabine Baring-Gould's *Iceland: Its Scenes and Sagas* (London: Smith, Elder and Co., 1863). In the pages of Baring-Gould, Morris would have been directed to books by William Hooker, Ebenezer Henderson and George Steuart Mackenzie. A reference to Richard Burton in the following letter indicates that he continued to read such works after his first visit: 'am curious to see what that humbug Burton has to say about Iceland' ('To Eiríkr Magnússon', 4 November 1872?, in *Collected Letters*, I, pp. 168–9 (p. 168)).
14 Morris, 'The Early Literature of the North – Iceland', p. 181.
15 E. J. Oswald, *By Fell and Fjord; or, Scenes and Studies in Iceland* (Edinburgh and London: William Blackwood and Sons, 1882), p. 1.
16 Morris, 'To Andreas Scheu', 15 September 1883, in *Collected Letters*, II, pp. 225–31 (p. 229).
17 Mackail, *The Life of William Morris*, I, p. 200.

1840, 'had Iceland not been burst-up from the sea'.[18] With this assertion, Morris could hardly have disagreed. But it is clear that he would have regretted the loss of certain relics Carlyle might happily have seen consigned to the depths of the ocean, the proto-democratic ethos of its early settlers, for one thing.

Morris's Iceland journals form a continuous record of his experiences rather than an account of what the country eventually meant to him. This is true despite the fact that the first journal was subsequently revised. Only in recollection, and after a second visit, did he assemble his memories into the kind of politically symbolic encounter with another culture that he described so confidently in 'The Early Literature of the North – Iceland'. In order fully to appreciate Iceland's appeal to Morris, it is necessary to look beyond the journals. They are treated in what follows as an experiential quarry, best considered in combination with later sources, with documents that indicate the uses to which Morris eventually put his memories of the country.

In *The Vikings and the Victorians*, Andrew Wawn identifies a discrepancy between comments Morris made in his letter to Andreas Scheu – in which he recalls that Iceland had taught him 'that the most grinding poverty is a trifling evil compared with the inequality of classes'[19] – and the lack of 'substantive references to the "trifling evil" of poverty' in the journals.[20] Wawn disputes the 'putative Icelandic origin' of Morris's socialism. In support of this view, he adduces 'Morris's bouts of dissatisfaction with the service provided by district guides; his obsession with lice whenever forced to enter a farmer's house; and the disdain directed at an ' "unsavoury idiot" at Barkarstaðir'. He implies that Morris idealized his experiences after the event, and that this process was aided by 'the inevitably limited nature of their exposure to the warp and weft of Icelandic society'. This tendency to idealize in retrospect, and an occasional discrepancy between the bad-tempered traveller and the wistful socialist of later years, really only indicate that the significance and meaning of Morris's experiences evolved in his mind as he moved through life. Even the possibility that his analysis of Icelandic culture was naïve does little to alter the basic fact that Iceland came, for Morris, to symbolize an alternative way of life.

Morris begins his first Iceland journal with entries detailing his progress on land from Queen Square to Granton Harbour in Scotland. It is a preliminary journey, framed, in some respects, as an infernal interlude, a necessary encounter with a landscape 'blotched by coal'.[21] At Newcastle, he describes the city's 'huge waste of station', a symbol of the modernity he wished to escape and an early reminder of his failure, in his capacity as a passenger, to achieve transcendence through travel. Once on board the *Diana*, he is plagued by seasickness and by a fear of drowning. While this preoccupation with the likelihood of personal catastrophe does not subside when he reaches Iceland, these early entries seem deliberately to highlight the contrast between his civilized, 'cockney' sensibilities and 'the

[18] Carlyle, 'The Hero as Divinity', *On Heroes, Hero-Worship, and the Heroic in History*, in *Works*, V, pp. 1–41 (p. 16).
[19] Morris, 'To Andreas Scheu', II, p. 229.
[20] Andrew Wawn, *The Vikings and the Victorians: Inventing the Old North in Nineteenth-Century Britain* (Cambridge: D. S. Brewer, 2000), pp. 276, 277.
[21] Morris, *Journals of Travel in Iceland 1871–1873*, in *Collected Works*, VIII, pp. 2, 11.

worship of courage' he so admired in the sagas.[22] The effect, as elsewhere in Morris's work, is to produce a contrast, a mutual elucidation of present-day Britain and pre-industrial Iceland.[23] Moreover, there are signs that this journey will take us back in time: of the Faroe Islands, for instance, he notes that 'the old life of the saga-time had gone, and the modern life [had] never reached the place'.[24]

Morris casts his sea voyage as an approach to a personal 'Holy Land'.[25] His first sighting of Iceland is recorded in a style that accords the event visionary significance (cf. Morris's later poem on the subject).[26] It is, he reports, 'the first sight of a new land'.[27] Though Morris's journals were not published in his lifetime, it remains useful to compare his views on the subject with those of a contemporary, Richard Burton. Burton first travelled to Iceland in 1872. In a book-length reflection on this journey, he suggested that the subject rarely avoided being 'of the sensational type'.[28] Referring principally to Sir George Steuart Mackenzie[29] and Revd Ebenezer Henderson,[30] Burton complained that previous travellers had 'Iceland on the brain'.[31] He blames exaggeration in their descriptions – a propensity to see a 'dreadful precipice' where he sees 'only the humblest ravine' – on their having 'seldom left home'. If, as Burton suggests, Mackenzie and Henderson had established Iceland as 'an exceptional theme', Morris himself clearly saw no reason to abandon their mode of treatment. The significance he attaches to his first sight of land is the first indication that he will not be putting Iceland into a more 'realistic' perspective; that he will be concerned to heighten, rather than to diminish or flatten out, the contrasts presented by the country's landscape and social conditions.

What, then, were Morris's reasons for considering Iceland 'an exceptional theme', and in what sense did he designate it an island of the past? The effect of the country's isolation should first be considered. Over the centuries, a peculiar lack of trade and immigration rendered Iceland a kind of language enclave. In consequence, modern Icelanders had little difficulty in understanding the rich crop of history and story surviving from the country's 'Golden Age' of saga literature. This was clearly an attractive idea for someone so actively interested in the reception of medieval culture as Morris. A similar situation forms the premise for the exchange of classical and medieval stories in *The Earthly Paradise*, whereby the

---

22 Morris, 'To Andreas Scheu', II, p. 229.
23 This strategy of comparison operates in accordance with Carlyle's view that the 'centuries too are all lineal children of one another; and often, in the portrait of early grandfathers, this and the other enigmatic feature of the newest grandson shall disclose itself, to mutual elucidation', *Past and Present*, in *Works*, p. 39.
24 Morris, *Journals of Travel in Iceland*, p. 15.
25 Morris, 'The Early Literature of the North – Iceland', p. 181.
26 Morris, 'Iceland First Seen', *Poems by the Way*, in *Collected Works*, IX, pp. 125–6.
27 Morris, *Journals of Travel in Iceland*, p. 19.
28 Richard F. Burton, *Ultima Thule; or, A Summer in Iceland*, 2 vols (London: William P. Nimmo, 1875), p. x.
29 Sir George Steuart Mackenzie, *Travels in the Island of Iceland during the Summer of the Year MDCCCX* (Edinburgh: Archibald Constable and Company, 1811).
30 Reverend Ebenezer Henderson, *Iceland; or, the Journal of a Residence in that Island During the Years 1814 and 1815*, 2 vols (Edinburgh: Oliphant, Waugh and Innes, 1818).
31 Burton, *Ultima Thule*, I, pp. ix, x, xi.

Wanderers discover a land in which the tongue of Ancient Greece has been preserved. While aware that a huge cultural gulf distanced pre-Reformation and pre-Christian Iceland from the society he was able to visit, Morris was nevertheless attracted by the thought that the country's linguistic and economic circumstances might offer him a rare glimpse of the past. The 'almost intact' language of old Iceland, he later stated, represented the 'instrument' of a wider preservation of Germanic tradition and religion.[32]

This emphasis on linguistic, and thus cultural, continuity extended even to his sense of identity. Influenced by a new generation of historians who were seeking the roots of the English 'constitution' in the woods of the German Dark Ages, Morris became increasingly interested in the notion of a common Teutonic heritage. Whig historians like William Stubbs and Edward Freeman had sought, through a study of Anglo-Saxon institutions, to underline the continuity and historical logic of English freedoms.[33] Such institutions, they claimed, had been transferred from the continental homelands of the Germanic tribes without significant alteration. Morris adopted the features of this argument he found attractive – namely its stress on the basic antiquity of freedom and democracy – whilst altering its polemical orientation, invoking a Teutonic tradition of liberty and equality in order to suggest the failure, rather than the present maintenance, of an ideal continuity. It becomes clear, as one reads Morris's most important statements on the subject, that he no more avoided the tribal conception of nationhood implicit in this thinking than did the historians who used it to advance a more conservative agenda. In the preface to their translation of *Völsunga Saga*, for instance, Morris and Eiríkr Magnússon outline a racially informed conception of the work's importance:

> we must again say how strange it seems to us, that this Volsung Tale, which is in fact an unversified poem, should never before have been translated into English. For this is the Great Story of the North, which should be to all our race what the Tale of Troy was to the Greeks.[34]

Such sentiments are echoed in Morris's surviving lecture on Iceland, in which he refers to the island's inhabitants as a people 'cognate to our own dominant race'.[35] Even in the nineteenth century, the idea of isolating the 'dominant' Anglo-Saxon and Norse strains from non-Germanic types represented an arbitrary and nonsensical approach to national genealogy. In fairness to Morris, he admits in the same lecture that the Icelanders were 'a little mingled with Irish blood'. This statement is of crucial significance, as it signals his primary interest in a continuity of ideas and sensibility, in the capacity of language to transmit culture.

---

[32] Morris, 'The Early Literature of the North – Iceland', p. 181.

[33] See John Mitchell Kemble, *The Saxons in England: A History of the English Commonwealth till the Period of the Norman Conquest*, 2 vols (London: Longman, Brown, Green, and Longmans, 1849); William Stubbs, *The Constitutional History of England in its Origin and Development*, 3 vols (Oxford: Clarendon Press, 1874–78); Edward A. Freeman, *The Growth of the English Constitution from the Earliest Times* (London: Macmillan and Co., 1872).

[34] William Morris and Eiríkr Magnússon, Preface, *Völsunga Saga: The Story of the Volsungs and Niblungs, with Certain Songs from the Elder Edda*, in *Collected Works*, VII, pp. 281–490 (p. 286).

[35] Morris, 'The Early Literature of the North – Iceland', p. 181.

Morris's belief that modern-day Britain had largely abandoned the customs enduring in Iceland should also free him partially from charges of racial determinism: for it suggests not that the British were untrue to their constitutional heritage because they lacked the requisite racial 'purity'; rather, that this was so because they had chosen a different manner of life. Ultimately, it would seem, Morris is interested in cultural continuity. He refers to race because Romantic philology encourages this identification, because race serves as a convenient shorthand for the political and cultural ideas he wishes to convey. Unpalatable and fallacious as this appears today, the biological model of continuity impresses on his audience the idea of a rightful, if neglected, cultural heritage.

On 26 August 1871, Morris visited Thingvellir, the ancient seat of Iceland's first general assembly, known as the Althing. There he saw the Lögberg (the Hill of Laws), an historic site he identifies as 'the heart and centre of the old Icelandic Commonwealth'.[36] It is important to stress that Morris had not yet begun to profess democratic convictions. Letters surviving from this year contain no references to the Paris Commune, an event that assumed great symbolic significance for him later in life. At Thingvellir, he seems more interested in the judicial combats once held at the 'Battle-Holm', and the dramatic 'Battle of the Althing', than in the republican mode of government pioneered there. Yet it is obvious that the notion of an Icelandic commonwealth did not offend him; he does not attempt, like George Dasent, to make it respectable by recalling that 'the government was really in the hands of a small aristocracy',[37] or, like Richard Burton, to denigrate it as a haunting ground for 'Sentimentalists' who 'would restore the obsolete practice, and transfer the legislators from their comfortable hall at Reykjavik'.[38]

Iceland's credentials as an early home to liberty were for Morris enhanced by its status as Europe's first settler society. In 'The Early Literature of the North – Iceland', he describes the country as an 'Isle of Refuge', an appellation inspired by its national myth of origin.[39] In the ninth century, Morris explains, King Harald Fairhair of Norway sought to unify his kingdom by imposing on it 'a kind of native feudalism'. Many chieftains resisted this policy, but their efforts were finally defeated, and they were forced to flee the country. In Iceland, they at last found a haven from persecution, and a means of preserving their old way of life. Again, the premise for *The Earthly Paradise* offers obvious parallels in its concern with the fortunes of a band of seekers who leave a ravaged land in search of a new world.[40] In the letter to Scheu, quoted above, Morris listed the 'independence' of the Icelanders, and their 'air of freedom' as the characteristics he most admired in them.[41] He was not the first person to seek explanation for the 'unconventionality' of the country's inhabitants in the story of its foundation. Dasent had argued that 'Freedom [. . .] was the final cause which drove the old freeman [. . .] to seek a new home'.[42] He thus dissociates this search for liberty from the 'impossible equality'

36 Morris, *Journals of Travel in Iceland*, pp. 170, 171.
37 George Webb Dasent, 'The Norsemen in Iceland', *Oxford Essays* (1858), 165–214 (p. 208).
38 Burton, *Ultima Thule*, II, p. 194.
39 Morris, 'The Early Literature of the North – Iceland', p. 181.
40 Morris, The Prologue, *The Earthly Paradise*, III.
41 Morris, 'To Andreas Scheu', II, p. 229.
42 Dasent, 'The Norsemen in Iceland', p. 168.

proselytised by 'theorists', stressing instead the desire 'to maintain the old state of things' that precipitated the exodus. In this respect, he reads Iceland's myth of origin differently from the later, democratically inclined, Morris of the 1880s. An emphasis on freedom, however, is common to the pronouncements of both men. Also of relevance is the stress Dasent places on the significance of the island's landscape. The isolation bred by a land 'cut up by natural features into a multi-tude of divisions' is presented as the chief guarantee of the loyalty, self-reliance and self-command the Northmen had sought to maintain in the face of autocratic rule. Dasent ascribes the importance of the household within Icelandic society – as opposed to the village, or the town – to a similar combination of geography and temperament:

> in Iceland, in the tenth century, there were no towns in this mediæval sense [. . .] Such herding together has always been repugnant to the free disposition of the people.

Samuel Laing also stressed the freedom-loving qualities of the Northmen.[43] Unlike Morris, he considered the 'civil, religious, and political liberty' of England to have been inherited directly from the Norse settlers of Danelaw, rather than from a common, proto-Germanic root (via the Anglo-Saxons). Again, Morris takes a subtly different position from previous commentators. He makes no attempt in his lecture to dissociate political freedom from equality. His tone is celebratory, and in this respect comparable to Charles Forbes's in *Iceland: Its Volcanoes, Geysers, and Glaciers*.[44] Quoting Arngrim Jonsen, Forbes had charac-terized the country as a 'Canaan of the north', describing New England and Iceland as 'the solitary instances of colonies being founded and peopled from higher motives than the love of gain'.

Morris's view of Iceland as a unique point of intersection between past and present stemmed partly from its possession of an ancient literature rooted funda-mentally in place. As soon as he reaches the Faroe Islands, he observes, 'it was like nothing I had ever seen, but strangely like my old imaginations of places for sea-wanderers to come to'.[45] Even the basic design of the boats, he reports, with 'the keel rib running up into an ornament at each end [. . .] cannot have changed in the least since the times of the Sagas'. As soon as the *Diana* reaches the coast of Iceland, Morris begins to bring the material world appearing before him into correspondence with the mythic topography he has gleaned from his reading. Picking out Ingólfshöfdi (Ingolf's Head), where 'Ingolf first sat down in the autumn of 874', he highlights the symbolic significance of this approach to land, and compares his own impending encounter with the unknown to that experi-enced by the first Norse settlers. This eagerness to bring out the mythic lie of the land is only encouraged when he notices how, in the minds of the Icelanders, the

---

43 Samuel Laing, Preliminary Dissertation, in Snorri Sturluson, *The Heimskringla; or, Chronicle of The Kings of Norway*, trans. by Samuel Laing, 3 vols (London: Longman, Brown, Green, and Longmans, 1844), i, p. 11.

44 Charles S. Forbes, *Iceland: Its Volcanoes, Geysers, and Glaciers* (London: John Murray, 1860), pp. 52, 53.

45 Morris, *Journals of Travel in Iceland*, pp. 12, 14, 21.

Saga Age operates as a kind of secondary reality.[46] Speaking of Sœmund, Ari and Snorri Sturluson, Morris remarks that the 'men who dwelt here or hereabouts still live in people's minds as the writers of most of the great stories and both the Eddas'.[47] Often the uncertainty surrounding a legend roughly associated with historical events encourages him to exercise poetic licence in his reconstruction of the sacred past. On 20 July 1871, he recalls seeing a long mound that 'rightly or wrongly, gave one strongly the impression of having been the site of Njal's house'. Following the map of 'historic' sites, of locations traditionally associated with Njal, Gunnar, Gudrun and Grettir, he is meticulous in his desire to access the past, and also conscious that he risks, in the process, constructing and concretizing one that never existed. Yet the reality of the 'old passion and violence' remains for him indisputable, in as much as 'one has no power to pass it by unnoticed'. In Iceland, then, Morris discovers a place in which the legendary past looms large: in the popular imagination, in place names, in his own mind. It is an island where reality and mythology coincide, a glorious exception because, for once, the world seems to match the story. His love of charts that show the phenomenally present lie of the land alongside the memorial imprints of its legendary life, would seem to originate in this experience. In the maps that accompany his late prose romances – *The Sundering Flood* (1897) especially – one can see the influence of the Icelandic mythic consciousness and a source for the cartographically under-pinned secondary worlds of J. R. R. Tolkien[48] and C. S. Lewis.[49]

Morris was most interested in expressions of folk consciousness that seemed to transform ordinary individuals into living receptacles of tradition:

> the shepherd boy on the hill-side, the fisherman in the firth still chant the songs that preserve the religion of the Germanic race, and the most illiterate are absolutely familiar with the whole of the rich literature of their country, and know more of the Haralds and the Olafs of the tenth and eleventh centuries than most of our 'culti-vated' persons know of Oliver Cromwell or William Pitt.[50]

Yet Iceland's special significance can be ascribed with as much justice to the social conditions prevailing in the country in the nineteenth century as to the apparent survival of its oral culture. Related to the absence of 'class degradation',[51] noted by Morris, were unusually high standards of literacy and learning among the general populace. The Revd Henderson, a representative of the Foreign Bible Society, observed earlier in the century with apparently unconscious irony that what really attracted him to Iceland was 'the exhibition of moral worth, and the strong features of superior intellectual abilities' noticeable in its inhabitants.[52] Of the people visiting Iceland in the mid to late nineteenth century, Morris was more or

---

46 In a letter to Louisa Macdonald Baldwin, Morris wrote: 'Our guides were very pleasant friendly fellows, as innocent of the great world as babies, and, apart from their daily labour, living almost entirely in the glorious past days of Iceland', 14 September [1873], in *Collected Letters*, I, pp. 198–200 (p. 200).

47 Morris, *Journals of Travel in Iceland*, pp. 41, 43, 108.

48 J. R. R. Tolkien, *The Hobbit* (London: Allen & Unwin, 1937).

49 C. S. Lewis, *The Lion, the Witch and the Wardrobe* (London: Geoffrey Bles, 1950).

50 Morris, 'The Early Literature of the North – Iceland', p. 181.

51 Morris, 'The Early Literature of the North – Iceland', p. 181.

52 Henderson, *Iceland*, II, p. 245.

less alone in lacking a desire to educate the Icelanders. The differences between his travelogue and Burton's are particularly revealing on this issue. Burton observes that the Icelander 'is what he was':[53] he had 'remained stationary' because education on that island 'ignored modern science' and was 'confined to Saga-history and theology'. Where Morris finds in Jón (the guide whom he met during his 1873 journey) a refreshing example of a working man proficient in foreign languages and thirsty for knowledge, Burton witnesses only anachronisms, a general failure to embrace the challenge of modernity.

Morris may also have grown to regard Iceland as a model for the holistic manner of life he was later to espouse. The traditional Icelandic dwelling was often built into a hillside. The back wall would consist of earth, and the roof would be covered in turf. At one point in the 1871 journal, he mentions a 'six-gabled house of the regular Icelandic type' and remarks that 'both walls and roof' are 'just as green as the field they spring from'.[54] The effect of such architecture on Morris may have been to suggest the possibility of a happy co-dependence between humanity and the environment, a challenge to dualism at once utopian and practical. There are certainly occasions when, in his descriptions of the scenery, he attributes a domestic quality to the most inhospitable of rock formations:

> often the wall would be cleft, and you would see a horrible winding street with stupendous straight rocks for houses on either side.

On 29 July, he sees a 'wall-sided mountain with a regular roof like a house' and, on 6 August, 'two strange-shaped mountains like a church-roof with a turret at the end of it'. In Iceland, Morris saw roofs that looked like meadows, and a landscape that 'mimicked' man-made structures. It is curious that he should have chosen to evoke this holistic, paradisal condition so determinedly, whilst also emphasizing the relentlessly threatening nature of the landscape, its 'grisly desolation'.

Iceland, then, was for Morris a strange survival, a society in which a medieval language and a store of heroic story were still common currency; a land isolated, and economically primitive; a land founded as a sanctuary for freemen, which for physical and economic reasons still demanded self-sufficiency of its inhabitants. For these reasons, it represented more than just another place: Iceland evoked a prior stage of civilization. One should distinguish between the country's actual state in the late nineteenth century (an economically depressed colony, which was, in its peripheral role, as much a product of modern capitalism as the imperial cities of Copenhagen and London) and Morris's view of it as a precious storehouse of linguistic and mythic culture.[55] For the moment, though, attention is

---

53 Burton, *Ultima Thule*, I, pp. 144, 155.
54 Morris, *Journals of Travel in Iceland*, pp. 40, 42, 53, 76, 107.
55 Magnús S. Magnússon draws attention to the constraints Danish colonial policy imposed on economic development in Iceland: 'the sheer necessity of foreign trade did not imply that the primitive economy became integrated into the world market in the 17th and 18th century. The existence of institutional factors, such as the Danish monopoly trade, combined with the efforts of the native landowning/ruling class effectively prevented any major technical and economical improvements. This social and economic framework did not alter until the late 19th century', *Iceland in Transition: Labour and Socio-Economic Change Before 1940* (Lund, Sweden: Skrifter Utgivna av Ekonomisk-Historiska Föreningen, 1985), p. 40.

confined to Morris's conception of the place. It is accordingly useful and legiti-mate to compare his position as a visitor to that of the narrator in *A Dream of John Ball*. Seemingly transported back to another time, he is conscious of being, in some respects, the bearer of bad news, a harbinger of the modernity he hopes his journey will allow him, temporarily, to elude.

In *Ultima Thule*, Richard Burton alludes to an invidious discrepancy between the interest travellers had shown in the Icelanders' surroundings and the 'scant attention paid to themselves'.[56] This situation, he suggests, had begun to produce noticeable disaffection among the inhabitants. In the preface to his book, Burton promises to 'remedy this grievance by ethnological descriptions'. While Morris also felt the need to combine appreciation of the Icelandic landscape with atten-tiveness to the lives of the people living amidst it, the 'anthropological' aspect of his journals is confined to the occasional observation, there being no scientific or classificatory purpose for his visit. Many of the travellers who visited Iceland before Morris were also keen to comment on the peculiar features of Icelandic society. Most complained of the inhabitants' unsanitary living conditions. While given to sentimental appreciation of the Icelanders' native 'innocence', an early traveller to the island, named William Hooker, conceded that 'to comfort and cleanliness in the persons of the natives' he had 'not been much accustomed'.[57] A German traveller, Ida Pfeiffer, recalled that she was quickly disabused of her hope that the country would prove 'a real Arcadia in regard to its inhabitants'.[58] The Icelanders, she complained, were 'second to no nation in uncleanliness'; further-more, she finds them 'insuperably lazy'. 'If a few German peasants were trans-ported hither', Pfeiffer is at one point drawn to reflect, 'what a different appearance the country would soon have!'. The most damning account of living conditions is provided by Sabine Baring-Gould, who asserts that 'there is neither order nor neatness in an Icelandic house: the porch is generally full of clothes, wash-tubs, turf-cutters [. . .] whilst the guest room is littered with brandy glasses, dresses, plates, and whips'.[59] It is against the background of successive expressions of horror at their abject living conditions that Morris formulates his quite different characterization of the populace. He frequently remarks on the cleanli-ness of the dwellings to which he is admitted, noting twice at the beginning of his first journal that the room in which he is staying is 'clean'.[60] These exclamations have a quality of surprise about them initially, but, as Morris begins to perceive the injustice previous travellers have done to their hosts, they become increasingly indignant:[61]

56 Burton, *Ultima Thule*, I, p. xii.
57 William Jackson Hooker, *Recollections of a Tour in Iceland in 1809/Journal of a Tour in Iceland in the Summer of 1809* (Yarmouth: J. Keymer, 1811), p. 226.
58 Ida Pfeiffer, *A Visit to Iceland and the Scandinavian North*, trans. by author (London: Ingram, Cooke, and Co., 1852), pp. 175, 179, 180.
59 Baring-Gould, *Iceland: Its Scenes and Sagas*, p. 62.
60 Morris, *Journals of Travel in Iceland*, pp. 16, 23.
61 Morris was probably thinking of this passage in Baring-Gould: 'loathsome forms of life teem in the unwholesome recesses of the bathstófa, and it is quite hopeless for the traveller to think of avoiding them [. . .] Unlike the Icelanders of the genus *homo*, these horrible parasites are endowed with a predilection for novelty, and in a moment scent out the blood of an Englishman, and come in eager hordes, from which he finds no escape till he reaches a boiling spring in which he can plunge his clothes and annihilate his tormentors wholesale', *Iceland*, pp. 61–2, 82.

later on I should have been surprised at the presence of a louse, but as aforesaid I
had been stuffed full of travellers' stories on this point and was troubled thereon.

It is worth noting that, later in his career, Morris was drawn to defend the
Icelandic character, apparently in response to comments of the kind made by
Richard Burton in *Ultima Thule*. Burton, it appears, had read Morris's translation,
The Story of Grettir the Strong:

> The 'Oxonian' abridges the prodigious long yarn spun by the Gretla, and shows the
> 'William Wallace of Iceland,' as the outlaw is called by the admirers of muscular
> un-Christianity, to have been, *pace* Mr Morris, even for Iceland, a superior ruffian.
> With few exceptions, we may say the same of the Saga heroes generally, and it is
> ethnologically interesting to contrast their excessive Scandinavian destructiveness
> with the Ishmaelitic turn of the Bedawin [. . .] the Arab, though essentially a thief
> and a murderer, [. . .] has a soft corner in his heart which the Iceland poet lacked; he
> was chivalrous as a knight-errant in his treatment of women; he was great upon the
> subject of platonic love.[62]

Morris would appear, indirectly, to be answering such charges in 'The Early Literature of the North – Iceland'. Here he concedes that 'a hard and grasping side to
the character of the heroes is not uncommon',[63] and admits that this 'contrasts
disagreeably enough with the heroes of Arab romance'. He attributes this to the
harshness of the northern climate and the grim realism favoured by Icelandic
story-tellers. He notes also that in the sagas, 'there are plenty of examples of
generosity and magnanimity', adducing in support of this assertion the friendship
between Gunnar and Njal at the centre of the action in *Njal's Saga*.

Morris's sense of the past enters a heightened state at those times when he is
received into the homes of the Icelanders. As one might expect, the antiquity of
domestic ritual, and the subject of hospitality in general, are topics broached in
most of the travelogues pre-dating Morris's visit. William Hooker, in his account
of the 'innocent' primitivism of the country, includes the prefatory remark, 'I am
indebted [. . .] for the truly hospitable entertainment I experienced from the
inhabitants of Iceland'.[64] He recalls how 'it was always the custom for the ladies of
the house to wait at table when any strangers are [*sic*] present', and tells of a priest
'who soon came down to welcome us, and offer any thing we might want that his
house would afford'. Mackenzie also speaks admiringly of Icelandic hospitality:

> Before commencing his journey, an Icelander takes off his hat, places it before his
> face, and repeats a prayer prescribed for such occasions. He is welcomed at every
> cottage he stops at, and it is seldom that any remuneration is required for his enter-
> tainment.[65]

At one stage in his journey, Mackenzie meets a priest whose offer of a sheep is
reported as a memorable 'mark of his hospitality and friendship'. Henderson's

---

62 Burton, *Ultima Thule*, II, pp. 124–5; Burton refers here to Frederick Metcalfe's *The Oxonian in
    Iceland* (London: Longman, 1861).
63 Morris, 'The Early Literature of the North – Iceland', p. 186.
64 Hooker, *Recollections*, pp. vii, 60, 104.
65 Mackenzie, *Travels in the Island of Iceland*, pp. 121, 267.

account of Iceland is the most laudatory in this respect. He experiences the help with undressing at bedtime (traditionally performed by the eldest daughter of the house) that Charles Faulkner, to the amusement of Morris and Evans, also receives.[66] Furnishing his reader with further proofs of 'the disinterestedness of Icelandic hospitality',[67] Henderson comments approvingly on the provisions made for poor relief:

> As there are no alms-houses for the reception of the poor in Iceland, every farmer is obliged to maintain such as are sent him by Hreppstiori, to whom the care of the poor is committed.

One is reminded of Cobbett's admiration for the 'traditional' English farmhouse, a capacious space able to accommodate under one roof a broad cross section of society. Similar sentiments are invoked defensively by George Dasent. Seeking to justify the old domestic arrangement, whereby the hall provides shelter for a whole household, along with livestock, he remarks:

> Off the hall, on the right, was the sleeping chamber (svefnhús), a spacious apart-ment in which let no delicate eyes be shocked to read that the whole family slept; for even modern refinement has heard of whole families huddled together in English farmhouses without the excuse of want.[68]

Charles Forbes witnesses remnants of this custom in Iceland, reporting that in places the 'entire establishment sleep together, as well as any strangers who may happen to drop in'.[69]

It is nevertheless significant that, by 1872, Richard Burton was complaining of a decline in traditional hospitality. In an unexpected reversal of his usual role as a proselytizer for modernity, he imputes its demise to the influence of the outside world:

> Fair visions of girls who kiss the stranger on the mouth, who relieve him of his terminal garments, and who place a brandy bottle under his pillow, and a bowl of milk or cream by his side, where are ye? Icelanders have allowed their pleasant prim-itive fashions to be laughed away by the jeering stranger, who little thought how much the custom told in favour of the hosts. The *naïve* modesty of antiquity, when Nestor's youngest daughter laved, anointed, and dressed Telemachus, and when the maids of Penelope had a less pleasant task with the elderly Ulysses, has departed

---

66 Henderson writes: 'A ceremony now took place, which exhibits, in the strongest light, the hospi-tality and innocent simplicity of the Icelandic character. Having wished me a good night's rest, they retired, and left their eldest daughter to assist me in pulling off my pantaloons and stockings [. . .] I remonstrated against it as unnecessary. The young woman maintained it was the custom of the country, and their duty to help the weary traveller' (I, pp. 114–15); Morris writes: 'I may mention here that a legend sprang up about this bedroom, to wit that C. J. F. was found in it when we were just come, having his boots and breeches pulled off by a female Icelander, after their ancient custom, he being resigned, owing to want of knowledge of the tongue: take said legend for what it may be worth', *Iceland*, p. 93.

67 Henderson, *Iceland*, I, pp. 128, 254.

68 Dasent, 'The Norsemen in Iceland', p. 204.

69 Forbes, *Iceland*, p. 85.

70 Burton, *Ultima Thule*, II, p. 160.

with the public bathings, in angelic attire, of Iceland, of Sind, and of Japan, and the kiss given to the guest by the young wife or the eldest daughter.[70]

Ida Pfeiffer also ascribes a pernicious influence to tourism in her travelogue, though she does so with less willingness to credit the Icelanders with a prior commitment to hospitality:

> As regards the hospitality of the Icelanders, I do not think one can give them so very much credit for it. It is true that priests and peasants gladly receive any European traveller, and treat him to every thing in their power; but they know well that the traveller who comes to their island is neither an adventurer nor a beggar, and will therefore pay them well [. . .] they take advantage of travellers with as much shrewdness as the landlords and guides on the continent.[71]

In this, as in most other areas, Morris's journals exhibit cognisance of what other travellers have said and a desire to present the Icelanders in the best possible light:

> the bonder is good tempered and invites us into the house, and offers us his parlour for our night's lodging: it rains so hard that we make few words about accepting the offer, though this was the first bonder's house we shall have slept in, and I had yet to shake off my dread of —, inspired principally by Baring-Gould's piece of book-making about Iceland.[72]

Time and time again, Morris is hospitably received in the homes of the Icelanders. There are even occasions when the warmth of the welcome prevents his party from keeping to their schedule.[73] Writing to Jane Morris on 11 August 1871, he predicts, 'we shan't get through above ½ our stores I fancy, people have been so hospitable.'[74]

The most important unit of settlement in Iceland remained the household. This fact, and the related scarcity of villages and towns, is emphasized by George Dasent in 'The Norsemen in Iceland'. Given the lack of inns, the few strangers arriving at any given habitation were accommodated in the priest's quarters, or in the main farmhouse. This unwillingness to hive outsiders and the poor off into institutional quarters obviously impressed Morris: the ready hospitality of the utopians in *News from Nowhere* incorporates something of this Icelandic attitude to the foreigner. And yet there are obvious differences between what hospitality means in an idyllic setting and its significance in a harsh environment such as Iceland. In the latter, hospitality is necessarily a matter of life and death. To turn a stranger away in this climate is to condemn him, whereas to admit him is to acknowledge a bond of humanity. May Morris, reflecting on this aspect of her father's experience, makes a similar point in emphasizing the importance of the country's harsh environment:

---

71 Pfeiffer, *A Visit to Iceland*, p. 178.
72 Morris, *Journals of Travel in Iceland*, p. 18.
73 'but I think it was more like two hours before any break in the hospitality would let us escape', *Journals of Travel in Iceland*, p. 124.
74 Morris, 'To Jane Morris', 11 August [1871], *Collected Letters*, I, pp. 145–6 (p. 146)).

everywhere, at the prosperous homesteads and at the poorer ones, the same idea of hospitality prevailed. It has sometimes struck me that there are certain similarities between travel in the deserts of the East (in Arabia, for instance) and that in Iceland: there are the same conditions that make a rigorous hospitality a necessity.[75]

In a footnote to his journal entry for 22 July 1871 Morris cites a custom that gives exemplary expression to this idea: he observes that 'an Icelander always talks of going *home* to any stead on the road, whether he is living there or not'.[76] One need look no further than Morris's translation of *Grettis Saga* to appreciate the convergence between the symbolic importance of hospitality in Icelandic folklore, and Morris's long-standing interest in the limits of privacy. Grettir, the archetypal saga outlaw, brings both salvation and destruction to those who give him shelter. He represents both the agent of humanity that considers every dwelling place a potential home, and the unhomely, superhuman, force that it is the purpose of every Icelander to shut out. Reflection on the openness of Icelandic society is most evident in Morris's journal, as with Henderson, in connection with the arrangements for poor relief. The Rabelaisian sight of an 'unsavoury idiot' greeting him at the porch of one dwelling prompts Morris to explain that, 'in Iceland where there are no workhouses or lunatic asylums, the paupers or lunatics are distributed among the bonders to be taken care of'.[77] The lasting impact of this distinctive approach to welfare and hospitality is best indicated by comments Morris made later in life, on writing to recommend the establishment of a British Consulate at Reykjavík. He stressed above all the 'many acts of kindness & hospitality' he had received from the country's inhabitants.[78]

Morris made every attempt to dissociate his experiences from the malicious travellers' stories that seemed to him such a travesty of Icelandic life.[79] Emphasizing the warmth of the welcome he received there represented one way of achieving this. Yet he remained uncomfortably aware that the very hospitality whose kindness he recommended should be reciprocated on an official level – through the institution of consulates and the like – was also a mark of the host society's vulnerability. Readers of the Iceland journals who are familiar with *News from Nowhere* will note that Morris's role as a traveller is analogous to the predicament of William Guest. This is never more true than in respect to the teasing remark Dick makes towards the end of Guest's stay, when he ventures to suggest that Guest had 'thrown a kind of evil charm' over him.[80] Despite Dick's assurance that his intentions were merely humorous, Guest feels 'somewhat uneasy at his words, after all'. James Buzard takes this passage as a key indication of how the '*interrupted narration*' of Morris's utopia functions 'as ethnography's textual analogue for its practitioner's dual role as Participant Observer, to some extent inside but finally out of what he studies':[81]

[75] May Morris, Introduction, *Collected Works*, VIII, pp. xv–xxxv (p. xxij).
[76] Morris, *Journals of Travel in Iceland*, p. 50.
[77] Morris, *Journals of Travel in Iceland*, p. 56.
[78] Morris, 'To the Consular Department, Foreign Office', 22 July 1880, in *Collected Letters*, I, pp. 574–5 (p. 575).
[79] Morris, *Journals of Travel in Iceland*, p. 82.
[80] Morris, *News from Nowhere*, p. 207.
[81] James Buzard, 'Ethnography as Interruption: *News from Nowhere*, Narrative, and the Modern Romance of Authority', *Victorian Studies*, 40 (Spring 1997), 3, 445–74 (p. 459).

Unlike Bellamy's hero but like the modern ethnographer, Guest knows himself for an unwilling agent of the forces behind him, the thin end of the wedge of that modernizing process which destroys the traditional culture he cherishes and studies: if for no other reason, he must go home again so as to limit the contamination he may spread in the field.

Claude Lévi-Strauss famously predicted that travel would ultimately prove self-defeating, that it would render itself redundant by producing a monoculture.[82] To what extent are such anxieties a feature of the material discussed here?

Most of the travelogues pre-dating Morris's journals contain passages in which doubt is cast on the advantage of the country's increasing links with the outside world, on its openness to the tourist and the trade emissary. Henderson reports that the Icelander's ' "good manners" are evidently getting corrupted by the "evil communications" of the strangers by whom they are visited'.[83] Ida Pfeiffer drew parallels with the effect produced by continental tourists in Switzerland, observing that the expression, 'no money, no Swiss' could be applied with equal justice to the Icelanders.[84] Burton compares the exaggerated accounts given by inexperienced travellers returning from Iceland to what 'Mr Cook's pilgrim-tourists' had done in 'the Holy Land'.[85] In his effort to guarantee the ethnological rigour and unsensational perspective of his study, Burton denigrates certain forms of tourism. He warns us, in the preface, that the 'cruise to the north coast, and the "Cockney trip" to Hekla and the Geysir' would be 'related with less circumstance' than was customary.[86] Morris was far from being a seasoned traveller, yet shows similar disdain for the touristic Iceland to which Burton alludes. His behaviour at Geysir, even then Iceland's most famous and most popular attraction, illustrates this point clearly enough:

> 'Why, I'm not going to camp here,' said I:
> 'You must,' said Eyvindr, 'all Englishmen do.'
> 'Blast all Englishmen!' said I in the Icelandic tongue.[87]

Morris's desire to distance himself from the conventional English tourist – a man, he assures us, who knew something of Iceland's geology, but had 'never heard the names of Sigurd and Brynhild, of Njal or Gunnar or Grettir or Gisli or Gudrun' (p. 66) – becomes even more pronounced when he realizes that the gushers at Geysir might actually be dangerous. His fears remind him of his own unheroic origins:

> . . . understand I was quite ready to break my neck in my quality of pilgrim to the holy places of Iceland: to be drowned in Markfleet, or squelched in climbing up

---

82 Rejecting the possibility of escapism, Claude Lévi-Strauss maintains that 'mankind has opted for monoculture'; that, in consequence, the 'so-called escapism of travelling' might do no more 'than confront us with the more unfortunate aspects of our history', *Tristes tropiques*, trans. by John and Doreen Weightman (London: Jonathan Cape, 1973), p. 38.

83 Henderson, *Iceland*, I, p. 377.

84 Pfeiffer, *A Visit to Iceland*, p. 175.

85 Burton, *Ultima Thule*, I, p. xi.

86 Burton, *Ultima Thule*, I, p. xii.

87 Morris, *Journals of Travel in Iceland*, pp. 66, 67, 68.

Drangey seemed to come quite in the day's work; but to wake up boiled while one was acting the part of accomplice to Mangnall's Questions was too disgusting. So there I sat on my horse, while the guides began to bestir themselves about the unloading, feeling a very unheroic disgust gaining on me.

Morris's wish to distinguish his journey from popular tourism, particularly from the kind promoted by entries on Iceland in such educational catechisms of the period as *Mangnall's Questions*,[88] is a symptom of his desire to leave England behind.[89] It is also a reminder that he would not be able to escape modernity in the way that the first Norse settlers had done in fleeing Harald Fairhair's 'kind of native feudalism'. He is consequently reduced to rejecting his origins in a negative sense. Faced with their omnipresence, he cannot disable them without engaging and invoking their presence in a way that spoils the illusion of escape.

In 'The Early Literature of the North', Morris had described Iceland as 'a country of no account whatever commercially'.[90] It is important to appreciate that this statement was not quite true. At this time, another kind of visitor was taking an interest in the country: prospectors arguably more threatening to Morris's sense of Iceland as an historic and immaculate place than were the Geysir devotees. As early as 1811, George Mackenzie recommended that the British annex Iceland. He argued that the 'exuberant and inexhaustible supply of fish from the sea, and the rivers, would alone repay the charitable action of restoring freedom to the inhabitants'.[91] In the preface to *Ultima Thule*, Richard Burton makes a similar statement. He explains that his main purpose in writing the book is 'to advocate the development of the island':[92]

> I hold three measures to be absolutely necessary; the first is the working of the sulphur deposits – not to mention the silica – now in English hands; the second, a systematic reform of the primitive means and appliances with which the islanders labour in their gold mines, the fisheries; and, thirdly, the extension of the emigrating movement, now become a prime need when population is denser than at any period of its thousand-year history.

Morris's restatement of Iceland's economic uselessness indicates in him a necessary blindness to the possibility and consequences of mineralogical exploitation. To have acknowledged the danger, after all, would have been to query the implied distance between its mythic terrain and that landscape 'haplessly blotched by coal' seen earlier from an English train window.[93] It would have destroyed the illusion that Iceland was an 'Isle of Refuge'.

---

88 R. Mangnall, *Historical and Miscellaneous Questions for the Use of Young People* (Stockport, [1800]).
89 Contrary to what Morris implies in *Journals of Travel in Iceland*, there is in fact no reference to Iceland in *Mangnall's Questions*. He was probably thinking of the entry on Iceland in Richmal Mangnall's *A Compendium of Geography with Geographic Exercises, for the Use of Schools, Private Families, and all those who Require Knowledge of this Important Science*, 2nd edn (London: Longman, Hurst, Rees, Orme, and Brown, 1822). It invokes Iceland's reputation as a 'land of wonders' (p. 219) and dwells on the attractions of the '*Great Geyser*' (p. 221).
90 Morris, 'The Early Literature of the North – Iceland', p. 180.
91 Mackenzie, *Travels in the Island of Iceland*, p. 271.
92 Burton, *Ultima Thule*, I, pp. xiii, xiv.
93 Morris, *Journals of Travel in Iceland*, p. 2.

Symptoms of Morris's unease with his role as a stranger are apparent from the point of his boarding the *Diana*. In fact, it is possible to regard the misunderstanding occurring when he arrives on the ship as the germ of his later interest in the difficulties faced by strangers:

> Magnússon, Faulkner and I got a boat presently, and boarded her, and saw a fat mild-faced steward, who refused five shillings which I had the bad manners, I don't know why, to offer him.[94]

One is reminded of the moment in *News from Nowhere* when William Guest attempts to pay his ferryman for carrying him on the Thames. This episode is glossed in the margin of the Kelmscott edition as, 'How to pay a stranger'.[95] In both cases, the recipient's refusal to accept a tip converts an act of *largesse* into a guilty consciousness of assumed patronage on the part of the giver. On boarding the *Diana*, Morris is not of course suggesting that he has entered a realm in which money holds no value (as in *News from Nowhere*). But this incident is cast as an example of the kind of disorientation and uncertainty that must beset the stranger; and, more importantly, of the possibility that a tourist may do harm in spite of hoping to do good. The recurrent mention of his fears concerning lice would appear to serve a similar purpose. On one level, these moments of self-parody enable Morris to critique what he sees as a 'civilized' sensibility and the 'travellers tales' that reflect it; on another, they incriminate him individually:

> I saw a Louse crawl just below my chin across the bed-clothes: the place was so clean that the inference was that I myself was lousy, which probability was plentifully rubbed in by my fellows, I assure you.[96]

A source of comedy maybe, but the decision to record this incident represents an acknowledgement, on Morris's part, that he arrives in Iceland tainted by 'civilized' preconceptions; that, in his capacity as a traveller, he is possibly a corrupting influence of the kind Henderson had identified.

In the Faroe Islands, Morris remarks, 'it affected me strangely to see all the familiar flowers growing in a place so different to anything one had ever imagined'. The sight of well-known flora serves here to intensify the experience of strangeness. Yet there are also occasions when Morris is forced to acknowledge that Iceland is not really a place apart – not historically, not geographically – and that this closed environment, this island space, is not immune to incursions of familiarity. At such moments, he is haunted by the uncanny in the Freudian sense of something 'which is secretly familiar [*Heimlich-heimisch*], which has undergone repression and then returned from it', by an awareness that origins exercise a tenacious control over present perception:[97]

94 Morris, *Journals of Travel in Iceland*, p. 6.
95 Morris, *News from Nowhere* (Hammersmith: Kelmscott Press, 1893), p. 12.
96 Morris, *Journals of Travel in Iceland*, pp. 13, 179.
97 Sigmund Freud, 'The Uncanny', in *The Standard Edition of the Complete Psychological Works of Sigmund Freud*, ed. by James Strachey, 24 vols (London: The Hogarth Press, 1981), XVII, pp. 219–56 (p. 245).

> I went into the little grassgarth at the back of the house and watching the fowls scratching about, felt a queer feeling something akin to disappointment of how like the world was all over after all: though indeed when I lifted my eyes the scene before me was strange enough.[98]

This recorded moment, more than any other, encapsulates the problem that troubles many of Morris's attempts to imagine, and to access, alternative worlds. This 'queer feeling', like the visions of the past and the uncanny resemblances that worry Guest as he travels through Nowhere, would seem to question the possibility of transcending one's immediate situation. A Janus-faced predicament complicates the dreamer's vision. Infected, all of a sudden, by a consciousness of the mundane, he is brought back to earth just at that moment when freedom seems to beckon.

In Iceland, Morris found a model for the political creed he was later to develop. Stressing at once the benefits of regionalism and the virtues of communality, the social vision he extracted from his experiences kept protective separatism in check through the incorporation of a countervailing openness. This early experience of being a recipient of hospitality also suggested the difficulty of preventing the intrusion of unwelcome elements, forces issuing from an outside world preordained, according to the logic of this isolationist strategy, as systemically inferior. In order to visit Iceland, and thereby derive benefit from it as an 'Isle of Refuge', Morris risked spreading a kind of disease in the field. The anxiety generated by this knowledge crystallizes in his mention of a 'queer feeling' of disappointment, a sudden awareness of the uncanny that would seem to challenge the very possibility of visiting difference.

The Difficulties of Translation and the Archaeology of 'un-degraded English'[99]

Morris approached the task of translating the primitive poetic epics of Iceland with concerns similar to those discussed in relation to his travel writing. He wanted to make the invigorating strangeness of heroic society known to his readership. He wanted to bring the good news home to them. And yet he was also conscious of the risk that his material would be sanitized in the process, brought into line with the expectations of a British audience. A suggestive paradox begins to emerge: in order to avoid compromising the distinctiveness of these works, Morris adopted strategies designed to refuse translation in its total sense. He aimed thus to retain in the new version certain aspects of the source text's foreignness. The mere fact that he believed it possible to represent the preserved remnants of a prior, 'untranslated' strangeness announces the utopian character of his activities in this area, the strength of his faith in the accessibility of an outside, of an alternative to prevailing forms.

It is important to recognize that Morris's approach to translation was in no sense unitary. The strategy he employed always responded to the linguistic chal-

---

[98] Morris, *Journals of Travel in Iceland*, p. 37.
[99] Morris, 'To Eiríkr Magnússon', 29 January 1874, in *Collected Letters*, I, p. 213.

lenges presented by the particular source text concerned. This becomes more apparent when a distinction is made between the translations Morris produced from languages whose contiguous relationship with English he wished to stress – the Icelandic sagas or *Beowulf*, for example – and those whose lineal connection to British culture he considered more problematic. Under this second heading may be included his translations of *The Odyssey* and *The Aeneid*, works whose canonical status lent them a deceptive aspect of familiarity.[100] Morris here resigns the attempt to translate in the traditional sense. He creates instead an aestheticist story-world whose setting is not always obviously classical and whose diction includes no 'untranslated' element. One apparently utopian mode of translation is thereby exchanged for another. The interventionist attempt to translate difference, and thus provoke change, gives way to an isolationist approach, by which I mean a translation that neither makes concessions to the audience's expectations nor attempts to evoke the work's original context. In both cases, there is a refusal of translation in its total sense. Where the former strategy is optimistic, in offering a sincere, if unconventional, route to achieving 'true translation', the latter is sceptical. It abandons the ideal of translation, favouring instead an irreverent attitude towards the source text.

What bearing might these questions have on the central concerns of this book? It is apparent that both modes of translation are intended to maintain a distance between the translated text and its host audience or culture. Each is premised on the idea that encounters with difference are on the whole positive, and that translation should not be used as an opportunity to cushion readers against shocks of this kind. Construed as a kind of openness, a sort of linguistic pluralism or hospitality, such a translation practice would seem to support the claims made for Morris's dialogic politics. Yet the reality of such an openness, particularly where effected by the preservation of an original, untranslated element, is contingent upon acceptance that it is possible to encounter difference on its own terms. In the divergence between the two modes of translation, it is possible to discern Morris's own fluctuating confidence in the possibility of an abrasive meeting of the past and the present, of heroic culture and modernity.

I begin by analysing the first mode of translation identified: that which purports to accommodate, in a new setting, the strangeness of the source text. Morris was faced, like all translators of poetry, with the intractable difficulty of rendering the diction and prosody of a foreign work in a medium necessarily unsuited to it. This is a problem to which Ezra Pound refers in his essay on Laurence Binyon's *Dante's Inferno* (1933).[101] Pound's remarks are of particular significance because they attempt the kind of comparison between translation and the husbandry of historic buildings that the structure of this chapter invites:

---

100 I do not propose discussing the translations of 'Old French Romances' that Morris published separately between 1893 and 1894 (in *Collected Works*, XVII, pp. 265–351). Stylistically and methodologically they reflect the preoccupations of his last years. They would benefit from a lengthy and separate treatment that, for reasons of brevity and structure, would not be possible here.

101 Ezra Pound, 'Hell', in *Literary Essays of Ezra Pound*, ed. by T. S. Eliot (London: Faber and Faber, 1954), pp. 201–13.

The devil of translating medieval poetry into English is that it is very hard to decide HOW you are to render work done with one set of criteria in a language NOW subject to different criteria.

Translate the church of St Hilaire of Poitiers into Barocco?

You can't, as anyone knows, translate it into English of the period.

For Pound, the architectural analogy demonstrates the impossibility of altering linguistic form without also altering style. Translating a text and altering a building are dissimilar in certain important respects, which will be discussed in the next section. But Pound's remarks are underpinned by a quite reasonable suspicion that textual translation is impossible in the way that is self-evident in the architectural sphere.

It is fair to argue that an able translator might never really make the source text known to their readership. Translation is more an ideal proposition than a practicable one; the best to be hoped for is a revealing, and sensitive, approximation to predominant semantic and prosodic features. A modern translation of Homer is not only formally and socially unrepresentative of the original, it also loses the markers of redundancy, the signs of pastness that locate it historically. In the nineteenth century, it was suggested by Matthew Arnold that no translation might hope to recreate the experience of a Sophocles reading Homer.[102] One might add, as a supplementary proposition, that no translation could ever incorporate the complex effects of proximity and distance to which a William Morris would be attuned in reading Malory. If the object of translating a text is to make it sufficiently familiar as to be comprehensible, the pursuit of this aim inevitably flattens out the texture of the original. It limits the possible interplay of familiarity and unfamiliarity within the text. Again, some kind of approximation to a historicized reading might be attempted, by employing archaism for example. But whatever strangeness one succeeds in reconstructing is always historically and contextually inauthentic. It will necessarily draw upon the resources of the host language. Before the implications of such a strategy are addressed in their minutiae, the translator must choose between different modes of treatment. One must decide whether the experience of reading the text as a contemporary of the author is to be evoked – that is, in producing a translation free of archaism – or whether to aim at that of a hypothetical, but modern-day native speaker, sensitive to the linguistic markers of pastness in the original. Again, there is no obviously correct way of proceeding. Morris's long-standing efforts to register the difference of past times, his Carlylean attempts to effect reform by bringing the past into contrast with society's present condition, led him in most instances to favour the latter approach. His translations include linguistic markers of pastness, effects that keep the story-matter at a social and historical distance from the present. Yet he was also concerned to make the past known to his readers, to make it idiomatic, to breathe life into it. So far as Morris's first mode of translation is concerned, there is a tension between this desire to render a text in a form that preserves its strange-

---

102 In 'On Translating Homer', Matthew Arnold asks, 'does Mr. Newman suppose that Homer seemed quaint to Sophocles, when he read him, as Sir Thomas Browne seems quaint to us, when we read him? or that Homer's diction seemed antiquated to Sophocles, as Chaucer's diction seems antiquated to us?', *Complete Prose Works*, I, pp. 97–216 (p. 119).

ness – and so its power to displace the claims of the present – and the utopian desire to *translate*, to open up 'realms of gold' and 'goodly states'.[103]

George Steiner's book, *Real Presences*, contains an observation germane to this topic.[104] He compares the act of translation to the reception of a stranger, to an encounter with strangeness that is formalized in some way, and thus rendered manageable:

> Oriental manuals of decorum, etiquette books of the European Renaissance and Enlightenment dwell on welcome. They detail the nuances of idiom and of gesture which define varying degrees and intensities of reception. [. . .] Translation comprises complex exercises of salutation, of reticence, of commerce between cultures, between tongues and modes of saying. A master translator can be defined as a perfect host.

There is a long-established analogy between the task of translation, and the challenge of hospitality. This is suggested by such English expressions as, the 'host language'. The validity of this comparison depends upon viewing the process of translation as a kind of domestication, a conversion of strangeness into something comprehensible, which the host culture understands on its own terms. Viewed according to Pitt-Rivers's hospitality scenario, the stranger-text enters into guesthood. And yet, some of its hostility, some of its essential difference (illusory or not), must be preserved in the new incarnation if one is to speak of translation, or reception, rather than wholesale possession or assimilation. As part of a general theory of translation, this last observation is clearly controversial, since it implies the possibility of retaining something of the original in the translated version. Perhaps correctly, the sceptic will assert that any residual strangeness is only an uncanny emergence of the familiar cloaked in unfamiliar forms; that it is not actually alien because the signs of difference available to the host language must come from within if they are to function as effective markers of the unknown. Lawrence Venuti, a notable theorist of translation, makes this point in relation to Ezra Pound's archaizing versions of Cavalcanti:

> The foreign can only be a disruption of the current hierarchy of values in the target-language culture, an estrangement of them that seeks to establish a cultural difference by drawing on the marginal. Translation, then, always involves a process of domestication, an exchange of source-language intelligibilities for target-language ones. But domestication need not mean assimilation, i.e., a conservative reduction of the foreign text to dominant domestic values. It can also mean resistance.[105]

In his efforts to represent the unknown, Morris, like Pound, was inevitably dependent upon the resources of the English language. Only by recruiting what seemed unfamiliar or uncanny in the already-known could he evoke the linguistic markers of a strangeness necessarily beyond representation.

103 John Keats, 'On First Looking into Chapman's Homer', in *Poetical Works*, p. 45.
104 George Steiner, *Real Presences: Is There Anything in What We Say?* (London: Faber and Faber, 1989), p. 146.
105 Lawrence Venuti, *The Translator's Invisibility: A History of Translation* (London: Routledge, 1995), p. 203.

What bearing might such realism have on the hospitality analogy? The term *guest*, as it functions in Pitt-Rivers's model of welcome, is applied in blind, rather than descriptive recognition of difference. The precise sense in which the stranger is foreign is not registered; only that he is so. In this respect, Venuti's subjectivist assertion of limits, his confidence in the inevitability of domestication, might seem applicable. But Pitt-Rivers's hospitality scenario is really far more amenable to the assertion of an alternative position. On the level of the house, of the accommodating institution, he emphasizes the guest's maintenance of a residual hostility, an inalienable difference from the host society. The analogy remains valid, then, because Morris believed in the possibility of accommodating a comparable strangeness within the 'house' of the target language. While not overwhelmingly hostile, the source text retains its integrity; it resists total assimilation. So interpreted, Pitt-Rivers's theorization of hospitality offers a useful framework within which to base an understanding of Morris's utopian aspirations as a translator.

Morris responded to the challenge of representing strangeness by devising a strange language. By these means, he aimed at maintaining the precarious distinction between the familiar and the unfamiliar that a reception – rather than a crude assimilation – of difference required. In this respect, the strategy of archaism offers a parallel to the pluralistic utopianism discussed in the introduction to this book. Morris hoped that a text in 'translation' would allow its readers to appreciate the alterity of the original. This aspiration is nowhere more clearly expressed than in the following excerpt from a letter to Georgiana Burne-Jones, in which he compares George Dasent's translation, *The Story of Burnt Njal*, to the Icelandic source text:

> I had been reading the Njala in the original before I came here: it is better even than I remembered; the style most solemn (Dasent now and then uses a word too homely I think, which brings it down a little).[106]

Using a 'word too homely', Morris suggests, would mean diminishing the stylistic solemnity of the saga. It would remove all markers of cultural difference, signs, in the words of Saint Jerome, that a translator has 'carried meaning over into his own language, just like prisoners, by right of conquest' (*sed quasi captivos sensus in suam linguam victoris jure transposuit*), that something foreign has been contained within familiar forms.[107] With the exception of those following Abraham Cowley[108] – whose technique of '*Imitation*' John Dryden dismissed as '*libertine*'[109] – most translators have aimed at faithfulness in rendering their sources. Whether this quality is achieved through literalism – '*Metaphrase*', in Dryden's terminology – or through a pursuit of the 'sense and spirit' of the original in '*Paraphrase*' – is

106 Morris, 'To Georgiana Burne-Jones', [27] January 1877, in *Collected Letters*, I, p. 344.
107 'Preface to the Book of Esther', quoted in George Steiner, *After Babel: Aspects of Language and Translation*, 3rd edn (Oxford: Oxford University Press, 1998), p. 281.
108 A. Cowley, Preface, *Pindarique Odes, Written in Imitation of the Stile & Manner of the Odes of Pindar*, in *Poems, The English Writings of Abraham Cowley*, ed. by A. R. Waller (Cambridge: Cambridge University Press, 1905), pp. 155–6.
109 John Dryden, Preface, *Ovid's Epistles Translated by Several Hands*, in *The Poems of John Dryden*, ed. by James Kinsley, 4 vols (Oxford: Clarendon Press, 1958), I, pp. 178–86 (p. 182).

still open to question. Most practitioners side with Cicero in arguing that a translation *verbum pro verbo* is more likely to produce distortion than it is to achieve accuracy.[110]

In the Victorian literary world, the most important exchange of views on this subject occurred between Matthew Arnold and Francis W. Newman. Arnold objected to Newman's declared aim in translating the *Iliad*, of 'attaining a plausible aspect of moderate antiquity, while remaining easily intelligible',[111] and retaining 'every peculiarity of the original [. . .] *with the greater care, the more foreign it may happen to be*'. Arnold prescribed instead, 'simple lucidity of mind',[112] a critical commitment to seeing 'the object as in itself it really is'. In many respects, Morris's approach seems to echo Newman's. Arnold's adversary had argued that 'the entire dialect of Homer being essentially archaic, that of a translation ought to be as much Saxo-Norman as possible, and owe as little as possible to the elements thrown into our language by classical learning'.[113] Morris did not pursue this rather unusual aim but he clearly wished to retain, in common with Newman, a suggestion of the original text's antiquity. On the other hand, there is something Arnoldian in his declared aim of achieving directness, of securing a link between the original and the new version. In a letter to Magnússon, Morris explained this aspect of his translation practice:

> I am deeply impressed with the necessity of making translations literal: only they must be in English idiom and in un-degraded English at the same time: hence in short all the difficulty of translation.[114]

In using the word *literal*, Morris seems not to advocate a word for word approach. Such a technique, after all, would not have admitted his wish to produce idiomatic English. Rather, there is in evidence here an Arnoldian desire to see beyond mere appearances, to penetrate into the 'spirit' of the original.

Despite wishing to achieve an idiomatic style, Morris was obliged to employ the ostensibly less direct technique advocated by Newman. This became necessary because he did not think fidelity could be achieved using modern-day English. It was senseless attempting to render 'the object as in itself it really is' through what he considered a debased medium. By preserving in the translation certain traces of the source text's original diction, he attempts to reconcile his notion of literality with the use of 'un-degraded English'. Magnússon, when speaking of the saga translations, confirms Morris's thinking on this matter:

---

110 Cicero, *De optimo genere oratorum*, in *Cicero in Twenty-Eight Volumes*, trans. by H. M. Hubbell, 28 vols (London: William Heinemann, 1968), p. 364; referring to his translations of Aeschines and Demosthenes, Cicero writes, 'I did not translate them as an interpreter, but as an orator, keeping the same ideas and the forms, or as one might say, the "figures" of thought, but in language which conforms to our usage. And in so doing, I did not hold it necessary to render word for word, but I preserved the general style and force of the language' (p. 365).

111 F. W. Newman, Preface, *The Iliad of Homer Faithfully Translated into Unrhymed English Metre* (London: Walton and Maberly, 1856), pp. x, xvi.

112 Arnold, 'On Translating Homer', in *Complete Prose Works*, I, pp. 140, 141.

113 Newman, Preface, *The Iliad of Homer*, p. vi.

114 Morris, 'To Eiríkr Magnússon', 29 January 1874, *Collected Letters*, I, p. 213.

There must be living many of his [Morris's] friends who heard him frequently denounce it as something intolerable to have read an Icelandic saga rendered into the dominant literary dialect of the day – the English newspaper language [. . .] This dignity of style cannot be reached by the Romance element in English. If it is to be reached at all – and then only approximately – it must be by means of the Teutonic element in our speech – the nearest akin to the Icelandic.[115]

This passage confirms the distinction made between the ostensibly similar strategies of archaism employed by Newman and Pound on the one hand, and by Morris on the other. The former approach represents an attempt only at producing the illusion of an authentic strangeness. Thus Donald Davie, commenting on Pound's later versions of Cavalcanti, argues that 'it is not enough to observe that the diction is archaic' because 'one is meant to ask also, "How archaic? Archaic of what period? What English precedents or analogues is this archaism meant to bring to mind?"'.[116] Just as Newman advocates using for Homeric translation a Saxo-Norman language as free as possible from the diction introduced by classical learning, so Pound 'makes us envisage [. . .] some non-existent, perhaps anonymous, English lyrist' a hundred years earlier than Surrey, a poet, like Cavalcanti, whose approach pre-dates the fashion for all things Petrarchan.[117] The latter strategy, Morris's strategy, is similar to Pound's in that it is predicated upon an attempt to recover a sensibility now lost. But Morris's quite distinct aims, and the significance he attaches to the interrelation of a cognate source-language and target-language, lead him to place less emphasis on available English analogues than do Newman or Pound. His Icelandic and Anglo-Saxon translations rest upon a confidence that it is possible to transfer 'foreign' elements without the need for a proxy in the host language, that an authentic link between the heroic past and the Victorian present might momentarily be opened.

Morris's desire to register the distant provenance of the original, and his concern not to pour it into a debased linguistic mould, coincide in recognizing the inadequacy of contemporary English for the task in hand, the task of accommodating an authentic strangeness. Such an attitude was absent from Newman's local confidence in the suitability of 'quaint' language, and from Arnold's conception of fidelity. While acknowledging that conventional poetic archaism is present in his earliest works, most critics trace Morris's development of a consistently archaic style to his translations of the sagas.[118] The effectiveness of the Morrisian literary tongue remains a point of critical dispute. The objections of rival translators to 'pseudo-Middle-English',[119] and the more sympathetic attitude to

---

115 Magnússon's words quoted in May Morris's introduction to *Collected Works*, VII, pp. xv–xx (pp. xvij–xviij).
116 Donald Davie, *Ezra Pound: Poet as Sculptor* (London: Routledge & Kegan Paul, 1965), p. 111.
117 Davie, *Ezra Pound*, p. 112.
118 Karl Litzenberg, 'The Diction of William Morris', *Arkiv för Nordisk Filologi*, 9 (1937), 327–63; Jessie Kocmanová, 'The Living Language of William Morris', *Brno Studies in English*, 9 (1970), 17–34.
119 Gudbrand Vígfússon and F. York Powell complained in the Introduction to *Corpus Poeticum Boreale*, 2 vols (Oxford: Clarendon Press, 1883) of 'the *affectation of archaism*, and the abuse of archaic, Scottish, pseudo-Middle-English words' that 'conceals all diversities of style and tone beneath a fictitious mask of monotonous uniformity', I, p. cxv.

archaism of C. S. Lewis[120] and Jessie Kocmanová,[121] continue to mark the parameters of today's debate. Whether or not it is an effective linguistic strategy, the use of archaic language poses more than the question of its stylistic suitability. Even in his youth, imagines Kocmanová, Morris was attuned to the politically inflected nature of language, and to the false neutrality of standard English in particular. She conjures a vision of the young Morris 'prancing down the glades of Epping Forest', 'busy even then with the contrast between the language of the Saxons and that of the hated Norman yoke'. Precisely when this suspicion of the conqueror's French developed is a moot point (Morris's early works evoke the Anglo-French tongue of the Hundred Years' War sympathetically enough). The point Kocmanová makes is sound in so far as a politically inflected view of language intersects, later in his career, with a theory of art and, then of revolution, identifying modern civilization as systemically corrupt. As Morris's comments to Magnússon indicate (quoted above), he was certainly applying this thinking to the linguistic sphere by the mid 1870s and, given the form of the earlier translations, had been doing so since 1869. It is only in the 1880s, at a time when he spoke regularly in public, that he begins to articulate this view of standard English as a debased currency:

> How often I have it said to me, You must not write in a literary style if you wish the working classes to understand you. Now at first sight that seems as if the worker were in rather the better position in this matter; because the English of our drawing-rooms and leading articles is a wretched mongrel jargon that can scarcely be called English, or indeed language; and one would have expected, *a priori*, that what the workers needed from a man speaking to them was plain English: but alas! 'tis just the contrary. I am told on all hands that my language is too simple to be understood by working-men; that if I wish them to understand me I must use an inferior quality of the newspaper jargon, the language (so called) of critics and 'superior persons'.[122]

Morris's point was simple: in an arena whose conditions of comprehension were not innocently predetermined, only dubious advantage attached to the virtue of being 'understood'. This problem was equally insoluble where the work of translation was concerned. Here, comprehensibility implied equalizing the register of the original, bringing it into conformity with a world whose conventions the point was to challenge, not reproduce in mirror image. He feared that a translation's status as *news* would be diminished if it was cast in an 'inferior quality of the newspaper jargon', in a language both unsuitably reflexive and ideologically suspect.

Morris's views on the condition of the English language were heavily influenced by those of Ruskin. In his attempts to displace the claims of the *status quo*, Ruskin employed an etymological method. The aim was to reclaim 'fallen' language, language whose shift in meaning testified to a pernicious shift in priorities. This implied using words in ways that forced to the surface their

---

[120]   C. S. Lewis, *Rehabilitations*, p. 38.
[121]   Kocmanová, *The Poetic Maturing of William Morris*, p. 82.
[122]   Morris, 'Monopoly; or, How Labour is Robbed', in *Collected Works*, XXIII, pp. 238–54 (p. 241).

long-forgotten, former senses. According to the logic of this strategy, the social system in which such words once signified would be momentarily recovered. The preface to *Unto this Last* contains Ruskin's most sustained attempt at reconfiguring language in this way. In it, he insists on offering his readers 'a logical definition of WEALTH', hoping thereby to undermine its ordinary, common-sensical, signification.[123] In 'The Veins of Wealth', similarly, he observes 'that men of business rarely know the meaning of the word "rich"'. Familiar terms are submitted to an analysis of their roots; economics is pared down to its origins in 'House-law'. By defamiliarizing the linguistic markers of the social order, he seeks to renovate a debased language, to widen the field of signification. Morris's indebtedness to Ruskin's strategy of defamiliarizing language is particularly apparent in the following excerpt from the lecture, 'Art, Wealth, and Riches':

> in the early days of our own language no one would have thought of using the word rich as a synonym for wealthy. He would have understood a wealthy man to mean one who had plentiful livelihood, and a rich man one who had great dominion over his fellow-men [. . .] Now, without being a stickler for etymological accuracy, I must say that I think there are cases where modern languages have lost power by confusing two words into one meaning, and that this is one of them.[124]

In this passage, Morris secures his argument against the etymological fallacy that undermined the credibility of Ruskin's strategy, the assumption that a word *should* mean now what it 'originally' meant. At the same time, he demonstrates the power a knowledge of the history of meaning offers to those who are victims of amnesiac and politically manipulative uses of language. In 'Art and its Produc-ers', he complains of the term *handicraftsmen*, that 'we have translated the word now in order to give it a meaning exactly opposite to its original one'.[125] In 'The Beauty of Life', he makes the critical remark that 'there are some rich men among us whom we oddly enough call manufacturers'.[126] In these passages Morris employs an unmistakeably Ruskinian mode of contrast to effect a disgruntled awareness of linguistic shift, and thus of social change.

By asking his audience leave, as he does in 'Art, Wealth, and Riches', to 'use the words wealth and riches somewhat in the way in which our forefathers did', Morris resists the call for total translation.[127] Insisting on the obsolete or repressed meaning of a familiar word, he effects the fleeting resurrection of a pre-capitalist world. Oscar Wilde, in his unsigned review of Morris's *The Odyssey of Homer*, made a similar point:

> language is apt to degenerate into a system of almost algebraic symbols, and the modern city-man who takes a ticket for Blackfriars Bridge, naturally never thinks of the Dominican monks who once had their monastery by Thames-side, and after whom the spot is named [. . .] Pope tried to put Homer into the ordinary language of his day, with what result we know only too well, but Mr. Morris, who uses his

---

123   Ruskin, Preface, *Unto this Last*, p. 18.
124   Morris, 'Art, Wealth, and Riches', in *Collected Works*, XXIII, pp. 143–63 (p. 143).
125   Morris, 'Art and its Producers', in *Collected Works*, XXII, pp. 342–55 (p. 346).
126   Morris, 'The Beauty of Life', in *Collected Works*, XXII, pp. 51–80 (p. 70).
127   Morris, 'Art, Wealth, and Riches', p. 143.

archaisms with the tact of a true artist, and to whom indeed they seem to come absolutely naturally, has succeeded in giving to his version by their aid that touch, not of 'quaintness,' for Homer is never quaint, but of old-world romance, and old-world beauty.[128]

The case against those who would condemn 'Wardour Street English' as useless ornamentation has a further dimension where Morris's saga translations are concerned. Karl Litzenberg, in his thoroughgoing analysis of Morris's language, has dismissed the charge that he used a ' "pseudo-", or "quasi-", or "bastard-", Middle English'.[129] Litzenberg argues instead that 'it is "belated"', a language 'super-imposed upon the literary English of the nineteenth century'. Where Morris translates from another Germanic language, albeit a different sub-branch,[130] this suggestion of belatedness becomes a tool, in Magnússon's words, for 'penetrating into the thought of the old language',[131] for bringing about 'such harmony between the Teutonic element in English and the language of the Icelandic saga as the not very abundant means at his command would allow'.[132] This peculiar attempt to render a foreign text on its own terms manifests itself, in the saga translations, and in Morris's version of *Beowulf*, as a frequent use of kennings, a preference for alliteration, a reliance on prepositional phrases and a willingness to employ typically Germanic rhetorical effects like litotes. In *The Tale of Beowulf*, compound words, like 'wave-holm',[133] 'word-hoard', 'man-kin', 'shade-goer' and 'were-gild' are commonplace. Similar effects are employed in the saga translations. A Germanic approach to word formation is combined with a recurrent use of words seen to derive from the Norse influence on English, like 'mickle' or 'soothly'.[134]

When Morris communicated with A. J. Wyatt, the Anglo-Saxon specialist with whom he co-translated *Beowulf*, he expressed concern that 'every word which it is necessary to substitute for the old one [. . .] *must* be weakened and almost destroyed'.[135] This anxiety is presented by Robert Boenig as evidence that Morris appreciated the central difficulty involved in translating Anglo-Saxon into English:

> The difficulty of vocabulary [. . .] is for Morris a function of linguistic change [. . .] For instance, there is an abundance of Old English words for 'warrior' – *secg, rinca, guma, hæleð*, etc., but Modern English only gives us one. There were presumably shadings of meaning among these words lost to us: hence 'warrior' weakens if not destroys the meaning of a given line.[136]

128 [Oscar Wilde], 'Mr. Morris's Completion of the Odyssey', *Pall Mall Gazette*, 24 November 1887, p. 3.
129 Litzenberg, 'The Diction of William Morris', p. 336.
130 English is classed by historians of language as West Germanic, and Icelandic as North Germanic.
131 Eiríkr Magnússon, Preface to the *Saga Library*, 6 vols (London: Bernard Quaritch, 1905), IV, pp. v–xvi (p. xiv).
132 Introduction to *The Story of Grettir the Strong*, in *Collected Works*, VII, pp. xv–xxxiv (p. xviij).
133 Morris, *The Tale of Beowulf*, pp. 185, 186, 200, 211.
134 I stress *seen to derive* as both were in fact already present in Anglo-Saxon, and thus available to English before the Norse invasions.
135 Morris, 'To Alfred John Wyatt', 28 August [1892], in *Collected Letters*, III, pp. 436–7 (p. 436).
136 Robert Boenig, 'The Importance of Morris's *Beowulf*', *Journal of the William Morris Society*, XII (Spring, 1997), 2, 7–13 (p. 7).

The preponderance of kennings in Morris's *Beowulf* might be interpreted, then, as a symptom of creative exuberance and a quite reasonable striving for accuracy and richness of expression. In *Beowulf*, more particularly, Boenig highlights the aptness of an archaizing vocabulary as applied to a poem that 'depicts an elegiac world in which lament for a lost past is a frequent mode'. Admittedly, it would be misleading to suggest that a reader of Morris's translation could, on the basis of its diction, discriminate accurately between the archaic tendencies of the translator and those of the *Beowulf* poet. Boenig nevertheless demonstrates that the 'plain English' approach, which has been in favour for most of the twentieth century, is not the only one that may lay claim to the aim of 'faithfulness'.

Occasionally the method by which Morris attempted to preserve the foreignness of the source text threatened to compromise his concurrent pursuit of directness. This is to say that the method of refusing translation in the conventional sense sometimes failed to produce a higher form of communication between past and present. The final text could be left suspended, ineffectually, somewhere in-between the two contexts. Such failures of translation can cause considerable problems. This is particularly so when the expressed aim is to capture the spirit of the original. In the preface to *The Story of the Volsungs and the Niblungs*, Morris hopes that the disjunction between archaic forms and the reader's expectations will momentarily free his audience from the prison house of contemporary usage:

> we think we may well trust the reader of poetic insight to break through whatever entanglement of strange manners or unused element may at first trouble him, and to meet the nature and beauty with which it is filled.[137]

Problems arise when Morris's intense awareness of continuity blinds him to the fact that what is cognate is not necessarily comprehensible. The result, as Andrew Wawn suggests in *The Vikings and the Victorians*, is that 'it is sometimes difficult to resist the sense that Morris was reaching out to an audience of initiates rather than seeking to win converts'.[138] Attending to the etymological pedigree of the host language, Morris worked to exclude aspects of English whose associations he deemed inappropriate, or actively detrimental, to the spirit of the Saga Age. By means of this selective approach to translation, he practised a separatism that was both unabashed and more effective in its exclusion of unwelcome elements than anything he had attempted before. Morris could do nothing to expunge the Latinate newspaper vocabulary already installed in the reader's mind. He could not restrict the social status of language, the ceaseless exchange of words that always defeats attempts to regulate or purify a tongue. His translations could at least produce the illusion of a pristine verbal icon. Like Lewis Carroll's Humpty Dumpty, he would for a season make words mean what he wanted them to mean.[139] In *News from Nowhere*, there are attempts to secure a dialogue between

---

137 Morris, Preface, *The Story of the Volsungs and the Niblungs*, pp. 285–6.
138 Wawn, *The Vikings and the Victorians*, p. 260.
139 In *Through the Looking-Glass*, Humpty Dumpty declares scornfully, ' "When *I* use a word," [. . .] "it means just what I choose it to mean – neither more nor less [. . .]" ', in Lewis Carroll, *Alice's Adventures in Wonderland and through the Looking-Glass* (London: Oxford University Press, 1971), pp. 113–245 (p. 190).

the world and the text.[140] Yet, even here, Victorian habits of language are temporarily shamed out of existence; the 'big words' of the British Empire are allowed to have no purchase on the lives of the utopians.

What Herbert F. Tucker has called Morris's 'macropoetic refusal to accommodate his contemporaries' is often in evidence on the level of pronouncements regarding the state of the English language.[141] In private, Morris sometimes admitted to a difficulty in composing his lectures. On one such occasion, he complained of 'those frogs [. . .] making such fools of us', a light-hearted objection to the French component in English that speaks of a serious interest in linguistic engineering.[142] Morris's attitude in these matters is epitomized by the disagreement he had with Wyatt over the inclusion of a glossary in their *Beowulf*. On 10 November 1894, Morris wrote:

> As to the glossary; I think our views as to what is wanted *in this case* differ; or rather we have not quite understood one another. *I* thought that all we wanted was a few very unusual words taken from M.E. such as brim or worth, and perhaps one or two sentences, though I think these would mostly explain themselves by the context except the few words aforesaid, almost all in the glossary I should not hesitate to use in an original poem of my own, you see: and *I* don't think it would need a glossary.[143]

Morris was alert to the dangers of an esoteric approach as applied to the visual arts, particularly with regard to the aestheticist failure to create an art for the people. Yet this desire to append only a limited glossary to *Beowulf* highlights his failure to appreciate that such a procedure was equally inadvisable in the linguistic sphere. The tragedy of his bid to revive the popular arts of the past, to translate what he called 'Bibles' (after Giuseppe Mazzini), was that in attempting to achieve community through a necessarily exclusionary focus on one tradition (in this case, a Germanic tradition), he was doomed to fail.[144] Far from jerking his readership into a pre-feudal, pre-capitalist state of mind – when the 'pig' in the peasant's yard was linguistically indistinguishable from the 'pork' on the noble's table – he risked the creation of a private language premised on the expectation that it would explain itself. Where the success of his translations depends upon their power to modify the consciousness of the reader, to facilitate communication with the past, such a strategy could only be counterproductive.

In his first Iceland journal, Morris blames the rebuff he receives at the hands of the steward who will not accept a tip on his own 'bad manners'.[145] Yet this embarrassing episode is not precipitated by any individual or moral shortcoming; it springs rather from a clash of expectations. Morris commits a *faux pas* in this situation not because his manners are bad but simply because they are applied in the

---

140 Morris, *News from Nowhere*, p. 49.
141 Herbert F. Tucker, 'All for the Tale: The Epic Macropoetics of Morris' *Sigurd the Volsung*', *Victorian Poetry*, 34 (Autumn, 1996), 3, 373–94 (p. 389).
142 Morris, 'To Jane Morris', 10 February [1881], in *Collected Letters*, II, pp. 14–16 (p. 15).
143 Morris, 'To Alfred John Wyatt', in *Collected Letters*, IV, p. 232.
144 Morris mentions Mazzini in a letter to the *Pall Mall Gazette*, 2 February 1886, in *Collected Letters*, II, pp. 514–18 (p. 515).
145 Morris, *Journals of Travel in Iceland*, p. 6.

wrong context. I suggested in the previous section that this incident might be taken as representative of the problems Morris faced in his attempts to 'visit' Icelandic culture. The encounter with the steward speaks eloquently of an unexpected failure of convertibility, a difficulty in exchanging not just money, but also the basic assumptions that regulate everyday behaviour. And yet the confusion is brought about as much by a persistence of familiar forms as by an encounter with difference. Morris's misreading of the situation dramatizes, in a displaced setting, a well-known translation problem: that of the illusory correspondence, or 'false friend'. It demonstrates that what we *do* know can mislead, that prior knowledge sometimes places a greater obstacle in the way of understanding than does ignorance. This mishap usefully illuminates a further impediment to any utopian, or transcendental, mode of translation. In a comparable way, Morris allowed his attention to a rightful inheritance, or the evocation of an ideal continuity, to blind him to the profound differences separating early Germanic prosody from post-medieval prosody. Boenig, though generally sympathetic to what Morris achieves in *Beowulf*, suggests the problem with this translation was 'not vocabulary but the imposition of an anachronistic prosody on the poem'.[146] This becomes a grave flaw when one realizes that it springs not from a desire to feudalize *Beowulf*, but simply from a failure to understand how Anglo-Saxon poetry worked. Boenig explains the matter as follows:

> Anglo-Saxon poets simply did not count unaccented syllables. The consequence is that some Old English lines are extremely short, some quite long.
>
> Morris, like so many others of his day, perceived the shorter lines as metrically deficient because something was missing – in short, grievous gaps. What Morris did in response was to regularize the length of the lines and thus fill in the perceived gaps.

The result, Boenig demonstrates, is that Morris's *Beowulf* is characterized by metrical regularity; that of the Old English *Beowulf*, by irregularity, with 'accents falling unexpectedly – perhaps as unexpectedly as a monster invading a great hall in the middle of the night'. Instead of confronting his readers with 'strange manners', and an 'unused element', instead of discomfiting them with the arrival of an unbidden guest, Morris holds up a mirror. Grendel is tamed; and the intersection between past and present effaced by a too familiar metrical pattern. It would be wrong to judge Morris too harshly for an oversight, or intervention, common among poets of his generation.[147] Yet the mere fact that he was unable to transcend the flawed Victorian understanding of Anglo-Saxon prosody serves as a further indication that accessing and representing a strange but 'kindred' past was less straightforward than he was willing to admit. Here, the inertia of form, even more so than that of meaning, becomes a symbol of untranslatability. In *After Babel*, George Steiner shows how instances of 'successful' translation have been used to support the idea that deep structures unite human beings from all

---

146 Robert Boenig, 'The Importance of Morris's *Beowulf*', pp. 8, 10, 11.
147 Gerard Manley Hopkins's experiments with accentual verse demonstrate that Morris's misconception was not universal.

cultures and all times.[148] Here he alludes to the early Bible translators, as well as to the work of Noam Chomsky.[149] Yet the general difficulty Victorian poets had in reproducing the classical hexameter in English, and Morris's apparent failure to transcend 'the Romance element in English',[150] would indicate that the surface structures facilitating poetic expression are not easily bypassed, that they are quite capable of frustrating demonstrations of cross-cultural continuity.

Morris's second mode of translation was applied to classical texts that, unlike the sagas, already enjoyed a secure and privileged position within Victorian literary culture. The argument that archaism is justifiable as an aid to achieving accuracy is no longer applicable here, as Morris makes no attempt to suggest the experience of reading Homer either as an ancient or a modern Greek. Since the languages concerned were only very remotely related to English, there was also no basis for an emphasis on linguistic continuity. Morris aimed less to point out an unacknowledged link with the present, than to defamiliarize such texts, to imbue them with romance. The principle of 'benign' exclusion is still applied, but here it produces a curious amalgam of Morris's ideal languages and period settings rather than a focused reference to any particular historical moment. In *The Odyssey of Homer* and *The Æneids of Virgil* (1876),[151] the diction conveys a powerful impression that these classical texts are intended to appear as the medievals received them, enacting a transformation of classical epic into 'medieval' romance. Relying in much of his published work upon authorities, upon existing tales, Morris's approach to composition was technically, as well as thematically, medievalist. A reliance on pre-existing material was redeemed by a loose adherence to the letter of the master text. In those translations that seem to filter the ancient world through a medieval world-view, he employs a diction remarkable for its bold defiance of the conventional vocabulary. In *The Odyssey of Homer*, 'wooers' is substituted for the standard term *suitors*; and Ilium is commonly described as 'the Holy Burg, Troy-town'.[152] Scattered through the text are references to minstrels' lays and heralds. It rhymes, though in this case one finds precedents in the rhymed translations of Chapman and Pope.[153] Morris clearly had no qualms about using such medieval techniques as rhyme and alliteration in the translation of works pre-dating their development. The result is not just an anachronistic form, but also the forging, through sound sympathy, of word relationships not obtaining in the original. This lack of deference to the classical resonance of the source text is not even securely underpinned by the alternative logic of a medievalized, romantic rendering. Such a procedure is not observed with sufficient consistency to suggest that Morris is attempting to produce a

148 Steiner, *After Babel*, p. 67.
149 Steiner explains this idea as follows: 'a translation from language A into language B will make tangible the implication of a third, active presence. It will show the lineaments of that "pure speech" which precedes and underlies both languages. A genuine translation evokes the shadowy yet unmistakable contours of the coherent design from which, after Babel, the jagged fragments of human speech broke off', *After Babel*, p. 67.
150 Magnússon, in *Collected Works*, VII, p. xvij.
151 Morris, *The Æneids of Virgil*, in *Collected Works*, XI.
152 Morris, *The Odyssey of Homer*, pp. 1, 11, 107.
153 Chapman, *The Odyssey* in *Chapman's Homer*; Alexander Pope, *The Odyssey of Homer*, ed. by Maynard Mack, 2 vols (London: Methuen & Co., 1967).

comprehensively 'feudal' version of the *Odyssey*. Distinctive features remain in evidence of the 'pre-feudal' tongue Morris devised for his saga translations. One finds words with Norse endings (like 'youngling'),[154] allusion to goodwives and alliterative compound expressions like 'death-day' and 'Burg-bane'. Noting the fact that 'Morris's poetry and his narrative prose are [. . .] markedly Teutonic', Magnússon recalls how his friend 'often used to say that the Teutonic was the poetical element in English, while the Romance element was that of law, practice and business'.[155] If this explains Morris's reasoning in allowing an otherwise unlikely language component to intrude, it also indicates his application of the technique Davie discusses in relation to Pound's translations:

> we seem required or invited to distinguish just what degree of archaism is being practised, precisely what period out of the long past of English poetry is being alluded to – and this so as to suggest that in just that period English approximated most nearly to such and such a Chinese perception, or cluster of perceptions.[156]

The comparison holds as applied to Morris's second mode of translation, but does not for the first. This is because the distance between the source-language, Ancient Greek, and the target-language, English, reduces Morris, in his attempts to evoke the 'poetic' heroism of Greece, to a dependence on the perceived carriers of equivalent feeling as they exist in English. It is the Teutonic strain that he selects for this task.

There is no attempt, then, to reproduce the linguistic circumstances of the original; nor to render these works in plain, modern English. Instead, *The Odyssey of Homer* and *The Æneids of Virgil* are cast in the mould of Morris's *Earthly Paradise* tales: classical stories being told in the Middle Ages by Norsemen who have settled in a land non-specific and far from home. Unlike these tales, they are nevertheless presented as translations. It would seem more useful, then, to consult Dryden's third mode of translation – what he calls *imitation* – in describing their nature:

> *The Third way is that of Imitation, where the Translator (if now he has not lost that Name) assumes the liberty not only to vary from the words and sence [sic], but to forsake them both as he sees occasion: and taking only some general hints from the Original, to run division on the ground-work, as he pleases.*[157]

In *The Poetic Maturing of William Morris*, Jessie Kocmanová defends Morris's version of *Laxdæla Saga*, 'The Lovers of Gudrun', according to the premise that such an approach is perfectly justifiable when considered strictly on its own terms.[158] Hence she argues that 'it would be absurd to criticise Morris in this case for not reproducing exactly the tone and method of the saga'. J. N. Swannell's complaint that Morris's Gudrun 'is not a Norse heroine', but a 'Pre-Raphaelite

---

154 Morris, *The Odyssey of Homer*, pp. 30, 43, 50, 133.
155 Magnússon, in *Collected Works of William Morris*, VII, pp. xv–xxxiij (p. xvij).
156 Davie, *Ezra Pound*, pp. 12–13.
157 Dryden, Preface, *Ovid's Epistles*, p. 182.
158 Jessie Kocmanová, *The Poetic Maturing of William Morris, From the Earthly Paradise to the Pilgrims of Hope* (Prague: Státní Pedagogické Nakladatelství, 1964), p. 82.

lady, if ever there was one!' is effectively answered by this argument, as is his objection that the 'love scenes and the emotional partings between Gudrun and Kiartan' suggest 'a romance of courtly love'.[159] Morris deploys these contrivances so freely that there would seem little sense in complaining, as does Geoffrey Riddehough that, 'the spirit of Northern poetry [. . .] had a distorting influence on the Englishing of Virgil'[160] or that Morris often refers to fighting as '"play" or as "the game of Mars," when nothing in his original justifies his doing so'. Such objections carry little weight when one accepts that Morris was attempting something quite different from translation as the term is normally understood.

How might the rationale implicit in this second mode of translation be explained? First of all, it is reminiscent of Pater's account, in *The Renaissance*, of attempts to combine the romance of medieval Christianity with the pagan spirit of Hellenism.[161] Translation of this kind provides Morris with a similar opportunity to fashion a hybrid sensibility. The approach taken can also be seen as a product of Ruskinian teaching. If it was both senseless and impossible to build a cathedral in a twelfth-century manner, then the same objection applied equally to recreating Homer in the modern age. Morris always preached against attempts to copy medieval or classical art. If one worked from a source text, there should come a point, he argued, when the authority was laid aside, and written out only from memory. In this way it would be transfigured, filtered through the consciousness of the recipient and thus remade. He did not consider his limited expertise as a linguist a serious impediment to his work because the theory applied here – his second mode of translation – no longer posits the dominance of the original work. Even when concerned to evoke a buried continuity, this attitude is borne out in his method of working. Magnússon and A. J. Wyatt wrote out plain English prose versions of the sagas and of *Beowulf*, respectively. Morris would then versify and adapt them according to the style and register he considered fitting. The text, as a result, would reach him in a mediated form even before he began work. That Morris was comfortable with this situation indicates his acceptance, in certain circumstances, of the essentially transformational nature of translation.

There are important differences between the utopian or transcendental aspect of Morris's attempt at gaining access to the past through translation, and the more sceptical approach, which subordinates the quite hopeless pursuit of accuracy or authenticity to a creative evocation of mood. What links the translation practice applied to the Germanic texts with that used to render *The Odyssey* and *The Aeneid* is their mutual recourse to a kind of linguistic separatism. As demonstrated, this approach occasionally becomes self-defeating. The exclusionary attempt to recover a buried continuity incurs its own particular problems. There is the danger that the seemingly familiar will mislead, and that the connection between past and present usage will depend solely upon the theoretic proof of a glossary. Where Morris makes no attempt to bring the present and a particular past into collision (as in *The Odyssey of Homer* and *The Æneids of Virgil*), the

---

159 J. N. Swannell, *William Morris & Norse Literature* (London: William Morris Society, 1961), p. 12.
160 Geoffrey B. Riddehough, 'William Morris's Translation of the *Aeneid*', *Journal of English and Germanic Philology*, XXXVI (1937), 338–46 (p. 338).
161 Pater, *The Renaissance*, pp. 26–7.

atmosphere of romance so created risks divorcing the text from the world of his readership, and distorting the register of the original. It may become, in consequence, a textual incarnation of the separatist utopia, a world sealed off and self-justifying. What remains clear, however, is that both strategies are designed to resist total translation, and that in consequence these texts act to displace the linguistic and cultural context of their readership. In this respect, they announce a confidence in the salutary effect of an encounter with strangeness, with strange manners and a strange language.

'Making the past part of the present': 'Ancient' Buildings, Preservation and the Romance of the Original[162]

In *The Shock of Medievalism*, Kathleen Biddick argues that Morris 'founded the SPAB [The Society for the Protection of Ancient Buildings] in 1877 to police the binary of copy and original in the Revival', 'to stop what its members regarded as a kind of parasitism in which industrially produced ornament fed off the historical Gothic by killing the host'.[163] 'Linear inheritance', she concludes, 'was restored through the SPAB's construction of the category of *the original*'. By locating an essentialism in Morris's position, Biddick starts from a sound basis: in so far as Morris believed ancient buildings were worth preserving, that they were substantively different from what might be constructed in his own day, his position was indeed essentialist. Yet it is hard to regard the essentialism of which Morris *was* 'guilty' – his acceptance of the inalienable difference embodied in an ancient building – as ideologically suspect in the way Biddick sees it. Here, the limitations of her reading begin to emerge. Any attempt to 'preserve' an artefact no longer inhabiting its 'original' setting must be regarded as a problematic gesture. But Morris could not have been further from promoting a single, 'authentic' form of Gothic. His efforts were directed mainly towards combating the naïve conception of 'originality' widespread among High Church clergymen and revivalist architects. Nor, indeed, was Morris's preservation work focused exclusively on Gothic remains. The remit of the SPAB was sufficiently catholic to admit the protection of Renaissance and baroque edifices, buildings for which Morris certainly had no personal taste.

In the previous section, attention was given to Matthew Arnold's call for translators to see 'the object as in itself it really is'. The assumptions informing this statement were to some extent present in what is termed Morris's essentialism: his confidence that ancient buildings constituted sites of real difference, structures that, if unmolested, would retain their historical integrity in the present. Morris believed artefacts of this kind were sufficiently intractable in their alterity as to be capable of interacting with the contemporary world without being assimilated. He hoped such strange survivals would act upon the present, that they would effect change in the environment surrounding them, and alter the perceptions of

162 Morris, 'Address at the Twelfth Annual Meeting; 3 July 1889 ("Anti-Scrape")', in *William Morris: Artist Writer Socialist*, I, pp. 146–57 (p. 148).
163 Kathleen Biddick, *The Shock of Medievalism* (Durham: Duke University Press, 1998), p. 37.

the people who viewed them. This position follows Arnold in cancelling the Kantian distinction between the thing as it appears and the thing in itself (if, like Arnold, one transfers the terms of Kant's epistemology to a diachronic axis of perceptions).[164] It suggests that individuals living in the present may see into what is ordinarily denied to them, that they may glimpse something of the past. Far from being trapped within our interpretative faculties, the essence of the object is available to cognition.

Morris nevertheless places historical constraints on this optimism. While the marooned condition of the artefact does not restrict the ability of the observer to witness aspects of the reality it inhabited in previous settings, its form is plural rather than unitary. The object testifies to no single past condition; it is, in its make-up, sedimentary. Furthermore, only phases of this continuum that survive in the present, and are recorded, offer themselves up to trans-historical perception. This process is not hampered by the inaccessibility of those networks of social meaning in which it was previously enmeshed, only by the fact that certain historical imprints have not endured. For Morris, then, there was no prison house of language, of history, or the perceptions: the object in its historically diverse essence was capable of breaking through to the sensory level. The inimitable but perceptible essence of historical relics opens a portal in the present, leading not necessarily to a privileged past, because it testifies to no one previous state, but at least to a consciousness that there *is* an outside, that what prevails in the present is not unassailable in its claim to validity. Officially, ancient buildings were to be preserved because the fallacious practice of 'restoration' (equally utopian in its way) was depriving them of their status as historical documents; because they should be regarded as public property; and because it was always safer to wait than to act where the prospect of irreversible work was concerned.[165] Beyond the rhetoric of persuasion and self-justification to which Morris was forced to resort in convincing those not in sympathy with his aims, he evidently believed that these buildings, these guests from another time, embodied real differences, real presences that constituted sources of reform and change. To restore them meant domesticating them, depriving them of their power to deliver a shock to the complacency of the age.

Preservationism as a ideal, and as a practical approach to conservation, had been current since the inception of the Gothic Revival. William Stukeley's campaign to save the stone circle at Avebury, Richard Gough's 1788 letter to the *Gentleman's Magazine* arguing for preservation of 'national objects',[166] and John

---

164 Kant writes that 'objects in themselves are not known to us at all, and [. . .] what we call outer objects are nothing other than mere representations of our sensibility', *Critique of Pure Reason*, trans. and ed. by Paul Guyer and Allen W. Wood (Cambridge: Cambridge University Press, 2000), p. 162.

165 As applied in Victorian architectural circles, the word *restoration* did not carry quite the meaning it has today. It implied a relatively aggressive bid to return buildings to a postulated 'original' state, a process that might involve extensive rebuilding, and the demolition of medieval or post-medieval work.

166 'I look upon these antique erections as national objects, and am as anxious about the preservation of, a cross, a tomb, an abbey, a church, or a castle, as some are about that of a coin, a picture, or a statue', Richard Gough ('D. N.'), 'A Plan for Preservation of Ancient Edifices', *Gentleman's Magazine*, LVIII (August, 1788), II, 689–91 (p. 690).

Britton's case for the protection of historic houses and Roman villas – presented before a House of Commons Select Committee in 1841 – were important stages in the formation of this approach to the past. In Morris's time, the work of the Commons Preservation Society (founded 1865), the Kyrle Society (founded 1875), the Lake District Defence Society, and of Percy Lubbock in attempting to get an Ancient Monuments Protection Act onto the statute book, all represented important departures. What distinguishes these efforts from Morris's activities is their lack of engagement with the mid- to late-nineteenth-century phenomenon of restoration. The SPAB had not, primarily, been founded to combat the wholesale destruction and commercial exploitation of national monuments. While it did become involved in campaigns to save historic buildings from demolition (notably Wren's City churches), it initially came into existence in outraged response to George Gilbert Scott's plan for a 'restoration' of Tewkesbury Abbey. Its *raison d'être* was defined more strongly, and more problematically, then, by the quarrel Morris had with a large section of those also professing themselves interested in the survival of historic buildings. The individuals towards whom Morris directed his wrath were antiquarian in their inclinations. They were not straightforward iconoclasts or vandals. As Morris explains in the following excerpt, the cause of the dispute lay rather in their singular approach to the wardenship of ancient buildings:

> After all, the issue is narrow between Sir Edmund Lechmere and the restorers, and myself and the anti-restorers. Neither side wants a building to lose its ancient character; only the restorers think it will look even more ancient if it be worked all over under the 'care' of Sir Gilbert Scott to-day.[167]

Fixated on a particular era of medieval history, the 'restorer' wished to expunge the accretions of subsequent ages from monuments lacking the desired period unity. The founding statement underpinning Morris's condemnation of restoration was contained in Ruskin's *The Seven Lamps of Architecture*.[168] Less exercised by evangelical outrage at the lie, or the deceit, of restoration, Morris was nevertheless indebted to Ruskin's views on the romance of decay, on the mysterious alterity of historical remains. Like Ruskin, he also acknowledged that where the survival of an ancient building was in question, it was acceptable to use industrial technology in undertaking essential repairs (to the roof, for example) and in propping up the foundations.

The arguments Morris borrowed from Ruskin do not smuggle a naïve conception of authenticity into the conservation debate. His opposition to restoration was rooted in a rejection of attempts to 'reinstate' a given building 'in a condition of completeness which could never have existed at any given time', this being the motivating aim Sidney Colvin ascribed to the French master of the art, Eugène

---

167 Morris, 'To the Editor of *The Athenaeum*', 4 April 1877, in *Collected Letters*, I, pp. 361–3 (p. 362).

168 In *The Seven Lamps of Architecture*, Ruskin states: 'neither by the public, nor by those who have the care of public monuments, is the true meaning of the word *restoration* understood. It means the most total destruction which a building can suffer', in *Works*, VIII, p. 242. Of the unrestored building, he asserts, 'there was yet in the old *some* life, some mysterious suggestion of what it had been, and of what it had lost', p. 243.

Emmanuel Viollet-le-Duc.[169] The objectives of the restorer implied a brutal disregard for both post-Reformation work, and for forms of the Gothic he happened to consider decadent (the perpendicular style, for example). This philosophy was nowhere more apparent than in the plan at Canterbury Cathedral to replace existing choir stalls of exceptional workmanship. Morris complained that 'in some people's minds' the stalls 'would be condemned as inherently unholy, because [. . .] a post-Reformation work'.[170] Colvin had referred, in his article on the subject, to a commonplace recognition – also present in Morris's lectures – that the nineteenth century was 'above all things an age of retrospect, of historical inquiry and historical science'.[171] This had led, he claimed, to an overweening desire among certain architects to apply what knowledge had been gleaned from such researches to the restoration of churches and cathedrals. They were attempting to return these buildings to their 'original' condition.

Biddick's reference to a fear of parasitism might be applied with more justice in describing the ideology motivating restoration than in attacking its opponents. One should acknowledge its wilful selectivity, its arbitrary prioritization of one past over another. The manifesto of the SPAB (written by Morris) referred to this aspect of the restoration project as the 'strange and most fatal idea [. . .] that it is possible to strip from a building this, that, and the other part of its history [. . .] and then to stay the hand at some arbitrary point, and leave it still historical, living, and even as it once was'.[172] Even Chris Miele, a commentator otherwise sympathetic to Morris's aims, ascribes to Morris's activism 'the assumption that authentic originals are in all circumstances superior to facsimiles'.[173] In a sense, this statement is justified: the SPAB had been formed according to a conviction that the inimitable relics of past ages were worth preserving. But the point is missed if one does not acknowledge that Morris's campaign was directed against a far less tolerant conception of originality. It should also be stressed that facsimiles, *per se*, were not the problem. Morris was objecting, rather, to the use of genuine churches as laboratories for the new science of architectural history, to the transformation of surviving buildings (buildings testifying to a plurality of pasts) into copies of 'some ideal state of perfection', of 'originals' that never existed:[174]

> I must needs think that a great building which is obviously venerable and weighty with history is fitter for worship than one turned into a scientific demonstration of what the original architects intended to do: I think that these learned restorations are good on paper to be kept in portfolios, but not good in new stone for the use of people who are busy & in earnest .[175]

What aroused Morris's concern was not the concept of a facsimile; but rather the fact that 'experimental' work of the kind described depended upon the creative

---

169 Sidney Colvin, 'Restoration and Anti-Restoration', *Nineteenth Century*, 2 (1877), 446–70 (p. 446).
170 Morris, 'To the Editor of *The Times*', 4 June 1877, in *Collected Letters*, I, pp. 374–5 (p. 374).
171 Colvin, 'Restoration and Anti-Restoration', p. 448.
172 Morris, 'To Dante Gabriel Rossetti', 3 April [1877], in *Collected Letters*, I, pp. 359–60 (p. 359).
173 Chris Miele, 'The First Conservation Militants: William Morris and the Society for the Protection of Ancient Buildings', in *Preserving the Past: The Rise of Heritage in Modern Britain*, ed. by Michael Hunter (Stroud: Sutton Publishing, 1996), pp. 15–37 (p. 18).
174 Morris, 'The Lesser Arts', p. 19.
175 Morris, 'To the Editor of *The Times*', 7 June 1877, in *Collected Letters*, I, pp. 375–6 (p. 376).

destruction of its object. Before the SPAB is charged with a fetishistic adulation of some vague, indeterminate past, it is prudent to recognize the nature of the naïve historicism it had been founded to combat. Morris's point in this respect was perfectly sound: that modern architecture cannot reproduce a workmanship inimical to its own processes; that modern architecture cannot transcend history.

Since the early 1980s, controversy has surrounded the issue of conservation. This debate is of relevance because Morris's name is often invoked dismissively by commentators of a 'sceptical' persuasion. Some have questioned the validity of preservation itself, others are concerned by the uses to which the more politically suspect category of 'heritage' has been put in national life. Martin Wiener's notorious critique of museum culture, *English Culture and the Decline of the Industrial Spirit, 1850–1980*, represents one such intervention.[176] Seeking to explain Britain's relative economic decline, Wiener argued that the passing of the high Victorian period saw among the English middle classes a loss of appetite for urban life and for industrialism. He ascribed this development, first, to the resurgent cult of rurality, and, second, to the attempts of the bourgeoisie to mimic their landed 'betters'. The factory-owning classes had begun to send their sons to Oxford. There, claims Wiener, they became 'gentlemen' ashamed of their earlier association with trade. According to this thesis, one sees as a result the formation of a culture in which entrepreneurship is actively discouraged. As might be expected, such figures as Cobbett, Ruskin and Morris are implicated in this turn towards nostalgic ruralism:

> With a declared 'passion for . . . the past,' Morris treasured the sense of continuity with earlier generations. [. . .] Near his country house at Kelmscott, in the upper Thames Valley, Morris found within a radius of five miles 'some half-dozen tiny village churches, every one of which is a beautiful work of art, with its own individuality.' These survivals of an earlier England seemed to bear witness to a vital popular culture that present-day England could not equal. They embodied for Morris, as for Tory writers, a vital reserve of social values for the nation [. . .] As the new elite adopted many trappings of the past, it also took on a peculiarly rural guise. It was in the same years in which the economy was losing its dynamism. (p. 46)

Behind this disdain for the nostalgic sentimentalists of English history, Wiener smuggles in a celebration of 'Crystal Palace' capitalism. In subsequent years, this curious mix of New Right ideology and Modernist veneration of the industrial emerges as an unlikely influence on the many avowedly leftist critiques of museum culture published during the 1980s and 1990s. 'Why "Heritage" is Right-Wing', an article Neal Ascherson published in the *Observer*, argued that 'the heritage industry, like the proposed "core curriculum" of history for English schools, imposes one ruling group's version of history on everyone'.[177] Building on the argument advanced by Robert Hewison in *The Heritage Industry*, this article decried the advent of 'theme park' Britain.[178] The distinction between 'heritage'

---

176 Martin J. Wiener, *English Culture and the Decline of the Industrial Spirit, 1850–1980* (Cambridge: Cambridge University Press, 1981), p. 46.

177 Neal Ascherson, 'Why "Heritage" is Right-Wing', *Observer*, 8 November 1987, p. 9.

178 Robert Hewison, *The Heritage Industry: Britain in a Climate of Decline* (London: Methuen, 1987), p. 1.

and 'history' as presented by Hewison is potentially unstable. It is sometimes difficult to distinguish his documentation of a politically directed packaging of the
past from a cruder modernism, a totalizing treatment of 'the past' as suspect. In
guarding against this outcome, it makes sense to follow Raphael Samuel, who
argues that neither preservationism, nor the past, is monolithic.[179] What needs to
be stressed is that Morris cannot fairly be identified with the 'heritage industry'.
Through his opposition to 'restoration', he undertook to debunk the popular
pursuit of historical authenticity. His position was not so different from
Hewison's or Ascherson's. Like them, he was sensitive to what is politically
expedient in domesticating 'historical' remnants, in effacing their 'hostility' or
difference from contemporary forms.

It is important, then, to appreciate just how willing Morris was to problematize
the very idea of preservation. Under certain conditions, he believed that some
kind of communion with another time might be possible; but he was also acutely
suspicious of the restorer's attempts to return ancient buildings to the ' "former
state" imagined [. . .] to be super-excellent'.[180] In this respect, Morris was moving
towards a theory of ideology, testing the limits of individual ability to transcend
the patterns of thought unique to one's age. He had his own 'super-excellent'
period, but quickly recognized that a policy of selectivity was not intellectually
sustainable, or indeed compatible with a wider public campaign. In the 'Report' to
the First Annual Meeting of the Society, Morris disclaimed any affiliation in the
'battle of styles', noting that amongst the organization's members were 'persons of
every shade of artistic opinion'.[181] The need to recruit the support of well-known
figures played a part in determining this policy. Replying to a letter from William
De Morgan on the subject of the SPAB campaign, Carlyle had alluded to the
endangered condition of Wren's City churches. Despite Morris's lack of affection
for the English baroque, a campaign to save the City churches was launched by the
SPAB, and Morris himself wrote publicly in its support. He made a similar intervention in the case of a plan to restore a 'medieval' high-pitched roof to Southwell
Minster. The flat ceiling, which had been installed in 1711, cannot have been to
Morris's taste. Yet he saw that it was in harmony with its setting, and that it made
little sense 'destroying a ceiling 167 years old' only 'to add one more to the many
imitations of ancient roofs'.[182]

Morris was attempting to place limits on the jurisdiction of present judge-
ments, querying the very possibility of an objective processing of historical
fragments. Yet, his questioning did not translate into a restrictive phenomenology.
The meaning of the marooned object was not conditioned exclusively by the
observer's sensory apparatus, or by his language system. This is to say that Morris
gave credence to the accessibility of the object where it constituted an inspiration
for reform or a source of instructive contrast. In such claims, we witness the
formation of a utopian epistemology:

[179] Raphael Samuel, *Theatres of Memory*, 2 vols (London: Verso, 1994), I, p. 306.
[180] Morris, 'To the Editor of *The Athenaeum*', 14 April 1877, in *Collected Letters*, I, pp. 361–3 (p. 362).
[181] Morris, 'Report', in 'The First Annual Meeting of the Society. Report of the Committee Thereat
Read', *Society for the Protection of Ancient Buildings*, 21 June 1878, 9–18 (p. 17).
[182] Morris, 'To the Ecclesiastical Commission for England and Wales', [29] July 1878, in *Collected
Letters*, I, pp. 490–3 (p. 492).

the honest man by the use of sufficient diligence can generally manage to see through the veil of sophistry into the genuine life which exists in those written records of the past; nay, the very lies themselves, being for the most part of a rough and simple nature, can often be dissolved and precipitated, so to say, into historical substance, into negative evidence of facts.[183]

There is therefore a conflict or, at the very least, a tension between Morris's acceptance of human captivity within present modes of thought, and the power to effect change he invests in historical fragments. It reproduces in a different medium the division between translations, like *The Odyssey of Homer*, that resign all attempt to represent Homeric diction in English, so abandoning the translator's conventional pursuit of 'the original', and the kind that render the heroic spirit of a poem like *Beowulf* in an 'authentic', archaically charged, English. However, the analogy is not perfect. The main difference between translation and preservation is that when one translates, there is no danger of inflicting damage on the original, unless to its reputation. The source text will always be available for consultation and further attempts at translation. A 'restored' building, on the other hand, no longer testifies to its former condition. By observing this distinction, Morris implied that historical artefacts could embody discernible otherness. This otherness was accessible to the present, accessible at least in so far as it could be destroyed by carelessness, arrogance or malign intention.

Even while a socialist, Morris attached a radical political value to the activity of preservation:

> Every one who tries to keep alive traditions of art by gathering together relics of the art of bygone times, still more if he is so lucky as to be able to lead people by his own works to look through Manchester smoke and squalor to fair scenes of unspoiled nature or deeds of past history, is helping us. Every one who tries to bridge the gap between the classes, by helping the opening of museums and galleries and gardens and other pleasures which can be shared by all, is helping us.[184]

As in the early short story, 'Frank's Sealed Letter', the importance of keeping memory 'green', of not succumbing to amnesia, is crucial to the argument Morris advances.[185] The events of this story also indicate that the process may be painful, that pain is often part of a useful remembering. The guardians of public buildings, Morris wrote in one letter, 'hold in their power the very seeds of Civilization to come'.[186] Yet the manner in which such structures coexist with the present must be awkward if they are to produce a response, a movement towards change. The relation between pain and redemption becomes most apparent at those moments when the issue of *convenience* arises.[187] The leading idea – that it was salutary to be 'startled into discomfort' by the contrast between past and present – could be a weak persuasive tool.[188] When justified in these terms, the case against insensitive

183   Morris, 'Architecture and History', in *Collected Works*, XXII (1884), pp. 296–317 (p. 297).
184   Morris, 'Art, Wealth, and Riches', p. 162.
185   Morris, 'Frank's Sealed Letter', p. 325.
186   Morris, 'Recipient Unknown', 4 September [1882], in *Collected Letters*, II, pp. 126–7 (p. 126).
187   See, for example, Morris, 'The Beauty of Life', pp. 68–9.
188   Morris, 'The Prospects of Architecture in Civilization', in *Collected Works*, XXII, pp. 119–52 (p. 122).

modernization was less effective in convincing architects to think again than were Morris's more compelling arguments against 'restoration'. This seems to have been the problem that dogged the SPAB's campaign to avert the widening of Magdalen Bridge in Oxford. Morris had argued that the proposed alterations would produce a permanent imbalance in the architectural harmony existing between the bridge and the buildings of the College. He also denied the necessity of increasing the capacity of this vital route into Oxford. In a letter to the *Pall Mall Gazette*, he stated that 'The Comm: of the S. P. A. B. do not hesitate to say [. . .] that they themselves believe it well worth keeping even at the expense of some considerable inconvenience to the neighbourhood'.[189] It is not surprising that an argument based on the primacy of aesthetic considerations should have gained no concessions from the planners. Unlike the restorers, they were motivated in the first instance by commercial convenience, by a desire to increase the flow of trade.

Morris states in 'Architecture and History' that 'this impossibility of reproduction is not accidental, but [. . .] essential to the conditions of life at the present day'.[190] This attention to the predicament of the nineteenth-century artist illuminates an apparent inconsistency at the heart of Morris's attacks on restoration. Celebrating the transhistorical character of a building, refusing to tie it down to a particular era, he asserted the value of a structure that testified to several pasts, rather than to the restorer's period-bound conception of a single, perfect past. (Morris regarded any given historical building as a 'tradition', best understood in T. S. Eliot's sense of the word, a sequence of additions harmonizing to form a greater whole that is continuously present.)[191] Sidney Colvin, in the article discussed earlier, argues along similar lines that 'a Gothic building [. . .] is like a living organism, naturally subject, in the course of its development, to successive adaptations and modifications of structure'.[192] The medieval parish churches beloved of Morris were particularly amenable to this way of thinking. Like the literary works he once compared to 'the kind of book which Mazzini called "Bibles"', they were 'in no sense the work of individuals', having 'grown up from the very hearts of the *people*'.[193] Unrestored churches, like Inglesham, near Kelmscot, attracted Morris's attention precisely because no original condition could be ascribed to them. The policy of the SPAB was nevertheless open to the objection that it did not accord nineteenth-century builders the right to make their own additions, even in the way that it accommodated eighteenth-century flat ceilings. This point was made in an unfavourable response to the SPAB's manifesto, which appeared in *The Builder*:

When, then, the society bids us, 'because we have no style of our own,' push the ancient buildings on to the by-ways of life, rather than touch one perishing stone

189 Morris, 'To the Editor of the *Pall Mall Gazette*', in *Collected Letters*, II, pp. 55–7 (p. 56).
190 Morris, 'Architecture and History', p. 299.
191 Eliot's theory of literary tradition recalls Morris's theory of architectural tradition: 'the existing monuments form an ideal order among themselves, which is modified by the introduction of the new (the really new) work of art among them', 'Tradition and the Individual Talent', in T. S. Eliot, *Selected Essays* (London: Faber and Faber, 1991), pp. 13–22 (p. 15).
192 Colvin, 'Restoration and Anti-Restoration', p. 456.
193 Morris, 'To the Editor of the *Pall Mall Gazette*', 2 February 1886, in *Collected Letters*, II, pp. 514–18 (p. 515).

that it contains, is not it exhibiting worship of the dead form instead of the living spirit in the most flagrant of ways? [. . .] to gather up our old buildings into a sort of *hortus siccus* for botanical study, – to extract from them the social life they may be made to retain, in order to put their skeletons in our museums.[194]

Why was it acceptable for the SPAB to freeze the development of Inglesham Church in the seventeenth century, when the last major additions were made to its furniture? Theoretically, Morris's position remains coherent if one accepts that some kind of fall has occurred, comparable to the linguistic 'fall' that necessitates the use of 'undegraded' English in his translations. This might be related to the division of labour, or to the advent of nineteenth-century historicism. Such a rupture in the continuity of history would disable the modern workman and prevent him from making his mark in a harmonious fashion. Nineteenth-century interventions might thus be condemned as 'unhistorical'.[195] There remains this problem, however: that Morris questioned the validity of modern additions solely in relation to the prevailing practice of attempting to recreate an imagined past. It is hard to say what he would have made of a Modernist, or at least non-historicist, approach. One suspects that the rigidity of this 'fall' narrative would have ruled out non-essential additions of all kinds.

In recent years, critics influenced by Michel Foucault's *Les mots et les choses*,[196] and by the New Historicism, have sought to question the positivistic, empirical mission informing the assemblage of artefacts in collections or museums. It is claimed that such institutions are based on the Baconian dream of '*a Model of the universal Nature made private*'.[197] In a similar spirit, Charles Saumarez Smith has written that 'one of the most insistent problems that museums face is precisely the idea that artefacts can be, and should be, divorced from their original context of ownership and use, and redisplayed in a different context of meaning, which is regarded as having a superior authority'.[198] Morris's concerned reflection that there is 'something melancholy about a museum' demonstrates that he was sensitive to issues of this kind.[199] Unable to reconcile modern calls for 'convenience' with the need to preserve the memory of the 'organic' ages, he felt obliged to advocate housing precious relics in public depositaries like the South Kensington Museum. Nevertheless, he remained uneasy with the idea of confining the once 'living' past within the distinctly inorganic bounds of a national collection. By

---

194 Horace Field, 'Protection of Ancient Buildings', *The Builder*, 8 September 1877, p. 915.
195 In contradistinction to the unhistorical modification of a building, Morris observes, in 'The Lesser Arts', that 'these old buildings have been altered and added to century after century, often beautifully, always historically; their very value, a great part of it, lay in that' (p. 19).
196 Michel Foucault, *Les mots et les choses: une archéologie des sciences humaines* (Paris: Éditions Gallimard, 1966).
197 In *Gesta Grayorum*, an account of the Gray's Inn revels of 1594–95, the advice of the Second Counsellor to the king, advocating the establishment of a large collection of objects housed in '*a small Compass*', is usually ascribed to Francis Bacon (William Canning, *Gesta Grayorum; or, The History of the High and Mighty Prince, Henry Prince of Purpoole* (London: W. Canning, 1688), p. 35).
198 Charles Saumarez Smith, 'Museums, Artefacts, and Meanings' in *The New Museology*, ed. by Peter Vergo (London: Reaktion Books, 1989), pp. 6–21 (p. 9).
199 Morris, 'The Lesser Arts', p. 17.

focusing on the preservation of *buildings* he also showed a determination to conserve at least the ghost of an 'original context'.[200]

Morris's concerns were nevertheless not those of the postmodern critic. He was unsettled by the idea that the object of preservation was *not* living, rather than worried that, in its effective inaccessibility, it was being cast as an observable presence. It is therefore important to recognize that he was responding less to the theoretical impossibility of such a project than to the fear that a distortion of the *true* past might be perpetrated. For, ideally, something of an earlier context was carried across in any Morrisian encounter with an artefact. Romance, as he defined it, was the 'capacity for a true conception of history, a power of making the past part of the present'.[201] A 'true conception of history' meant for Morris a living history. Museums, and campaigns for preservation, were the only means of achieving this in an age hostile to 'romance'. But such resorts were themselves symptoms of the same 'disease', that paralysis of historicism and self-consciousness diagnosed as the cause of the 'restoration' phenomenon. In the absence of an organic tradition, he was forced to conclude that his contemporaries had 'been simply filling windbags and weaving sand-ropes [. . .] in founding schools of art, National Galleries, South Kensington Museums, and all the rest of it'.[202]

Morris's work with the SPAB reflected his hope that historic relics might retain their integrity in the present; that, if left 'unrestored', they would remain exceptions to the logic of an 'inorganic' age. In so far as he associated surviving medieval buildings with 'romance', with a discernible alterity, the redemptive function attached to such structures might indeed be termed essentialist. It is important to distinguish this position from attempts to honour an original, authentic moment of production, located in a scientifically accessible past. The SPAB wanted to accommodate ancient buildings without assimilating them. Such a policy might be described as pluralistic in its conception of an ancient building as an historical continuum. The Society's determination not to take sides in the 'battle of styles' would also support this conclusion. Morris's quite legitimate opposition to the 'illiberal' procedures of 'restoration' does not then place any limits on the extent of stylistic tolerance. It is only through his hostility to modern additions that such limits are disclosed. By dividing the history of architecture into organic and inorganic ages, Morris invalidated present efforts in such a way that he produced a contradiction at the heart of his policy. The link between past and present, whose preservation the SPAB had worked towards, was thereby annulled. The hope that ancient buildings might serve to redeem the modern world was, by extension, cast into doubt.

---

[200] In 'How I Became a Socialist', Morris rejects attempts to 'make art a collection of the curiosities of the past which would have no serious relation to the life of the present' (p. 280).
[201] Morris, 'Address at the Twelfth Annual Meeting; 3 July 1889 ("Anti-Scrape")', p. 148.
[202] Morris, 'Art and the Beauty of the Earth', in *Collected Works*, XXII, pp. 155–74 (p. 171).

Conclusions

By travelling to Iceland, translating heroic literature, and preserving medieval buildings, Morris found methods of approaching difference, and thus of challenging the dominance of contemporary social forms. Implicit in this project was a confidence in the possibility of anachronism, of encounters in the present with the embodied fragments of a stranded past. In order to redeem the present, Morris applied the Götzist principle of instructive contrast. Yet just as the hero of Goethe's play eventually falls victim to the wiles of his guest, Weislingen, so Morris begins to appreciate the past's fragility. His confidence in the transcendental logic of Götzism is undermined by a growing suspicion that comparisons between past and present might not be managed on equal terms. This former optimism, Morris came later to believe, had been incompatible with the scale and nature of the problem. In the 1880s, he became convinced that variety, romance, and the other virtues he associated with unrestored buildings, would not succeed in challenging the *status quo*. Rather, they would succumb to it and reinforce it in the manner of most other attempts at reform. Hence his anti-parliamentary position, and his otherwise baffling lack of enthusiasm for the activities of the Arts and Crafts pioneers. The suspicion that radical politics would be co-opted or domesticated if it attempted to ' "moralize" capital' marked his most distinct movement away from the Ruskinian legacy.[203] It announced the faltering of his confidence in the redemptive power of the guest from another time, a challenge to his faith in the residual and salutary hostility of what hailed from elsewhere. Morris had begun to dismiss 'reactionary plans for importing the conditions of the production and life of the Middle Ages';[204] he was to speak instead of a necessary, apocalyptic, 'burning up of the gathered weeds'.[205] Even in these years, his creative activity continues unabated, exhibiting a practical recognition of the need, occasionally, to live life in the present, to put aside fears of palliation.[206] One might read into this stance some concurrent dissatisfaction with the official rhetoric of deferral, a determination, at least in his own life, to accommodate and enjoy the sources of romance still available to him. As will be demonstrated, Morris found various ways of maintaining, alongside an acceptance of dialectical materialism, his prior faith in the power of contrast and the utopian method of juxtaposing the past and the present.

203   Morris, 'The Hopes of Civilization', in *Collected Works*, XXIII, pp. 59–80 (p. 78).
204   Morris, 'The Hopes of Civilization', p. 77.
205   Morris, 'The Lesser Arts', p. 11.
206   Morris discussed this need in 'Making the Best of It'.

Chapter 4

UTOPIAN HOSPITALITY:
THE TEUTONIC 'HOUSE COMMUNITY'
AND THE HAMMERSMITH GUEST HOUSE

Introduction

The previous chapter explored three comparatively abstract manifestations of Morris's confidence that strangers or receptacles of alterity might serve to redeem a host society. Attention now returns to the arena of the idyllic society and the formal utopia. To what extent did Morris use the medieval and Teutonic language of hospitality to represent the dilemma of the stranger in utopia? Considering the accustomed hostility shown by ideal societies towards outsiders, what advantages and what dangers might attend such an approach? The first section of this chapter explores these questions in the context of the Germanic societies portrayed by Morris in *The House of the Wolfings* and *The Roots of the Mountains*. The focus then shifts to the similarly contained community of the medieval guild. The final section addresses the difficult question of representing dissent within a formal utopia. *News from Nowhere* plays on the outlandish, yet familiar, appearance of the emissary entertained within its limits. What might the experiences of William Guest, and the machinery of reception through which he progresses, disclose about the role of hospitality in fashioning tolerance?

H. G. Wells's speculative novel, *A Modern Utopia*, contains a discussion with an obvious bearing on the notion of 'utopian hospitality'. In order to 'maintain itself intact from outward force', the book's narrator asserts, the pre-Darwinian utopia was usually situated in 'a mountain valley or [on] an island'.[1] Indeed, the high value placed on isolation was reflected in a suspicion of strangers: the 'Republic of Plato', he notes, 'stood armed ready for defensive war', and 'the New Atlantis and the Utopia of More [. . .] like China and Japan [. . .] held themselves isolated from intruders'. These statements serve to bolster the narrator's central proposition that 'universal Toleration is certainly a modern idea', that conditions in a modern utopia were bound to be quite different from those obtaining in earlier republics.

This conscious rejection of the vulnerable static society in favour of the fully transformed *world* is in some respects the transition Morris's prose writings undergo in the 1880s. The primitive communities discussed in the first part of

---

[1] Wells, *A Modern Utopia*, pp. 11, 12, 31.

this chapter are in many respects dissimilar from the jealous city-states mentioned by Wells's narrator. Morris's formal utopia, in its defiant regionalism, has little in common with the 'World-state' proposed as an alternative. The relation Wells draws between past and present, between the old utopia and the new, nevertheless constitutes a useful way of distinguishing one phase of Morris's career from the next. He moved from the evocation of an idyllic but threatened existence in the Teutonic romances, to the portrayal of a utopian *world* in *News from Nowhere*. In the former, the problem of openness is explored in relation to the threat posed by an alien civilization (whether Romans or massing hordes); in *News from Nowhere*, it arises with regard to the 'modern' difficulty of accommodating 'strangers', of reconciling diversity with a unity sufficient to ensure social cohesion. I therefore discriminate in what follows between the society that, in its dealings with strangers, takes into account the 'breeding barbarian or the economic power' beyond its gates, and the society in which hospitality refers fundamentally to the internal question of tolerance, and to the tension between community and individuality. As Morris was a confirmed socialist by the time these romances were published, the division in treatment I propose might also refer to that between the utopian, but nevertheless pre-revolutionary situation described in *The House of the Wolfings* and *The Roots of the Mountains*, and the fully communist one, the global, post-revolutionary epoch portrayed in *News from Nowhere*.

Hospitality, Conflict and Social Change in *The House of the Wolfings* and *The Roots of the Mountains*

In the first chapter of *Socialism from the Root Up* – an explicatory tract written by Morris in collaboration with Ernest Belfort Bax – it is stated that 'history has no lessons' for the opponents of change.[2] To socialists, on the other hand, 'it gives both encouragement and warning'. This statement has a particular bearing on the works discussed in the first two sections of this chapter, in that they constitute idealizations of prior social forms written by a man who had converted to Marxian socialism, to an acceptance that history discloses a progressive momentum. In *The House of the Wolfings* and *The Roots of the Mountains*, there exists an obvious tension between Morris's primitivism and his recognition that the degeneration of ancient communism was a precondition for the expected triumph of communism in the modern era. The past is not accorded a privileged status because it exhibits a superior way of life or because it represents a site of loss and yearning. Its special status resides instead in its power to exhibit previous dialectical stages, evidences of the revolutionary reality to come.

   For Morris, whose intellectual roots were in Gothicist resistance to the cruder forms of utilitarianism, this insistence on forward movement inevitably raised questions. How was he to reconcile his desire to invest positive value in prior human types, like the medieval mason, and the Icelandic hero, with the Marxian recognition that the pre-commercial forms of most value – those, in fact, that

---

[2] 'Ancient Society' (*Commonweal*, 15 May 1886, p. 53) was the first chapter of *Socialism from the Root Up*, instalments of which appeared in *Commonweal* from 15 May 1886 to 19 May 1888.

defined the pre-capitalist era – were precisely those that had to give way if historical 'progress' was to be made? Accepting the necessity of a period of capitalism meant discounting the claim of individuals born into the wrong era to realizable hopes. It implied a rejection of the 'unrealistic', untimely, dreams of a Pelagius or a Robert Owen, a rejection of those 'castles in the air' condemned by Marx and Engels in *The Manifesto of the Communist Party* (1848).[3] But Morris was never quite able to substitute a cold, teleological acceptance of necessary waste in place of his accustomed, humanistic concern for the plight of the historically compromised individual. His prose romances of the 1880s dramatize a conflict between immediate hopes and historical necessity. They idealize a past era, but also, reluctantly, indicate its impending destruction. Indeed, the primitive virtues Morris valued most were precisely those implicated in the great change, in the subsequent 'degeneration' of tribal life into commercialism. Of these, it is the Teutonic love of hospitality famously recorded by Tacitus that he presents as the most admirable pre-commercial value and the most productive of change.[4] Hospitality emerges in these romances both as a humanizing force and as a stimulus to the 'necessary' but painful advent of feudalism, and then capitalism.

In the 'Ancient Society' chapter of *Socialism from the Root Up*, Morris and Bax describe the life of the Gothic *gentes* and tribes. These were the people about whom Tacitus wrote in his *Germania*. It is important to recognize that the information contained in 'Ancient Society' relied implicitly upon a particular scale of human development: that which Bax, who knew German, found summarized in Engels's *The Origin of the Family, Private Property and the State* (1884).[5] Details of this historiographic model were also available to both men in their original form, as set out in Lewis H. Morgan's book, *Ancient Society*.[6] Whether or not Morris read Morgan, he certainly had intelligence, via Bax, of the principles the American ethnologist had expounded.[7] Indeed, the strength of Bax's influence on the text of *Socialism from the Root Up* is obvious in its unsentimental account of the primitive life led by the German 'kindreds':

> the land was common in the sense that it was not the property of individuals, but it was not common to all comers; primitive society was formed, and man was no longer a mass of individuals, but the groups of this primitive society were narrow and exclusive; the unit of Society was the *Gens*, a group of blood-relations at peace among themselves, but which group was hostile to all other groups; within the Gens wealth was common to all its members, without it wealth was prize of war [. . .] The Tribe now took the place of the Gens; this was a larger and more artificial group, in which blood relationship was conventionally assumed [. . .] Finally, ancient Barba-

3 Karl Marx and Frederick Engels, *Manifesto of the Communist Party*, in *Collected Works*, 49 vols (London: Lawrence & Wishart, 1975–2001), Vol. 6, pp. 476–519 (p. 516).
4 Cornelius Tacitus, *Germania*, in *Tacitus in Five Volumes*, trans. by M. Hutton (London: William Heinemann, 1970), pp. 117–215 (p.165).
5 Frederick Engels, *The Origin of the Family, Private Property and the State, in the Light of the Researches by Lewis H. Morgan*, trans. by Alick West (London: Lawrence and Wishart, 1940).
6 Lewis H. Morgan, *Ancient Society; or, Researches in the Lines of Human Progress from Savagery through Barbarism to Civilization* (New York: Henry Holt and Company, 1878).
7 Morris was also in contact with Edward Carpenter, who acknowledged a debt both to Engels's *The Origin of the Family* and to Morgan's *Ancient Society* in his *Civilisation: Its Cause and Cure and Other Essays* (London: Swan Sonnenschien & Co., 1889), p. 5.

rism was transformed into ancient Civilisation, which, as the name implies, took the form of the life of the city.[8]

That the communism of the Teutonic past might hold lessons for the socialist is made clear in this passage. And yet the passing of 'barbarism' is never presented as a cause for regret. The brisk tone of the chapter betrays the conceptual importance of a progressive momentum, a forward movement whose underlying logic is not simply dialectical materialism, but also Morgan's upward scale of human development. Had Morris been the sole author of the piece, it is difficult to say how far he might have allowed a regretful tone to colour his account of this epoch. It is notable that his two Germanic romances encourage one to linger in the period, to dwell on its advantages in a way that the above description of 'narrow and exclusive' social groups does not. Indeed, these works take as their premise the one conceivably sentimental feature of Engels's account: his contention that the barbarians 'rejuvenated' northern Europe, that they bequeathed to it 'a genuine piece of gentile constitution, in the form of mark communities'.[9] According to this thesis, the political legacy of Teutonic life gave 'the oppressed class, the peasants, even under the harshest mediæval serfdom, a local centre of solidarity and a means of resistance such as neither the slaves of classical times nor the modern proletariat found ready to their hand'. Further to this, Engels argued that the 'milder form of servitude' current among the Gothic tribes allowed northern Europe to bypass the classical era of aristocracy and slavery. His analysis culminates in this concluding assertion, quoted from Morgan:

> Democracy in government, brotherhood in society, equality of rights and privileges, and universal education, foreshadow the next higher plane of society to which experience, intelligence and knowledge are steadily tending. *It will be a revival, in a higher form, of the liberty, equality and fraternity of the ancient gentes.*
>
> (Engels's italics, p. 204; quoting Morgan, p. 552)

In the light of Engels's optimism, Morris's decision to breathe life into the two stages of barbarism described by Morgan (that of the gens and that of the tribe) begins to seem less like an anti-progressivist gesture. To accept the broader, intellectual, significance of the material upon which the Teutonic romances are based is to admit a new complexity to any conception of Morris's purpose in eulogizing the past. One witnesses the extent to which his work reflected a wider concern, in socialist circles, to evoke continuities between the primitive past and the socialist future. It also becomes possible to understand his otherwise perverse celebration of a distant epoch, upon the passing of which present revolutionary hopes might seem to have depended. Signs nevertheless remain in Morris's work of a pained hesitation between the merits of the Teutonic past, and the doctrinal necessity of enacting its demise.

These romances are works of fiction, rather than serious attempts at historical reconstruction. It would nevertheless be a mistake, as Nicholas Salmon observes, to read *The House of the Wolfings* and *The Roots of the Mountains* 'out of context'.

---

[8] 'Ancient Society', *Socialism from the Root Up*, p. 53.
[9] Engels, *The Origin of the Family*, pp. 177, 178.

Salmon implies that 'they could not help but be inspired by his [Morris's] wider concerns and his impressive knowledge of late nineteenth century historiography'.[10] It is clear, first of all, that Morris found in certain historians of his time an alternative to the monastically inspired communism of More's *Utopia*, where 'nothing is private property anywhere'.[11] Nineteenth-century scholarship often differs from the work of twentieth-century historians in its unapologetic reliance on classical authorities, on documents that would no longer be considered reliable foundations for historical knowledge. Morris, and the historians of early German life contemporary with him, made considerable use of Julius Caesar's *De bello Gallico*[12] and Tacitus's *Germania*. Whether considered a serious attempt at ethnological description or a satirical attack on Roman decadence, it is obvious why the latter should have appealed to Morris: Tacitus's report that the Germans placed little value on silver and gold[13] provided him with suitable material upon which to base his own utopian rejection of civilized life. Crucially related to this conception of a society in which 'to exploit capital and to increase it by interest are unknown' is the stress on communality evident in Morris's Teutonic romances. This emphasis encompasses several important aspects of barbarism as described in nineteenth-century historiography: the organization of society along lines of blood relation, the territorial concept known as 'the mark', and the importance of the 'house' as a place of common resort and communal life. These features all imply a social life far removed from the propertied, nuclear family of the nineteenth century.

What, then, did Morris borrow from contemporary historians of Teutonic life? It is important at the outset to stress both his selectivity and the fact that the theories of marriage and kinship upon which he relied were sometimes incompatible. Matters are also complicated by the decision, in *The House of the Wolfings* and *The Roots of the Mountains*, to depict primitive peoples plotted at different points on Morgan's historical scale. In the former work, the narrator states that 'the men of one branch of kindred dwelt under one roof together', and that there were not 'many degrees amongst them as hath befallen afterwards, but all they of one blood were brethren and of equal dignity'.[14] The house here is the unchallenged centre of the community, a 'great hall', comparable to 'a church of later days that has a nave and aisles'. In *Ancient Society*, Morgan makes a related point:

> House architecture, which connects itself with the form of the family and the plan of domestic life, affords a tolerably complete illustration of progress from savagery to civilization. Its growth can be traced from the hut of the savage, through the communal houses of the barbarians, to the house of the single family of civilized nations, with all the successive links by which one extreme is connected with the other.[15]

10 Nicholas Salmon, 'A Study of Victorian Historiography: William Morris's Germanic Romances', *Journal of the William Morris Society*, XIV (Spring, 2001), 2, 59–89 (p. 84).
11 More, *Utopia*, p. 121.
12 Julius Caesar, *The Gallic War*, trans. by H. J. Edwards (London: William Heinemann, 1966).
13 Tacitus, *Germania*, pp. 137, 169.
14 Morris, *The House of the Wolfings*, pp. 5, 6.
15 Morgan, *Ancient Society*, p. 6.

According to what Morris gleaned from Bax, the reference to 'one branch of kindred' in *The House of the Wolfings* and the description of a totally communal living space would suggest that he had in mind a single gens.[16] Under normal circumstances, such a group would show hostility towards other groups within the tribe. (This much is also suggested by the passage quoted earlier from *Socialism from the Root Up.*) The communality achieved within the gens is thus balanced against the mercenary war-making it would pursue as a collective agent. Only with the removal of this state of assumed hostility could a utopian era of *tribal* communality commence.

The house community was an important category in the historiography of the period. It had been invoked, as was seen in Chapter Three, by George Dasent in his essay, 'The Norsemen in Iceland'.[17] In the form that Morgan and Engels understood it, the term originated in Heusler's concept of the 'Hausgenossenschaft':

> Among the Germans also, according to Heusler (*Institutionen des deutschen Rechts*), the economic unit was originally not the single family in the modern sense, but the 'house community', which consisted of several generations or several single families, and often enough included unfree persons as well.[18]

Since Morris could not read German, it seems likely that he derived his knowledge of primitive communal arrangements, first, from his reading of the sagas, and second, from the several histories of the mark readily accessible to him.[19] His lecture, 'The Revival of Architecture', contains a reference to 'the late John Richard Green and Professor Freeman'.[20] This allusion to two prominent historians of English history demonstrates a familiarity with the literature surrounding what John Kemble, in *The Saxons in England*, identified as one of 'the principles upon which the public and political life of our Anglosaxon [*sic*] forefathers was based'.[21] Kemble refers here to the mark, an area of 'waste' regarded as 'the property of the community', 'a space or boundary by which its own rights of jurisdiction are limited, and the encroachments of others are kept off'.

In *The Growth of the English Constitution from the Earliest Times*, Edward Freeman aimed to demonstrate that England's 'ancient history' was 'the possession of the Liberal'.[22] For him, the English parliament and the Swiss '*Gemeinde* or *Commune*', were descended from institutions originally transferred to England by the Anglo-Saxons, among them the democratic assembly and the respect for property enshrined in the mark. William Stubbs made a similar point in *The Constitutional History of England in its Origin and Development*:

> the mark system preserves in itself the two radical principles of German antiquity, the kindred and the community of land; and their primitive appurtenances, the

---

16 Morris, *The House of the Wolfings*, p. 5.
17 Dasent, 'The Norsemen in Iceland', p. 203.
18 Engels, *The Origin of the Family*, p. 62.
19 The word *mark* appears in the title of Morris's earlier romance, *A Tale of the House of the Wolfings and All the Kindreds of the Mark*.
20 Morris, 'The Revival of Architecture', in *Collected Works*, XXII, pp. 318–30 (p. 319).
21 Kemble, *The Saxons in England*, I, pp. v, 44, 46.
22 Edward A. Freeman, *The Growth of the English Constitution from the Earliest Times* (London: Macmillan and Co., 1872), pp. viii, 10.

wergild and compurgation, in which the kindred share the rights and responsibilities of the individual freemen; the right and obligation are based on the kindred, regulated by the land tenure, and subject to the general administration of the peace.[23]

The above sources informed John Green's description of the mark, in his *A Short History of the English People*:

> Each little farmer-commonwealth was girt in by its own border or 'mark,' a belt of forest or waste or fen which parted it from its fellow-villages, a ring of common ground which none of its settlers might take for his own.[24]

The historians mentioned thus far (Green, Freeman, Stubbs) depended in their conclusions upon a Whig interpretation of English history. In contrast to the progressive historical model posited by other dominant strands of liberalism, the emphasis was here placed on continuity, on a legitimizing continuum linking Anglo-Saxon 'liberty' to the institutions of nineteenth-century England. From the earlier works inhabiting this tradition – Sharon Turner's *The History of the Anglo-Saxons*, in particular – these historians inherited an agenda that remained more or less intact until the late Victorian period.[25] The idea was to establish a pre-Norman precedent for parliamentary democracy, and thereby challenge the traditional Tory claim to lineal primacy in constitutional matters.[26]

Morris, on the other hand, had by this time lost all faith in the idea of reform or restitution. His interest in the mark had more in common with the revolutionary stance of Engels. He recognized in it a method of challenging the universalist claims of the bourgeois family, and of establishing a precedent for the sharing of property. Morris's second Teutonic romance, *The Roots of the Mountains*, opens with a passage of description that associates the story with a later stage on Morgan's scale of development. There is no reference to the mark. The living arrangements are still communal, it being the case that 'many men dwelt in each house'.[27] However, numbers of houses are now clustered within a defined area, the result being that the single focus of the ancestral hall is replaced by a comparatively dispersed pattern of settlement. There is also a strong suggestion that the bond of communality has ceased to be strictly filial, becoming instead conventional. People are included in the community because they are '*deemed* to be of the kindred' (my emphasis), not because they are strictly of it. The gens, it seems, has melted into the tribe, producing a union of households retaining at least the notional acceptance of shared ancestry. Basing itself on the assumption of interrelatedness, the communistic way of life of the earlier stage is retained, but it lacks sure bonds of blood, and the state of assumed hostility between households of the previous stage no longer obtains.

23 William Stubbs, *The Constitutional History of England in its Origin and Development*, 3 vols (Oxford: Clarendon Press, 1874–78), I, p. 53.
24 J. R. Green, *A Short History of the English People* (London: Macmillan, 1874), p. 3.
25 Sharon Turner, *The History of the Anglo-Saxons from their First Appearance above the Elbe to the Death of Egbert*, 4 vols (London, 1799–1805).
26 For an account of the complex, shifting history of Whig historiography see J. W. Burrow, *A Liberal Descent: Victorian Historians and the English Past* (Cambridge: Cambridge University Press, 1981).
27 Morris, *The Roots of the Mountains*, pp. 8, 18.

It is with respect to customs of hospitality that Morris's idealization of primitive societies becomes truly apparent. In this area, the behaviour of his fictional subjects departs from the factual account of a 'narrow and exclusive' society contained in *Socialism from the Root Up*.[28] This subject may be broken down into two parts: the first dealing with the status of the stranger in these societies; the second, with their marriage customs and the times at which members of the kindred were obliged to venture beyond their immediate social group. Tacitus, in his *Germania*, ascribed to the German tribes the typically utopian characteristics of isolation and racial purity, noting that they had only 'very slightly blended with new arrivals from other races or alliances'.[29] Kemble, with his insistent stress on territory, carries this 'state of isolation' over into his own account of Germanic institutions.[30] The mark, he states, was 'unsafe, full of danger', a piece of ground that would not suffer profanation by the stranger: 'death lurks in its shades and awaits the incautious or hostile visitant'. Green treats this theme in his descriptions of settlements 'jealous' of their 'independence', and in his reference to the lawful slaying of unannounced strangers.[31]

Tacitus, however, notes a contrary impulse among the Germans. There is, he finds, a concurrent concern for the rights of the outsider; or, at least, of outsiders who are members of the wider tribe or nation. This is expressed partly through an emphasis on the traditionally integrative activities of banqueting and admitting guests:

> No race indulges more lavishly in feasting and hospitality: to close the door against any human being is a crime. Every one according to his property receives at a well-spread board: when it has come to an end, he who had been your host points out your place of entertainment and goes with you. You go next door, without an invitation, but it makes no difference; you are received with the same courtesy. Stranger or acquaintance, no one distinguishes them where the right of hospitality is concerned.[32]

The Teutonic unwillingness to make a distinction between the stranger and the acquaintance was discussed first by Morgan, and then by Engels, who notes that 'Tacitus' description of hospitality as practised among the Germans is identical almost to the details with that given by Morgan of his Indians'.[33] Morgan attributed '*The right of adopting strangers into the gens*' to most of the early societies he analysed, but gave special attention to the Iroquois.[34] In that case, sufficient remnants of ancient practices survived to form the basis of an ethnographic study. Morgan's thesis was premised upon the assertion that 'since mankind were one in origin, their career has been essentially one'. This equivalence of experience meant that the particular might function to illuminate the general. The 'history and experience of the American Indian tribes', he assured his readers, 'represent, more

---

[28] 'Ancient Society', *Socialism from the Root Up*, p. 53.
[29] Tacitus, *Germania*, p. 131.
[30] Kemble, *The Saxons in England*, I, pp. 46, 47, 48.
[31] Green, *A Short History of the English People*, p. 3.
[32] Tacitus, *Germania*, pp. 163–5.
[33] Engels, *The Origin of the Family*, p. 157.
[34] Morgan, *Ancient Society*, pp. vii, 80.

or less nearly, the history and experience of our own remote ancestors when in corresponding conditions'. The fact that the Iroquois occasionally adopted captives taken in war into the gens, and that 'women and children taken prisoners usually experienced clemency in this form' was supposed, according to this proposition, to yield something quite specific about the customs of the Teutonic tribes. This followed because they were deemed to inhabit a similar stage of civilization as the Iroquois.

Morris's Teutonic romances demonstrate a far from superficial engagement with these debates. In the opening description of the Wolfing people, one learns that 'they had servants or thralls [. . .] men of alien blood'.[35] It is then stated that 'from time to time were some of such men taken into the House, and hailed as brethren of the blood'. References to 'the guesting cup' and the 'guest-fain cooking-fire', and several instances of 'adoption', including that of Fox the Red, indicate that Morris wanted his fictional subjects to share the flexibility Morgan and Engels attributed to kindred societies. At the same time, there is a revealing omission of the more extreme measures mentioned by Green, notably those designed to protect the mark from profanation.[36] This selectivity of approach reveals what is utopian in Morris's depiction of primitive life. The taste for violent solutions exhibited in *The Defence of Guenevere* and *Sigurd the Volsung* confirms that Morris's modification of sources stemmed less from squeamish or sentimental proclivities than from a concern to evoke a particular kind of fellowship, one combining the communal feeling arising from a shared sense of kinship with receptivity to what is alien. A version of this principle is articulated at one point by Hall-Sun:

> Surely, mother: all men who bring peace with them are welcome guests to the Wolfings: nor will any ask thine errand, but we will let thy tidings flow from thee as thou wilt. This is the custom of the Kindred, and no word of mine own.[37]

Both the hero who leads the tribe to victory, and Hall-Sun, the vestal warden of the communal household, are outsiders fostered by the kindred. The willingness of the Wolfings to cancel the hostility one might expect them to show towards outsiders reaches a climax at the end of the tale. As soon as the outcome of the great battle is clear, the reader is told that 'without the Roof feasted the thralls and the strangers, and the Roman war-captives'. The continuation of the feast beyond the walls of the hall seems to herald a new era of inclusiveness.

One might expect even fewer restrictions to limit hospitality in a society where the bond between household members has become more conventional, less dependent on blood. In *The Roots of the Mountains*, the people of Burgstead maintain useful trading relations with their neighbours. Among these are a Shepherd-Folk, who deck their halls 'mostly with the handiwork of the Woodland-Carles their guests'.[38] The rhythms and conventions of hospitality also inform Gold-mane's visit to the Mountain Hall, where the descendants of the

---

35 Morris, *The House of the Wolfings*, pp. 5, 61, 63.
36 Green, *A Short History of the English People*, p. 3.
37 Morris, *The House of the Wolfings*, pp. 76, 207.
38 Morris, *The Roots of the Mountains*, pp. 7, 38.

Wolfings live. Here he must overcome an initial show of hostility – in effect, a test of his worthiness – that culminates in his assuring Sun-beam he will be her guest, not her stranger (cf. *The Winter's Tale*).[39] Henceforth, he is known to them as *Guest*. When the Burgdalers hold a 'Yule-tide play', it is a scene of hospitality that they choose to enact.[40] In the conventional announcement, 'Enter ye, whether ye be friends or foes: for if ye be foemen, yet shall ye keep the holy peace of Yule, unless ye be the foes of all kindreds and nations, and then shall we slay you', the broad embrace is made explicit. It is qualified only by the contingency of self-defence.

The suggestion that communal units will rely for deliverance and renewal upon either a guest, a stranger (as in the case of Thiodolf and Hall-Sun), or a captive, is relevant to Morris's attempt at lessening the more exclusive implications of kindred society. Such matters should be viewed in the context of the controversy documented by Nicholas Salmon,[41] concerning the competing claims of Morgan and the British ethnologist, John F. McLennan. In *Primitive Marriage*, McLennan outlined his thesis that among tribes whose normal state was that of mutual enmity – where no 'distinction is drawn between strangers and enemies' – a principle of exogamy was observed.[42] He defined this principle as one that '*prohibited marriage within the tribe*'. It followed, necessarily, that 'while this state of enmity lasted, exogamous tribes never could get wives except by theft or force'. He contrasts this rule with that observed by endogamous tribes, which prohibited their members from marrying out. McLennan's theory of early marriage practices found no favour with Engels, whose emphasis on the early supremacy of 'mother-right' – a form of social organization conveniently opposed to bourgeois conventions of patriarchy and monogamy – relied upon Morgan's denial of any distinction between exogamous and endogamous tribes.[43] Morgan proposed the alternative thesis that while members of any given gens were obliged to take partners from a different gens, marriages would not extend beyond the umbrella of the tribe. Hence no policy of abduction, actual or conventional, would be required. Salmon argues that Morris '*must* have been aware of these conflicting accounts'.[44] He bases this conviction on May Morris's recollection that her father read 'with critical enjoyment the more important modern studies' of the period covered loosely by *The House of the Wolfings*.[45] He also refers to Morris's discussion of marriage customs in 'The Development of Modern Society' (in which Morris states that 'it used to be thought that violent robbery was the method, but I believe the second method was the one used' [i.e. Morgan's method]).[46] Having considered the evidence, Salmon reaches the following conclusion:

39 Shakespeare, *The Winter's Tale*, I.ii.54.
40 Morris, *The Roots of the Mountains*, pp. 68, 69.
41 Salmon, 'A Study of Victorian Historiography'.
42 John F. McLennan, *Primitive Marriage: An Inquiry into the Origin of the Form of Capture in Marriage Ceremonies* (Edinburgh: Adam and Charles Black, 1865), pp. 53, 54, 133.
43 Engels, *The Origin of the Family*, p. 41.
44 Salmon, 'A Study of Victorian Historiography', p. 65.
45 May Morris, Introduction, *Collected Works*, XIV, pp. xv–xxix (p. xxv).
46 Morris, 'The Development of Modern Society', *Commonweal*, 19 July 1890, pp. 225–6 (p. 226).

Although the above would seem to suggest that by 1890 Morris had come down firmly on the Engels/Morgan side of the debate, in the Germanic romances he displays a knowledge of both sides of the argument and makes a number of important contributions of his own.[47]

The details of this controversy have a direct bearing on the question of hospitality, on the regulations governing the admission of strangers into a household and the circumstances under which such an event might take place. Engels, commenting on the marriage customs of Australian Aborigines, makes this relationship transparent:

> wandering hundreds of miles from his home among people whose language he does not understand, [he] nevertheless often finds in every camp and every tribe women who give themselves to him without resistance and without resentment; the law by which the man with several wives gives one up for the night to his guest. Where the European sees immorality and lawlessness, strict law rules in reality. The women belong to the marriage group of the stranger.[48]

In Morris's Germanic romances, there is no sign of any 'marriage group of the stranger', but there are several direct allusions to 'matters of kinship and affinity'.[49] The reader learns that the 'men of one House might not wed the women of their own House', that 'to the Wolfing men all Wolfing women were as sisters'. They must wed instead with 'such Houses of the Mark as were not so close akin to the blood of the Wolf', a 'law that none dreamed of breaking'. In *The Roots of the Mountains*, Gold-mane's romantic dilemma is expressed succinctly in his insistence, prior to breaking off the match, on calling his intended bride, 'kinswoman':

> 'Nay,' said Iron-face, 'call her not kinswoman: therein is ill-luck, lest it seem that thou art to wed one too nigh thine own blood. Call her the Bride only: to thee and to me the name is good'.[50]

Gold-mane is here rebuked for confusing the categories of the marriageable and the unmarriageable. The 'bride', it is asserted, 'was a woman born to be the ransom of her Folk'. She is sufficiently far away in kin to represent a suitable token of the household's reliance on the system of gentes.

By incorporating the regulations governing marriage described by Morgan, Morris announces an extension of his concern with hospitality, with a formalized accommodation of what is external, but also essential to, the continuance of household life. It is accordingly significant that Morris also finds a place for McLennan's less co-operative account of marriage customs. The description of the 'Dusky Men', the hordes who threaten to overwhelm the peaceable society cradled in Burdgale, shows clear signs of this influence:

> Whereas both the Markmen and the Burgdalers conform to the type of endogamous tribe composed of interrelated gens described by Engels in *The Origin of the Family*,

---

47 Salmon, 'A Study of Victorian Historiography', p. 65.
48 Engels, *The Origin of the Family*, p. 45.
49 Morris, *The House of the Wolfings*, p. 5.
50 Morris, *The Roots of the Mountains*, pp. 17, 68.

Morris's description of the sexual practices of the Dusky Men (the Huns) is based on McLellan's [*sic*] alternative definition of a strictly exogamous tribe in which inter-marriage is impermissible and wives had to be forcibly obtained by abducting them from the neighbouring hostile tribes.[51]

The 'Dusky Men' do not value women of their own blood, and therefore slay their female children. They procure mates by beguiling 'wayfarers', and invading neighbouring settlements.[52] Morris ascribes to this marauding race a mixture of cruelty, deviant sexuality, and parasitism. They threaten to disrupt the flow of partners between the remaining gens, replacing a system based on exchange with one relying purely upon consumption.

The Teutonic societies Morris treats in these romances stand in obvious opposition to the 'civilized' existence of urban life. The popular Victorian myth of Germanic freedom and independence (discussed in Chapter Three) emerges here as an approach to land settlement and decision-making distinct from that associated with the classical polis. Other than in the sagas, Morris would have found this idea articulated by Tacitus, who restated the apparently commonplace assertion that 'none of the German tribes live in cities'.[53] In the ethnological work known to Morris, these two forms of society – the village and the city – were also seen as diametrically opposed:

> The experience of mankind, as elsewhere remarked, has developed but two plans of government [. . .] Under the first a gentile society was created, in which the government dealt with persons through their relations to a gens and tribe. These relations were purely personal. Under the second a political society was instituted, in which the government dealt with persons through their relations to territory, *e.g.* – the township, the country, and the state. These relations were purely territorial. The two plans were fundamentally different. One belongs to ancient society, and the other to modern.[54]

Describing Solon's legendary division of Athenian society into 'three classes, irrespective of gentes', Morgan argued that the growth of cities was intertwined with 'recognition of property' and the formation of an 'aristocratic element' or class system. Morris's statement of his aims in writing historical romances confirms the inference encouraged by this research: that in dramatizing a conflict between the Gothic tribes and the Romans, he was illustrating 'the melting of the individual into the society of the tribes', and portraying an alternative to urban life.[55]

Explicit reference is made to this conflict at several points in *The House of the Wolfings*. The Romans are described as 'the folk of the cities'.[56] In the eyes of the kindreds, they do not simply live amidst material, and architectural, confusion (in

---

51 Salmon, 'A Study of Victorian Historiography', p. 81.
52 Morris, *Roots of the Mountains*, p. 203.
53 Tacitus, *Germania*, p. 155.
54 Morgan, *Ancient Society*, pp. 62, 260.
55 Morris, 'To [Thomas James Wise?]', 17 November [1888], in *Collected Letters*, II, pp. 835–6 (p. 836).
56 Morris, *The House of the Wolfings*, pp. 21, 45.

dwelling 'mid confusion of heaped houses'); they have also violated the old familial system (the organization of a people into gentes whose emphasis on blood ties confers a self-reinforcing, self-naturalizing identity). At one point in the tale, an Elking warrior informs the Wolfings that the correspondence between habitation and kindred has ceased among the Romans. Their unit of settlement, the city, comprises no system of gentes:

> they have forgotten kindred, and have none, nor do they heed whom they wed, and great is the confusion amongst them. And mighty men among them ordain where they shall dwell, and what shall be their meat, and how long they shall labour after they are weary [...] and though they be called free men who suffer this, yet may no house or kindred gainsay this rule and order. In sooth they are a people mighty, but unhappy.

Morris's polemical intent becomes increasingly apparent as the parallels between the Marxist account of nineteenth-century capitalism and the slave society of Rome accumulate. Individualism, and a worship of gold, effectively render the Roman legions a mercenary force (cf. Edward Gibbon's *The Decline and Fall of the Roman Empire*).[57] The Wolfings find ways to exploit these characteristics.[58] The Roman Captain fights in pursuit of fame, but 'he had no will to die among the Markmen, either for the sake of the city of Rome, or of any folk whatsoever', being happier 'to live for his own sake'.[59] At the crucial moment, 'the faint-heart folly of the Roman Captain' saves his foes. The implied distinction is that between the kind of selfhood produced by an atomized society and that nurtured by the collective, transhistorical life of the tribe.

However, the comparison Morris invites is not between a stratified, individualistic society and a purely communistic utopia. As John Goode argues, he gave particular attention to this epoch precisely because 'it seemed to offer a point in time when the needs of the individual for private freedom were balanced with maximum equilibrium against the coherence of the community'.[60] Goode adds that the 'Germanic *gens* is used ideologically as an example of what is good or might be good in a social structure'. In a similar vein, Salmon argues that 'Morris's intention in detailing the customs of the tribes is not to establish a link with modern institutions but to provide his readers with a model against which to judge their legitimacy'.[61] Nevertheless, the comparison with modern society is only advantageous, and thus politically effective, because Morris makes it clear that the rigidity of kinship is qualified by hospitable, social impulses. What might be considered the merits of city life – the scope for individuality amidst

---

57 Gibbon wrote: 'Barbarians are urged by the love of war [...] but the timid and luxurious inhabitants of a declining empire must be allured [...] by the hopes of profit', *The History of the Decline and Fall of the Roman Empire*, 6 vols (London, 1776–88), II, p. 48.
58 In 'The History of Pattern-Designing', Morris writes of the Roman Empire in its declining years: 'the old classical exclusiveness is gone for ever [...] when the Roman army goes afield, marching now as often to defeat as victory, it may well be that no Italian goes in its ranks to meet the enemies of Rome', in *Collected Works*, XXII, 206–34 (p. 223).
59 Morris, *The House of the Wolfings*, pp. 133–4, 155.
60 John Goode, 'William Morris and the Dream of Revolution', in *Collected Essays of John Goode*, ed. by Charles Swann (Keele, Staffordshire: Keele University Press, 1995), pp. 272–319 (p. 305).
61 Salmon, 'A Study of Victorian Historiography', p. 73.

anonymity, for instance – are not then sacrificed. Instead, they are successfully spliced with the benefits of communality. It is significant, in the light of these remarks, that Morris retains the comparison with the urban way of life in *The Roots of the Mountains*. Gold-mane frequently expresses a suspicion of 'the Plain and its Cities'.[62] Despite the absence of Romans, a similar contrast between forms of political and kindred life is maintained. Morris also chooses to introduce a new enemy, one embodying the opposite extreme, a communism at once demeaning and hostile to expressions of individuality:

> thou must not deem of these felons as if they were of like wits to us [. . .] Rather they move like to the stares in autumn, or the winter wild-geese, and will all be thrust forward by some sting that entereth into their imaginations.

This characterization of the Dusky Men would seem to vindicate Goode's emphasis on the Morrisian avoidance of extremes, whether of selfishness or absolute conformity. Both romances illustrate the achievement of what he calls a 'maximum equilibrium' between individualism and communality.[63] This attribute neither derives from, nor fosters, immunity to change; it resides instead in the shock dealt to the societies depicted, a threat to the integrity of community sufficient to deliver them from complacency and monotony. This effect is achieved in *The House of the Wolfings* and *The Roots of the Mountains* by means of an outbreak of armed struggle. The arrival of a new opponent strengthens solidarity and sociability among the defenders. 'Folkmotes' are held, feasts are given, and leaders are elected. When the mass of fighting men and women act in unison, heroes emerge whose actions reinforce the suggestion that the virtues of community have reached some sort of reconciliation with individuality. Amidst societies existing with their neighbours in a perpetual state of mutual hostility, the growth of hierarchy is continually restrained by the levelling impact of war.

In *The House of the Wolfings* and *The Roots of the Mountains*, this consideration is less important than the extraordinary situation presented by the arrival, respectively, of the Romans and the Dusky Men. In *The House of the Wolfings*, individual gentes combine in order to meet the threat, thereby forming an enormous host of warriors. Scenes of hospitable entertainment highlight the role ritual plays in softening differences and laying them in abeyance.[64] The 'joy of fighting for the kindred' becomes the primary impulse in the conflict that follows. This phrase evokes both Morris's attempts to reconcile work and play, and his less palatable conviction that conflict has an integrative social function. When the battle ends in triumph for the kindreds, the formation of a new collective, a social group born of the struggle, is marked by a great feast:

> But ye kindreds of the Markmen, the Wolfing guests are ye,
> And to-night we hold the high-tide, and great shall the feasting be.

By the time of events in *The Roots of the Mountains*, this formalized unity – where the laws of hospitality continue to police the congregation of separate social

62 Morris, *The Roots of the Mountains*, pp. 20, 253.
63 Goode, 'William Morris and the Dream of Revolution', p. 305.
64 Morris, *The House of the Wolfings*, pp. 74, 145, 200.

entities – has given way to a less exclusive form of society. As in *The House of the Wolfings*, an outbreak of war serves to catalyse further aggregation of communal units. The people of Burgdale form an alliance with the folk Gold-mane meets in the mountains. The two peoples become 'friends and brothers in arms'.[65] Beyond the circumstances of Gold-mane's love affair, and its responsibility for forging fellowship between kindreds, the new collaborative effort is justified by 'the old saw' that 'grief in thy neighbour's hall is grief in thy garth'. When the Burgdalers meet escaped captives, and when they liberate large numbers of slaves from the valley occupied by the Dusky Men, the integrative function of hospitality is again made evident. One 'runaway' is dealt with in the fashion of 'a woman cherishing a son', a comparison that highlights the flexible conception of *kindred* employed by Morris. When the escapees reach Burgdale, the inhabitants compete to make the newcomers feel at home:

> some of the good folk that lived hard by must needs fare home to their houses to fetch cakes and wine for the guests; and they made them sit down and rest on the green grass by the side of the Portway, and eat and drink to cheer their hearts.

The hospitality is rehabilitating. The physical health of these freed slaves begins to improve. Indeed, it becomes symbolical of Burgdale's accommodating, life-enhancing civilization:

> The Alderman laughed, and said: 'If they be Gods they are welcome indeed; and they shall grow the wiser for their coming; for they shall learn how guest-fain the Burgdale men may be. But if, as I deem, they be like unto us, and but the children of the Gods, then are they as welcome, and it may be more so, and our greeting to them shall be as their greeting to us would be.

The new arrivals are given gifts from the treasury and, in this way, reabsorbed into a culture of ceaseless exchange.

The emergence of a struggle in scale above and beyond the means of any individual gens has further significance. Speaking of the mark-community in *The Saxons in England*, Kemble wrote that 'the natural tendency [. . .] of this state of isolation is to give way'.[66] As the countryside becomes more populous, the clearings expand until 'the next step is the destruction of the Marks themselves, and the union of the settlers in larger bodies'. When the herdsmen from different communities first meet, 'one of three courses appears unavoidable: the communities must enter into a federal union; one must attack and subjugate the other; or the two must coalesce into one on friendly and equal terms'. This process, as it concerns Saxon England, is repeated 'until the family becomes a tribe, and the tribe a kingdom'. In Morris's romances, the combination of gentes is provoked not by scarcity of land, but by conflict. The immediate consequences of assimilation include victory in war and a season of sociability. Morris's decision to locate his romances on Morgan's scale of development also encourages the conclusion that permanent assimilation of the gentes into a tribe (or of the tribes into a nation) is

---

65 Morris, *The Roots of the Mountains*, pp. 117, 196, 210, 236, 249.
66 Kemble, *The Saxons in England*, I, pp. 48–9.

only a short step away.[67] At the end of *The Roots of the Mountains*, many Burgdale men choose to stay in Rosedale, never returning to Burgdale, 'save as guests'.[68] The Burgdale men, equally, promise a home and livelihood to the 'once-enthralled folk of Rosedale'. These suggestions of loosening exclusivity culminate in the following agreement between the two peoples:

> since ye have joined yourselves to us in battle, and have given us this Dale, our health and wealth, without price and without reward, we deem you our very brethren, and small shall be our hall-glee, and barren shall our Doom-ring seem to us, unless ye sit there beside us. Come then, that we may rejoice each other by the sight of face and sound of voice; that we may speak together of matters that concern our welfare; so that we three Kindreds may become one Folk.

In the closing paragraph, it is stated that the 'Men of Burgdale and the Sheepcotes; and the Children of the Wolf, and the Woodlanders, and the Men of Rosedale' were 'friends henceforth, and became as one Folk'.

When describing the Saxon conquest of England, Green argued that the need for organization and leadership among allied tribes meant that 'war begat the King and the military noble', and 'all but begat the slave'.[69] In both romances, Morris describes the election of a tribal leader according to a similar linkage of circumstances. The event is portrayed as a positive development because it seems to harness the freely expressed will of the 'people'. It is unlikely, however, that Morris was blind to the wider changes portended by the arrival of kings, notably the emergence of aristocracy and private property. The unification of peoples described at the end of *The Roots of the Mountains* presents a similar case. The end result of a hospitality that extends the concept of 'brethren' beyond the bounds of possible kinship is weakening of the kindred qualification, the social bond presented as the basis for community and equality between group members. In *The House of the Wolfings*, Thiodolf's defiant speech gestures towards a pluralistic conception of the gens at the same time as it announces a vital weakening of the blood ties upon which the group is founded:

> For whereas thou sayest that I am not of their blood, nor of their adoption, once more I heed it not. For I have lived with them, and eaten and drunken with them, and toiled with them, and led them in battle and the place of wounds and slaughter; they are mine and I am theirs.[70]

The course of events that makes possible Thiodolf's role as an alien war-leader is linked directly to the change described in *Socialism from the Root Up*, whereby 'The Tribe [. . .] took the place of the Gens'.[71]

This move towards a more flexible and more accommodating conception of the social group contains the germ of several events conducive to adverse change. Engels's explanation of the fall of kindred society among the Romans was based

[67]   Morgan, *Ancient Society*.
[68]   Morris, *The Roots of the Mountains*, pp. 394, 408, 411.
[69]   Green, *A Short History of the English People*, pp. 12–13.
[70]   Morris, *The House of the Wolfings*, p. 170.
[71]   'Ancient Society', *Socialism from the Root Up*, p. 53.

upon the understanding that dissolution of blood ties brought about a loss of social coherence.[72] He points to the subsequent emergence of private property, to the development of cities, the growth of slavery, and the rise of a merchant class in the final stage of barbarism. The Germanic tribes are thus seen to pass through the points in the scale of development already reached by classical civilization. This course of events is also described in *Socialism from the Root Up*, as the moment when 'ancient Barbarism was transformed into ancient Civilisation, which [. . .] took the form of the life of the city'.[73] According to Engels, the vacuum created by the weakening gens encouraged the development of new evaluative systems, among them the economic method of classifying individual worth. With the ceasing of the kindred qualification, people could be traded and exchanged in the same way that commodities were. Hence, the fall of the gens meant a collapse of the limits placed on human exchangeability. In *The House of the Wolfings*, it is possible to infer a hint at the eventual degeneration of kindred civilization from the doom-laden poem declaimed by an ancient man of the Daylings.[74] He narrates a symbolic encounter between a weary, hungry man, and a stranger:

> I came to the house of the foeman when hunger made me a fool;
> And the foeman said, 'Thou art weary, lo, set thy foot on the stool;'
> And I stretched out my feet, – and was shackled: and he spake with a
>   dastard's smile,
> 'O guest, thine hands are heavy; now rest them for a while!'
> So I stretched out my hands, and the hand-gyves lay cold on either wrist:
> And the wood of the wolf had been better than that feast-hall, had I wist
> That this was the ancient pitfall, and the long expected trap,
> And that now for my heart's desire I had sold the world's goodhap.

Here, the naïve assumptions and the nascent desires of the barbarian lead him into a state of slavery. This course of events fits with Morgan's analysis of the development of property. He states that 'when property had become created in masses, and its influence and power began to be felt in society, slavery came in; an institution violative of all these principles, but sustained by the selfish and delusive consideration that the person made a slave was a stranger in blood and a captive enemy'.[75] Morgan thus highlights the crucial link between the development of property and the growth of an attitude of ownership towards strangers.

In *The House of the Wolfings* and *The Roots of the Mountains* captives and outsiders are treated very well. At the end of each romance a large number are either absorbed into the gens or kept as thralls, thereby compromising the assumption of interrelatedness. It is fair to read this outcome as an indication that the Burgdalers, in particular, are moving into the next stage of civilization. Morgan describes this as the phase when 'the creation and protection of property became the primary objects of the government, with a superadded career of

---

72 Engels, *The Origin of the Family*, p. 146.
73 'Ancient Society', *Socialism from the Root Up*, p. 53.
74 Morris, *The House of the Wolfings*, p. 73.
75 Morgan, *Ancient Society*, pp. 339, 341.

conquest for domination over distant tribes and nations'. Morris himself classified it as 'the time [. . .] when warring tribes began to make their conquered enemies slaves instead of killing them'.[76] The difficulty of combining a secure and self-contained order of society with a policy of openness arises as a result. It is in many ways the central problem presented by utopian hospitality. In *Comparative Politics*, Edward Freeman considers this question as it concerns the growth of cities in the Teutonic lands, conglomerations that were eventually forced to restrict the franchise of their membership:

> There is commonly a stage in the history of a city Commonwealth, that stage which in the Roman legend is represented by the Asylum of Romulus, in which the new-born city is liberal of its franchise to strangers who are ready to throw in their lot to the new community, and so to add to its strength. Then comes a stage in which citizenship begins to be too highly valued to be given to all who ask for it, when the original citizens shrink up into an oligarchic body, with a large mass around them, who share only an imperfect citizenship, or no citizenship at all. [. . .] Thus there arises an excluded class, strangers in the place where perhaps they were born, where their forefathers may even have lived for several generations.[77]

Freeman's argument depends elsewhere on the assertion that 'the nations of the Teutonic race, alike in Germany, in Britain, and Scandinavia, grew from tribes into nations without ever going through the Greek stage of a system of isolated cities', and that the affinity and rights accorded by a membership of nation mitigated the effects of exclusion from the civic franchise. Yet whether one speaks of ancient Greece or feudal England, in 'neither case does the civic franchise belong to every man who chooses to go and dwell within the civic boundary'. Admission to the citizenry 'always requires that particular qualification which is fixed by the custom of the civic community, be that qualification birth, marriage, servitude, special purchase, or special grant'. This analysis would suggest that it was precisely the growth of cities, stimulated by an initially liberal bestowal of the franchise, that necessitated the development of a less flexible conception of citizenship, a hospitality no longer absolute or unconditional. With this division of the populace into a privileged and an excluded class, a new significance attaches to the stranger: he joins the ranks of a revolutionary body. In 'True and False Society', Morris made explicit the connection between the modern situation and the ancient class struggle, arguing that 'much the same thing is going on in the relations of employers to the employed as went on under the slave society of Athens or under the self-sustained baronage of the thirteenth century'.[78]

A revolution caused by generous hospitality might not seem to pose problems for Morris the Marxist. Yet these Germanic romances evoke neither the degeneration of a classical model of government, nor a modern explosion of class consciousness. The focus falls instead on tribal networks consistently presented in an ideal light. The old order is not by definition illegitimate or corrupt, therefore.

---

76 Morris, 'How We Live and How We Might Live', p. 15.
77 Edward A. Freeman, *Comparative Politics: Six Lectures with The Unity of History* (London: Macmillan, 1873), pp. 116, 279–81, 283.
78 Morris, 'True and False Society', in *Collected Works*, XXIII, pp. 215–37 (p. 220).

Given this idyllic treatment, it is difficult to imagine Morris welcoming the disintegration of kindred society as a salutary development. A helpful comparison is offered by the account Morgan gives of the overthrow of the gentes among the Greeks:

> As early as the time of Lycurgus there was a considerable immigration into Greece from the islands of the Mediterranean [. . .] which increased the number of persons unattached to any gens. When they came in families they would bring a fragment of a new gens with them; but they would remain aliens unless the new gens was admitted into a tribe [. . .] The gentes and phratries were close corporations, both of which would have been adulterated by the absorption of these aliens through adoption into a native gens [. . .] There can be no doubt that as far back as the time of Theseus, and more especially in the time of Solon, the number of the unattached class, exclusive of the slaves, had become large [. . .] It is not difficult to see in this class of persons a growing element of discontent dangerous to the security of society.[79]

Referring later to the same situation, as presented before the Roman authorities, Morgan adds that such a state of affairs, 'admitting of no remedy under gentile institutions', 'must have furnished one of the prominent reasons for attempting the overthrow of gentile society, and the substitution of political'. This version of events seems to have influenced Morris, either through Bax's reading of Engels, or through Edward Carpenter's reading of Morgan.[80] There is, then, good reason to suspect that Morris appreciated how an admission of freed captives might hasten the fall of Burgdale society. Considerable textual evidence exists to suggest that he wished to incorporate this uneasy awareness within the tale itself: hospitality is celebrated as an admirable social virtue, but Morris's readers are not allowed to ignore its attendant dangers. One is alerted, in particular, to the risk that a growing mass of strangers will eventually make even a formalized acceptance of interrelatedness untenable, that it will usher in a more exclusive, urban constitution.

Engels pays particular attention to two effects of this change. The first concerns the shift from 'the old communistic household'[81] – in which 'the task entrusted to the women of managing the household was as much a public, a socially necessary industry as the procuring of food by the men' – to the patriarchal and monogamous family amidst which 'household management' had 'lost its public character'. Although stress is laid on the dignified nature of household affairs (as in *News from Nowhere*), and on the matriarchal power of such figures as Hall-Sun, Morris's communism never stretches quite so far as to challenge the assumption that sexual relations between humans are ideally monogamous, as might be

---

79 Morgan, *Ancient Society*, pp. 266–7, 324.
80 Carpenter, whom Morris knew and liked, relied upon the researches of Morgan and Engels in narrating the transition from 'barbarism' to 'civilization'. 'Lewis Morgan in his *Ancient Society* adds the invention of writing and the consequent adoption of written History and written Law; Engels in his *Ursprung der Familie, des Privat-eigenthums und des Staats* points out the importance of the appearance of the Merchant, even in his most primitive form, as a mark of the civilisation-period', *Civilisation – Its Cause and Cure and other Essays* (London: Swan Sonnenschein & Co, 1889), p. 5.
81 Engels, *The Origin of the Family*, pp. 78, 79.

implied by a celebration of primitive communality. The second development relates to the growth of a merchant class. This is an event that Morris does choose to represent. It becomes clear, particularly in *The Roots of the Mountains*, that the figure of the merchant is of considerable significance. These outsiders are given licence to visit a community and then leave. In *The Origin of the Family*, Engels argued that the emergence of private property 'creates a class which no longer concerns itself with production, but only with the exchange of the products'.[82] With the merchants, 'a class of parasites comes into being'. There is some evidence to suggest that Morris, unlike Engels, saw a distinction between bourgeois mercantilism and the earlier activities of trade emissaries. The positive vision of Chaucer signing bills of lading at the beginning of *The Earthly Paradise* supports this argument, but Morris also referred directly to the question in his lectures. 'Architecture and History' contains the assertion that the medieval merchant 'was not a mere gambler in the haphazard of supply and demand as he is to-day, but an indispensable distributor of goods'.[83] At the beginning of *The Roots of the Mountains*, the trading habits of the peoples living in and around Burgdale are described without disapproval. There is nevertheless an essential distinction between kindred members and merchants. The latter are not selfless in contemplating war, or in serving the wider social group. The chapman who visits Burgdale before the fight with the Dusky Men finds battle 'loathsome'.[84] Not 'for all the gain of his chaffer had he come into the Dale, had he known that war was looked for'. War interrupts the flow of trade. In this sense, it is hostile to the mercantile enterprise. War also marks the point at which tribal unity becomes incontrovertible, when the Morrisian virtue of fellowship suspends any faltering of social coherence resulting from the weakening of kindred ties. Coming from the cities, the merchants represent the strengthening claims of the outside world. Gaining admission to the kindreds' settlement via the primitive commitment to hospitality, they introduce a new kind of bond not in the least concerned with blood affinity. This bond approximates to commercial contract and, eventually, usury.[85] Parasitic or not, the presence of the merchants in *The Roots of the Mountains*, and their temporary absence during the conflict with the Dusky Men, announce the inception of a new way of life.

In Morris's Teutonic romances, the emergence of a less communal civilization is initially suspended by the waging of war. Battle preparations appear at first to strengthen the tribe's sense of identity, and the atmosphere of crisis is marked by

82 Engels, *The Origin of the Family*, pp. 188, 189.
83 Morris, 'Architecture and History', p. 304.
84 Morris, *The Roots of the Mountains*, p. 236.
85 This usurious attitude to strangers is explored by David-Everett Blythe in an article that treats the influence on Ruskin of Shakespeare's *The Merchant of Venice*: 'the prejudicial Deuteronomic usury-sanction makes foreigners eligible victims: "Unto a stranger thou mayest lend upon usury, but unto thy brother thou shalt not lend upon usury" (Deuteronomy 23:20). On one side Antonio is a free-lender to any man; on the other, Shylock and Tubal are incorporated to lend usuriously to Venetian Gentiles. This is but the racial entrenchment of Ruskin's "Competition or Evil Commerce" (17.210) which "makes all men strangers" (17.183)', 'A Stone of Ruskin's Venice', in *New Approaches to Ruskin*, pp. 157–73 (pp. 168–9). Later in the same article, Blythe writes: 'It is not just that Shylock isolates himself from social affection: there is no social disaffection so universally ill-meant as a hospitality which courts the statistical but denies the essential spirit of men' (p. 169).

feasting and storytelling. When combat finally commences, its effect is socially levelling. Only in the immediate aftermath of war do we witness its deeper impact. For, in both romances, there are signs that war catalyses a shift towards a new social formation. Once hostilities have ended, the process begins with the admission of a large number of captives to the gens. Whilst presenting this as a laudable act, Morris also hints that it will weaken the kindred ties that guarantee unity and communality. The creation of new battle alliances has a similar effect, initiating the unification of gentes, which eventually produces the tribe; and, in turn, the consolidation of tribes, which gives birth to the nation.

Morris's 'holy flame of discontent': The Dialectic of Hope and Defeat in *A Dream of John Ball*[86]

Late Teutonic society was not the only period Morris associated with a brief reconciliation of freedom and community. Similar virtues and similar vulnerabilities are invoked by him in describing late medieval times, though the focus here falls less on the household than on the activities of trade guilds. In both cases, a form of fellowship or combination, portrayed as positive and worthwhile in itself, is revealed as an engine of change, an expression of fellowship ultimately conducive to its own demise.

In 'Art and Industry in the Fourteenth Century', Morris identified the guilds with 'The poor remains of the old tribal liberties, the folkmotes, the meetings round the shire-oak, the trial by compurgation, all these customs which imply the equality of freemen'.[87] The 'constitution of the craft-gild [*sic*] was at first thoroughly democratic or fraternal'.[88] In this respect, it resembled the early form of the gens: narrow and exclusive, but communal, with 'workmen not belonging to the commune not admitted unless hands fell short'.[89] This was one of many rules 'considered to have been made in the direct interest of the workmen'. What Morris called 'the spirit of combination' acts here in unison with an attempt to regulate and protect certain branches of trade.[90] Under these conditions, 'the accumulation of capital is impossible' and 'was meant to be impossible'.[91] As a result, the 'commune of the Middle Ages, like the classical city' existed in a bounded condition: 'the means of intercourse were lacking, and men were forced to defend the interests of small bodies against all comers, even those whom they should have received as brothers'. The same spirit of association is linked by Morris to the slow birth of the middle classes and the destruction of the old feudal hierarchy, events fostering equalitarianism and comparatively unrestricted forms of exchange.[92] Far from representing a reactionary attempt to establish a monopoly over production,

---

86 Morris, 'The Hopes of Civilization', p. 72.
87 Morris, 'Art and Industry in the Fourteenth Century', in *Collected Works*, XXII, pp. 375–90 (p. 380).
88 Morris, 'Architecture and History', p. 307.
89 Morris, 'Art and Industry in the Fourteenth Century', pp. 385–6.
90 Morris, 'Architecture and History', p. 303.
91 Morris, 'Art and Industry in the Fourteenth Century', pp. 386, 388.
92 Morris, 'Art and its Producers', p. 347.

argues Morris, the guilds were the 'progressive part of the society of the time'.[93] As such, they contained the seeds of capitalism, and promoted a form of fellowship that served, despite itself, to quicken the end of association:

> its own success in developing the resources of labour ruined it; it opened chances to men of growing rich and powerful if they could succeed in breaking down the artificial restrictions imposed by the gilds [*sic*] for the sake of the welfare of their members.[94]

The breaking down of trade restrictions eventually has the same effect as the bypassing of the kindred qualification among the Gothic tribes: at first it appears to shore up the commune, giving 'an appearance of strengthening it by adding to its members, increasing its power of production, and so making it more stable for the time being'.[95] But this effect is only temporary. In the name of solidarity, it destroys association; in the interests of sociability, it becomes the harbinger of a mercantile spirit that removes regulations and ushers in an age of universal commensurability or free exchange.

Why does Morris celebrate the virtues of a society, whether the gens or the guild, only to imply that these virtues were responsible for its demise? Were kindred, community, and association not considered sufficient in themselves? John Goode's reference to a state of 'maximum equilibrium' would certainly suggest the inadequacy of a primitive household unaffected by social forces.[96] Surveying the historical meaning of Morris's Germanic romances, Florence Boos sheds light on this question. Accepting that 'there is something vaguely ominous about the extinction of the Dusky Men in *Roots*', she finds nevertheless that 'its simple patterns of kinship, sacrifice, tolerance, and eventual union of the four branches of "Folk" provide a miniature model for Morris's internationalism'.[97] Morris understood that victory could not be depicted in a wholly favourable light unless some concession to liberal values took effect at the end of the tale. In *The House of the Wolfings*, the dilemma posed by Thiodolf's acceptance of the dwarf-wrought hauberk raises similar questions. Boos concludes that the problems caused by this love-token – notably its tendency to make him faint before he enters a potentially fatal phase of combat – constitute the key symbol in 'an allegory of the need to subordinate the exclusiveness of erotic attachment to love of the kindred'. Goode suggests that it is Thiodolf's eventual decision to discard the hauberk, to recognize that a 'totally individuated individual loses his identity' that 'makes the story a *revolutionary* Romance rather than a reactionary one'.[98] Both critics are justified in asserting the ultimate triumph of communal values. The difficulties Thiodolf faces in reconciling his position as war-leader with his status as an alien, and in fulfilling his role as a warrior at the same time as his role as a lover, allow Morris to denigrate the social model represented by the Dusky Men,

---

93   Morris, 'The Revival of Architecture', p. 325.
94   Morris, 'Art and Industry in the Fourteenth Century', p. 389.
95   Morris, 'Feudal England', in *Collected Works*, XXIII, pp. 39–58 (p. 55).
96   Goode, 'William Morris and the Dream of Revolution', p. 305.
97   Florence Boos, 'Morris's German Romances as Socialist History', *Victorian Studies*, 27 (Spring, 1984), 3, 321–42 (p. 342).
98   Goode, 'William Morris and the Dream of Revolution', p. 311.

among whom communality has eliminated individuality. The inwardness encouraged by the hauberk is not presented as a valid alternative to self-sacrifice, but the
mental struggle it initiates nevertheless demonstrates Morris's concern to accommodate alternative paths, even where they are not actually taken. Face-of-god, in
The Roots of the Mountains, is led by amorous feeling to risk committing a similar
offence against tribal convention. By failing to marry the Bride, the woman from a
marriageable gens marked out as a future wife, he provokes anger among the
Burgdale elders. In the last analysis, Face-of-god's actions still achieve legitimacy.
The union of the Rosedale people and the Burgdalers brings into being a marriage
group capable of accommodating his inclinations. Here, as elsewhere, Morris
allows for the possibility of transgression, while making no commitment to its
final necessity.

There exists a yet more compelling explanation for Morris's paradoxical
combination of dialectical materialism and primitivism. He wished to invest
defeat with an unconventional significance, attaching value to untimely hopes,
even where they ended in disappointment. In an article devoted to the similarities
between Morris's politics and the philosophy of Ernst Bloch,[99] Ruth Levitas
proposes an argument that helps to explain this strategy:

> It would be a mistake to claim that the positions implied by Bloch and Morris's
> commentators are identical, although they are remarkably similar [. . .] In both
> cases, there is an attempt to argue that dreaming is an activity necessary to tran-
> scending our present sorry state, and that such dreams have both an educative and a
> transformative function; that the goal of that transformation is the transcendence of
> alienation; that art can prefigure that experience (Bloch), and will be fundamental to
> its realisation (Morris); and that these claims are, if not already contained within
> Marxism, at least compatible with and a necessary adjunct to it.[100]

Levitas considers Bloch's political philosophy alongside that of E. P. Thompson.
Thompson's commentary on M. M-H. Abensour's doctoral thesis, 'Les Formes de
L'Utopie Socialiste-Communiste', provides the groundwork for her contention
that 'utopia is not simply about the expression and pursuit of desire, but about its
education'.[101] This comparison of Morris and Bloch highlights their mutual
adherence to the view that economic determinism could not and should not
attempt to order the human imagination, a faculty capable, independently, of
nurturing revolutionary forms of hope. Marxism, that is, needed to encompass
both a 'cold' and a 'warm' stream of thought.[102]

How does this emphasis on hope explain the disjunction between Morris's
evocation of utopian conditions and the doomed status of primitive happiness
among the German tribes? The best way of proceeding is to consider his portrayal
of the Peasants' Revolt in *A Dream of John Ball*. In lectures dealing with this
episode, Morris wrestles with a problem similar to that posed by hospitality in

---

[99] Ernst Bloch, *The Principle of Hope*, trans. by Neville Plaice, Stephen Plaice and Paul Knight, 3 vols
      (London: Basil Blackwell, 1986).
[100] Ruth Levitas, 'Marxism, Romanticism and Utopia: Ernst Bloch and William Morris', *Radical
      Philosophy*, 51 (1989), 27–36 (p. 34).
[101] E. P. Thompson, 'Postscript: 1976', *William Morris*, pp. 763–816.
[102] Bloch, *The Principle of Hope*, 3, p. 1369.

tribal society. On the one hand, he idealizes the period, subscribing to Thorold Rogers's view that the fourteenth century was for the labouring class a period of unparalleled comfort in conditions and earnings.[103] On the other, he invests positive value in the very rebellion Green and Rogers regarded as the death knell of feudalism.[104] In his commentary on *A Dream of John Ball*, John Goode argues that Morris would have known 'from Marx that the major precondition of capitalist production is the freeing of labour' and that the 'release from serfdom was part of a process which retarded "fellowship" by disruption of a sense of community'.[105] This is to say that 'whatever "communism" Ball was preaching was dialectically opposed to the direction his rebellion took'.

In one sense, there is no inconsistency. Goode himself argues, 'if the ideology of the rebels is what makes for the opposite of John Ball's dream, the spirit of solidarity which he inspires among them is a recognition in action of the change beyond the change'. In an effort to redeem the defeated hopes of the tribes who battle with the Romans, and of the priest who leads the serfs into battle with their feudal masters, Morris honours revolt as a universal. In 'The Arts and Crafts Of To-day', he demonstrates the necessity of viewing the imperfection and defeat of past efforts as cumulative steps towards a better future:

> Yet the world has not gone back; for that old object of desire was only gained in the past as far as the circumstances of the day would allow it to be gained then. As a consequence the gain was imperfect; the times are now changed, and allow us to carry on that old gain a step forward to perfection: the world has not really gone back on its footsteps, though to some it has seemed to do so. Did the world go back, for instance, when the remnant of the ancient civilizations was overwhelmed by the barbarism which was the foundation of modern Europe? We can all see that it did not. Did it go back when the logical and orderly system of the Middle Ages had to give place to the confusion of incipient commercialism in the sixteenth century? Again, ugly and disastrous as the change seems on the surface, I yet think it was not a retrogression into prehistoric anarchy, but a step upward along the spiral, which, and not the straight line, is, as my friend Bax puts it, the true line of progress.[106]

Morris resolved the difficulty expressed most clearly in 'Art and Industry in the Fourteenth Century' – that 'the Middle Ages, so to say, saw the promised land of Socialism from afar, like the Israelites, and like them had to turn back again into the desert' – by placing a higher value on hope than on immediate success or timeliness.[107] This emphasis is explained by his related assertion that 'brave men never die for nothing, when they die for principle':[108]

103 James E. Thorold Rogers, *Six Centuries of Work and Wages: The History of English Labour*, 2 vols (London: W. Swan Sonnenschein & Co., 1884), p. 415.
104 In 'Feudal England', Morris states, 'serfdom came to an end in England, if not because of the revolt, yet because of the events that made it, and thereby a death-wound was inflicted on the feudal system' (p. 56).
105 Goode, 'William Morris and the Dream of Revolution', pp. 295, 299.
106 Morris, 'The Arts and Crafts Of To-day', in *Collected Works*, XXII, pp. 356–74 (p. 371).
107 Morris, 'Art and Industry in the Fourteenth Century', p. 388.
108 Morris, 'The Hopes of Civilization', p. 74.

Chartism therefore, though a genuine popular movement, was incomplete in its aims and knowledge; the time was not yet come and it could not triumph openly; but it would be a mistake to say that it failed utterly: at least it kept alive the holy flame of discontent.[109]

According to this invocation of a 'holy flame', the value of hope, in all eras, is redeemable. Even where Morris exhibits a stubborn historicism, it is not hard to detect a parallel acceptance of universal categories or, at least, continuities immune to defeat. The 'Fellowship of Men' mentioned in *A Dream of John Ball* stands as an obvious example, a transhistorical standard offering the consolation of future success.[110]

It is worth returning to Morgan's assertion that remnants of the defeated barbarian constitution lingered in medieval Europe, and then became dormant, destined to return to form the basis of a higher plane of society. Whether Morris derived his emphasis on a continuity of institutions and hopes from Engels[111] or from the Whig historians he certainly did read, is not of crucial significance. More important is that he ensured the theoretical coherence of his position by recruiting past hopes to present needs. This is not to suggest that the tension between the immediate results of the combination of tribes (or the revolt of serfs) and his fictional treatment of them was entirely resolved. The tragedy of *A Dream of John Ball*, and of Morris's own unwillingness to abandon the historically compromised individual in the face of economic determinism, lay in the necessity of supporting causes that inadvertently aided the destruction of 'fellowship'.[112] Morris's narrator demonstrates cognizance of this when he reflects on 'how men fight and lose the battle, and the thing that they fought for comes about in spite of their defeat, and when it comes turns out not to be what they meant, and other men have to fight for what they meant under another name'. The effect of this philosophy of continuity, of transhistorical fellowship, is to rescue from the obscurity of local defeat such potential substitutes for alienation as hope, struggle, hospitality and combination, without invalidating a basic adherence to dialectical materialism. Hence Morris's historical subjects are able to express both discontent and the right to bring about self-betterment in the present. This becomes possible because the immediate defeat is redeemed by the ultimate, cumulative, victory. Such a resolution would be impossible were it not for the involvement of otherwise stranded individuals in the production of previous crises.

Morris never overcame the tension between his desire to credit the individual with historical agency and his acceptance of a theory of history that substituted social forces for a personal striving after hope. This unwillingness to subordinate hope to economic determinism need not be interpreted as a conflict between Marxism and something else. As E. P. Thompson[113] and Ruth Levitas[114] have argued, it may constitute the expression of two, quite distinct, forces within Marxism. It is not even necessary to regard these forces as mutually exclusive.

---

109   Morris, 'The Hopes of Civilization', p. 72.
110   Morris, *A Dream of John Ball*, p. 284.
111   Note that Engels quotes Morgan's prediction at the close of *The Origin of the Family*.
112   Morris, *A Dream of John Ball*, pp. 284, 231–2.
113   E. P. Thompson, 'Postscript: 1976', *William Morris*.
114   Levitas, 'Marxism, Romanticism and Utopia', p. 34.

They may simply govern different and discrete domains. Morris idealized the life of the Germanic gentes and the fourteenth-century peasant (or guild member) in the knowledge that these forms of existence were both inferior to the socialist era about to be born, and objects that must by definition be destroyed *en route* to the earthly paradise. Levitas's distinction between hope and necessity helps to explain Morris's strategy. The communism of the German tribes provided inspiration for the socialist cause, and their bid for self-defence in the face of marauding forces was valid in this respect. But a painful break with their way of life has to occur if 'progress' is to be made. A similar truth is implied by Guest's departure at the end of *News from Nowhere*.

The attractiveness of the past depicted by Morris indicates his reliance on a liberalism more commonly associated with the commercial age. Yet his tendency to locate utopia in periods during which the exclusiveness of traditional society is weakening under the influence of a nascent mercantile culture indicates that he was not blind to the relationship between the growth of political freedom and the development of capitalism. Those forms of behaviour most wedded to the practices of a traditional society – namely, hospitality and armed conflict – are also those most responsible for ushering in an epoch of 'alienation'. They operate as carriers for the communality *and* the liberalism Morris hoped would combine to guarantee community and freedom in the new socialist era. By aligning the interests of the contemporary working classes with those of a transhistorical fellowship, by stressing the continuity of the Germanic constitution within the hopes of this body, he secured the relevance of this fruitful dialectical encounter to his own day, and blurred somewhat the distinction between the discontented of past and present.

The Laws of Hospitality: Liberty, Generosity, and the Limits of Dissent in *The Tables Turned* and *News from Nowhere*[115]

In recent decades, successive critical movements and social changes have fashioned a cultural situation particularly amenable to the sympathetic reception of Morris's first formal utopia.[116] The collapse of communism in Eastern Europe also served to strengthen critical interest in *News from Nowhere*. While undoubtedly encouraging fresh scepticism regarding 'socialistic' solutions to economic or ethical problems, the end of the Cold War prompted, in certain quarters, a renewed and liberated reconsideration of alternative communist traditions.[117] Morris's utopia appealed precisely because it represented a political dead end, a socialism that, by virtue of its purism, could not be said to have influenced either the British Labour Movement or Marxist-Leninist communism. By 1990, this

---

[115] A version of this section appeared in *The Yearbook of English Studies*, under the title, 'The Laws of Hospitality: Liberty, Generosity, and the Limits of Dissent in William Morris's *The Tables Turned* and *News from Nowhere*', 36 (2006), 2, 212–29.

[116] Among these may be counted deconstruction, neo-anarchist/environmentalist politics and governmental devolution.

[117] See, for example, Krishan Kumar's comments in 'News from Nowhere: The Renewal of Utopia', quoted in the Introduction.

process had reached fruition. For the first time in its history, *News from Nowhere* was being hailed as a timely production, 'A Vision for our Time'.[118]

In *William Morris & News from Nowhere*, a collection of essays issued to mark the centenary year of the work's publication, Morris is presented as an anarcho-communist forebear of recent trends.[119] The views of the volume's editor, Stephen Coleman, are especially germane. He suggests that 'the matter of the freedom to dissent' is central to the question of whether Morris accomplishes 'unenforced social harmony'.[120] He concludes, first, that 'in Nowhere cohesion is not the product of compulsion'; and second, that recurrent failure to endorse Morris's insistence on the achievability of political liberty is merely 'a reflection of the intensity of the modern fear of freedom'. Later in the decade, the proceedings of a conference held at Exeter College, Oxford, were published in a volume entitled *William Morris: Centenary Essays*.[121] A similar version of Morris emerged here. Contributing to the collection, Ady Mineo suggests that a 'lack of compulsory, prescribed codes of behaviour' ensures the 'dialectical quality' of Morris's utopia.[122] It conveys the impression of a society 'where individual freedom presides over every aspect of human activity'. Such features 'prevent *News from Nowhere* from presenting a unified and autocratic point of view'. They confer on it 'the character of a polyphonic text, according to Mikhail Bakhtin's definition, where the reader is confronted by a plurality of ideological positions and discourses'. Mineo highlights the 'important function' of this dialogism in facilitating 'the incorporation of dissent', referring to 'Boffin, who can write "reactionary" novels', to 'Ellen's grandfather in his nostalgia for the competitive and aggressive society of the past', and to 'the "obstinate refusers"'.

In a different article, Mineo has argued that human activity in Morris's utopia 'is regulated by the pleasure principle in so far as compulsion, repression and alienation no longer shape the lives of individuals'.[123] This emphasis on the liberating function of desire is in part traceable to the influence of Herbert Marcuse's *Eros and Civilization*.[124] In this work, Freud's deference to the claims of the 'reality principle', and the economistic assumption of scarcity, are rejected as self-imposed limitations. In the area of Morris studies, the faculties that pertain here – the faculties of *desire* and *hope* – have received most attention from E. P. Thompson and Ruth Levitas. In the Postscript to the revised edition of *William Morris: Romantic to Revolutionary*, Thompson glosses M. M-H. Abensour's 'education of desire' argument (discussed in the previous section), recommending it as a useful way of reappraising Morris's utopianism.

118 These words were applied by Coleman and O'Sullivan, as the subtitle of their anthology of essays, *William Morris & News from Nowhere: A Vision for Our Time*, ed. by Stephen Coleman and Paddy O'Sullivan (Bideford, Devon: Green Books, 1990).
119 Coleman and O'Sullivan, *William Morris & News from Nowhere*.
120 Coleman, 'How Matters are Managed: Human Nature and Nowhere', in *William Morris & News from Nowhere*, pp. 87, 89.
121 *William Morris: Centenary Essays*, ed. by Peter Faulkner and Peter Preston (Exeter: University of Exeter Press, 1999).
122 Mineo, 'Beyond the Law of the Father: The "New Woman" in *News from Nowhere*', pp. 200, 201.
123 Ady Mineo, 'Eros Unbound: Sexual Identities in *News from Nowhere*', *The Journal of the William Morris Society*, IX (Spring, 1992), 4, 8–14 (p. 8).
124 Herbert Marcuse, *Eros and Civilization: A Philosophical Inquiry into Freud* (London: Routledge & Kegan Paul, 1956).

Thompson's enthusiasm for Abensour has not been uncontroversial. Perry Anderson, for one, notoriously characterized his emphasis on desire as a brief insinuation of that 'Parisian irrationalism' which favours 'metaphysical vacancy' over 'clear and observable meaning'.[125] Ruth Levitas, in her article, 'Marxism, Romanticism and Utopia: Ernst Bloch and William Morris', takes into account the views of both Thompson and Anderson, and synthesizes them: Morris's utopianism, she argues, is no vague expression of frustrated desire; but rather a disciplined, politically effective, form of dream.

Yet in recent discussions of *News from Nowhere*, one hears less of discipline than of Morris's openness, his pluralism and his playfulness. What limits he may have placed on the scope of these freedoms, or, more specifically, on the conduct of his utopians, have received comparably little attention. The troubled history of utopian experimentation in the twentieth century makes this emphasis unsurprising: it is now a precondition of any favourable appraisal of Morris's work that it echo A. L. Morton's assertion that 'Morris' is the first Utopia which is not utopian'.[126] All the same, it is my purpose to insist on the limited nature of Nowhere's openness. This does not mean that I dispute the common assertion that *News from Nowhere* constitutes a libertarian utopia. As the first part of this discussion should serve to demonstrate, much evidence exists to support such a reading. It is simply necessary to register the fact that, in certain respects, Nowhere remains typically utopian, that it constitutes a vision of happiness achieved by means of an act of exclusion. Morris, this is to say, exercises his sovereignty as a utopist: he leaves out what displeases him.[127]

In its self-proclaimed capacity as a 'utopian romance',[128] *News from Nowhere* inhabits a political tradition that has been assailed by a long sequence of opponents. The bourgeois critique of utopianism traditionally takes the form of a rejection of what is impractical or fanciful. The Marxist critique, outlined in *The Manifesto of the Communist Party*, urges an abandonment of Owenite and Fourierist projects, blueprints for paradise devised, it is argued, by individuals who gave no thought to the dynamic effect of social forces.[129] Later in the century, Edward Bulwer Lytton's *The Coming Race*,[130] Samuel Butler's *Erewhon*[131] and William Hudson's *A Crystal Age*[132] built on the Swiftian tradition, offering satirical treatments of ordered societies. Intended in part as displaced attacks on the world occupied by their readership, these works also explored the hostile attitude 'utopian' societies have traditionally shown towards outsiders. The link between perfectionism and intolerance thereafter becomes a staple of dystopian fiction. It is nevertheless important to recognize that attempts to enforce communities of

---

125 Perry Anderson, *Arguments within English Marxism* (London: Verso, 1980), pp. 161–2.
126 Morton, *The English Utopia*, p. 164.
127 By invoking the doctrine of sovereignty, I suggest not that Morris enjoys unqualified 'legislative' power, only that the world he creates is willed selectively into being. For an account of the less controlled aspects of Morris's authorship, see my article, 'News from Nowhere, Utopia and Bakhtin's Idyllic Chronotope', *Textual Practice*, 16 (Winter 2002), 3, 459–72.
128 Morris, *News from Nowhere*, p. 41.
129 Marx and Engels, *Manifesto of the Communist Party*, pp. 515–16.
130 Edward Bulwer-Lytton, *The Coming Race* (Edinburgh: William Blackwood and Sons, 1871).
131 Samuel Butler, *Erewhon* (London: Trübner & Co., 1872).
132 William Hudson, *A Crystal Age* (London: T. Fisher Unwin, 1887).

belief were in no sense exclusively modern phenomena. Thomas More, the author of the first utopia proper, wrote *A Dialogue Concerning Heresies* in 1529 to justify the persecution of Protestants.[133] In *Utopia*, More did not adopt the principles of Plato's *Republic* wholesale, but he certainly retained the Platonic emphasis on the need to enforce social unity.[134]

In the first half of the twentieth century, Karl Popper and Friedrich Hayek began to express the view that the crimes of fascism and communism were directly attributable to this heritage. The misgivings prompting such critiques were only strengthened by the publication of Yevgeny Zamyatin's *We* (1921), Aldous Huxley's *Brave New World* (1932) and George Orwell's *Nineteen Eighty-Four* (1949), all three of them dystopias. These works fuelled a growing distrust of social engineering, imaginative or otherwise.[135] With the collapse of faith in post-war welfarism, this strand of modern scepticism served to underpin the gathering postmodern critique of utopianism, an attack on optimism exemplified by Jean-François Lyotard's condemnation of 'grand narrative' in *La Condition Postmoderne* (1979). Rejecting the work of Ernst Bloch, and the Frankfurt School, Lyotard argued that 'the critical model in the end lost its theoretical standing and was reduced to the status of a "utopia" or "hope," a token protest'.[136] More importantly, he claimed, past reliance on a transcendent, guiding force – Hegelian, Marxist or theological – had led to a recurring rule of terror. In exchange for this costly 'nostalgia of the whole', Lyotard urged the waging of 'war on totality'. Whether or not the validity of these arguments is accepted, the sub title of *News from Nowhere* – 'a utopian romance'[137] – invokes a literary and political tradition now so controversial as to have an unavoidable bearing on the reception of Morris's vision. While the understandable dominance of anti-utopian sentiment in the twentieth century does not automatically render *News from Nowhere* a prototype for totalitarian politics, consideration of these issues is essential if one is to appreciate the background against which claims for Morris's unique status as a utopist are made. The grounds for these claims must now be examined.

There is, to begin with, considerable evidence to support the assertion that Morris attempted to reconcile liberalism, or a spirit of tolerance, with his medievalism and his socialism. This comes as no surprise once it is known that he began his career in politics under the aegis of the Liberal Party, and that it was in

---

133 More wrote: 'And surely as the prynces be bounden yt they shall not suffer theyr people by infydels to be inuaded so be they as depely bounden that they shall not suffer theyr people to be seduced and corrupted by heretykes [. . .] All whiche maye in the begynnynge be ryght easely auoyded by punysshment of those fewe that be the fyrste', *A Dialogue Concerning Heresies*, in *The Yale Edition of the Complete Works of St. Thomas More*, ed. by Thomas M. C. Lawler, Germain Marc'hadour and Richard C. Marius, 14 vols (New Haven: Yale University Press, 1981), VI, pp. 415–16.

134 More's *Utopia* shares with Plato's *Republic* an emphasis on the need for collective education and for uniformity of social life.

135 This trend is documented in the following works: Judith N. Shklar, *After Utopia: The Decline of Political Faith* (Princeton, N. J.: Princeton University Press, 1957); George Kateb, *Utopia and its Enemies* (London: Collier-Macmillan, 1963).

136 Jean-François Lyotard, *The Postmodern Condition: A Report on Knowledge*, trans. by Geoff Bennington and Brian Massumi (Manchester: Manchester University Press, 1992), pp. 13, 81.

137 Morris, *News from Nowhere*, p. 41.

reading J. S. Mill's judiciously fair 'Chapters on Socialism' that he reached a final acceptance of socialism's precepts.[138] One might even regard Ruskinian medievalism (at least in the modified, non-hierarchical form that Morris received it) as the source for this unusual synthesis. Insisting on the individual value of every human soul, the teachings of Morris's 'master'[139] were distinguished by a celebration of variety, complexity and growth, both in nature and in the productions of man. In many spheres of activity, Morris took Ruskin's famous chapter on 'The Nature of Gothic' in *The Stones of Venice* as a guide in his attempts to reconcile justice with beauty.[140] Though utopian in effect, the Gothic virtues identified by Ruskin – changefulness, imperfection, variety[141] – were not susceptible to the kind of criticisms detailed above (since these are levelled exclusively at the classical, city-state tradition associated with Plato). Employment of the organic metaphor may be interpreted, then, as a way of symbolizing complexity. The static utopia is thereby rejected in favour of something more accommodating to diversity. In 'Making the Best of It', Morris specified that 'all patterns [. . .] meant to fill the eye and satisfy the mind' should contain 'a certain mystery'.[142] In 'Art and Socialism', similarly, he demanded that the society of the future have 'waste places and wilds in it'.[143]

This reluctance to drive mystery or romance out of the world marks an important point of divergence between Morris's political vision and the so-called 'Enlightenment project' attacked by recent opponents of utopia. The point, in a sense, is unexceptional: with the nineteenth-century emphasis on progressive development, most utopists were compelled to come to terms with history. Even the impersonal, evolutionary momentum of Darwinian theory militated against social models founded on the undesirability of change – like the static city-state of the Renaissance – or on the Enlightenment conception of a law-governed world tending towards equilibrium. What *does* set Morris's utopia apart is his rejection of crude progressivism. In *News from Nowhere*, the 'teeming garden' that surrounds each of the medieval-style houses,[144] and the 'wild spot' at Kensington, reflect a determination to reserve space for growth, whilst renouncing the aim of total knowledge. Moreover, Ruskin's high valuation of the Gothic's 'confession of Imperfection' finds expression in the Nowherean toleration of flawed human nature, in an acceptance that 'hot blood will err sometimes':

138   In 'How I Became a Socialist', Morris recalls: 'I *had* read some of Mill, to wit, those posthumous papers of his [. . .] in which he attacks Socialism in its Fourierist guise. In those papers he put the arguments, as far as they go, clearly and honestly, and the result, so far as I was concerned, was to convince me that Socialism was a necessary change' (pp. 277–8).
139   Morris, 'How I Became a Socialist', p. 279.
140   Ruskin, 'The Nature of Gothic', *The Stones of Venice*.
141   There may appear difficulty in applying the word *utopian* to Ruskin's seemingly Augustinian emphasis on imperfection. The contradiction recedes when one considers that Ruskin's theory of Gothic is a celebration of *earthly* imperfection, not an argument for deferring all hopes of paradise to the next life.
142   Morris, 'Making the Best of It', p. 109.
143   Morris, 'Art and Socialism', in *Collected Works*, XXIII, pp. 192–214 (p. 209).
144   Morris, *News from Nowhere*, pp. 23, 26, 82.

Surely if we, in dread of an occasional rare homicide, an occasional rough blow, were solemnly and legally to commit homicide and violence, we could only be a society of ferocious cowards.

Central to Morris's medievalism is the contention that bravery and beauty cannot be achieved without a measure of disorder. Passionate behaviour may occasionally have adverse consequences, but it is in general the function of a more positive, a more productive imperfection that both complicates and redeems human actions.

Morris's decision to emphasize the theme of hospitality also has a crucial role in suggesting the 'openness' of his utopia. It is not sufficient simply to stress the idea of welcome. Morris adopts wholesale neither the paternalist bent of Ruskinian criticism, nor the forms of heroic hospitality. On arrival in Nowhere, William Guest is not forced to pay his respects to a feudal chieftain. He enjoys a hospitality that, if inspired by pre-commercial forms, is nonetheless devoid of authoritarian associations. Morris creates a society that offers openness without the expectation of kinship or marriage. He proffers a citizenship devoid of Roman or modern-day legalism. As William Guest travels through Nowhere, he encounters many tokens of this openness. The first person he meets, Dick the ferryman, calls him 'neighbour'. Though clearly a convention, this form of address operates as a marker of equality, social harmony and friendliness. Its significance is confirmed by the speed with which the word enters Guest's active vocabulary.[145] (It is hard to imagine that Morris did not intend his readers to recognize *neighbour* as a post-revolutionary replacement for *comrade*, an appellation whose military origin made it inappropriate as a marker of Nowhere's less conscious, less embattled, modes of fellowship.) He is then conveyed to a 'Guest House', a building providing welcome and respite. It represents the beginning, rather than the end of his journey, a place of fair welcome, rather than official reception or quarantine. When Guest arrives at the British Museum, he is assured that, 'wherever you come from, you are come among friends'. Later, when the boating party visits Hampton Court, they find 'tables spread for dinner' that are available to all comers. Its venerable interior highlights a favourable disparity between monarchical hospitality and the egalitarian present. The contrast between older forms of welcome and those practised in Nowhere is never more evident than when Guest notices a 'village guest-house' that 'still had the sign of the Fleur-de-luce which it used to bear in the days when hospitality had to be bought and sold'. The openness suggested by Guest's initial reception is reinforced by the ease with which Nowhere's inhabitants cross once prohibitive boundaries. It is implied that the natural world has come to roost inside the dwellings of Morris's happy folk. People no longer regard 'nature' as 'their slave' or as something distinct from humankind. In recognition of this, Guest remarks that the sky 'looked really like a vault', like the roof of one great communal hall. The effect of these scenes is to impress on the reader the truth of the observation that Guest must have been travelling in 'unsocial countries', that he is not just a stranger, but someone from 'a place very unlike England'. At such moments one is able to interpret hospitality as a sign less of sociability than of tolerance: Guest comes from a

---

145 Guest remarks a little later, ' "But neighbours" (I had caught up that word)'.

place not simply different from Nowhere but antagonistic to it. The conventions of the utopian form, of course, require some interaction between the transformed reality and the *status quo*, so this observation is not altogether conclusive as a proof of a modified, 'utopian' hospitality. More clear cut is the hospitality shown to Mr Justice Nupkins in *The Tables Turned* (1887), the socialist play Morris wrote and performed for his comrades at the Socialist League.[146] Mary Pinch, a victim of injustice under the old regime, shows her forgiveness of the man who once sentenced her to imprisonment by inviting him into her house, and insisting that he have 'something to eat and drink'.

In the preface to *The Growth of the English Constitution from the Earliest Times*, Edward Freeman asserts that 'freedom is everywhere older than bondage', and, indeed, that 'toleration is older than intolerance'.[147] Having considered the possibility that Morris's medievalism encouraged a kind of pluralism, and discussed his evocation of a modified, non-hierarchical hospitality, it is now essential that the origins of his 'liberal' credentials are investigated. In earlier chapters, I argued that Morris was influenced by historians in the Whig tradition, and that his fascination with Icelandic culture was informed by a respect for what he considered the exemplary freedom of the Teutonic constitution and spirit. Yet the sources of Morris's liberalism were not restricted to this narrow area of convergence between medievalism and liberal thought. In 1897, Edward Caird insisted that it was 'altogether a mistake to think that at the present time individualists and socialists generally stand to each other as absolutely opposed sects'.[148] It is 'impossible', he explains, 'for a society to be strong, if its members are weak, or for the members to be strong, except through the same means which secure the greatest material and moral unity of the society.' Caird's essay clearly contains the resources for a more sensitive reading of *News from Nowhere* than would be allowed for by other, less flexible conceptions of socialism. And yet Morris's objections to the coercion of individuals were not simply based on an apprehension that actions of this kind might be socially deleterious. His concerns were of a more principled, humanitarian nature than the comparison with Caird might be taken to imply. After all, the reports of atrocities committed by the Bashi-Bazouks in Bulgaria in 1876 formed the principal stimulus for his first involvement in party politics. In the face of Turkish support for these outrages, and British backing for the regime under whose authority they were committed, the rights of minorities had become a preoccupation for Morris. This same preoccupation led him to become disillusioned with the subsequent Liberal government of Gladstone when it introduced an Irish Coercion Bill in 1881 and ordered a naval bombardment of Alexandria.[149]

While less influenced by German idealism than by Ruskin's theory of medieval

---

[146] Morris, *The Tables Turned; or, Nupkins Awakened*, in *William Morris: Artist Writer Socialist*, II, pp. 528–67.

[147] Freeman, *The Growth of the English Constitution*, p. viii.

[148] Edward Caird, 'The Present State of the Controversy between Individualism and Socialism', in *Collected Works of Edward Caird*, ed. by Colin Tyler, 12 vols (Bristol: Thoemmes Press, 1999), 11, pp. 1–30 (p. 15).

[149] In his letter to Andreas Scheu (15 September 1883), Morris recalled, 'the action and want of action of the new Liberal Parliament, especially the Coercion Bill and the Stockjobbers' Egyptian War quite destroyed any hope I might have had of any good being done by alliance with the radical party' (II, p. 230).

labour.[150] Morris shared with Caird a conviction that liberalism and socialism might be compatible. During the 1880s, members of the Social Democratic Federation gave considerable attention to this matter.[151] In an issue of *Justice* published in 1884, it was reported that George Bernard Shaw gave a lecture entitled 'Socialism *versus* Individualism'.[152] Shaw's lecture dealt with a question that had risen to prominence in the wake of Herbert Spencer's influential attack on socialism in *The Man versus the State* (1884). Here, Spencer argued that 'no form of co-operation, small or great, can be carried on without regulation, and an implied submission to the regulating agencies'.[153] He warned that the victory of socialism would bring about a 'revival of despotism'. Responding to these charges, Morris wrote an article, entitled 'The Dull Level of Life'. Far from nurturing individuality, he argued, capitalism's boasted emphasis on choice – in matters of life as well as taste – merely substituted monotony for pleasure:

> The crushing weight of this pleasureless labour laid with cruel indifference on our lives by the present anarchy is what individuality is languishing under; from Socialism it has nothing to fear, but all to gain.[154]

Time and again, Morris reiterated his belief that compulsion was a chief characteristic of capitalism, not socialism. The capitalist, he stated, was 'the monopolist of the means of productive labour', who 'can *compel*' his workforce 'to make a bargain better for him and worse for them'.[155] The subsequent course of history does not flatter the position Morris assumes. It would now be hard to argue that Spencer was wrong in predicting that socialism would foster a dangerous aggregation of state power. In Soviet Russia, state socialism presided over class liquidation, forced collectivization, the gulag system of labour camps and a police state whose chief instruments were denunciation, deportation and terror. Morris defends socialism in the abstract, conflating his own suspicion of engineered solutions to social problems with the wider socialist project in the hope that policy discussions, then ongoing, would be decided his way. It is precisely because he misread the flow of events, and failed to win the argument, that he avoids acting as an apologist for totalitarian politics. The picture is complicated still further by Morris's recognition of a distinction between the transition phase and the era of mature communism. He did not rule out a measure of centrally directed compulsion in the immediate aftermath of revolution. This matter is discussed at more length later in the chapter. For the moment, it is sufficient to stress Morris's refusal to accept the incompatibility of mature socialism and individualism.

During the 1880s, Morris and his comrades at the League found several opportunities to promote a libertarian agenda. The long-running controversy

---

150 Ruskin, 'The Nature of Gothic', *The Stones of Venice*.
151 The SDF was the socialist party to which Morris belonged before he left to form the Socialist League; its official organ was called *Justice*.
152 The title of this lecture was announced in *Justice*, 19 July 1884, p. 7. Its content was reported as being 'on Socialism and Individualism, the alleged antagonism between which he denied', in *Justice*, 26 July 1884, p. 6.
153 Herbert Spencer, *The Man versus the State*, in *Social Statistics, Abridged and Revised; Together with The Man versus the State* (London: Williams and Norgate, 1892), pp. 322, 325.
154 Morris, 'The Dull Level of Life', *Justice*, 26 April 1884, p. 4.
155 Morris, 'Useful Work *versus* Useless Toil', p. 109.

surrounding Bismarck's institution of anti-socialist laws in Germany represented an obvious inspiration for these efforts. Of even greater importance was the 'free speech' campaign waged in response to the so-called 'police-war against the open-air speaking of the Socialists'.[156] This period of agitation came to a head with the events of Bloody Sunday, 1887, during which protesters were violently dispersed from Trafalgar Square by police and soldiers. As championed here, the cause of free speech was pursued in response to specific curtailments of *socialist* speech. Though hardly a disinterested defence of civil liberties, the framing of this partisan grievance in general terms establishes a standard against which to assess Morris's own record. One might also consider in this light his campaign for the preservation of ancient buildings. When arguing for the preservation, rather than the hasty destruction of unfashionable structures, Morris proposed that it was 'reasonable for the minority' – the minority to which he belonged – to 'appeal to the public to wait'.[157] Applying the language of political tolerance to the business of architectural preservation, these comments echo one of the central principles articulated by J. S. Mill in his famous essay *On Liberty* (1859): that orthodox or prevailing opinions are not by virtue of popular adherence correct or socially beneficial.[158] In 'The Art of the People', Morris appears to invoke the terms of Mill's argument, asserting the possibility that the preservationists might 'represent a small minority that is right, as minorities sometimes are'.[159] It is difficult to determine the extent to which commitment to this principle transcended the situational rhetoric of socialist agitation. When the tables were turned, when the Morrisian position was no longer the minority position, would unorthodox opinion still enjoy the right to be heard? The details of life in *News from Nowhere* are hardly likely to answer this question. Nevertheless, they represent a sincere account of Morrisian communism, which should not be ignored. To deal first with the architectural analogy, it is clear that Morris's utopians do 'not grudge a few poorish buildings standing'.[160] They act according to the principle that 'the name of a dead folly doesn't bite', that there is no need to efface the built memory of the preceding age. On a political level, Nowhere seems not to repeat the 'common sin of all Utopias hitherto' identified by H. G. Wells's narrator in *A Modern Utopia*, of ignoring 'difference' and 'individuality'.[161] It avoids this failure, first, in respect to its accessibility, an issue that returns attention to the concept of hospitality.

In *Perpetual Peace*, Immanuel Kant establishes a theoretical paradigm for the tolerant reception of outsiders. This description of the principles to which any just society would adhere is printed under the heading, '*World citizenship shall be limited to conditions of universal hospitality*':

> hospitality means the right of a foreigner not to be treated with hostility by mere reason of his arrival on foreign soil. The natives may turn him away – if this can be

---

156 Morris, 'Free Speech in the Streets', *Commonweal*, 31 July 1886, p. 137.
157 Morris, 'To the Editor of the *Athenaeum*', 4 April 1877, in *Collected Letters*, I, pp. 361–2 (p. 362).
158 J. S. Mill, *On Liberty*, in *The Collected Works of John Stuart Mill*, ed. by John M. Robson, 33 vols (Toronto: Toronto University Press, 1963–91), XVIII, pp. 213–310.
159 Morris, 'The Art of the People', p. 31.
160 Morris, *News from Nowhere*, pp. 32, 42.
161 Wells, *A Modern Utopia*, p. 36.

done without his perishing – but so long as he behaves peaceably they may not show hostility towards him. A foreigner cannot claim the right of a guest (a special benev-olent treaty would be needed to give him, for a certain time as it were, the 'freedom of the house'), but only the right of a visitor. This right to offer himself as a companion pertains to all mankind by virtue of the communal possession of the earth's surface.[162]

Kant makes a distinction here between hospitality proper – in speaking of the freedom of the house – and extra mural hospitality. This does not fit particularly well with Morris's blurring of the two jurisdictions: Morris's point, surely, was that strangers should be treated as guests in the public *and* the private realm. Moreover, Kant's emphasis on an inalienable *right* to hospitality is both more limited than Morris's in the freedom it accords to the guest and devoid of his emphasis on generosity, on the *gift* of hospitality. Yet it is clear that this treatment of hospitality constitutes an important precedent for the link between political liberty and a warm welcome located in Morris's work. Particularly pertinent is Kant's condemnation of the injustice shown by 'civilized' states 'in their visits to foreign countries and peoples'. In Morris's Nowhere, a liberalistic conception of hospitality serves, in a similar way, to illuminate the ethical failings of the modern social apparatus.

In his correspondence, it is notable how often Morris aligns himself with the figure of the grumbler or obstinate complainant. Writing to Georgiana Burne-Jones, he once confessed, 'I don't quite agree with you in condemning grumbling against follies and ills that oppress the world at large.'[163] In 'How We Live and How We Might Live' (1884), he insists, 'I won't submit to be dressed up in red and marched off to shoot at my French or German or Arab friend in a quarrel that I don't understand; I will rebel sooner than do that'.[164] These senti-ments reflect the defiant sense of individuality to which May Morris recalls her father giving voice: 'if they brigaded *him* into a regiment of workers he would just lie on his back and kick'.[165] What is the position of strangers and dissenters in Morris's utopia? In *News from Nowhere*, the issue surfaces in the form of old Hammond's jibe, 'A terrible tyranny our Communism, is it not?', made in response to Guest's scepticism regarding decision-making arrangements.[166] Morris's willingness to permit rash actions in Nowhere – marital infidelity and occasional violence, for example – is equalled by his toleration of figures whose 'atavism' would make them hospital cases in Edward Bellamy's *Looking Back-ward*.[167]

In the chapter entitled 'HAMPTON COURT. AND A PRAISER OF PAST TIMES', Morris's most belligerent dissenting voice is first heard. Ellen's grandfa-ther, 'the old grumbler', complains that in Nowhere he feels compelled to lead a

162 Kant, *Perpetual Peace*, 1795, pp. 33–4.
163 Morris, 'From a Letter to Georgiana Burne-Jones', 16 September 1881, in *Collected Letters*, II, p. 65.
164 Morris, 'How We Live and How We Might Live', p. 20.
165 May Morris, Introduction, *Collected Works*, XVI, pp. xj–xxix (p. xxviij).
166 Morris, *News from Nowhere*, p. 90.
167 Morris's objections to Bellamy's *Looking Backward 2000 to 1887* (Boston: Ticknor & Company, 1888), inspired him to supply his own vision of the socialist future as a corrective.

dull and unadventurous life.[168] Jan Holm has addressed the implications of this scene in an article entitled 'The Old Grumbler At Runnymede'. Holm argues that Morris's motives are purely strategic, that he uses Ellen's grandfather as a straw man, a figure who, in the course of the dialogue, is manoeuvred 'in a manipulative way that makes the critic of his world appear silly'.[169] There is much to be said for this reading of the encounter, but it is not altogether sufficient. Morris uses the grumbler's dissenting voice to do more than contain and neutralize audience scepticism. He provides more than a 'comic relief' antidote to old Hammond's prolonged, sage-like discourse.[170] The members of the boating party have already travelled some way upstream, and Guest is no longer contemplating Nowhere's social arrangements. He is instead considering his 'enjoyment of the beautiful time' and his 'own lazily blended thoughts'.[171] When the party finally meet the old man, his abrupt manner comes as a shock. Clara makes 'some commonplace remark about the beauty of the day', and the old man replies, 'You really like it then?' Holm rightly observes that these outbursts recur so often that they become a cause of merriment, a familiar and unthreatening form of words. The grumbler's unconventional manners nevertheless serve to question the maturing complacency of Guest, Clara and Dick. Clara is 'astonished' and later breaks into laughter. The old man soon finds himself caught in the tangled web of his own inconsistency; but one should not ignore the jolt effected by his first appearance, or the power of his most convincing argument: that life in Nowhere lacks 'a spirit of adventure', that people would be 'brisker and more alive' were they living in a competitive arena. Morris's willingness to allow the old grumbler temporarily to supplant Dick in his role as 'host' evinces his confidence that these arguments will not find fertile soil in the reader's mind, that by voicing them they may more effectively be debunked.

Even if one accepts that the appearance of this figure has the effect of immunizing Nowhere against criticism, Morris's decision to place a grumbler in his utopia, a man representative for Dick of past 'nuisance', helps him to characterize Nowhere as a land where tolerance is taken for granted. If the old grumbler wishes to dissent from pleasure in his surroundings, then nobody is going to penalize him. If he approaches the activity of grumbling with peculiar relish, in stubborn perpetuation of that discontent rendered obsolete by the revolution, then he has every right to do so. Morris makes a similar point in *The Tables Turned*. The former Mr Justice Nupkins is treated in the subsequent socialist era as if he were 'Citizen Nupkins'.[172] The celebratory mood of the play supports the now unfortunate jest that he will be shot like a dog, a detail apparently designed to parody the treatment socialist rebels expected to receive at the hands of the British government. But ultimately he is humoured as a curiosity, a piece of local colour: 'You are queerly rigged', declares William Joyce on first seeing Nupkins, 'You're like an ancient ruin, a dream of past times'. Nupkins, like the Houses of Parliament in

---

168 Morris, *News from Nowhere*, p. 153.
169 Jan Holm, 'The Old Grumbler at Runnymede', *The Journal of the William Morris Society*, 10 (Spring 1993), 2, 17–21 (p. 21).
170 Holm, 'The Old Grumbler at Runnymede', p. 18.
171 Morris, *News from Nowhere*, pp. 146–50.
172 Morris, *The Tables Turned*, pp. 556, 559, 563, 565, 567.

News from Nowhere, is allowed to retain his essential character, only he must change his title, and apply himself to some useful work. The irony is that Nupkins never is successfully *awakened*. He remains an obstinate complainant:

> C.N. (*bursting into tears*). A world without lawyers! – oh, dear! oh, dear! To think that I should have to dig potatoes and see everybody happy.

Nupkins is nevertheless treated impartially. He is not sent to a firing squad or a mental asylum. As in Nowhere, if people wish to denounce the new social arrangements, or even the very notion of a paradisal community, they are free to do so.[173] No matter how misguided Morris might think these figures, readers are invited to acknowledge that they are entitled to their own '*theories* about the change which has taken place'.[174]

The humorous atmosphere that pervades the scene at Runnymede reveals the pleasure Morris takes in dissenting, if only momentarily, from his own political programme. The figure of the reactionary, of the staunch opponent, becomes a useful mask, enabling him to put self-criticism to an instructive purpose. It is also productive of revelry and misrule. In *The Tables Turned*, Morris has himself described by Lord Tennyson as 'a stumpy little fool in blue'.[175] Mr Hungary, the barrister acting for the prosecution in the play's riotous courtroom scenes, becomes the mouthpiece for much satirical comment on the varied fortunes and pretensions of the socialist movement. *News from Nowhere* itself begins with a savagely comic representation of affairs at the League:

> there were six persons present, and consequently six sections of the party were represented, four of which had strong but divergent Anarchist opinions.[176]

The schismatic character of British socialism is here the object of Morris's generous ridicule, the prevailing mindset of divergence ironically endorsed by the logical formulation, 'consequently'. Even in their anarchic individualism, the 'four' appear unable to agree. Caricature surfaces in the description of this scene as another method of self-parody. Morris, quite obviously, is the friend of a friend, the stormy personality who ends by 'damning all the rest for fools'. Old Hammond, in his role as explicator and historian, is also aligned with the author. In this capacity, he is rendered susceptible to anarchic self-interruption:

> 'to the time when Africa was infested by a man named Stanley, who –'
> 'Excuse me,' said I, 'but as you know, time presses; and I want to keep our question on the straightest line possible; [. . .]' [. . .] the old man [. . .] was rather peevish at being cut short in his story.

All too conscious of his own capacity for rambling polemic, Morris ensures that old Hammond is stopped in full stride. He does not just cut short in their story

---

173 At one point, the old grumbler remarks, 'I think one may do more with one's life than sitting on a damp cloud and singing hymns' (p. 152).
174 Morris, *News from Nowhere*, p. 156. This stands in contrast to life in the utopias of Plato and More, where opinion is regulated and enforced by an intellectual elite.
175 Morris, *The Tables Turned*, p. 549.
176 Morris, *News from Nowhere*, pp. 3, 65, 96–6, 146, 190.

those characters who approximate most closely to his own extra-textual persona. He also combines interruption with comic deflation. The irreverent atmosphere so produced reassures us that there are no sacred personages in this world, no experts unwilling to tolerate good-humoured mockery.

Notwithstanding the emphasis on openness, it is clear that a respect for *home*, for a limited, to some extent private, realm, remains a crucial precondition of the happiness Morris envisages. When Guest suggests that 'households' recall for him 'the customs of past times', that is, Victorian times, old Hammond replies that 'separate households are the rule amongst us', that 'they differ in their habits more or less, yet no door is shut to any good-tempered person who is content to live as the other house-mates do'. Guest's implicit suggestion that 'Fourierist phalangsteries' [*sic*] might be more in keeping with Nowhereian communality meets the retort that refuges from destitution are no longer required. Why, then, in a utopia, amidst a humanity no longer alienated by a hostile environment, should the notion of *home* remain so crucial? Guest observes, on visiting Hampton Court, that the people there had 'an indefinable kind of look of being at home and at ease'. Ellen later contrasts this settled existence with the 'great deal of changing of abode' she suspects was typical of nineteenth-century life. The ethos determining this veneration of homeliness is revealed most clearly in old Hammond's reference to the different 'habits' that distinguish households. The persistence of individual dwellings, and their capacity to offer 'ease', reflects Morris's concern to preserve individual identities and group-specific 'habits'. Thresholds offer a convenient means of preserving the cultural integrity enjoyed by separate households. So while Morris increases the permeability of the average dwelling, and extends the constituent meaning of *home* far beyond what was achieved at Red House, he retains spaces where hospitality can be practised meaningfully. This depends, of course, upon the survival of the guest-host relationship, and of the differing claims designated within it.

In seeking to explain another strange survival – the persistence of occasional violence in this utopia – it helps to consider the influence on Morris of Norse mythology. It has been suggested by Hartley Spatt that he 'rejected the very assumption [. . .] that transcendence was the ultimate goal'.[177] The clash of ice and fire that animates the created world of Norse mythology may be regarded as one source of this unwillingness to 'transcend dialectic'.[178] As implied by the alternative title of his utopia, an 'Epoch of Rest', Morris also found the prospect of synthesis attractive. The passionate intensity of his utopians nevertheless ensures that the possibility of unpremeditated conflict is preserved. In his lecture, 'Monopoly: or, How Labour is Robbed' (1887), Morris addressed this matter directly, arguing for 'a society in which [. . .] we shall live among friends and neighbours, with whom indeed our passions or folly may sometimes make us quarrel'.[179] Spatt's emphasis on content is echoed by Mineo, who stresses the text's

---

[177] Hartley S. Spatt, 'William Morris's Late Romances: The Struggle Against Closure', in Florence S. Boos, ed., *History and Community: Essays in Victorian Medievalism* (New York: Garland Publishing, 1992), pp. 109–35 (p. 110).

[178] Spatt, 'William Morris's Late Romances', p. 110.

[179] Morris, 'Monopoly; or, How Labour is Robbed', p. 254.

formal resistance to narrative closure.[180] Such arguments find some justification in the original circumstances of publication. Morris wrote *News from Nowhere* at speed. It first appeared as a series of instalments in *Commonweal*, the newspaper of the Socialist League. This procedure encouraged a less meticulous approach to planning than might otherwise have been expected, as suggested by certain factual inconsistencies.[181] It also allowed for the easy interpolation of new episodes in later editions. Morris's success in producing a text responsive to the changing current of debate is best illustrated by the addition of the 'The Obstinate Refusers' (Chapter XXVI) to the Reeves and Turner edition of 1891.[182] One suggested reason for the change is that Morris felt compelled, in the face of anarchist domi-nance at the Socialist League, to register the possibility that comrades may choose to go their own way.[183] Morris's own capacity for wilfulness is demonstrated by the altered inscription at the Hammersmith Guest House. Today's standard edition reads 'Guests and neighbours, on the site of this Guest-hall once stood the lecture-room of the Hammersmith Socialists'.[184] The inscription in the *Common-weal* edition refers instead to the 'Hammersmith Branch of the Socialist League', a detail that reflects the secession of Morris's local association from the parent body.

If this utopia does indeed represent an open-ended text, of the type Umberto Eco has sought to theorize,[185] there would seem to be grounds for the claim that Morris does not impose meaning; that in resisting the 'sense of an ending',[186] he encourages the reader to determine the import of the text. *News from Nowhere* contains two episodes that would appear to support such an account. The first occurs near the end of Guest's journey, when Ellen speculates that, 'happy as we are, times may alter; we may be bitten with some impulse towards change, and many things may seem too wonderful for us to resist'.[187] The second comes at the close of the tale, at that point when the narrative voice stresses the personal char-acter of this dream of a better life. Only 'if others can see it' will it become 'a vision' of the future, one which is socialistic, which invites and requires participa-tion. This accords with Morris's assertion, in his review of *Looking Backward*, that the 'only safe way of reading a utopia is to consider it as the expression of the temperament of its author'.[188] Indeed, his proliferating self-representation may be viewed as an attempt at dramatizing this point. Old Hammond, the old grumbler, and even Dick are all reminiscent of the author. In this way, one is reminded that such projects have their narcissistic side, that *News from Nowhere* is a work of creative prose rather than a manifesto. There seems to be some basis, then, for the

---

180 Mineo, 'Beyond the Law of the Father', p. 200.
181 Andrew Belsey provides detailed justification for the observation that 'the totality of temporal references in *News from Nowhere* do not add up to a coherent whole' in 'Getting Somewhere: Rhetoric and Politics in *News from Nowhere*', *Textual Practice*, 5 (Winter 1991), 3, 337–51 (p. 347).
182 Morris, *News from Nowhere* (London: Reeves and Turner, 1891).
183 See Michael Liberman's article, 'Major Textual Changes in William Morris's *News from Nowhere*', *Nineteenth Century*, 41 (1986–87), 3, 349–56 (p. 355).
184 Morris, *News from Nowhere*, p. 16.
185 Umberto Eco, *The Open Work*, trans. by Anna Cancogni ([London]: Hutchinson Radius, 1989).
186 Frank Kermode, *The Sense of an Ending: Studies in the Theory of Fiction* (New York: Oxford University Press, 1967).
187 Morris, *News from Nowhere*, pp. 194, 211.
188 Morris, 'Looking Backward', *Commonweal*, 22 June 1889, pp. 194–5 (p. 194).

claim that Morris's decentralist politics find expression in the form of a textual strategy that seeks to devolve meaning, that uses an open-ended plot as a suitable vehicle for the description of an open society and employs the form of a literary utopia to produce a vision sufficiently enigmatic and personalized to discourage dogmatic interpretation.

Thus far, evidence has been considered in support of the claim that Morris created a uniquely libertarian utopia. It should be clear that the post-revolutionary communities depicted in *News from Nowhere* and *The Tables Turned* enjoy levels of freedom uncustomary at least in those utopias derived from the tradition of the Platonic or Spartan ideal republic. This investigation must now move into its second phase. In Morris's utopia we abandon the realm of oppressive laws, of happiness jealously guarded, only to discover that the gift of freedom is a Trojan horse for a different kind of regulation. By accommodating old grumblers and obstinate refusers in Nowhere, Morris would seem to display, according to the critics I have discussed, a hospitable *largesse*. And yet, as soon as these liberties are viewed in terms of generosity, in terms of something unnecessary but gracious, one begins to wonder whether such acts can ever be purely disinterested. There is, in other words, the danger of allowing the selfless connotations of hospitality to obscure the otherwise *interested* and *individual* nature of this utopia (which Morris himself stressed). In his New Historicist account of the hospitality rituals evoked in Renaissance drama, Daryl Palmer stresses 'the ideological commitments of hosts, guests, and onlookers'.[189] In the plays of the period, he suggests, 'hospitality encourages a benign description of the world, even as it supports strategies of exploitation'. Is hospitality in *News from Nowhere* applied towards the furtherance of a genuine pluralism, or does it serve the purposes Palmer would ascribe to it; projecting power and thus achieving assent, even as it parades a formalized dissent?

To explore this point further, I now consider the insights afforded by Marcel Mauss's influential discussion of gift exchanges in *Essai sur le don* (1925; rev. edn 1954).[190] Mauss opens his investigation with an assertion that has direct bearing on the kind of 'generosity' that might characterize the operations of a utopist who deliberately includes hostile or subversive elements within his vision of the good society. 'In Scandinavian civilization', he writes, 'exchanges and contracts take place in the form of presents'. In theory, such gifts 'are voluntary'; but 'in reality they are given and reciprocated obligatorily'. How might this realistic, or sceptical, theory of generosity help to modify understanding of Mr Justice Nupkins's position, or that of the old grumbler? Mauss suggests that to be seen to give is 'to show one's superiority, to be more, to be higher in rank'. 'To accept without giving in return, or without giving more back', he adds, 'is to become client and servant.' As a form of generosity, hospitality involves its participants in an unspoken agreement of a similar nature. It instils an understanding that certain forms of behaviour are not acceptable whilst the role of guest is maintained. It also confers definite power on the host.

---

189 Daryl W. Palmer, *Hospitable Performances: Dramatic Genre and Cultural Practices in Early Modern England* (West Lafayette, Indiana: Purdue University Press, 1992), pp. 7, 28.
190 Mauss, *The Gift*, pp. 3, 6, 69, 95.

Mauss's argument depends upon a rejection of the assumption that among 'primitive' peoples a system of barter everywhere preceded the advent of mercantile exchange. Against this view, he asserts that 'there has never existed, either in an era fairly close in time to our own, or in societies that we lump together somewhat awkwardly as primitive or inferior, anything that might resemble what is called a 'natural' economy'. By a ' "natural" economy', Mauss means that model of society postulated by classical economists wherein simple exchanges of goods, wealth and products are concluded between individuals without wider ramifications. Arguing that the Romans and the Greeks 'invented the distinction between personal and real law, separated sale from gift and exchange, isolated the moral obligation and contract', he implies that the logic of these procedures should not be allowed to cloud understanding of cultures predating their discovery. It is first of all notable how close the portrait of economic life contained in *News from Nowhere* is to the state of affairs described by Mauss. Morris's utopians make no 'distinction between obligations and services that are not given free, on the one hand, and gifts, on the other'.[191] Their way of life resembles Mauss's 'archaic society', in which the 'whole economy of the exchange-through-gift lay outside the bounds of the so-called natural economy, that of utilitarianism'. The significance of this comparison becomes clearer when it is seen that Mauss, like Morris, describes the prospect of a return to this state of affairs in terms of the recovery of a kind of 'group morality':

> Thus we can and must return to archaic society and to elements in it. We shall find in this reasons for life and action that are still prevalent in certain societies and numerous social classes: the joy of public giving; the pleasure in generous expenditure on the arts, in hospitality, and in the private and public festival.

The part of Mauss's thesis that applies most readily to the economy of *News from Nowhere* – it too substitutes hospitable gestures for utilitarian exchange – is the argument that it would be wrong to equate a lack of legal limits or formal contract with a situation in which no limits whatsoever obtain. Classing Morris's Nowhere as a primitive economy of sorts, one may begin to appreciate the implications of Mauss's theory of the gift, his assertion that acts of generosity should not be considered in isolation from the society in which they are performed, his contention that such acts are really 'total services' whose character, whilst apparently 'free and disinterested' is 'nevertheless constrained and self-interested'. In the light of this comparison, one might first ask whether it is reasonable to construe Morris's accommodation of dissent as a selfish act masquerading as a disinterested one. Do the liberties bestowed on the old grumbler, for instance, serve Morris's political ends – in his role as host, as a figure who invites us into his world – even as he seems to undermine them in an act of self-immolation or potlatch?[192]

191 Mauss, *The Gift*, pp. 4, 6, 61, 87, 88–9, 92.
192 Mauss writes of chiefs and nobles who in their rivalry 'go as far as the purely sumptuary destruction of wealth that has been accumulated in order to outdo the rival chief as well as his associate', *The Gift*, p. 8. He proposes 'to reserve the term potlatch for this kind of institution'.

Mauss,[193] and Pitt-Rivers after him,[194] regard hospitality as a momentary peace, a temporary suppression of residual hostility. What happens when this thinking is applied to a reading of Morris's own utopian act, his attempt to open a momentary corridor between two hostile realms, to maintain an 'unstable state between festival and war'?[195] Most obviously, it clarifies Morris's need to impress upon his readers – his guests – the attractiveness of a realm culturally hostile to their own place of domicile. He must do this in order to obtain from them what he wants: a transfer of allegiance. Of course there is nothing unique in comparing an imperfect past with an improved future. Most utopists, after all, must install an agent of the external world in an ideal realm in order to convey their news. Morris's guest from the nineteenth century receives a hospitality that is warm, but the gesture is not necessarily disinterested, at least on the level of the text's function as a persuasive utopia. There is, then, a functional rationale governing Morris's representation of dissent, implying that 'grumbling and wishing yourself back again in the good old days', in the style of Ellen's grandfather, provides convenient opportunity for the instructive refutation of heresy.[196] This strategy suggests unfortunate parallels with the 'repressive tolerance' Herbert Marcuse located in affluent post-war societies, societies in which 'modes of protest and transcendence' were 'no longer contradictory to the status quo',[197] but rather 'part of its healthy diet'.

Morris's inclusion of 'dissenting' voices is also functional in so far as it prevents Nowhere from degenerating into the kind of 'happy valley' described by Samuel Johnson in *The History of Rasselas* (1759).[198] Considered in these terms, the appearance of the old grumbler is undoubtedly an 'event'. His incredulous enquiry, 'you like heaven, do you?' at once announces that it is possible to have too much peace and quiet, and fends off that possibility.[199] Though a familiar objection to the prospect of untrammelled pleasure, the suggestion that heaven would actually be a very dull place was then assuming new resonance against the backdrop of social Darwinist controversy. H. G. Wells, only five years later, predicted that a humanity no longer challenged by its environment would face new dangers. In *The Time Machine*, the Eloi, or Upper-worlders, have lost all their habits of curiosity.[200] Their defensive capacities have wasted away and they live, as a result, in fear of a carnivorous coming race. The old grumbler's satiric sketch of heaven would not, in its realization, have offered Morris any satisfaction. A world without work was for him a lifeless prospect, a place of the undying, like that encountered by Hallblithe in *The Story of the Glittering Plain* (1891).[201] The sympathetic narra-

---

193 Mauss argues that at a certain point in the evolution of society people started 'substituting alliance, gifts, and trade for war, isolation and stagnation', *The Gift*, p. 105.

194 Pitt-Rivers, 'The Stranger, the Guest and the Hostile Host'.

195 Mauss, *The Gift*, p. 105.

196 Morris, *News from Nowhere*, p. 150.

197 Herbert Marcuse, *One Dimensional Man* (London: Abacus, 1972), pp. 21, 25.

198 Samuel Johnson, *The History of Rasselas, Prince of Abyssinia*, in *The Yale Edition of the Works of Samuel Johnson*, ed. by Gwin J. Kolb, 16 vols (New Haven: Yale University Press, 1990), XVI, pp. 1–212.

199 Morris, *News from Nowhere*, p. 152.

200 H.G. Wells, *The Time Machine: An Invention* (London: Heinemann, 1895).

201 Morris, *The Story of the Glittering Plain; or, The Land of Living Men*, in *Collected Works*, XIV, pp. 209–324.

tion of Hallblithe's flight from paradise suggests that the old grumbler is not used exclusively as a mouthpiece for the views of opponents. His presence can be iden- tified with the use of variety outlined by Ruskin in 'The Nature of Gothic'. He serves to disrupt and to ward off 'monotony',[202] to express a vision of what Nowhere would become without work and without incident.

The distinction Mauss makes, between a society run according to principles of generosity and one in which absolute freedom of action is enjoyed, underlines the point made by several critics that Morris's decentralist politics[203] did not equate to anarchism in the most literal sense the word.[204] Doing away with legalism, shifting emphasis away from the state and the city towards the commune and the house- hold, did not mean dispensing with forms of regulation altogether. Anarchism was not a word with which Morris felt comfortable. It suggested to him a disre- gard for his most cherished concepts, for society and the commonweal. Indeed, *News from Nowhere* can itself be interpreted as an attack on anarchism, as a lament for the disunity then plaguing the leadership of the Socialist League. Even while instalments were still appearing in *Commonweal*, Morris was ejected from his position as editor by representatives of the strengthening anarchist wing. When Guest and old Hammond discuss the various forms of government avail- able to a society, his host responds in a way that leaves Morris's views on the subject in no doubt:

> 'Well,' said I, 'there is a third possibility – to wit, that every man should be quite independent of every other, and that thus the tyranny of society should be abol- ished.'
>
> He looked hard at me for a second or two, and then burst out laughing very heartily; and I confess that I joined him.[205]

It would then be a mistake to interpret the apparent openness of Nowhere, and Morris's enthusiasm for certain aspects of the anarchists' programme – such as communes, decentralization, regionalism – as an indication that he intended the freedom of his utopians to go entirely unrestricted. In Nowhere there is no government to enforce social behaviour, but it does not follow that the individual pursues life in a social vacuum devoid of necessity and responsibility.

The reminiscences of Bruce Glasier include a passage, attributed to Morris, that casts further light on this matter. Glasier's claim to be able to quote his old comrade word for word so many years after the event might lead us to treat his

---

202 Ruskin, 'The Nature of Gothic', *The Stones of Venice*, p. 207.

203 In 'Dawn of a New Epoch', Morris suggests that socialism is only the most recent expression of a broader decentralist tendency: 'It is clear that, quite apart from Socialism, the idea of local administration is pushing out that of centralized government: to take a remarkable case: in the French Revolution of 1793, the most advanced party was centralizing: in the latest French Revo- lution, that of the Commune of 1871, it was federalist' in *Collected Works*, XXIII pp. 121–40 (p. 138).

204 Rowland McMaster suggests that, in the end, Morris could not quite believe 'the innocence of the paradisal vision' and 'accepted a compromise, as Mill had done, between total freedom and coer- cion', 'Tensions in Paradise: Anarchism, Civilization, and Pleasure in Morris's *News from Nowhere*', *English Studies in Canada*, XVII (March, 1991), I, 73–87 (p. 84).

205 Morris, *News from Nowhere*, p. 89.

reports with some scepticism. Yet the following passage contains nothing that could not be gleaned from Morris's extant writings:[206]

> But, mark you again, what I aim at is Socialism or Communism, not Anarchism. Anarchism and Communism, notwithstanding our friend Kropotkin, are incompatible in principle. Anarchism means, as I understand it, the doing away with, and doing without, laws and rules of all kinds, and in each person being allowed to do just as he pleases. I don't want people to do just as they please; I want them to consider and act for the good of their fellows – for the commonweal in fact. Now what constitutes the commonweal, or common notion of what is for the common good, will and always must be expressed in the form of laws of some kind – either political laws, instituted by the citizens in public assembly, as of old by folk-moot, or if you will by real councils or parliaments of the people, or by social customs growing up from the experience of Society [. . .] I am not going to quibble over the question as to the difference between laws and customs.[207]

Echoing Chapter II ('Doing as One Likes') of Matthew Arnold's *Culture & Anarchy*, the expression, 'to do just as he pleases' stipulates that anarchy was exactly what Morris considered himself to be attacking.[208] In his opinion, it was capitalism that was anarchic. This was to underestimate the robust and systematic nature of the force he was opposing. It also ignored the organized quality of a related foe, which Morris never tired of criticizing: namely, utilitarianism. It is nevertheless significant that he chose to characterize capitalism as the enemy of civilization, rather than as the bulwark of some familiar and established order.

The reference, in Glasier's account, to a distinction between laws and customs is of crucial importance, as it indicates the method by which Morris rejected modern legal forms without renouncing the need for regulation. Michael Holzman makes a related point when he observes that Morris accommodates 'rules to deal with unreasonable situations' that eventually 'will become "half-forgotten"'.[209] 'In Utopia, or Nowhere,' he continues, 'minorities will have better manners than they appear to have had within the Socialist League.' Mauss's analysis of the gift supplies a way of demonstrating the limits of Morris's 'generosity'. It also highlights the relationship between manners and regulation, and demonstrates how, under certain conditions, manners might be regarded as a viable alternative to more formal regulatory methods. Given Morris's determined resistance to 'anarchistic' solutions, it is ironic that the same conception of manners underpins the ideas of William Godwin. Commonly regarded as the father of anarchism, Godwin's work resists crude categorization. *Caleb Williams* narrates

---

[206] See, for example, the exchange between Morris and Blackwell in the letters pages of *Commonweal*. It established the parameters of the debate between the anarchist wing of the Party and the group that eventually broke away to form the Hammersmith Socialist Society. Note in particular, 'Correspondence', *Commonweal*, 18 May 1889, p. 157; and Morris's letter, 'Communism and Anarchism', *Commonweal*, 17 August 1889, p. 261.
[207] J. Bruce Glasier, *William Morris and the Early Days of the Socialist Movement* (London: Longmans, 1921), pp. 63–4.
[208] Matthew Arnold, *Culture & Anarchy: An Essay in Political and Social Criticism*, in *The Works of Matthew Arnold*, V, pp. 85–256 (pp. 115–36).
[209] Michael Holzman, 'Anarchism and Utopia: William Morris's *News from Nowhere*', *ELH*, 51 (1984), 589–603 (p. 595).

the serial misfortunes of a self-educated servant who becomes a fugitive from justice after incurring the wrath of his tyrannical employer.[210] The novel contains a passage in which a captain of thieves, faced with the dilemma of sheltering the eponymous hero, warns his followers against 'violating the laws of hospitality'. He distinguishes adherence to these laws from servile compliance with the laws of the state. His ignoble companion offers the retort that, 'After having violated other laws, I do not see why we should be frightened at an old saw.' This passage demonstrates the risk Morris ran of unfairly caricaturing the anarchist tradition, elements of which could be construed as proximate, even identical, to his own political outlook. Godwin's implicit message, after all, is that liberty does not justify the dissolution of all social bonds and loyalties. Through the speech of the less sympathetic thief, he also denigrates the extreme position Morris crudely terms, 'anarchist'. The confusion is partly one of terminology and partly a symptom of Morris's need to distinguish his own attachment to minimal regulation from the position of his opponents.

In his short work, *Of Hospitality*, Jacques Derrida argues that 'absolute hospitality requires that I open up my home and that I give not only to the foreigner [. . .] but to the absolute, unknown, anonymous other, and that I *give place* to them, that I let them come [. . .] without asking of them either reciprocity (entering into a pact) or even their names'.[211] How might this definition illuminate the interrelation between regulation and hospitality so far discussed? It is apparent, first of all, that Derrida's account precludes all forms of law (both the formal and the informal). While Morris modifies hospitality in such a way as to make it less exclusive, Guest's welcome is not of the absolute kind described here. Morris makes a concerted effort to demonstrate the regulatory effect of the hospitality Guest receives, its conferral of an unofficial, but nonetheless real, code of conduct.[212] Mauss's assertion that 'it is not individuals but collectivities that impose obligations of exchange and contract upon each other' goes some way towards explaining why Guest never feels the need to reciprocate when he is given gifts at the market (the pipe and tobacco, for instance).[213] In his capacity as a favoured visitor, he is not obliged to give in return to any one individual; he instead enters into a contract of mutual respect and responsibility with Nowherian society as a whole. It is at this point that Nowherian hospitality and Derrida's absolute or unconditional hospitality diverge.

In the opening scenes of *News from Nowhere*, Morris draws attention to the themes of courtesy and good manners. Robert wonders whether there is 'any indiscretion in asking' Guest his name.[214] He eventually receives a reprimand for this persistent questioning, and a kick under the table from Dick. That Robert is able to persist in asking questions, whilst 'almost aware of his breach of good

210 William Godwin, *Caleb Williams* (Oxford: Oxford University Press, 1982), p. 222.
211 Derrida, *Of Hospitality*, p. 25.
212 Engels's analysis of Australian Aboriginal law, considered in Part I of this chapter, is of relevance to this discussion of informal regulation. Engels argued that the European who sees 'immorality and lawlessness' in the custom 'by which the man with several wives gives one up for the night to his guest' misinterprets a situation in which 'strict law rules in reality', *The Origin of the Family*, p. 45.
213 Mauss, *The Gift*, p. 6.
214 Morris, *News from Nowhere*, pp. 16, 17, 157.

manners', at once indicates the flexibility Morris builds into his system of informal regulation, and demonstrates that even those who commit minor transgressions are always *aware* that they are doing so, implying that they have not failed to internalize the social rhythms of their society. It is important to recognize that even the old grumbler is aware of his obligations and is willing to adhere to them. After making his views known, and causing general upset in the process, he remarks, apologetically, 'all I can see is that you are angry, and I fear with me: so if you like we will change the subject'. Guest thinks 'this kind and hospitable in him, considering his obstinacy about his theory'. In the margin of the Kelmscott edition, this episode is glossed as 'Courtesy amidst obstinacy'.[215] Thus it is possible to commit transgressions or to behave impolitely in this society without becoming an outlaw; but an unavoidable awareness of obligation ensures that such actions are followed by repentance.[216]

Morris expressed his views on the subject of social regulation in a letter to *Commonweal*, dated 18 May 1889.[217] In it he considers the place of authority in a communist society. With 'equality of condition assured' and an 'ethics based on reason', he argues, 'the political side of the question would take care of itself'. By confining the enactment of criminal justice to a personal level, he also expresses admiration for the Icelandic equivalent of the wergild.[218] In 'The Early Literature of the North – Iceland', Morris explained how this system of atonement and reparation operated during the Age of Settlement:

> The morality of the time was enforced purely by public opinion, a shabby or treacherous action was looked upon as something quite different from a legal offense [*sic*], condemnation for which latter involving no kind of disgrace: and even when a man slew his enemy in a just quarrel he had to pay for him; though where the wrong was flagrant he could kill him at a less expense than otherwise (Gunnar). All this you must understand was not mere private war and revenge and consequent confusion but simply a different system to our politico-territorial system, and was based as I said on the equal personal rights of all freedmen.[219]

In *News from Nowhere*, similarly, a transgressor is required 'to make any atonement possible to him'.[220] This personalizing of grievance and redress finds its parallel in the system of self-regulation Morris describes in his Teutonic romances. In *The House of the Wolfings*, the marriage customs of the gens are explained in great detail. We are told that 'this was a law that none dreamed of breaking'.[221] A similar phrase is used by old Hammond when he explains that in

---

215 Morris, *News from Nowhere*, Kelmscott edition, p. 227.

216 In answer to Guest's question as to whether anyone ever 'transgresses this habit of good fellowship' (*News from Nowhere*, p. 80), Hammond replies that 'when the transgressions occur, everybody, transgressors and all, know them for what they are; the errors of friends, not the habitual actions of persons driven into enmity against society'.

217 Morris, 'Correspondence', *Commonweal*, p. 157

218 The *OED* defines Wergild as follows: 'In ancient Teutonic and Old English law, the price set upon a man according to his rank, paid by way of compensation or fine in cases of homicide and certain other crimes to free the offender from further obligation or punishment.'

219 Morris, 'The Early Literature of the North – Iceland', pp. 183–4.

220 Morris, *News from Nowhere*, p. 82.

221 Morris, *The House of the Wolfings*, p. 5.

Nowhere 'the regulations of the markets' vary 'according to the circumstances': they are guided by a 'general custom' that 'nobody dreams of objecting to'.[222] In a fully developed communist society, Morris implies, it will be impossible to dissent from the values of the wider social conscience without committing an act of self-harm.

Harmonization of the social and the individual good, and a conviction that all members of a 'true society' can enjoy happiness in common, combine to underpin Morris's new world, to guarantee its stability. But there is a problem here. When old Hammond makes specific reference to the importance of happiness, he betrays in the process a crucial assumption, the belief that all members of humanity are naturally made happy by the same things:

> What is the object of Revolution? Surely to make people happy. Revolution having brought its foredoomed change about, how can you prevent the counter-revolution from setting in except by making people happy?[223]

Morris makes a similar point in his letter to *Commonweal* of 18 May 1889: 'The bond of Communistic society will be voluntary in the sense that all people will agree in its broadest principles when it is fairly established, and will trust to it as affording mankind the best kind of life possible'.[224] Morris's wish to accommodate the diverse propensities of humanity begins to pull against his perception that only a common experience of happiness will supply a self-regulating 'true society'. The assumption that people will not seek to damage their own interests secures the settlement under which the Nowherians live. Morris himself remarks in 'How We Live and How We Might Live' that, 'in a state of social order I shall have no need to rebel'.[225] In other words, the inhabitants of Nowhere will have no wish to escape, because the conditions exist for them all to be happy. Again, it is necessary to state that this stable consensus is not achieved through an abolition of rules, but via the optimistic assumption that reasonable, politically free individuals will not discriminate between the personal and the social logic of such rules. Like hospitality, manners already existed in Victorian society as a non-legal standard of conduct. As such, they represented a suitable aid for imagining the otherwise inconceivable: a situation in which an abolition of official legality had not resulted in an outbreak of disorder or antisocial behaviour.

The consequences of Morris's reliance on informal law are at their most interesting and problematic as they affect William Guest. His arrival in a world regulated by a highly developed sense of good conduct poses an obvious difficulty: originating from elsewhere, he is in danger of doing what must be unthinkable for his hosts: he risks breaking a rule without being aware that he has done so. Morris exploits this situation for comic effect, but not in such a way that its serious aspects are obscured. The appearance of Guest does not precipitate or encourage an unravelling of the codes that govern Nowherian life. Instead, he is gradually directed towards conformity with them; he becomes a test case for the possibility

---

[222] Morris, *News from Nowhere*, p. 84.
[223] Morris, *News from Nowhere*, p. 92.
[224] Morris, 'Correspondence', *Commonweal*, p. 157
[225] Morris, 'How We Live and How We Might Live', p. 20.

of socializing the denizens of a commercial nation. Every time he commits a *faux pas*, every time he contravenes the unspoken rules that define polite behaviour, he is troubled by a feeling of awkwardness. He engages, as a result, in a process of self-censorship. Anxious to maintain his role as a guest – unwilling to lose this status by causing offence to his hosts – he begins to suppress aspects of his past that seem either factually inconsistent with his role as a stranger or politically unacceptable in a communist society. As soon as he realizes he has crossed over to another time, this process of self-regulation begins:

> The date shut my mouth as if a key had been turned in a padlock fixed to my lips; for I saw that something inexplicable had happened, and that if I said much, I should be mixed up in a game of cross questions and crooked answers.[226]

Guest's socialization is not seamless, however. His sense of frustration occasionally gets the better of him. At one point, he thinks to himself, 'Hang it! [. . .] I can't open my mouth without digging up some new complexity'. Henceforth he chooses silence over humiliation, holding his peace, 'for fear of fresh entanglements'. Even after the initial confusion presented by the ferryman's refusal to accept any payment for his services, Guest occasionally slips up. His sense that it would be a mistake to repeat such displays too often is expressed in the thought that he 'had no mind for another lecture on social economy and the Edwardian coinage'. The unease produced by his ignorance of Nowhereian mores comes to a head when he attempts to pay for the pipe and tobacco given to him at the market:

> I took it out of her hand to look at it, and while I did so, forgot my caution, and said, 'But however am I to pay for such a thing as this?'
> Dick laid his hand on my shoulder as I spoke, and turning I met his eyes with a comical expression in them, which warned me against another exhibition of extinct commercial morality; so I reddened and held my tongue, while the girl simply looked at me with the deepest gravity, as if I were a foreigner blundering in my speech, for she clearly didn't understand me a bit.

Guest's worst display of extinct morality occurs when he asks Dick whether there are any prisons in Nowhere. His enquiry prompts the angry reply, 'Man alive! how can you ask such a question?'. Moments of this kind influence Guest's response to his environment. They impress on him the need to recognize and adapt to a distinct culture, a new set of rules. A particularly revealing episode occurs when Guest remarks casually on the great kindness shown to him by Dick. Old Hammond's reply reminds readers that in Nowhere – as in Mauss's 'archaic society' – hospitality is governed by obligations, unspoken rules, which neither guests, nor hosts, may ignore with impunity:

> 'Well,' said old Hammond, 'if he were not "kind," as you call it, to a perfect stranger he would be thought a strange person, and people would be apt to shun him.'

---

226 Morris, *News from Nowhere*, pp. 9, 28, 31, 34, 37, 44, 55, 65.

It is also explained to Guest that Nowhere is an open society, that though people may live in 'separate households', 'no door is shut to any good-tempered person who is content to live as the other house-mates do'. The chief responsibility guests must accept is that 'it would be unreasonable for one man to drop into a house-hold and bid the folk of it to alter their habits to please him'. Again, the provision of freedom is premised upon the assumption that its beneficiaries will accept the obligations conferred by it.

In *La Pensée utopique de William Morris* (1972), Paul Meier studies the detail of Morris's revolutionary theory,[227] in particular his attempt to distinguish between the two phases that would constitute the change: between the '*machinery*' that 'Socialism *must* use in its militant condition' and the 'essence' of the true socialism that will finally be realized.[228] The actions Morris was prepared to countenance over the course of the transition phase must be of considerable significance to us, given the horrors perpetrated in the name of transition in the old Soviet Union. Meier's most important statements relate to the notion of a dictatorship of the proletariat. Arguing that Morris openly accepted the need for post-revolutionary compulsion, he writes that 'The new order, indubitably, will have many difficulties to overcome, and many among them will be the heritage of the old society, of which it will bear the 'stigmata' as Marx put it'.[229] When one examines the letter used by Meier to support these assertions, it becomes clear that Morris's under-standing of *compulsion* was by no means equivalent to what is meant, ordinarily, by *coercion*:

> [. . .] I admit the necessity for a transitional stage of progress. During that stage before the *habit* of working for the whole was formed some compulsion would have to be exercised; that compulsion would be found in the very remains of competition which would render the stage imperfect; only it would be comparatively a fair competition.[230]

This passage takes seriously the idea of forcibly 'educating' a populace, but stops short of advocating employment of physical force. A similar reluctance to *coerce* informs Morris's emphasis on impersonal sources of discipline. In 'Dawn of A New Epoch' (1886), he explains that people of all classes would need to respond to 'the tyranny of Nature'.[231] They would need to accept the same environmental imperative faced by Citizen Nupkins (that is, dig for potatoes or go hungry). It is only when the freedom of the individual is actually threatened that Morris sees a place for coercive measures. This is to say, before a mature *public conscience*, stem-ming from the combined 'aspirations of our better selves' could be established, some provision would need to be made for the protection of society's weaker members:[232]

---

227 Paul Meier, *William Morris: The Marxist Dreamer*, trans. by Frank Gubb, 2 vols (Sussex: Harvester Press, 1978).
228 Morris, 'Communism', in *Collected Works*, XXIII, pp. 264–76 (p. 264).
229 Meier, *William Morris*, II, p. 296.
230 Morris, 'To George Bainton', 6 May 1888, in *Collected Letters*, II, pp. 776–8 (p. 777).
231 Morris, 'Dawn of a New Epoch', in *Collected Works*, XXIII, pp. 121–40 (p. 125).
232 Morris, 'Correspondence', *Commonweal*, p. 157.

> If individuals are not to coerce others, there must somewhere be an authority which is prepared to coerce them not to coerce; and that authority must clearly be collective.

Again, one begins to discern the limits of the freedom Morris is able to espouse. He was further from advocating coercive social engineering than is implied by Meier's account. The alternative conception of the transition phase I have outlined nevertheless distinguishes his position from an anarchistic one. For Morris, all individuals were social actors. All had a responsibility to carry their share of the burden imposed by 'nature', and to refrain, whilst at leisure, from compromising the liberty of their neighbours.

Even when attention is confined to the internalized morality of mature Morrisian communism, the levels of consensus achieved in Nowhere (sufficient to leave individuals in no doubt concerning the ethical value of their actions) can appear a little sinister. It seems to leave limited room for the exercise of practical freedom, or for morality. Accepting that Morris devoted much of his energy to combating the strictures of Victorian morality, this recourse to an extralegal regulatory level becomes even less palatable when one considers that many oppressive features of life in nineteenth-century England issued not from law, but from customs and conventions.[233] Morris did foresee occasional exceptions to the rule that people would be naturally self-regulating, but these exceptions are dealt with under the heading of illness: Guest is told that when an 'ill-doer' is 'sick or mad', he 'must be restrained till his sickness or madness is cured'.[234] Such passages bring the Soviet practice of sending dissidents to mental hospitals uncomfortably to mind, as well as the Victorian willingness to incarcerate people guilty of moral failings (in debtors' prisons, workhouses . . .). That the form of regulation proposed by Morris is entirely consensual should not obscure the fact that his community is founded upon certain principles, principles necessarily exclusive of identifiable social types.

Earlier in this chapter I suggested that Morris's medievalism was compatible with the pluralism many critics would ascribe to him. It is necessary now to consider an alternative view. Medievalism, with its concern for fellowship, for a fixed network of social bonds, is equally apt to inspire a suspicion of outsiders. It is possible, for example, to view Morris's agitation during the Eastern Question crisis in this light. The outrage provoked in 1876 by the massacre of Bulgarian Christians was intensified by a widespread – conceivably 'medievalist' – suspicion of 'the Turk' ('the common enemy', as Gladstone termed him).[235] Indeed, 'Wake, London Lads', the rousing song Morris penned for the occasion of an anti-war meeting (16 January 1878), included such lines as 'cast the Turk away!'[236] It is, moreover, hard to ignore the relationship between intolerance, medievalism and the calls of J. A. MacGahan – the journalist whose reports on the events in Bulgaria had prompted the crisis – for 'the redemption of the Christian races of

---

233 Victorian treatment of 'fallen' women is one example of oppressive social convention.
234 Morris, *News from Nowhere*, p. 83.
235 William Ewart Gladstone, *Bulgarian Horrors and the Question of the East* (London: John Murray, 1876), p. 13.
236 Morris, 'Wake, London Lads', in *Collected Letters*, I, pp. 436–7 (p. 437).

South-eastern Europe', in effect, for a new crusade.[237] Associated in the medieval mind with moneylending and usury, the Jews retained a similar role as scapegoats in the discourse of nineteenth-century medievalism.[238] As Morris became politically active, the figure of the Jew as capitalist came to inform his dismissive references to Disraeli as 'the Jew',[239] and the unashamedly anti-Semitic quip contained in a letter to May Morris, dated 10 December 1881.[240] The idea of tolerance becomes particularly significant when one considers the portrayal, in *The Roots of the Mountains*, of a character called Penny-thumb. Described as 'long, stooping, gaunt and spindle-shanked', he is 'a man whom the kindreds had in small esteem'.[241] The narrator states that he was a 'notable close-fist' and that his nose was 'long like a snipe's neb', features that draw on the conventions of anti-Semitic caricature. When it is revealed that Folk-might was responsible for ransacking his hoarded goods, he justifies his actions according to the failure of the alien to circulate treasure:

> As for the ransacking of Penny-thumb, I needed the goods that I took, and he needed them not, since he neither used them, nor gave them away, and, they being gone, he hath lived no worser than aforetime.

The stereotype is hardly mitigated by the willingness of one Burgdaler, called Bristler, to take up the feud against the thieves who have robbed him. This action merely reinforces the suggestion that open-handedness is a racially selective characteristic. Any fair account of this matter would need first to show that, in accordance with the 'English' form of anti-Semitism discussed by Anthony Julius, these prejudices were not programmatic, that they stopped well short of advocating violence or coercion; and, second, that on an individual level Morris's anti-capitalism did not find expression in consistent or practical anti-Semitism.[242] His letter to John Simon, dated 26 January [1882], demonstrates the level of outrage he felt on hearing of the pogroms being perpetrated in Russia.[243] His friendship with Emma Lazarus, a Zionist, complicates the picture still further.[244] The point of discussing this matter is not to convict Morris of anti-Semitism on the strength of what must be decidedly mixed evidence. It is, rather, in moving towards a more subtle conception of the limits on tolerance inherent in his anti-capitalism that

[237] J. A. MacGahan, *The Turkish Atrocities in Bulgaria* (London: Bradbury, Agnew, & Co., 1876), p. vii.

[238] In Carlyle's *Past and Present*, the Jews are expelled from the Abbey of St Edmundsbury (p. 92).

[239] Morris, 'To Jane Morris', 11 April 1878, in *Collected Letters*, I, p. 476.

[240] 'How do you like brass-headed she-Jews, May dear?', Morris, 'To May Morris', 10 December 1881, *Collected Letters*, II, p. 88.

[241] Morris, *The Roots of the Mountains*, pp. 62, 281.

[242] In *T. S. Eliot, Anti-Semitism and Literary Form* (Cambridge: Cambridge University Press, 1995), Anthony Julius writes, 'English anti-Semitism was, and remains, an affair of social exclusion. Jews have not been harried, but kept at a distance' (p. 12).

[243] Morris, 'To John Simon', 26 January [1882], in *Collected Letters*, II, pp. 95–6.

[244] Once, in a letter to Emma Lazarus, Morris reflected, 'I feel very deeply your kindness both as an individual and as a representative of another country & another race' (5 March [1884?], *Collected Letters*, II, pp. 267–8 (p. 267)). If further reassurance is needed, J. Bruce Glasier's memoir, *William Morris and the Early Days of the Socialist Movement*, contains a passage in which Morris is reported to have said: 'I'm no Jew-hater [. . .] As likely as not I belong to one of the lost ten tribes' (p. 107).

such issues must be taken into account. A further example, taken from *The Roots of the Mountains*, serves to illustrate this point. Where Penny-thumb is 'tolerated', the Dusky Men remain firmly beyond the pale. Their appearance is wholly abject. Described as 'crooked-legged [. . .], snubbed-nosed, wide-mouthed, thin-lipped, very swarthy of skin, exceeding foul of favour', these invaders do not qualify, at any point in the tale, for mercy.[245] They seem to inhabit a space beyond the limits of the human as the Burgdalers define it.

One episode in particular is apt to set alarm bells ringing in the modern reader. Travelling by carriage to Bloomsbury, Dick and Guest are joined, unexpectedly, by an old man. It is clear that he is not altogether welcome. In the course of the ensuing discussion, Dick mentions a form of dissent that has never been tolerated in Nowhere, not during the transition phase, and not afterwards:

> in the early days of our epoch there were a good many people who were hereditarily afflicted with a disease called Idleness [. . .] I believe that at one time they were actually *compelled* to do some such work, because they [. . .] got so ugly and produced such ugly children if their disease was not treated sharply, that the neighbours couldn't stand it.[246]

Dick seems to regard idleness as an environmental hazard, a negative externality or private failing with manifest public effects. He is happy that all this is in the past, in the transition phase identified by Morris as a time of compulsion, and so presents this story as a curiosity lacking in real significance. But then the old man breaks in and explains that 'it was thought at the time that it was the survival of the old mediæval disease of leprosy'. Dick gets 'restive' here 'under so much ancient history', as if extended contemplation of such matters might hold danger. Morris seems to be stressing the historically specific nature of idleness in order to justify the extraordinary changes evident in popular habit. Human nature has not changed, but the diseases that once impaired it have been eliminated. Morris's leper, then, is the gouty rich man who chooses to seclude himself, to keep himself apart. He is excluded from Nowhere according to the assumption that his disease is self-induced, that it belongs to a past era that cannot be reconciled with a new age more or less defined by common involvement in pleasurable work. Considered in the light of the above discussion, Morris's 'generosity' may not now seem boundless. It is possible to read 'reactionary novels' in Nowhere. But their being classed as such indicates that the freedoms proposed are limited precisely by the fact that they are cast in recognizable opposition to nineteenth-century ways, that they are defined against different kinds of freedom (the freedom to trade for profit, for example).

In common with Coleman, Mineo and Kumar, I have argued that Morris's Nowhere enshrines many of the principles that one associates with a tolerant, liberal society. Moreover, the problem of scarcity, as Thompson suggests, has been overcome. In this respect, *News from Nowhere* might be said to be 'open' and 'exploratory' in character.[247] But it cannot be sufficient to stress this aspect of

---

245 Morris, *The Roots of the Mountains*, p. 88.
246 Morris, *News from Nowhere*, pp. 22, 39, 40.
247 E. P. Thompson argues that 'one part of Morris's achievement lies in the open, exploratory character of Utopianism: its leap out of the kingdom of necessity into an imagined kingdom of

Morris's work without also registering the obligations life in his community confers. I have differed with recent critics in emphasizing the limits implicit to this dream of a hospitable society. For Morris, there is no 'natural' economy to which one might resort, no state of society devoid of individually felt responsibility or obligation. The key to understanding the complex nature of Nowhere's openness lies, then, in recognizing the persistence of informal laws and customs. Morris had no intention of evoking a Cockaigne of desires endlessly fulfilled. This aspect of his work, I would suggest, is best demonstrated by the closing sequence of *News from Nowhere*. Guest and the boating party have just joined their 'up-river hosts'.[248] Preparations are being made for a feast in the church. Just at that moment when the atmosphere of welcome and sociability is intensifying, Guest begins to suspect that his position is not secure, that he is about to be ejected from his dream. Soon, his friends are no longer able to perceive him. This moment of closure demonstrates that certain things might never be accommodated in Nowhere, that if a utopia is to be meaningful, its borders will eventually need to be enforced. On a practical level, this final reassertion of a limited freedom and of laws (however informal or customary) designed to prevent the exercise of selfish liberties, appears a sound policy. Expressing Morris's sophisticated political vision, it contains a recognition of the need for compromise in social life. But one also sees that the 'tolerance' of *News from Nowhere* is only ever offered on the author's own terms. This is to say that utopian hospitality presumes the prior exclusion of unwanted elements. In the context of a speculative fiction, the banishment of past 'diseases' may make absolute sense: in order to convey its 'news', such a text needs to differentiate itself firmly from the world of its readership. As part of a private thought experiment, such formal constraints need not be listed under the heading of 'intolerance'. It is only when one starts to take *News from Nowhere* seriously as a blueprint, to consider its social arrangements in a way Morris never intended, that his vision begins to intersect with the present. At that point, those excluded from his world – 'lepers', ugly people, the victims of idleness or 'Mulleygrubs' – begin to seem less like formal devices.[249] They take on a human appearance, and become, in their predicament, uncomfortably resonant of a darker vision.

Conclusions

In Morris's Teutonic romances, in *A Dream of John Ball*, and in *News from Nowhere*, hospitality operates to break down barriers. It weakens the kindred ties that underpin traditional societies. At the same time, it has an integrative function, a role in cementing community. This is achieved, primarily, through the maintenance of a regulatory framework, and through the absorption of the threat to social unity posed by strangers. On the level of his work as a whole, this

---

freedom in which desire may actually indicate choices or impose itself as need; and in its innocence of system and its refusal to be cashed in the same medium of exchange as "concept", "mind", "knowledge" or political text', *William Morris*, pp. 798–9.

248 Morris, *News from Nowhere*, Kelmscott edition, p. 288.
249 Morris, *News from Nowhere*, p. 40.

complex motif should be viewed in terms of Morris's attempts to graft a basic belief in liberty onto a rooted conception of community or fellowship. Such efforts to reconcile individualism and socialism were in certain respects problematic, both practically and politically. Yet in *News from Nowhere*, in Morris's most conscious attempt to overcome this familiar nineteenth-century dichotomy, his approach remains refreshingly flexible. Here one witnesses a bid to forge from a modified, or utopian, hospitality a world where the paternalistic *and* anarchic extremes of 'unconditional' welcome no longer obtain, where the logic of the gift supplies a form of exchange at once interested and non-utilitarian.

Chapter 5

LEGACIES

This final chapter addresses the legacy of Morris's lifelong experimentation with utopian forms. What influence did his 'utopia of strangers' have on the work of his contemporaries, and on that of his immediate successors? To what extent does it offer an alternative resource to utopists wishing to draw on a tolerant or open tradition of the ideal society? While the unhappy course of twentieth-century political history imposes strict limits on the scope for arguing points of this kind, Morris's hospitable socialism influenced a wide range of writers, thinkers and architects in the years leading up to the First World War. Knowledge of this influence is an obvious prerequisite for determining what might helpfully be salvaged from his legacy.

The course of events, it is true, did not follow a trajectory Morris would have countenanced. In Britain, socialism disregarded the revolutionary method. Its leaders opted instead for political compromise, founding the parliamentary Labour Party to further their objectives under the existing structure. Intellectually, it drifted from the anarchism of the SDF and the Socialist League towards the Fabian path advocated by George Bernard Shaw. In parts of the world where an immediate agenda of transformation was pursued, the results were bloody, and utopian only in the sense condemned by Karl Popper. It is even possible to trace a line of continuity between the Arts and Crafts fascination with vernacular architecture and folkways, and the romantic nationalism of National Socialism.[1] The emphasis on welcome was shed along the way, and the line of inheritance was selective: Hitler's genocidal conceptualization of the outsider, and Stalin's adherence to Socialism in One Country had far more affinity with the isolationism and purism of the classical utopia than with the liberal instincts of Morris and his peers. And yet the association between a neo-feudal veneration of 'home-place' and fascist philosophies of being is not entirely accidental, whether one considers Martin Heidegger's concern with authentic dwelling[2] or Hitler's cruder notion of *Lebensraum*.

---

[1] In 'The Nazi Garden City', Gerhard Fehl notes that while 'the brutal Nazi occupation and spatial re-ordering of Poland between 1939 and 1944 would appear to be the complete antithesis of the garden city tradition [. . .] the Nazi planners were, in reality, applying elements taken from the conceptual repertoire of the garden city [. . .] which had been technicalized and divorced from their original reformist mission', *The Garden City: Past, Present and Future*, ed. by Stephen V. Ward (London: E. & F. N. Spon, 1992), pp. 88–106 (p. 88).

[2] Martin Heidegger, 'Building Dwelling Thinking', in *Poetry, Language, Thought* (New York: New Perennial, 2001), pp. 141–60.

In the artistic sphere, Morris's emphasis on handicraft endured in isolated contexts. Its most potent resurgence took the form of Mahatma Gandhi's support for spinning wheels as an alternative to the imperial trade in textiles. Yet the general tide of events did not favour Morris's view of things. Even the Bauhaus, an artistic project manifestly and avowedly indebted to the Arts and Crafts Movement, sought to achieve high design standards by means of modern manufacturing techniques. Only in the styles favoured by 1930s suburban development, and in recent imitations, does Morris's preference for the vernacular persist. The commercial spirit and environmentally insensitive nature of these developments nevertheless distance them from their source of inspiration. Thus consolidation of Morris's immediate legacy occurred in the context of pressure from historical forces militating against absorption of his aesthetic and political ideas into the cultural mainstream. If his hospitable socialism is identified as a resource attractive to other utopists operating at the turn of the century, it must be regarded as a counter-tradition, an 'alternative' whose opportunity to exert lasting influence was at best fleeting.

I begin this chapter by analysing the influence of *News from Nowhere*'s hospitable ideal on H. G. Wells's *A Modern Utopia*, and on other utopists writing at the end of the nineteenth century and the beginning of the twentieth. The focus then moves away from formal utopias, towards more concrete evocations of the good society. What influence did medievalist veneration of hospitality have on the architecture and planning of English Garden Suburbs and Garden Cities? To what extent did Red House serve as a design ideal for the architects involved? The final section and the Conclusion address the central question posed, in determining the extent to which the medievalist ideal of unconditional hospitality, and the Morrisian interpretation of it, offered an alternative to the values of control, enclosure and exclusivity associated with the classical utopia, and with modern totalitarian thought.

Strangers in H. G. Wells's *A Modern Utopia*

The impact of *News from Nowhere* on H. G. Wells's exploratory work, *A Modern Utopia*, is worthy of sustained consideration. Wells's title is evocative of a problem that lay at the root of the political troubles Morris faced in the last years of his life. What was a 'modern utopia'? Morris's answer to this question – a collective society governed by informal laws, in which each person enjoys the opportunity to develop their individuality – did not accord with the views of his anarchist colleagues in the Socialist League. It could not have been further from the statist perspective favoured by writers like Edward Bellamy, and indeed by the forms of socialism that rose to prominence around the world in the early twentieth century. Nor did it tally with the evolutionary perspective of Fabian friends like Shaw.

An obvious difficulty confronted Morris in promoting his vision of the good society. How could a medievalist conception of labour and social relations ever tackle the problems posed by modernity, rooted as they were in the predicament of mass society, of an industrial economy oiled by production and consumption?

A lazy analysis of Morris's position might characterize it as 'backward', a repudiation of technology and modern life that by definition failed to meet the challenge of the times. It makes more sense to regard medievalism as a peculiar outgrowth of modernity, an instance of that self-consciousness and historical angst that accompanied the crises of authenticity provoked by mass production and the builder's pattern book. In this respect, *News from Nowhere* assuredly is a 'modern utopia'. It is modern precisely because it is not practicable, precisely because it is premised upon the notion that we might access some part or parts of the past in our efforts to remake the present.

Morris's favoured response to modernity did not endure in spirit beyond the First World War, even if its formal qualities persisted for some time after. A brief analysis of utopian fiction from the time of *News from Nowhere*'s publication to the disillusion precipitated by the Somme reveals the impact of this short ascendancy. A number of works engage with popular forerunners to Morris's work. Conrad Wilbrandt's *Mr. East's Experiences in Mr. Bellamy's World*[3] responded to the utilitarian future mapped by Edward Bellamy in *Looking Backward*. Samuel Butler published *Erewhon Revisited Twenty Years Later*,[4] a sequel to his satirical masterpiece, *Erewhon* (1872). Others simply extended Bellamy's utilitarian principle. Bradford Peck attempted this in *The World a Department Store*.[5] There were also works that followed Herbert Spencer,[6] in warning of the uniformity and ugly majoritarianism attending the triumph of socialism. Of these, Jerome K. Jerome's 'The New Utopia'[7] and Eugen Richter's *Pictures of the Socialistic Future*[8] are notable examples.

Other writers chose the path of optimism, enthusiastically harnessing the pastoral vision suggested by *News from Nowhere*. Attention is typically devoted to the proper scope of individuality in a utopian society. Foremost among such works is Oscar Wilde's playfully crude extension of Morris's emphasis on individual potentiality, in 'The Soul of Man under Socialism'.[9] Much of the effect of Wilde's piece hinges on the counter-intuitive claim that '*Socialism itself will be of value simply because it will lead to Individualism*'. Even accepting that he is concerned most of the time to derive dramatic effect and comic value in yoking together apparently contrary political ideas, there is a serious side to Wilde's message. The scenario posited by Marx – that man under communism might 'hunt in the morning, fish in the afternoon, rear cattle in the evening, criticise after dinner [. . .] without ever becoming hunter, fisherman, shepherd or critic'[10]

3   Conrad Wilbrandt, *Mr. East's Experiences in Mr. Bellamy's World* (New York: Harper & Bros, 1891).
4   Samuel Butler, *Erewhon Revisited Twenty Years Later; Both by the Original Discoverer of the Country and by his Son* (London: A. C. Fifield, 1901).
5   Bradford Peck, *The World a Department Store. A Story of Life Under a Cooperative System* (London: Gay & Bird, 1900).
6   Spencer, *The Man versus the State*.
7   Jerome K. Jerome, 'The New Utopia', in *Diary of a Pilgrimage and Six Essays* (Leipzig: Bernard Tauchnitz, 1892), pp. 235–54.
8   Eugen Richter, *Pictures of the Socialistic Future, Freely Adapted from Bebel*, trans. by H. Wright (London: Sonnenschein & Co, 1893).
9   Oscar Wilde, 'The Soul of Man under Socialism', in *The Artist as Critic: Critical Writings of Oscar Wilde*, ed. by Richard Ellmann (London: W. H. Allen, 1970), pp. 255–89.
10   Karl Marx, *The German Ideology*, in *Collected Works*, 5 (1976), p. 47.

– finds an equivalent in Wilde's assertion that 'Every man must be left quite free to choose his own work',[11] as do Morris's objections to *Looking Backward*.[12] 'If the Socialism is Authoritarian; if there are Governments armed with economic power as they are now with political power', Wilde insists, 'then the last state of man will be worse than the first'.[13] Although Wilde's 'new Individualism' approximates more closely to the 'new Hellenism' promulgated by Pater,[14] than to Morris's brand of aesthetic socialism, the respect for individual rights and self-development is a common feature.

More obviously reliant on Morris's contribution to utopian literature is the work of William Dean Howells. Howells published two fictions based not on the usual premise of an everyman visiting utopia, but rather upon the visit of a utopian – in this case, an Altrurian – to late-nineteenth-century America.[15] The contrast between the expectations of the Altrurian concerning life in the United States, and its gradually unfolding reality, provides a subtle and satirical springboard for Howells' political agenda. In the second of the two novels, *Through the Eye of the Needle*, the reader is given access to the homeward correspondence of the same visitor. Apart from the various references to Morris included in these works, the emphasis on hospitality is the most obvious marker of his influence. The Altrurian is particularly scathing in his account of domestic manners in American high society:

> Our fashion of offering hospitality on the impulse would be as strange here as offering it without some special inducement for its acceptance. The inducement is, as often as can be, a celebrity or eccentricity of some sort, or some visiting foreigner; and I suppose that I have been a good deal used myself in one quality or the other. But when the thing has been done, fully and guardedly at all points, it does not seem to have been done for pleasure, either by the host or the guest. The dinner is given in payment of another dinner; or out of ambition by people who are striving to get forward in society; or by great social figures who give regularly a certain number of dinners every season. In either case it is eaten from motives at once impersonal and selfish.

The second half of this work consists of letters sent by an American woman who has followed the Altrurian to his home country. The result is a more conventional 'stranger-in-utopia' scenario. The country she describes is remarkably similar to Morris's Nowhere. Like the iron bridges crossing the Thames in *News from Nowhere*, 'The old steam-roads of the capitalistic epoch have been disused for generations, and their beds are now the country roads'. Just as Morris stressed the importance of an active life, so '*work* is the ideal'. The Altrurians 'do not believe in [. . .] labor-saving devices'. It is also notable that the 'people have a perfect inspiration for hospitality':

11 Wilde, 'The Soul of Man under Socialism', p. 257.
12 Morris, 'Looking Backward'.
13 Wilde, 'The Soul of Man under Socialism', p. 257.
14 Pater, *The Renaissance*, pp. 26–7.
15 William Dean Howells, *A Traveller from Altruria* (Edinburgh: D. Douglas, 1894); William Dean Howells, *Through the Eye of the Needle: A Romance* (New York: Harper & Brothers, 1907), pp. 73, 157, 158.

Their hospitality is a sort of compromise between that of the English houses where you are left free at certain houses to follow your own devices absolutely, and that Spanish splendor which assures you that the host's house is yours without meaning it. In fact, the guest-house, wherever we go, *is* ours, for it belongs to the community, and it is absolutely a home to us for the time being. It is usually the best house in the village, the prettiest and cosiest, where all the houses are so pretty and cosey [*sic*].

There are distinct echoes here of the Hammersmith Guest House in *News from Nowhere*, and of John Ruskin's ideal village inn. This is most evident in relation to the sense of ownership and of being-at-home endowed by communal arrangements.

Of all Edwardian utopias, Robert Blatchford's *The Sorcery Shop: An Impossible Romance* draws most directly on the spirit of *News from Nowhere*.[16] The wizard who opens the door to this 'impossible country, inhabited by impossible people' explains that, while 'there are no laws here', 'there are customs'. Combined with the reference to *News from Nowhere* in the Author's Note, this governing principle signals the kindred ties with Morris's vision. As one might expect, Blatchford is also keen to stress the open and hospitable nature of the world he portrays. It is stated that 'children can find homes in a hundred households', because 'Every house is open, every table free to them'; and Chapter Fourteen bears the familiar title, 'In the Guest House':

> The dining hall of the Guest House stood in the middle of a cherry orchard, and through its open casements floated in the delicate but searching perfume of the wonderful blossoms.
>
> It was a large room, of oblong shape, with windows running in a band the whole length of the walls on both sides. Above the windows was a frieze of dim cobalt blue, with here and there a painted swallow flying.

The communal arrangements, the harmony between architecture and nature, and the emphasis on dining as a path to healthy sociability, are elements reminiscent of the Morrisian utopia. For all this, Blatchford's work is heavy-handed by comparison. It lacks the enigmatic quality that ensures Morris's vision is more than a polemic.

In assessing the broader impact of Morris's contribution, there is danger in lingering too long on the work of his disciples. More can be gained from examining critical consolidations of his ideas and influence. This service is provided by H. G. Wells's ground-breaking work, *A Modern Utopia*. Wells's contribution is distinguished by its success in combining the traditions of satire, of unreliable and multilayered narration, of playfulness, and of idealism, characteristic of the form in its various manifestations.[17] It is also notable for consolidating the previous

---

[16] Robert Blatchford, *The Sorcery Shop; An Impossible Romance* (London: The Clarion Press, 1907), pp. 13, 45, 47.

[17] The work closes with an explicit reference to the ironized and fragmented nature of this utopia: '*Why could not a modern Utopia be discussed without this impersonation – impersonally? It has confused the book, you say, made the argument hard to follow, and thrown a quality of insincerity over the whole. Are we but mocking at Utopias, you demand, using all these noble and generalised hopes as the backcloth against which two bickering personalities jar and squabble? [. . .] But this Utopia began upon a philosophy of fragmentation, and ends, confusedly, amidst a gross tumult of immediate*

hundred years of speculation as well as for prefiguring much of what would follow. Most of all, Wells achieves success in creating one of the first meta-utopias. Only W. H. Mallock in *The New Republic* achieves a comparably sustained analysis of the ideal society in its many political, technical and formal incarnations.[18] Wells manages to combine this critical approach with the optimism of his own vision, albeit filtered through the narrative distancing device of 'The Voice'. Wells's contribution is also unusual for its position within a corpus whose main tendency has been dystopian. The fate of the Eloi in his novella, *The Time Machine*, the dark future suggested by *When the Sleeper Awakes*,[19] and the unfortunate end of the British cabinet minister in 'The Door in the Wall' (1904) (whose search for dreamland results in a broken neck at the bottom of an excavation shaft),[20] establish Wells's credentials as a writer capable of deep pessimism. He nevertheless saw grounds for optimism early in his career. This fact finds no better illustration than in the title of the work under consideration. For Wells, the word *modern* carried no necessary slight or warning. A *modern* utopia would be a true utopia, a world comprising remedies for the faults of all preceding 'utopias'. Although he finds many of the resources for this vision in Morris's *News from Nowhere*, it is also clear what must be left behind:

> we must needs define certain limitations. Were we free to have our untrammelled desire, I suppose we should follow Morris to his Nowhere, we should change the nature of man and the nature of things together; we should make the whole race wise, tolerant, noble, perfect – wave our hands to a splendid anarchy, every man doing as it pleases him, and none pleased to do evil, in a world as good in its essential nature, as ripe and sunny, as the world before the Fall. [. . .] We are to restrict ourselves first to the limitations of human possibility as we know them in the men and women of this world to-day, and then to all the inhumanity, all the insubordination of nature. We are to shape our state in a world of uncertain seasons, sudden catastrophes, antagonistic diseases, and inimical beasts and vermin, out of men and women with like passions, like uncertainties of mood and desire to our own.[21]

Thus Wells seeks to retain a measure of realistic imperfection within his world. While Morris sought to achieve something similar where human relations are concerned – in representing the impassioned circumstances surrounding a homicide – Wells wants nothing to do with the Nowherian assumption of reasonable conduct, or with the idyllic taming of the seasons implicit in William Guest's account. Wells's portrait of the Eloi in *The Time Machine* served as his most explicit repudiation of Morris's elimination of competition, a vision of aesthetic man reduced to pathetic and vulnerable simplicity. Given this resistance to 'naïve' conceptions of human nature, it is odd that he attracted criticism for a perceived abolition of original sin. Writing in *Heretics*, G. K. Chesterton argued that 'the

---

realities [. . .] this so-called Modern Utopia is a mere story of personal adventures among Utopian philosophies, A Modern Utopia, pp. 371–2.

18   W. H. Mallock, *The New Republic; or Culture, Faith, and Philosophy in an English Country House* (London: Michael Joseph, 1877).

19   H. G. Wells, *When the Sleeper Awakes* (Leipzig: Bernard Tauchnitz, 1899).

20   H. G. Wells, *The Door in the Wall, and other Stories* (London: Grant Richards, 1911).

21   Wells, *A Modern Utopia*, pp. 7–8.

weakness of all Utopias is this, that they take the greatest difficulty of man and assume it to be overcome, and then give an elaborate account of the overcoming of the smaller ones'.[22] His criticisms centred on a passage in Wells's utopia, in which it is stated that 'The leading principle of the Utopian religion is the repudiation of the doctrine of original sin'.[23] Just as Wells fails to appreciate the space Morris leaves to the disruptive side of human nature, so Chesterton is neglectful of Wells's opening remarks, the limitation implicit in the assertion that the 'Utopians hold that man, *on the whole* [my italics], is good'.

It follows that the methodological difference between Morris and Wells is not as pronounced as might at first seem the case. Undoubtedly, the two men disagreed on the need for, and nature of, competition, and they foresaw quite different futures for the state and for public authorities. These fundamental differences only make the remaining similarities more striking. Although the purpose of this analysis is to explore parallels in the handling of political liberty and tolerance, it is worth noting at the outset that Wells depicts a world where it is 'unlikely there will be any smoke-disgorging steam railway trains', and where 'Cycle tracks will abound'. A mischievous remark that the steam train's 'obsolescence' will 'endear them to the Ruskins of to-morrow' underlines Wells's adherence to the proto-environmental aesthetic of the Arts and Crafts Movement, even if the extensive role accorded to mass transportation, using 'double railways', and to cycle use does not adhere strictly to Morris's vision in *News from Nowhere*. The emphasis on 'pleasant ways over the scented needles of the mountain pinewoods, primrose-strewn tracks amidst the budding thickets of the lower country' and 'paths running beside rushing streams' ensures that Wells's society remains within the tradition of the pastoral utopia, reinvigorated fifteen years earlier by Morris.

More significant than these superficial similarities is the emphasis that Wells's narrator places on individuality. It is in this respect, primarily, that principles tested in *News from Nowhere* emerge in a clear light, equated by Wells with the fundamental characteristics of a 'modern' utopia. His approach is to contrast life in a 'modern utopia' with the 'symmetrical and perfect cultivations' and 'multitude of people [. . .] without any personal distinction whatever' to be found in the utopias of earlier ages. It is argued there 'are no individualities' in 'almost every Utopia – except, perhaps, Morris's "News from Nowhere"'. The allusion to Morris prepares the way for an unfolding conception of what individuality might mean in a modern utopia, which is thoroughly Morrisian, founded upon the exercise of developing faculties, a pursuit of potentiality that stops short of interference with the freedoms of one's neighbour:

> To the classical Utopists freedom was relatively trivial. Clearly they considered virtue and happiness as entirely separable from liberty, and as being altogether more important things [. . .] To have free play for one's individuality is, in the modern view, the subjective triumph of existence, as survival in creative work and offspring is its objective triumph. But for all men, since man is a social creature, the play of will must fall short of absolute freedom. Perfect human liberty is possible only to a despot who is absolutely and universally obeyed.

22 G. K. Chesterton, *Heretics* (London: Bodley Head, 1905), p. 79.
23 Wells, *A Modern Utopia*, pp. 9, 10–11, 32, 33, 36, 45, 47, 299, 300.

Wells follows Morris's line remarkably closely. He adopts the position, examined in Chapter Four, that 'A socialism or a communism is not necessarily a slavery, and there is no freedom under Anarchy'. Reflections of this kind move Wells towards one of the book's more memorable and useful remarks, which is that it 'has been the common sin of all Utopias' to ignore 'difference' and 'individuality'. The new society will overcome this problem by encouraging an 'evolving interplay of unique individualities'.

The nature and constitution of the household is a central concern in *News from Nowhere*. A subtle combination of communality and privacy emerges, achieved through the sharing and habitation of small, individual dwellings. *A Modern Utopia* handles this subject in a similar way. Comparable emphasis is placed on an enhanced form of communality, tempered in this case by sufficient privacy to ensure the survival of healthy individuality. Again, Wells notes a favourable comparison with the earlier tendency of imagined communities towards extinguishment of private life:

> I doubt if anyone could stand a month of the relentless publicity of virtue planned by More . . . No one wants to live in any community of intercourse really, save for the sake of the individualities he would meet there. The fertilising conflict of individualities is the ultimate meaning of the personal life, and all our Utopias no more than schemes for bettering that interplay. At least, that is how life shapes itself more and more to modern perceptions. Until you bring in individualities, nothing comes into being, and a Universe ceases when you shiver the mirror of the least of individual minds.

Morris is seen as the herald of a new respect for individual separation, a movement away from the situation described in More's *Utopia*, whereby 'folding doors, easily opened by hand [. . .] give admission to anyone':[24]

> Compared with the older writers Bellamy and Morris have a vivid sense of individual separation, and their departure from the old homogeneity is sufficiently marked to justify a doubt whether there will be any more thoroughly communistic Utopias for ever.[25]

Wells thus borrows from, and pays homage to, Morris. His utopia exhibits medievalist respect for the wealth, beauty and mystery of privacy, for the desire 'to form households and societies'. It confers on its denizens the right to establish 'gardens and enclosures and exclusive freedoms for our like and our choice'. The only departure from Morris's vision is the fiscal method devised for regulating the growth of such privacies.

Like Morris, Wells preserves a right to movement and access. He gives the inhabitants of his world a Romantic 'freedom of going to and fro', 'to go wherever the spirit moves them, to wander and see'.[26] This will be a world with 'no unclimbable walls and fences'. Wells seems to propose far more mobility than Morris ever considers desirable, a 'migratory population' in fact, detached from

---

24 More, *Utopia*, p. 121.
25 Wells, *A Modern Utopia*, pp. 38, 87.
26 Wells, *A Modern Utopia*, pp. 11–12, 23–4, 31, 35, 40, 44, 123, 215, 216, 217.

the 'the fetters of locality'. Yet he shares a medievalist concern for the lot of the wanderer and wayfarer. The 'whole Utopian world', it transpires, 'will be open and accessible [. . .] for the wayfarer'. There is corresponding emphasis on the importance of inns. As the following description demonstrates, reliance is placed on the model of the Hammersmith Guest House in *News from Nowhere*. The hostel and meeting place portrayed here blend the best of 'old world' hospitality with the communality and efficiency of the new age:

> This particular inn is a quadrangle after the fashion of an Oxford college; it is perhaps forty feet high, and with about five stories of bedrooms above its lower apartments; the windows of the rooms look either outward or inward to the quadrangle, and the doors give upon artificially-lit passages with staircases passing up and down. These passages are carpeted with a sort of cork carpet, but are otherwise bare. The lower story [*sic*] is occupied by the equivalent of a London club, kitchens and other offices, dining-room, writing-room, smoking and assembly rooms, a barber's shop, and a library. A colonnade with seats runs about the quadrangle, and in the middle is a grass-plot. In the centre of this a bronze figure, a sleeping child, reposes above a little basin and fountain, in which water lilies are growing. The place has been designed by an architect happily free from the hampering traditions of Greek temple building, and of Roman and Italian palaces; it is simple, unaffected, gracious.

This 'quadrangle type of building is the prevalent element in Utopian Lucerne'. There are households and flats with communal cooking areas, since 'the ordinary Utopian would no more think of a special private kitchen for his dinners than he would think of a private flour mill or dairy farm'. And it appears that a 'common garden, an infant school, play rooms, and a playing garden for children, are universal features of the club quadrangles'.

A Modern Utopia invests hospitality with a political resonance also familiar from Morris's work. This is most apparent when Wells extends his migratory theme to cover a generally tolerant attitude towards outsiders. The paragraph in question is worth quoting now at greater length:

> Time was when a mountain valley or an island seemed to promise sufficient isolation for a polity to maintain itself intact from outward force; the Republic of Plato stood armed ready for defensive war, and the New Atlantis and the Utopia of More in theory, like China and Japan through many centuries of effectual practice, held themselves isolated from intruders. Such late instances as Butler's satirical 'Erewhon,' and Mr. Stead's queendom of inverted sexual conditions in Central Africa, found the Tibetan method of slaughtering the inquiring visitor a simple, sufficient rule. But the whole trend of modern thought is against the permanence of any such enclosures. We are acutely aware nowadays that, however subtly contrived a State may be, outside your boundary lines the epidemic, the breeding barbarian or the economic power, will gather its strength to overcome you. The swift march of invention is all for the invader. Now, perhaps you might still guard a rocky coast or a narrow pass; but what of that near to-morrow when the flying machine soars overhead, free to descend at this point or that? A state powerful enough to keep isolated under modern conditions would be powerful enough to rule the world, would be, indeed, if not actively ruling, yet passively acquiescent in all other human organisations, and so responsible for them altogether. World-state, therefore, it must be.

Wells is not insensible to the age-old irreconcilability of openness and perfection. He solves the problem in a radical way, by abolishing borders and creating a 'World-state'. It may be argued that he abolishes strangers in the process. He nevertheless intends to address the fact that it was 'Towards the Stranger' that 'the Utopias of the past displayed their least amiable aspect', replacing it with 'a modern idea' equivalent to 'universal Toleration'. 'Utopia', it appears, will be 'saturated with consideration'. Indeed, 'Utopian manners will not only be tolerant, but almost universally tolerable.' This is 'a Utopia as wide as Christian charity, and white and black, brown, red and yellow, all tints of skin, all types of body and character, will be there'. And as for the question of dissent, there are signs that Wells, like Morris, is prepared to regard its articulation as a virtue:

> is not this too one of the necessary differences between a Modern Utopia and those finite compact settlements of the older school of dreamers? It is not to be a unanimous world any more, it is to have all and more of the mental contrariety we find in the world of the real; it is no longer to be perfectly explicable, it is just our own vast mysterious welter, with some of the blackest shadows gone, with a clearer illumination, and a more conscious and intelligent will.

Just as the willingness to accord room for dissent is present, so also is the suggestion that its more excessive varieties – whether 'the blackest shadows' or in the Nowherian lexicon, 'mulleygrubs'[27] – will not be represented. Much as Morris does, Wells preserves his interests as a utopist by proscribing elements hostile to the integrity or stability of his vision.

Fifteen years after its publication, *News from Nowhere* remained a vital resource for other utopists, offering inspiration on questions related to political tolerance and individuality. Some caution is nevertheless warranted. Wells's main affinities were not with the socialistic tradition of medievalism, but with the Fabian brand of social optimism. His approach to the task of constructing a new world is far less dismissive of the existing apparatus, and in that sense more practical. This applies particularly to the financial settlement under which Wells's modern utopians live. In the face of established utopian hostility to gold coinage, a long section on economics serves to justify the use of a currency. The evil, Wells notes, resides not in money or its inherent functioning, but in the way that it has been used. Moreover, Wells envisages a pattern of nationalization and state provision of such needs as electricity, with 'All natural sources of force' and 'all strictly natural products, coal, water power [. . .] inalienably vested in the local authorities'.[28] This sounds far closer to the kind of socialism that achieved dominance in post-war Britain than to anything Morris would have countenanced. The tendency towards agglomeration is also reflected in Wells's conception of the 'World State', 'the sole landowner of the earth'. Morris's sympathies are more closely wedded to medievalist regionalism, the mystical resonance of locality and place. Wells's attention to ideal economic and fiscal arrangements also highlights differences. He acknowledges that 'Work has to be done', but suggests nevertheless that the freedom to be idle will be open to the Utopian, 'like, privacy, locomotion, and

---

[27] Morris, *News from Nowhere*, p. 40.
[28] Wells, *A Modern Utopia*, pp. 77, 89, 147–9.

almost all the freedoms of life, and on the same terms – if he possess the money to pay for it'. This controversial assertion is justified according to the assumption that money is not a necessary evil, and that its possessors would not obtain it by foul means in this society. Equally, Wells envisages welfare provisions like a minimum wage, state support for the unemployed, and, for the destitute, 'simple but comfortable inns with a low tariff'. Where Morris places his confidence in the wise and charitable spirit of human nature, Wells finds most of his solutions in the state, an organization run and directed by an elite group of benevolent citizens who bear the rather sinister appellation, Samurai. Thus Wells draws on the Platonic model of a society overseen by esteemed and virtuous 'Guardians',[29] whilst rejecting the elitist and exclusive connotations that come with it, and incorporating the very emphasis on individuality, tolerance and receptivity present in the Morrisian utopia.

It was argued in Chapter 4 that the commitment to hospitality and tolerance that characterizes *News from Nowhere* is at once suggestive of straightforward political generosity and an inevitable engine of self-interest. Morris's emphasis on the value of receptivity, whether unselfish or pragmatic, fell out of favour in political circles as the new century progressed. With the general introduction of passports during the First World War, and the growth of economic protectionism in the 1930s, borders and national populations became more, not less, fixed. The optimism of the Edwardian utopia gave way to despair, induced by war and by the seeming failure of utopian ideology in the Soviet Union and in Germany. A strand of medievalism nonetheless leads from Morris to Wells. This strand emerges strongly in *A Modern Utopia*, a work that incorporates many features indicative of the new statism, welfarism, and worship of technology, which nevertheless accords a crucial role to individuality and to the ethics of hospitality.

Garden Suburbs: An Architecture of Welcome?

In Chapter 2, the structural symbolism of Morris's first family home was examined. Red House, it was argued, suggested a disjunction between the archaic ideal of unconditional hospitality and the realities of nineteenth-century social conditions and mores. Whatever openness was incorporated in the plan of the building could not serve as a meaningful intervention. It could not rise above the status of a conceit. What remained, however, was a suggestion of altered relations between the domestic sphere and the wider world. The value and influence of Red House inhered in this exemplary function. While it is no longer fashionable to place confidence in Pevsner's conception of Red House as a proto-modernist building, it did exercise a powerful influence on the development of Arts and Crafts architecture. It is worth assessing the legacy of Morris's hospitable medievalism in the sphere of architectural experimentation, both as expressed at Red House, and in later pronouncements and works of art. To what extent did a veneration of hospitality influence the architects and planners of England's emerging Garden

---

[29] Plato, *The Republic*.

Suburbs and cities? Did they achieve an openness any more socially significant than that projected by Red House?

One of the claims made for Red House is that it achieves a greater level of responsiveness and connectedness to its environment than buildings in the classical style. There is ample evidence in Morris's writings, and later in the work of garden reformers like Gertrude Jekyll (in such works as *Home and Garden*), to suggest a conscious push towards better integration of the two realms.[30] Attempts to incorporate existing features of the land and 'built heritage' were another aspect of a less narrow conception of domestic space. At Red House, this concern is expressed solely in the determination to retain within the grounds of the new house elements of the orchard that once covered the site. Later in his career, Webb extended this integrationist philosophy. The results are most obvious in his designs for Standen, the West Sussex mansion referred to in Chapter 2. Built for the wealthy London solicitor, James Beale, in 1894, the house incorporates within its network of steep gables and rising chimneys an original fifteenth-century building, called Great Hollybush farmhouse. As well as retaining existing buildings, Webb used sandstone quarried on the site. He also employed bricks and hanging tiles characteristic of the Arts and Crafts vernacular style. There is, no doubt, a gulf between an aesthetic approach to 'holistic' architecture and one that fosters social intercourse between the house and the wider environment. It is not surprising that this chasm was rarely bridged in the context of projects aimed solely at providing wealthy individuals with quiet, inoffensive country seats. Whilst often engaged, as Morris would have it, in satisfying the 'swinish luxury of the rich', the Arts and Crafts Movement nevertheless possessed a social dimension, whose character repays analysis.

The most widespread expression of this awareness took the form of a challenge to the traditional division of labour between the domestic and the public sphere. Webb's plans for Red House reflect an attempt to combine the functions of workshop, artists' community and family home. This philosophy passed to the workers' communes of the Arts and Crafts Movement, typified by the collective schemes of C. R. Ashbee. In 1902, Ashbee moved his Guild of Handicraft – an organization based on the University Settlement operating from Toynbee Hall, Whitechapel – to Chipping Campden in the Cotswolds. He did so precisely in order to maximise the conditions for effective co-operation. The century had already seen schemes designed to bring work and family life into closer harmony. Robert Owen's experiments at New Lanark, and Sir Titus Salt's construction of a model workers' community around his mill at Saltaire, achieved particular notoriety. However, these projects placed as much emphasis on control as upon philanthropy. It may well be that the distinction is meaningless, as would be implied by the Foucauldian critique of institutions, from almshouses to hospitals.[31] If attention is confined to the realm of intentions rather than effects, it remains historically meaningful to discriminate between the earlier and later phase of Victorian public

---

[30] Gertrude Jekyll, *Home and Garden. Notes and Thoughts, Practical and Critical, of a Worker in Both* (London: Longmans & Co., 1900).

[31] In *Surveiller et punir: naissance de la prison* (Paris, Gallimard, 1975), Michel Foucault proposes the thesis that discipline is all pervasive. In this respect, he does not discriminate between penal institutions and educational or charitable establishments.

spiritedness. For it was only in the last two decades of the century that the emphasis on co-operation and equality, which the Pre-Raphaelites derived from the Nazarene model of an artist's workshop, rose to prominence.

The workers' community laid out at Bourneville by Joseph Cadbury bears all the hallmarks of the new spirit. Whilst questions of productivity are rarely far away from conceptions of worker health and happiness, the spirit of the scheme invoked the vernacular preferences of late-Victorian medievalism, with a corresponding concern to relieve poverty and provide a healthy environment. Elsewhere, almshouses were being erected. This was admittedly not an activity unique to the late-Victorian period, as the many institutions surviving from earlier in the century testify. It is nevertheless true that the Arts and Crafts style of architecture, so attuned to the mixture of communality and fortification characteristic of these early modern institutions, lent itself to the task as readily as did the architects' taste for social engineering.

Arts and Crafts planning was in general characterized by a concern to achieve greater integration of the working world and the domestic one. It sought to harmonize the functional spaces of home life and lent emphasis to sociability and charity. This was expressed through attention to communal dining areas and gardens, as well as through provision of almshouses and workman's cottages. Of these features, many were most fully realized in the Garden Suburb and Garden City architecture of R. Norman Shaw, and in that of Barry Parker and Raymond Unwin. Here, one finds a direct chain of influence stretching from the ideas promoted earlier by Morris. It is worthwhile considering the detail of their schemes, first at Shaw's Bedford Park, and then at Letchworth, the town planned by the prophet and initiator of the Garden City movement, Ebenezer Howard. Features indicative of hospitable medievalism are highlighted and assessed with regard to their success in fostering a less exclusive conception of the domestic sphere.

Bedford Park represents the first of many Garden Suburbs developed in Britain and the United States towards the close of the nineteenth century. Jonathan T. Carr, the property speculator who conceived the scheme, was not seeking a revolution in social relations or a radical alteration of the relationship between town and country. His effort to exploit the possibilities created by the railway for commuting from suburb to city was nonetheless ground-breaking in effect. The well-spaced, healthy, and attractively designed dwellings provided first by the Aesthetic Movement architect, E. W. Godwin, and then by Shaw, succeeded in establishing Bedford Park's reputation. Free-thinkers, artists, and writers found life there congenial. Among those who moved to the area were W. B. Yeats and the Russian anarchist, S. Stepniak. It was not long before the neighbourhood became a testing ground for Morris's decorative schemes, inhabited as it was by the 'enlightened' middle classes who patronised his shop. The 'Ballad of Bedford Park' was penned as a satiric homage to this new community, a place where the virtues of taste and poetic inspiration reigned supreme.[32]

---

[32] Originally published in St James's Gazette, 17 December 1881, the Ballad is reproduced in M. J. Bolsterli, *Early Community at Bedford Park: 'Corporate Happiness' in the First Garden Suburb* (Ohio: Ohio University Press, 1977), pp. 123–6.

Figure 6. Gate and porch of 17 Blenheim Road, Bedford Park, 1880s

The area was laid out in separate phases, with several architects involved. There is nevertheless a striking continuity of design, the work of Shaw and his former student, E. J. May, being almost indistinguishable. Most buildings represented typical examples of the 'Queen Anne Revival' style. The houses that line the streets at the heart of the estate borrow many of the features pioneered by Webb and his mentors, but without involvement in overt medievalism. In general, the preference is for clarity of line and classical elegance, rather than extravagant outgrowth. The white painted wood in evidence on most houses stands out clearly against red brick. There are, all the same, features that prefigure the Arts and Crafts devotion to the medieval. Despite the classical and Dutch influence, many dwellings have steep gabled roofs. The regular wooden fencing that runs throughout the residential area borrows from the Ruskinian emphasis on redemptive enclosure. Gates are lavished with detail, and frequently open onto a path leading to a pronounced porch, roofed and glazed with attractive green glass [figure 6]. The example pictured here is particularly indebted to Webb's porch at Red House, in that a set of benches is built into the sheltered area. Given the exclusive nature of the development, it is hard to imagine this as a gesture to the passing 'wayfarer', even in the time when Bedford Park's reputation was fairly Bohemian. The symbolism suggests enclosure and privacy far more strongly than it does the opening of an exquisitely sheltered space. The echoes of Red House are nonetheless worth noting.

For the purposes of this study, the most significant feature of Bedford Park is the Tabard Inn at 2 Bath Road (1880) [figure 7]. Named after the pilgrims'

Figure 7. T. M. Rooke, The Tabard Inn and stores, 1881

meeting place in *The Canterbury Tales*, this public house exhibits all the emphasis on medieval sociability one might expect of a building by Shaw. Its features are represented in a suitably ideal light in T. M. Rooke's contemporary watercolour. Rooke's composition includes a large banner, decorated with a tabard motif, which hangs from one side of the inn. Passers-by and a fiddler linger outside, and a sign, depicting a herald blowing on his trumpet, hangs above the entrance, invoking the idea of Merry England. Unlike other structures on the estate, the building forms part of a gabled, Tudor-style terrace. Each floor hangs forward of the one below, thereby mimicking the appearance of a London house before the Fire. The windows have small, Renaissance-style lights, and there is a handsome entrance that leads into a tiled reception area [figure 8]. Just as Ruskin had advocated several decades earlier, this porch provides a comfortable midway point between the outside world and the interior. The Tabard was handsomely furnished in wood and decorated with tile schemes designed by William De Morgan and Walter Crane. These featured such nursery rhyme themes as Little

Figure 8. Entrance porch of the Tabard Inn, Bedford Park, 1880, designed by R. Norman Shaw

Bo-peep, pastoral subjects reminiscent of the tiles that Morris, Marshall, Faulkner & Company designed for the hall of Queens' College, Cambridge.

The home-like interior of the Tabard, with its division into distinct areas and rooms, and the Ruskinian attention to porches and gates elsewhere on the estate, do not alter the essentially private and exclusive nature of Carr's ambitious scheme. This point may be raised in relation to most developments of this kind, including the later, more geometric, Hampstead Garden Suburb. It is apparent that efforts were made in some quarters to overcome this effect, in the hope of achieving a genuinely open form of community. The Garden City movement was given programmatic direction by the publication of Howard's architectural manifesto, *To-morrow: A Peaceful Path to Social Reform*.[33] Although he advocated a geometric and rational method of combining the virtues of town and country in one economically contained community, the involvement of men like Parker and Unwin ensured that the medievalism of Morris infused the new wave of developments. As Mervyn Miller has argued, the Morris-influenced Unwin worked subtly to subvert Howard's geometric plan through continual reversion to, and development of, the English vernacular.[34]

It is important to consider the role of Unwin in accounting for Morris's influence on the Garden City movement. An admirer of Morris from the time of his youth, he had been a member of the Socialist League in the 1880s. He was greatly influenced by Morris's formulation of the ideal home, and he had faith in the connections Ruskin drew between art and society. The notion that architecture might at once reflect, affect, and effect social relations is a principle materialized in all his work, forming a link between Ruskin's dictum that 'All good architecture is the expression of national life and character'[35] and the Edwardian emphasis on environmental determinism, the idea that neighbourliness and community might be engineered through good planning. Speaking of the internal court, the continuous open corridor, protruding window bays and internal porch at their C. F. Goodfellow house in Northwood, Staffordshire (1899–1902), Frank Jackson argues that Parker and Unwin 'saw the principle of design as crucial to the development of society in general, and an expression of the interplay between cultural form and social and individual life'.[36]

In the course of his career, Unwin undertook work at Joseph Rowntree's model village of New Earswick, near York; at Ebenezer Howard's Letchworth; and at Henrietta Barnett's Hampstead Garden Suburb. Instead of providing a detailed account of the history of these developments, attention here is focused on Unwin's recurrent emphasis on sociability and the need to reform domestic life. An early Parker and Unwin building, the 'Homestead', was constructed in 1903, in Ashgate, near Chesterfield. The house illustrates several important principles. In

---

[33] Ebenezer Howard, *To-morrow: A Peaceful Path to Social Reform* (London: Swan Sonnenschein & Co., 1898); Ebenezer Howard, *Garden Cities of To-morrow: Being the Second Edition of 'To-morrow: A Peaceful Path to Real Reform'* (London: Swan Sonnenschein & Co, 1902).

[34] Miller made this observation in a paper entitled 'Building the Earthly Paradise: William Morris and Raymond Unwin', given at the William Morris Society Conference (Royal Holloway, University of London), 'William Morris in the 21st Century', 8 July 2005.

[35] Ruskin, 'Traffic', p. 434.

[36] Frank Jackson, *Sir Raymond Unwin: Architect, Planner and Visionary* (London: A. Zwemmer Ltd, 1985), p. 32

his design tract, *The Art of Building a Home*, Unwin followed Morris in noting the way old buildings 'seem almost to grow out of the ground'.[37] One explanation for this phenomenon may lie in the use of 'local stone', and other 'material common to the district'. At the 'Homestead', Parker and Unwin worked within the constraints of local materials to evoke the wider notion of 'Homeplace', a word that suggests the perceived authenticity, rootedness and secure being-in-place deriving from this method of construction. The paramount concern is not aesthetic, therefore, but social. The primary endeavour is to provide, through thorough consolidation of home-life, an effective bulwark against alienation.

The concept of home is explored in depth by Unwin in his Fabian Tract, *Cottage Plans and Common Sense*.[38] Here he identifies 'desire for shelter, comfort and privacy' as the primary motivations for living in a house. Privacy and comfort, in combination with the necessity of shelter, form a potent mixture, evoking the idealized Romantic and mid-century preoccupation with 'home and hearth'. Unwin is careful not to leave matters there. He identifies the problem that 'the roof and walls which shut out the driving rain, the searching wind and the neighbors' prying eyes, at the same time exclude fresh air and sunlight'. Unwin's wish not to exclude air and light speaks of typically Edwardian environmental concerns. Once it is appreciated that he was equally determined not to exclude social life, his position seems less commonplace. Miller notes that Unwin's preoccupation with the idea of home furthered the 'democratisation of architecture' rather than the repudiation of public space:

> In 1911 Unwin declared 'the basis for all good city planning is the home of the citizen' (*Proceedings*, 1911, p. 97). This summed up the Parker and Unwin approach, in which they worked outwards from the individual home and hearth to the grouping of housing, the design of outdoor space and ultimately the Garden City and Garden Suburb. Unwin's concern for detail and quality in the design of working-class housing accomplished what Sir Frederic Osborn called 'the democratisation of architecture'.[39]

The primary means of averting unhealthy exclusions took the form of a new attention to corporate life, and the possibilities of association. Unwin began by looking at the plan of the old English village. Here he found an 'expression of a small corporate life in which all the different units were personally in touch with each other, conscious of and frankly accepting their relations, and on the whole content with them'.[40] Hoping to engineer functional relations through a duplication of traditional spatial relations, he observes that 'the most successful plan might be to gather the houses and other buildings on three sides of an open space, adopting the village green as the model'. The openness created by shared aspects on common land would also be applied to curb the zone of privacy surrounding individual dwellings. Unwin writes that 'A good number of the houses too might

---

37   *The Art of Building a Home: A Collection of Lectures and Illustrations by Barry Parker and Raymond Unwin* (London: Longmans, Green & Co., 1901), p. 86.
38   Raymond Unwin, *Cottage Plans and Common Sense* (London: Fabian Society, 1902), p. 2.
39   Mervyn Miller, *Raymond Unwin: Garden Cities and Town Planning* (Leicester: Leicester University Press, 1992), p. 25.
40   Parker and Unwin, *The Art of Building a Home*, pp. 92, 97, 98.

be open to the road or green' with the 'unfenced common coming right up to one's doorstep', giving a 'sense of openness whether viewed from within or from without'.

In addition to encouraging spatial openness, Unwin identified the unexploited potential for co-operation between residents. Tapping this resource would be key to mitigating the harmful effects of privacy. Whether applied to cottage and workman's developments or to middle-class estates, 'associated action' aimed to secure common interests and to 'give the sense of cohesion to the whole settlement which is so lamentably wanting when each struggles ineffectually to secure as much as he can [. . .] for himself alone'.[41] He derived this conviction, that co-operation would ensure 'the maximum of these advantages' for 'every individual house, be it large or small', from an analysis of historical and especially feudal precedent:

> Association for mutual help in various ways is undoubtedly the growing influence which is destined to bring to communities that crystalline structure which was so marked a feature of feudal society, and the lack of which is so characteristic of our own. When our new settlements begin to feel this influence they will again take on some of the unity which comes from organic growth. And as this influence increases in force, and interest and thought become more and more centred in the communal institutions and buildings, so will these begin to grow in beauty; for the people will wish to adorn them.

Given Unwin's interest in the 'crystalline' nature of 'feudal society', it comes as no surprise that he esteemed the architectural form of the quadrangle and the medieval college. Unwin's early life in Oxford left him with a profound admiration for these hybrid urban units. Instead of mourning a lost age of cohesive town life, he set about highlighting the proximity between the normal layout of tenement housing and the alternative model he was proposing. Simple alterations, he implied, might deliver a revolution in living conditions:

> What more satisfactory town buildings could one desire than some of the old colleges? Yet these consist primarily of rows of small tenements grouped round quadrangles or gardens with certain common rooms attached. The hall, the chapel, and the gatehouse, are prominent features; while the cloisters, where such exist, affording covered ways from the tenements to the common rooms, help to give a sense of unity to the whole. Why should not cottages be grouped into quadrangles, having all the available land in a square in the centre?

These new quadrangles would foster new social relations, being structures peculiarly suited to 'the provision of small laundries, baths, reading-rooms, and other such simple and easily managed co-operative efforts'.[42] Unwin's ideas are demonstrated graphically in *Cottage Plans and Common Sense* by a plan for artisan houses [figure 9]. Each of the dwellings depicted is carefully situated so as to form a quadrangle. There is 'something at once homely and dignified about a quadrangle', explains Unwin. It lends 'a sense of unity, of a complete whole, which lifts it

---

41 Parker and Unwin, *The Art of Building a Home*, pp. 96, 100, 103–4.
42 Unwin, *Cottage Plans and Common Sense*, pp. 4, 14.

Figure 9. Quadrangle of artisan homes, 1902, Plate 3 from Raymond Unwin's
Cottage Plans and Common Sense

out of the commonplace in a manner that nothing can accomplish for a mere street of cottages'. The quadrangle comes thus to symbolize many of the social aims he hoped to achieve through his architecture, offering at the same time a route to their practical realization.

As well as designing configurations of housing that would allow for association and communal interaction, Unwin was interested in the layout of communal facilities. His first move was to return to the revivalist form of the great hall, reducing it to a size appropriate to a family home, but retaining the roof space, exposed beams, hearth and ministrels' gallery [figure 10]. Parker and Unwin's 'The Art of Designing Small Houses and Cottages', an essay included in *The Art of Building a Home*, grants particular attention to the planning of halls and living rooms. The fireplace should be 'placed in a deep recess or ingle', so 'that a thorough sense of cosiness may always be obtainable'.[43] And it should serve its original function, providing 'the charm of the ruddy fire-lit space glowing red in the grey ill-lighted building, and the cosiness of the sheltered low recess in the wide and lofty hall'. It must also be 'large enough to be comfortable for one to sit in regularly, a place where one can live, not merely sit to be roasted'. The fire itself 'must be so designed as to have something of the feeling of the old fire on the hearth'.

As Parker and Unwin progressed to the planning of whole communities, their attentions turned to designing spaces that might play host to the inter-household

[43] Parker and Unwin, *The Art of Building a Home*, pp. 117, 118–19.

Figure 10. Preliminary sketch for a hall in Buxton, Derbyshire, 1901, Plate 20 from Barry Parker and Raymond Unwin's *The Art of Building a Home*

'association' upon which their architectural theories depended. In *Cottage Plans and Common Sense*, Unwin states that these spaces should 'supply somewhat the place of the individual parlor, the bakehouse, and even the common kitchen'.[44] Crucially, the number of functions catered for would rise with 'the growth of self-restraint and the co-operative spirit', a set of manners encouraged and developed over time by the layout of the community. This notion is familiar from the fictional exploration of utopian manners and informal regulation in *News from Nowhere*, and it is hard to imagine that such an ardent admirer of its author could have written these words without indebtedness. Also comparable to Morris's vision is the material realization of these ideas. Unwin's plan for a village common room near Leeds [figure 11] borrows heavily from the Morrisian ideal of the barn, an adaptable rural space, traceable to no single period, which is seen as having grown up from the soil and the souls of the people. Unwin built structures with a similar function in the course of his work on garden cities and suburbs. At New Earswick, he constructed a 'Folk Hall'. At Letchworth, the planners paid homage to Ruskin's favourite archetype, the village inn. Named the Skittles Inn, it was billed as an unlicensed public house 'conducted on the lines of the Old-fashioned Inns' that catered for 'Fellowship; Rest & Recreation'.[45] At Letchworth, a kind of hall for theatricals and other activities was provided in the form of the Mrs Howard Memorial Hall, and at Hampstead Garden Suburb 'The Clubhouse' at

---

[44] Unwin, *Cottage Plans and Common Sense*, p. 15.
[45] Mervyn Miller, *Letchworth: The First Garden City* (Chichester, West Sussex: Phillimore & Co Ltd, 1989), p. 93.

Figure 11. Design for a proposed village common room near Leeds, 1901, Plate 36 from Barry Parker and Raymond Unwin's *The Art of Building a Home*

Willifield Green served the function of a public meeting place and forum for the mixing of classes.

In retrospect, it is evident that Letchworth and Hampstead Garden suburb were as prone to the progressive privatization of the 'enlightened' suburb as any other. This reflects the love of house and home identified with the English social model by the German architectural critic, Hermann Muthesius. While Muthesius notes that the English hall surrounds the guest with a 'sense of comforting hospitality and open-armed welcome',[46] he also stresses that 'The Englishman sees the whole of life embodied in his house' and that the 'great store that the English still set by owning their home is part of this powerful sense of the individual personality'. Such attitudes were always likely to assert themselves in ways that precluded the very communal provisions Unwin hoped would accompany and redeem them. To this day, covenants and trust arrangements limit the scope for changing the character of some Garden City properties, and for profiting from unearned rises in value. However, attempts to create altered conditions have always been vulnerable to the power of habit. Just as Morris's William Guest finds it difficult to rid himself of nineteenth-century manners, so the inhabitants of these new communities carried elements of the 'old world' with them. Social integration schemes encouraged by the architects enjoyed questionable success. Frank Jackson notes of Hampstead Garden Suburb that it 'never attained the mixture of

46 Muthesius, *The English House*, pp. 7, 203.

classes and social equality that Unwin felt was a necessary complement to aesthetic quality, partly due to its enclosed nature and the superior quality of its environment, which attracted the better-off'.[47] This reference to the problems associated with enclosure is telling. Unwin was not blind to the issue, and accordingly employed less fortified methods of achieving a sense of 'homeplace' than the quadrangle. Letchworth and Hampstead Garden Suburb contain examples of buildings constructed on an 'L'-shaped plan. These are particularly common on corner plots. A variant is the open courtyard layout, with wings comprising separate dwellings. An intention to promote intercourse and interdependence between the private space and the public sphere is obvious in such architecture.

The welcoming embrace evoked structurally in so many cases has an underpinning philosophy more profound than straightforward nostalgia for village life. The ideas at stake go beyond a simple love of quaintness or cosiness. Unwin, in particular, was keen to stress the pragmatic nature of his recourse to historical forms. He was looking for design solutions that would work to mitigate individualism, and it therefore made sense that he should look beyond the architecture of modern society in his search. One must nevertheless register the power of the market and of habit to disrupt this process. The point is made succinctly by Mervyn Miller when he observes, with regard to Letchworth, that 'Despite attempts to break down class barriers with receptions for newcomers, distinctions remained'.[48] Old lines of status continued to run 'through many aspects of Garden City Life, particularly the "improving" lectures and the temperance question'.

None of these facts invalidates the worth of the attempt. They merely indicate the difficulties of building a utopia that is bounded, as opposed to comprehensive, in scope. Morris recognized this problem; it is clear that it informed his thinking in opting for a distinctly revolutionary brand of socialism. H. G. Wells responded to the unsustainable nature of an isolated or autarkical society by abolishing frontiers within his vision of the good society. Utopia, for him, would necessarily be a 'World-state'.[49] In this respect, the earthly endeavours of Norman Shaw, and of Unwin, are closer to the fanciful medievalism of Morris's Red House period. The seriousness of their approach, and their determination to transform social relations, mark their efforts out from Webb's first commission. They were nevertheless susceptible to the same difficulties connected with extending utopian content and practice beyond the parameters of utopian form. By taking a less systemic approach and daring to free Morris's thinking from the straitjacket of the Marxist teleology, they left a greater mark on the physical landscape and on patterns of life than might otherwise have been possible. This enduring legacy should be borne in mind when assessing the more obvious shortcomings of the Garden City project.

---

[47] Jackson, *Sir Raymond Unwin*, p. 98.
[48] *Letchworth: The First Garden City*, p. 88.
[49] Wells, *A Modern Utopia*, p. 12.

William Morris: A Tolerant Utopianism?

The crimes of fascism and Stalinism have impelled critics wishing to advance a favourable reading of Morris's work to distinguish his vision from totalitarian forms of utopianism. The arguments of those who assert the exceptional tolerance of Morris's vision were discussed and summarized in the main Introduction. It was one aim of this study to reach definite conclusions as to the validity of such claims.

My approach has been to historicize the tendency towards openness identified by these critics, to remove it from the sphere of abstract speculation and to express it in a language compatible with Morris's aesthetic and political context. This has involved grounding the liberalism that modern readers detect in *News from Nowhere* in a more complex ideal than mere tolerance. It would be suggestive of enlightened generosity and yet recognizably medievalist. It would be rooted in the conservative as well as radical strains of nineteenth-century thought. This book has been concerned with the development and significance of the unconditional and idealized hospitality with which Morris and so many others were preoccupied. Before proceeding to general conclusions, several issues need to be addressed. To what extent did the medievalist ideal of unconditional hospitality allow Morris to move beyond the values of control, enclosure and exclusivity associated with the classical utopia, and with totalitarian thought? Can Morris really be said to have initiated a tolerant utopianism?

Similar ground was covered in Chapter 4, but it is necessary to pose the question with a perspective on Morris's entire career. The findings of the previous chapter may then be incorporated into a wider, cumulative, set of conclusions. Morris's efforts to mitigate the exclusivity of his utopian projects are expressed in the structures of welcome at Red House; in attempts to represent difference through travel and translation; in the balanced application of preservationist principles to pre- and post-Renaissance buildings; and in the principles of unconditional – even, occasionally, self-defeating – hospitality promoted in the Teutonic romances and in *News from Nowhere*. On an exemplary, if not strictly practical level, his approach throughout his career is to remain open to 'the stranger at the gate'. In this respect, his creative vision does not employ the model of the ordered, closed society criticized by Popper;[50] it seems rather to draw inspiration from the Homeric, Biblical and medieval traditions of hospitality.

Such observations, alone, do not provide a sufficient basis for asserting Morris's 'special' status. This book has given expression to a sustained counter-argument whose validity must also be acknowledged. A literary tradition that stresses the dangers inherent to the act of admitting strangers has been identified. Morris's works contain many instances of the disruptive and dangerous guest, a type explored most obviously in his early renderings of the Arthurian legend. On the whole, Morris's treatment of the anarchic quality of sexual attraction, from the Guenevere of his early poems to Ellen in *News from Nowhere*, is tolerant, in so far as he allows it redemptive significance. Guenevere is given a voice, and her plight as a captive bride tempers the transgression enacted by Launcelot's court-

---

50 Popper, *The Open Society and its Enemies.*

ship. In *News from Nowhere*, the reader learns that Ellen has 'often troubled men's minds disastrously'.[51] Morris's willingness to accommodate the disruptive nature of sexuality, in his fiction as well as his personal life, may be construed as yet another instance of his much lauded 'tolerance'. And yet he also gives representation to the view that strangers are a source of trouble. His version of the fleece legend features a diabolic Medea;[52] and even in *News from Nowhere*, Guest's tendency to commit *faux pas* would seem to hold dangers for the host society. Morris's experiences in Iceland are also relevant. As a traveller, he felt frustration at being an unwilling agent of the very culture he was seeking to escape.

These qualifying remarks do not add up to a refutation of Morris's credentials as a believer in the virtues of openness and generous hospitality. They do, however, encourage consideration of a side of Morris rarely registered in appraisals of his utopianism. A simple stress on his exceptional capacity for tolerance cannot account for the persistence of the aestheticist or separatist component also present, if not necessarily dominant, in his work. Chapter Two located this tendency in the complex interplay of openness and inwardness running through *The Earthly Paradise*. While Morris moved beyond Rossetti's aestheticism to embrace more engaged political and artistic standpoints, he never abandoned it entirely. His reasons for continued confidence in the dream for the dream's sake are partly temperamental. They were also pragmatic, however. In an age that Morris considered artistically debased, inwardness and aestheticism had their uses. They protected the practices and values of artists whose work was by definition counter to the values of the mass market. To reach a measured view of Morris's commitment to tolerance, one must recognize, by analogy, the functionality of this component where his developing utopian socialism was concerned. By locating Nowhere at a future time, and refusing to grant Guest indefinite asylum, the integrity of utopian borders is preserved. The eradication of 'Mulleygrubs' and the elimination of idleness have a similar effect.[53] Acting in defence of Morrisian values, these later manifestations of inwardness provide a source of discipline strong enough to prevent openness from degenerating into disorder.

Morris's aestheticism should not therefore be dismissed as a longing for the apolitical. Only by maintaining a basic reliance on the principles governing this early separatism does he avert the formation of a utopia fatally compromised by its vulnerability to constant intrusion. It would seem that Morris's approach is not so very different from that of other utopists. Formally speaking, this is clearly the case: his utopia is another place; and it is monologic in so far as it springs from the mind of one identifiable author. On the level of content, there are some forms of behaviour that would never appear (trading for profit, for instance). Readers witness the reception of only one kind of guest, a man who bears striking resemblance to the author. Morris nevertheless does just about everything possible within the limits of the form to move away from the static social model of the classical utopia, jealous of its achievements and its territorial integrity. Morris's version of the good society does exhibit high levels of tolerance. His opposition to state socialism and his liberalistic concern for the rights of minorities indicate a

51 Morris, *News from Nowhere*, p. 188.
52 Morris, *The Life and Death of Jason*.
53 Morris, *News from Nowhere*, p. 40.

commitment to social pluralism. It is hard to think of many utopias that include figures like the old grumbler and the obstinate refusers. This much is not in question. Morris's many attempts to incorporate a measure of disorder successfully inhibit the advent of the kind of closed society condemned by twentieth-century critics of utopia. By problematizing the validity of an unconditional hospitality, of a generosity not rooted to some extent in self-interest, I have not sought to overturn this reading of Morris's significance in the history of utopian thought. I have attempted instead to refine understanding of the limits implicit in that position.

There remains, nevertheless, some instability at the heart of Morris's creative project. The potential for conflict between the defensive or separatist tendency and the extension of welcome to an imperfect world is never fully resolved. There is always the danger that openness will lead to a collapse of the distinction between the improved situation and the *status quo*, that extending utopian content beyond the parameters of utopian form will appear authoritarian, or that it will end, simply, in self-defeat, in a violation of the ideal. Morris, despite retaining informal laws and a commitment to social co-operation, takes a risk in seeking to combine perfection with a measure of 'redemptive' disorder.

Conclusions

This chapter tells a complex story of influence and discontinuity. H. G. Wells borrowed heavily from the Morrisian commitment to tolerance and to reviving medieval forms, such as the roadside inn and the quadrangle. He nevertheless had little time for the abolition of a monetary system, and his sympathies were closer to contemporary formulations of state intervention and redistributive taxation than to anything Morris proposed. Differences cluster, then, around the mechanics of the new era. Arguably more important is their shared confidence that a modern utopia would, by definition, be a tolerant utopia. The legacy of Morris's 'Hammersmith Guest House' and of the co-operative households he imagined is evident in the work of Parker and Unwin. Quadrangles, village greens, communal wash houses and 'folkhalls' express Morris's confidence in the vernacular path to cohesive communities. Both conceptions – that a modern utopia is in essence tolerant, and that folkways and village layout would foster a new co-operative consciousness – appear naïve now. In the immediate wake of the First World War, they would have seemed positively obsolete. The catastrophe of mechanized conflict had more or less extinguished the optimism of the Edwardian utopia. Morris and his disciples would have to wait until the 1970s before benefiting from the reaction against Modernism and the emergence of a new environmentalism. Some critics see the Morrisian brand of socialism, which stresses individuality and quality of life in preference to crude measures of economic growth, as a way of understanding and overcoming the 'wrong turn' of the command economy. Krishan Kumar has argued to this effect.[54] While the validity of this view is hard to verify, it *is* possible to argue that Morris and his disciples bestowed intellectual and practical resources capable, if nothing else, of providing inspiration.

---

[54] Kumar, 'News from Nowhere: The Renewal of Utopia'.

CONCLUSION

Morris placed a premium on the openness and tolerance of any society worthy of the adjective, *utopian*. Individuality would be prized above conformity; neighbourliness and fellowship would prevail over self-interest and resignation; hospitality would guard against insularity and protectionism. Although these values are most fully expressed in Morris's late political fictions, there is a close affiliation between them and the medievalism that informs the achievements of his entire career. One facet of this medievalism – a recurring interest in the archaic ideal of unconditional hospitality – proves particularly responsive to analysis of Morris's 'tolerance'. I have argued that Morris moved from a medievalist concern with monarchical, monastic and aristocratic largesse towards less hierarchical formulations of this ideal. The first change occurs when Morris visits Iceland and witnesses the extramural conception of home favoured by the society of farmers he found there. With the growth of his interest in socialism, he came to favour a communitarian attitude towards guests, informed less by *noblesse oblige* or tribal conceptions of the folk than by the traditions of the socialist meeting house and the popular myths of collective effort invoked by guild socialism. The great hall thus becomes the guest house. It is clear, nevertheless, that Morris's capacity for accommodating difference was not limitless; and indeed that the concept of hospitality itself depends upon exclusivity, no matter which interpretation of it one considers. Morris unashamedly emphasizes the continued importance of the home and the household in the utopian situation. In so doing, he confesses pragmatic as well as principled reliance on limits, on a sense of belonging and community.

Considered in a wider historical context, Morris's interest in 'guesting' represents but one of a range of aesthetic and political evocations of hospitality, taking as their source the Romantic fascination with, and re-evaluation of, outsiders. When combined with the social organicism favoured by commentators like Pugin and Cobbett, and with the age-old tendency to associate a perceived decline in manners with a descent into atomism, this way of conceiving relations between house and world informs a range of agendas. What Radicals, Tory Radicals, neo-Catholics, Pre-Raphaelites, ethnographers of the Germanic world and guild socialists had in common was a conception of the Middle Ages that emphasized a superior way of organizing relations between men. As Morris's example, and that of the Arts and Crafts pioneers demonstrates, this did not necessarily imply favouring a hierarchical method of socializing individuals over an equalitarian one. The Middle Ages were just as readily imagined as a nineteenth-century liberal's paradise.

Whether a commitment to unconditional hospitality can serve as a robust political ideal in the modern age is questionable. Even when one ignores the weaknesses inherent to Morris's vision of a revolutionized society, it would be unwise to extrapolate the virtues of his outlook in considering the problems of the present. Morris's solutions, like those proposed by the architects who sought to materialize his conception of fellowship, are locked within a social and political milieu long since past. What remains clear is that the conditions upon which communities offer hospitality are as controversial as ever. In a new century troubled by the social implications of immigration and asylum, the solutions that Victorian thinkers formulated in the face of modernity remain topical and challenging. Indeed, the world has never stood in greater need of a 'utopia of strangers', a means of conceptualizing the meaning of home for a mobile workforce driven from one location to another by the exigencies of life in a global economy.

BIBLIOGRAPHY

Manuscripts

Print Room, Victoria and Albert Museum, Webb E58–1916 DD22–Webb E68–1916 DD22

Books and Articles

Anderson, Perry, *Arguments within English Marxism* (London: Verso, 1980)

Anon., 'Spring in the Olden Time. – The Maypole', *Illustrated London News*, 27 May 1843, p. 367

Anon., 'Oxford', *The Oxford and Cambridge Magazine* (April, 1856), pp. 234–57

Anon., *Spectator*, 12 March 1870, pp. 332–4

Anon., *Justice*, 19 July 1884, p. 7

Anon., *Justice*, 26 July 1884, p. 6

Anon., *The Arabian Nights' Entertainments*, trans. by Edward William Lane, 3 vols (London: John Murray, 1859)

Armstrong, Isobel, *Victorian Poetry: Poetry, Poetics and Politics* (London: Routledge, 1993)

Armstrong, Nancy, *Desire and Domestic Fiction: A Political History of the Novel* (New York: Oxford University Press, 1987)

Arnold, Matthew, *The Complete Prose Works of Matthew Arnold*, ed. by R. H. Super, 11 vols (Ann Arbor: University of Michigan Press, 1962)

Ascherson, Neal, 'Why "Heritage" is Right-Wing', *Observer*, 8 November 1987, p. 9

[Austin, Alfred], 'The Poetry of the Period. Mr. Matthew Arnold. Mr. Morris.', *Temple Bar*, XXVII (November 1869), 35–51

Banham, Joanna and Jennifer Harris, eds, *William Morris and the Middle Ages: A Collection of Essays, Together with a Catalogue of Works Exhibited at the Whitworth Art Gallery, 28 September–8 December 1984* (Manchester: Manchester University Press, 1984)

Baring-Gould, Sabine, *Iceland: Its Scenes and Sagas* (London: Smith, Elder and Co., 1863)

Baudelaire, Charles, *Selected Writings on Art and Artists*, trans. by P. E. Charvet (Cambridge: Cambridge University Press, 1981)

Beeton, Mrs Isabella, *The Book of Household Management; Comprising Information for the Mistress . . . Also, Sanitary, Medical, & Legal Memoranda; with a History of the Origin, Properties, and Uses of all Things Connected with Home Life and Comfort* (London: S. O. Beeton, 1861)

Behlmer, George K., *Friends of the Family: The English House and Its Guardians, 1850–1940* (Stanford, California: Stanford University Press, 1998)

Bellamy, Edward, *Looking Backward 2000 to 1887* (Boston: Ticknor & Company, 1888)

Belsey, Andrew, 'Getting Somewhere: Rhetoric and Politics in *News from Nowhere*', *Textual Practice*, 5 (Winter 1991), 3, 337–51

Benveniste, Emile, *Indo-European Language and Society*, trans. by Elizabeth Palmer (London: Faber and Faber, 1973)

Berneri, Marie Louise, *Journey through Utopia* (London: Freedom Press, 1982)

Biddick, Kathleen, *The Shock of Medievalism* (Durham: Duke University Press, 1998)

Blake, William, *William Blake's Writings*, ed. by G. E. Bentley, Jr, 2 vols (Oxford: Clarendon Press, 1978)

Blatchford, Robert, *The Sorcery Shop: An Impossible Romance* (London: The Clarion Press, 1907)

Bloch, Ernst, *The Principle of Hope*, trans. by Neville Plaice, Stephen Plaice and Paul Knight, 3 vols (London: Basil Blackwell, 1986)

Boccaccio, Giovanni, *The Decameron*, trans. by Guido Waldman (Oxford: Oxford University Press, 1993)

Boenig, Robert, 'The Importance of Morris's *Beowulf*, *Journal of the William Morris Society*, XII (Spring, 1997), 2, 7–13

Bolsterli, M. J., *Early Community at Bedford Park: 'Corporate Happiness' in the First Garden Suburb* (Ohio: Ohio University Press, 1977)

Boos, Florence Saunders, *The Design of William Morris' The Earthly Paradise* (Lewison/ Queenston/Lampeter: The Edwin Mellen Press, 1990)

——, ed., *History and Community: Essays in Victorian Medievalism* (New York: Garland Publishing, 1992)

——, 'Victorian Response to *Earthly Paradise* Tales', *Journal of the William Morris Society*, V (Winter, 1983–84), 4, 16–29

——, 'The Evolution of the "The Wanderers' Prologue"', *Papers on Language and Literature*, 20 (1984), 4, 397–417

——, 'Morris's German Romances as Socialist History', *Victorian Studies*, 27 (Spring, 1984), 3, 321–42

Brantlinger, Patrick, '*News from Nowhere*: Morris' Socialist Anti-Novel', *Victorian Studies*, 19 (1975), 35–49

Browne, Thomas, *The Works of Sir Thomas Browne*, ed. by Geoffrey Keynes, 4 vols (London: Faber & Faber, 1978)

Bruckner, Matilda Tomaryn, *Narrative Invention in Twelfth-Century French Romance: The Convention of Hospitality (1160–1200)* (Lexington, Kentucky: French Forum Publishers, 1980)

Bulwer-Lytton, Edward, *The Coming Race* (Edinburgh: William Blackwood and Sons, 1871)

——, *The Last of the Barons* (London: George Routledge and Sons, 1875)

Burne-Jones, Georgiana, *Memorials of Edward Burne-Jones*, 2 vols (London: Macmillan and Co., 1904)

Burrow, J. W., *A Liberal Descent: Victorian Historians and the English Past* (Cambridge: Cambridge University Press, 1981)

Burton, Richard F., *Ultima Thule; or, A Summer in Iceland*, 2 vols (London: William P. Nimmo, 1875)

Butler, Samuel, *Erewhon* (London: Trübner & Co., 1872)

——, *Erewhon Revisited Twenty Years Later; Both by the Original Discoverer of the Country and by his Son* (London: A. C. Fifield, 1901)

Buzard, James, 'Ethnography as Interruption: *News from Nowhere*, Narrative, and the Modern Romance of Authority', *Victorian Studies*, 40 (Spring 1997), 3, 445–74

Caesar, *The Gallic War*, trans. by H. J. Edwards (London: William Heinemann, 1966)

Caird, Edward, *Collected Works of Edward Caird*, ed. by Colin Tyler, 12 vols (Bristol: Thoemmes Press, 1999)

Calhoun, Blue, *The Pastoral Vision of William Morris: The Earthly Paradise* (Athens: University of Georgia Press, [1975])

Campanella, Tommaso, *The City of the Sun: A Poetical Dialogue*, trans. by Daniel J. Donno (Berkeley: University of California Press, 1981)

Canning, William, *Gesta Grayorum; or, The History of the High and Mighty Prince, Henry Prince of Purpoole* (London: W. Canning, 1688)

Carlyle, Thomas, *The Works of Thomas Carlyle* ('Centenary Edition'), ed. by H. D. Traill, 30 vols (London: Chapman and Hall, 1896–1901)

Carpenter, Edward, *Civilisation – Its Cause and Cure and other Essays* (London: Swan Sonnenschein & Co, 1889)

Carroll, Lewis, *Alice's Adventures in Wonderland and through the Looking-Glass* (London: Oxford University Press, 1971)

Casson, Sir Hugh, 'Red House: The Home of William Morris', *The Listener*, 1 October 1953, pp. 536–7

Chapman, George, *Chapman's Homer*, ed. by Allardyce Nicoll, 2nd edn, 2 vols (Princeton, N. J.: Princeton University Press, 1967)

Chaucer, Geoffrey, *The Riverside Chaucer*, ed. by Larry D. Benson, 3rd edn (Oxford: Oxford University Press, 1987)

Chesterton, G. K., *Heretics* (London: Bodley Head, 1905)

Cicero, *Cicero in Twenty-Eight Volumes*, trans. by H. M. Hubbell, 28 vols (London: William Heinemann, 1968)

Cobbett, William, *A History of the Protestant 'Reformation,' in England and Ireland, Showing How that Event Has Impoverished and Degraded the Main Body of the People in those Countries* (London: John Dean, 1825)

——, *Rural Rides*, 2 vols (London: J. M. Dent & Sons, 1941)

Coleman, Stephen and Paddy O'Sullivan, eds, *William Morris & News from Nowhere: A Vision for Our Time*, (Bideford, Devon: Green Books, 1990)

Coleridge, Samuel Taylor, *The Collected Works of Samuel Taylor Coleridge*, ed. by J. C. C. Mays, 16 vols (Princeton, N. J.: Princeton University Press, 2001)

Collingwood, W. G., *The Life of John Ruskin*, 7th edn (London: Methuen, 1911)

Colvin, Sidney, 'Restoration and Anti-Restoration', *Nineteenth Century*, 2 (1877), 446–70

Constant, Benjamin, *Journal intime précédé du cahier rouge et d'Adolphe* (Monaco: Éditions du Roucher, 1945)

Corelli, Marie, 'The Decay of Hospitality', *The Bystander*, 29 June 1904, pp. 203–5

Cowley, A., *Poems, The English Writings of Abraham Cowley*, ed. by A. R. Waller (Cambridge: Cambridge University Press, 1905)

Dasent, George Webb, 'The Norsemen in Iceland', *Oxford Essays* (1858), 165–214

Davey, Peter, *Arts and Crafts Architecture: The Search for Earthly Paradise* (London: The Architectural Press, 1980)

Davidoff, Leonore, *The Best Circles: Society Etiquette and the Season* (London: Croom Helm, 1973)

Davie, Donald, *Ezra Pound: Poet as Sculptor* (London: Routledge & Kegan Paul, 1965)

Davis, J. C., *Utopia and the Ideal Society: A Study of Utopian Writing 1516–1700* (Cambridge: Cambridge University Press, 2002)

Derrida, Jacques, *Adieu to Emmanuel Levinas*, trans. by Pascale-Anne Brault and Michael Naas (Stanford, California: Stanford University Press, 1999)

——, and Anne Dufourmantelle, *Of Hospitality*, trans. by Rachel Bowlby (Stanford: Stanford University Press, 2002)

Dickens, Charles, *The Posthumous Papers of the Pickwick Club* (London: Chapman and Hall, 1837)

Disraeli, Benjamin, *Sybil; or, The Two Nations*, 3 vols (London: Henry Colburn, 1845)

——, *Coningsby; or, The New Generation*, 3 vols (London: Henry Colburn, 1844)

Donne, John, *The Poems of John Donne*, ed. by Herbert J. C. Grierson, 2 vols (Oxford: Oxford University Press, 1966)

Donnelly, Dorothy F., *Patterns of Order and Utopia* (Basingstoke: Macmillan, 1998)

Dryden, John, *The Poems of John Dryden*, ed. by James Kinsley, 4 vols (Oxford: Clarendon Press, 1958)

Dunlop, Beth, ed., *Arts and Crafts Houses I* (London: Phaidon, [n.d.])

Eco, Umberto, *The Open Work*, trans. by Anna Cancogni ([London]: Hutchinson Radius, 1989)

Eliot, T. S., *Selected Essays* (London: Faber and Faber, 1991)

Engels, Frederick, *The Origin of the Family, Private Property and the State, in the Light of the Researches by Lewis H. Morgan*, trans. by Alick West (London: Lawrence and Wishart, 1940)

Evans, Robin, *Translations from Drawing to Building and Other Essays* (London: Architectural Association, 1997)

Faulkner, Peter, *Against the Age: An Introduction to William Morris* (London: Allen and Unwin, 1980)

——, and Peter Preston, eds, *William Morris: Centenary Essays* (Exeter: University of Exeter Press, 1999)

Field, Horace, 'Protection of Ancient Buildings', *The Builder*, 8 September 1877

Foisner, Sabine, *The Redeemed Loser: Art World and Real World in William Morris* (Salzburg: Institut für Anglistik und Amerikanistik, Universität Salzburg, 1989)

Forbes, Charles S., *Iceland; Its Volcanoes, Geysers, and Glaciers* (London: John Murray, 1860)

Fortes, Meyer, and Sheila Patterson, eds, *Studies in African Social Anthropology* (London: Academic Press, 1975)

Foucault, Michel, *Les mots et les choses: une archéologie des sciences humaines* (Paris: Éditions Gallimard, 1966)

——, *Surveiller et punir: naissance de la prison* (Paris, Gallimard, 1975)

Fouqué, Frederic La Motte, *Sintram and his Companions: A Romance*, trans. by J. C. Hane (London: C. and J. Ollier, 1820)

Franklin, Jill, *The Gentleman's Country House and Its Plan, 1835–1914* (London: Routledge, 1981)

Freeman, Edward A., *The Growth of the English Constitution from the Earliest Times* (London: Macmillan and Co., 1872)

——, *Comparative Politics: Six Lectures with The Unity of History* (London: Macmillan, 1873)

Freud, Sigmund, *The Standard Edition of the Complete Psychological Works of Sigmund Freud*, ed. by James Strachey, 24 vols (London: The Hogarth Press, 1981)

Gautier, Théophile, *Mademoiselle de Maupin*, trans. by Joanna Richardson (Harmondsworth: Penguin Books, 1981)

Gerard, David, *John Ruskin & William Morris: The Energies of Order and Love* (London: Nine Elms, 1988)

Gibbon, Edward, *The History of the Decline and Fall of the Roman Empire*, 6 vols (London, 1776–88)

Girouard, Mark, *The Victorian Country House*, rev. edn (New Haven: Yale University Press, 1979)

——, 'Red House, Bexleyheath, Kent', *Country Life*, 16 June 1960, pp. 1382–5

Gladstone, William Ewart, *Bulgarian Horrors and the Question of the East* (London: John Murray, 1876)

Glasier, J. Bruce, *William Morris and the Early Days of the Socialist Movement* (London: Longmans, 1921)

Godwin, William, *Caleb Williams* (Oxford: Oxford University Press, 1982)

Goethe, Johann Wolfgang von, *Goethe's Plays*, trans. by Charles E. Passage (London: Ernest Benn, 1980)

——, *Goetz of Berlichingen, with the Iron Hand: A Tragedy*, trans. by Walter Scott (London: J. Bell, 1799)

Goode, John, *Collected Essays of John Goode*, ed. by Charles Swann (Keele, Staffordshire: Keele University Press, 1995)

Gough ('D. N.'), Richard, 'A Plan for Preservation of Ancient Edifices', *Gentleman's Magazine*, LVIII (August, 1788), II, 689–91

Green, J. R., *A Short History of the English People* (London: Macmillan, 1874)

Jekyll, Gertrude, *Home and Garden. Notes and Thoughts, Practical and Critical, of a Worker in Both* (London: Longmans & Co., 1900)

Joyce, James, *Dubliners* (Oxford: Oxford University Press, 2001)

Haarhoff, T. J., *The Stranger at the Gate: Aspects of Exclusiveness and Co-operation in Ancient Greece and Rome, with Some Reference to Modern Times*, 2nd edn (Oxford: Blackwell, 1948)

Hall, Michael, 'Red House, Bexleyheath, London', *Country Life*, 10 July 2003, 66–71

Hallam, Henry, *View of the State of Europe during the Middle Ages*, 3 vols (London: John Murray, 1853)

Hardy, Thomas, *Jude the Obscure* (London: Osgood, McIlvaine, 1896)

Hartley, L. P., *The Go-Between* (London: Hamish Hamilton, 1953)

Harvey, Charles and Jon Press, *William Morris: Design and Enterprise in Victorian Britain* (Manchester: Manchester University Press, 1991)

——, *Art, Enterprise, and Ethics: The Life and Work of William Morris* (London: Frank Cass, 1996)

Hayek, Friedrich, *The Road to Serfdom* (London: G. Routledge & sons, 1944)

Heal, Felicity, *Hospitality in Early Modern England* (Oxford: Clarendon, 1990)

Heidegger, Martin, *Poetry, Language, Thought* (New York: New Perennial, 2001)

Henderson, Ebenezer, *Iceland; or, the Journal of a Residence in that Island During the Years 1814 and 1815*, 2 vols (Edinburgh: Oliphant, Waugh and Innes, 1818)

Henderson, Philip, *William Morris: His Life, Work and Friends* (London: Thames & Hudson, 1967)

Heraud, John A., 'Christmas Eve, and Welcome to Old Friends', Supplement to *Illustrated London News*, 23 December 1848, p. 411

Herbert, Karen, 'Dissident Language in *The Defence of Guenevere*', *Victorian Poetry*, 34 (Autumn, 1996), 3, 313–27

Herodotus, *Herodotus*, trans. by A. D. Godley, 4 vols (London: William Heinemann, 1966)

Hewison, Robert, ed., *New Approaches to Ruskin* (London: Routledge & Kegan Paul, 1981)

——, *The Heritage Industry: Britain in a Climate of Decline* (London: Methuen, 1987)

Hilton, Tim, *John Ruskin: The Later Years* (New Haven and London: Yale University Press, 2000)

Hodgson, Amanda, *The Romances of William Morris* (Cambridge: Cambridge University Press, 1987)

Holm, Jan, 'The Old Grumbler at Runnymede', *The Journal of the William Morris Society*, 10 (Spring 1993), 2, 17–21

Holzman, Michael, 'Anarchism and Utopia: William Morris's *News from Nowhere*', *ELH*, 51 (1984), 589–603

Hooker, William Jackson, *Recollections of a Tour in Iceland in 1809/Journal of a Tour in Iceland in the Summer of 1809* (Yarmouth: J. Keymer, 1811)

Howard, Ebenezer, *To-morrow: A Peaceful Path to Social Reform* (London: Swan Sonnenschein & Co., 1898)

——, *Garden Cities of To-morrow: Being the Second Edition of "To-morrow: A Peaceful Path to Real Reform"* (London: Swan Sonnenschein & Co, 1902)

Howells, William Dean, *A Traveller from Altruria* (Edinburgh: D. Douglas, 1894)

——, *Through the Eye of the Needle: A Romance* (New York: Harper & Brothers, 1907)

Hudson, William, *A Crystal Age* (London: T. Fisher Unwin, 1887)

Hunter, Michael, ed., *Preserving the Past: The Rise of Heritage in Modern Britain* (Stroud: Sutton Publishing, 1996)

Hutton, Ronald, *The Rise and Fall of Merry England: The Ritual Year 1400–1700* (Oxford: Oxford University Press, 1993)

Huxley, Aldous, *Brave New World* (London: Chatto & Windus, 1932)

Ignatieff, Michael, *The Needs of Strangers* (London: Chatto & Windus, 1984)

Jackson, Frank, *Sir Raymond Unwin: Architect, Planner and Visionary* (London: A. Zwemmer Ltd, 1985)

Jerome, Jerome K., *Diary of a Pilgrimage and Six Essays* (Leipzig: Bernard Tauchnitz, 1892)

Johnson, Samuel, *The Yale Edition of the Works of Samuel Johnson*, ed. by Gwin J. Kolb, 16 vols (New Haven: Yale University Press, 1990)

Julius, Anthony, *T. S. Eliot, Anti-Semitism and Literary Form* (Cambridge: Cambridge University Press, 1995)

Kant, Immanuel, *Critique of Pure Reason*, trans. and ed. by Paul Guyer and Allen W. Wood (Cambridge: Cambridge University Press, 2000)

——, *Perpetual Peace*, trans. by Helen O'Brien (London: Sweet & Maxwell, 1927)

Kateb, George, *Utopia and its Enemies* (London: Collier-Macmillan, 1963)

Keats, John, *The Poetical Works of John Keats*, ed. by H. W. Garrod, 2nd edn (Oxford: Clarendon Press, 1958)

Kelvin, Norman, ed., *The Collected Letters of William Morris*, 4 vols (Princeton: Princeton University Press, 1984–96)

——, 'Morris, the 1890s, and the Problematic Autonomy of Art', *Victorian Poetry*, 34 (Autumn, 1996), 3, 425–32

Kemble, John Mitchell, *The Saxons in England: A History of the English Commonwealth till the Period of the Norman Conquest*, 2 vols (London: Longman, Brown, Green, and Longmans, 1849)

Kermode, Frank, *The Sense of an Ending: Studies in the Theory of Fiction* (New York: Oxford University Press, 1967)

Kinna, Ruth, *William Morris: The Art of Socialism* (Cardiff: University of Wales Press, 2000)

Kirchhoff, Frederick, *William Morris* (Boston: Twayne Publishers, 1979)

——, *William Morris: The Construction of a Male Self, 1856–1872* (Athens, Ohio: Ohio University Press, 1990)

Kirk, Sheila, *Philip Webb: Pioneer of Arts & Crafts Architecture* (Chichester, West Sussex: Wiley-Academy, 2005)

Kocmanová, Jessie, 'Some Remarks on E. P. Thompson's Opinion of the Poetry of William Morris', *Philologica Pragensia*, III (1960), 3, 168–78

——, 'The Living Language of William Morris', *Brno Studies in English*, 9 (1970), 17–34

——, *The Poetic Maturing of William Morris, From the Earthly Paradise to the Pilgrims of Hope* (Prague: Státní Pedagogické Nakladatelství, 1964)

Koenig, John, *New Testament Hospitality: Partnership with Strangers as Promise and Mission* (Philadelphia: Fortress Press, 1985)

Kristeva, Julia, *Étrangers à nous-mêmes* (Paris: Gallimard, 1988)

Kumar, Krisan, *Utopia and Anti-Utopia in Modern Times* (Oxford: Basil Blackwell, 1987)

——, 'News from Nowhere: The Renewal of Utopia', *History of Political Thought*, XIV (Spring, 1993), 1, 133–43

——, 'A Pilgrimage of Hope: William Morris's Journey to Utopia', *Utopian Studies: Journal of the Society for Utopian Studies*, 51 (1994), 1, 89–107

Langland, Elizabeth, *Nobody's Angels: Middle-Class Women and Domestic Ideology in Victorian Culture* (Ithaca: Cornell University Press, 1995)

Langland, William, *The Vision of Piers Plowman* (London: J. M. Dent, 1995)

Lashley, Conrad and Alison Morrison, *In Search of Hospitality: Theoretical Perspectives and Debates* (Oxford: Butterworth-Heinemann, 2000)

Lefebvre, Henri, *The Production of Space*, trans. by Donald Nicholson-Smith (Oxford: Blackwell, 1991)

Lethaby, W. R., *Philip Webb and his Work* (London: Oxford University Press, 1935)

Lévi-Strauss, Claude, *Tristes tropiques*, trans. by John and Doreen Weightman (London: Jonathan Cape, 1973)

Levitas, Ruth, 'Marxism, Romanticism and Utopia: Ernst Bloch and William Morris', *Radical Philosophy*, 51 (1989), 27–36

——, *The Concept of Utopia* (Hemel Hempstead: Philip Allan, 1990)

Levy, Harry L., 'The Odyssean Suitors and the Host-Guest Relationship', *Transactions and Proceedings of the American Philological Association*, 94 (1963), 145–53

Lewis, C. S., *Rehabilitations and Other Essays* (Oxford: Oxford University Press, 1939)

——, *The Lion, the Witch and the Wardrobe* (London: Geoffrey Bles, 1950)

Liberman, Michael, 'Major Textual Changes in William Morris's *News from Nowhere*', *Nineteenth-Century Literature*, 41 (1986), 3, 349–356

Lindsay, Jack, *William Morris: His Life and Work* (London: Constable, 1975)

Litzenberg, Karl, 'The Diction of William Morris', *Arkiv för Nordisk Filologi*, 9 (1937), 327–63

Lockhart, John Gibson, *Memoirs of the Life of Sir W. Scott*, 10 vols (Edinburgh: 1839)

Longfellow, Henry Wadsworth, *Tales of a Wayside Inn* (London: Routledge, Warne, and Routledge, 1864)

Lowenthal, David, *The Past is a Foreign Country* (Cambridge: Cambridge University Press, 1985)

Lyotard, Jean-François, *The Postmodern Condition: A Report on Knowledge*, trans. by Geoff Bennington and Brian Massumi (Manchester: Manchester University Press, 1992)

MacCarthy, Fiona, *William Morris: A Life for Our Time* (London: Faber and Faber, 1994), [n.p.])

——, 'Garden of Earthly Delights', *Guardian* ('Review' section), 26 July 2003, pp. 4–6

Macdonald, Jean, *Red House: A Guide*, 2nd edn (London: William Morris Society, 1993)

MacGahan, J. A., *The Turkish Atrocities in Bulgaria* (London: Bradbury, Agnew, & Co., 1876)

Mackail, J. W., *The Life of William Morris*, 2 vols (London: Longmans, Green, and Co., 1899)

Mackay, Charles, *The Collected Songs of Charles Mackay* (London: G. Routledge & Co., 1859)

Mackenzie, Sir George Steuart, *Travels in the Island of Iceland during the Summer of the Year MDCCCX* (Edinburgh: Archibald Constable and Company, 1811)

Magnússon, Eiríkr, *Saga Library*, 6 vols (London: Bernard Quaritch, 1905)

Magnússon, Magnús S., *Iceland in Transition: Labour and Socio-Economic Change Before 1940* (Lund, Sweden: Skrifter Utgivna av Ekonomisk-Historiska Föreningen, 1985)

Mallock, W. H., *The New Republic; or Culture, Faith, and Philosophy in an English Country House* (London: Michael Joseph, 1877)

Malory, Thomas, *Works*, ed. by Eugène Vinaver (London: Oxford University Press, 1971)

Mandler, Peter, *The Fall and Rise of the Stately Home* (New Haven and London: Yale University Press, 1997)

Mangnall, R., *Historical and Miscellaneous Questions for the Use of Young People* (Stockport, [1800])

——, *A Compendium of Geography with Geographic Exercises, for the Use of Schools, Private Families, and all those who Require Knowledge of this Important Science*, 2nd edn (London: Longman, Hurst, Rees, Orme, and Brown, 1822)

——, *Historical and Miscellaneous Questions, for the Use of Young People; with a Selection of British and General Biography, etc. etc.*, adapted for the use of schools by Rev. G. N. Wright (London: William Tegg & Co., 1856)

Manners, John, *England's Trust and other Poems* (London: J. G. F. & J. Rivington, 1841)

——, 'A Plea for National Holy-days' (London, 1843)

Mannheim, Karl, *Ideology and Utopia: An Introduction to the Sociology of Knowledge* (London: K. Paul, Trench, Trübner & Co., 1936)

Marcuse, Herbert, *Eros and Civilization: A Philosophical Inquiry into Freud* (London: Routledge & Kegan Paul, 1956)

——, *One Dimensional Man* (London: Abacus, 1972)

Marsh, Jan, *William Morris & Red House* (National Trust Books, 2005)

Marshall, John, and Ian Willox, *The Victorian House* (London: Sidgwick & Jackson, 1989)

Marshall, Roderick, *William Morris and his Earthly Paradises* (New York: George Braziller, 1981)

Marx, Karl and Frederick Engels, *Collected Works*, 49 vols (London: Lawrence & Wishart, 1975–2001)

Mauss, Marcel, *The Gift*, trans. by W. D. Halls (London: Routledge, 1990)

McLennan, John F., *Primitive Marriage: An Inquiry into the Origin of the Form of Capture in Marriage Ceremonies* (Edinburgh: Adam and Charles Black, 1865)

McMaster, Rowland, 'Tensions in Paradise: Anarchism, Civilization, and Pleasure in Morris's *News from Nowhere*', *English Studies in Canada*, XVII (March, 1991), I, 73–87

Meier, Paul, *William Morris: The Marxist Dreamer*, trans. by Frank Gubb, 2 vols (Sussex: Harvester Press, 1978)

Metcalfe, Frederick, *The Oxonian in Iceland* (London: Longman, 1861)

Meynell, Esther, *Portrait of William Morris* (London: Chapman & Hall, 1947)

Migeon, Jacques, 'Red House and Ruskin', *Journal of the William Morris Society*, III (Spring, 1977), 3, 30–2

Mill, J. S., *The Collected Works of John Stuart Mill*, ed. by John M. Robson, 33 vols (Toronto: Toronto University Press, 1963–91)

Mineo, Ady, 'Eros Unbound: Sexual Identities in *News from Nowhere*', *The Journal of the William Morris Society*, IX (Spring, 1992), 4, 8–14

More, Thomas, *The Yale Edition of the Complete Works of St. Thomas More*, ed. by Edward Surtz and J. H. Hexter, 14 vols (New Haven: Yale University Press, 1965)

Morgan, Lewis H., *Ancient Society; or, Researches in the Lines of Human Progress from Savagery through Barbarism to Civilization* (New York: Henry Holt and Company, 1878)

Morris, Barbara, 'William Morris and the South Kensington Museum', *Victorian Poetry*, 13 (1975), 3–4, 159–175

Morris, William, *The Collected Works of William Morris*, ed. by May Morris, 24 vols (London: Longmans Green and Company, 1910–15)

——, *William Morris: Artist Writer Socialist*, ed. by May Morris, 2 vols (Oxford: Basil Blackwell, 1936)

——, *The Unpublished Lectures of William Morris*, ed. by Eugene D. LeMire (Detroit: Wayne State University Press, 1969)

——, *News from Nowhere* (Hammersmith: Kelmscott Press, 1893)

——, *News from Nowhere* (London: Reeves and Turner, 1891)

——, 'Report', in 'The First Annual Meeting of the Society. Report of the Committee Thereat Read', *Society for the Protection of Ancient Buildings*, 21st June 1878, 9–18

——, 'The Dull Level of Life', *Justice*, 26 April 1884, p. 4

——, 'Free Speech in the Streets', *Commonweal*, 31 July 1886, p. 137

——, 'Looking Backward', *Commonweal*, 22 June 1889, pp. 194–5

——, 'Communism and Anarchism', *Commonweal*, 17 August 1889, p. 261

Morton, A. L., *The English Utopia* (London: Lawrence & Wishart, 1952)

Mumford, Lewis, *The City in History* (Harmondsworth: Penguin Books, 1966)

Muthesius, Hermann, *The English House*, trans. by Janet Seligman (London: Crosby Lockwood Staples, 1979)

Myers, Hilary and Richard Myers, *William Morris Tiles: The Tile Designs of Morris and his Fellow-workers* (Shepton Beauchamp: R. Dennis, 1996)

Nash, Joseph, *The Mansions of England in the Olden Time* (London: Thomas Mclean, 1849)

Newman, F. W., *The Iliad of Homer Faithfully Translated into Unrhymed English Metre* (London: Walton and Maberly, 1856)

Nozick, Robert, *Anarchy, State, and Utopia* (Oxford: Basil Blackwell, 1974)

Oberg, Charlotte H., *A Pagan Prophet, William Morris* (Charlottesville: University Press of Virginia, 1978)

Orwell, George, *Nineteen Eighty-Four* (London: Secker and Warburg, 1949)

Oswald, E. J., *By Fell and Fjord; or, Scenes and Studies in Iceland* (Edinburgh and London: William Blackwood and Sons, 1882)

Palmer, Daryl W., *Hospitable Performances: Dramatic Genre and Cultural Practices in Early Modern England* (West Lafayette, Indiana: Purdue University Press, 1992)

Parker, Barry and Raymond Unwin, *The Art of Building a Home: A Collection of Lectures and Illustrations by Barry Parker and Raymond Unwin* (London: Longmans, Green & Co., 1901)

Parry, David, *Households of God: The Rule of St Benedict with Explanations for Monks and Lay-people Today* (London: Darton, Longman & Todd, 1980)

Parry, Linda, *William Morris Textiles* (London: Weidenfeld and Nicolson, 1983)

——, *William Morris* (London: Philip Wilson in Association with the Victoria and Albert Museum, 1996)

Passmore, John, *The Perfectibility of Man* (London: Duckworth, 1970)

Pater, Walter, *The Works of Walter Pater*, 8 vols (London: Macmillan and Co., 1900)

[Pater, Walter], 'Poems by William Morris', *Westminster Review*, XXXIV (October, 1868), 300–12

Peck, Bradford, *The World a Department Store. A Story of Life Under a Cooperative System* (London: Gay & Bird, 1900)

Peristiany, J. G., *Contributions to Mediterranean Sociology: Mediterranean Rural Communities and Social Change* (Paris: Mouton & Co., 1968)

Pevsner, Nikolaus, *Pioneers of the Modern Movement: From William Morris to Walter Gropius* (London: Faber and Faber, 1936)

——, *Pioneers of Modern Design: From William Morris to Walter Gropius*, 2nd edn (Harmondsworth: Penguin Books, 1960)

——, *The Sources of Modern Architecture and Design* (London: Thames and Hudson, 1968)

Pfeiffer, Ida, *A Visit to Iceland and the Scandinavian North*, trans. by author (London: Ingram, Cooke, and Co., 1852)

Plato, *The Republic*, trans. by Paul Shorey, 2 vols (London: William Heinemann, 1963)

Plutarch, *Plutarch's Lives*, trans. by Bernadotte Perrin, 11 vols (London: William Heinemann, 1959)

Poe, Edgar Allan, *The Works of Edgar Allan Poe*, 10 vols (New York: Funk & Wagnalls, 1904)

Pointon, Marcia, *William Dyce, 1806–1864: A Critical Biography* (Oxford: Clarendon Press, 1979)

Poovey, Mary, *Uneven Developments: The Ideological Work of Gender in Mid-Victorian England* (London: Virago Press, 1989)

Pope, Alexander, *The Odyssey of Homer*, ed. by Maynard Mack, 2 vols (London: Methuen & Co., 1967)

Popper, K. R., *The Open Society and its Enemies*, 2 vols (London: Routledge, 1945)

Pound, Ezra, *Literary Essays of Ezra Pound*, ed. by T. S. Eliot (London: Faber and Faber, 1954)

Power, Mary, 'A Note on Hospitality and "The Dead"', *James Joyce Quarterly*, 13, Fall 1975, 1, p. 109

Pugin, A. Welby, *Contrasts; or, A Parallel Between the Noble Edifices of the Middle Ages, and Corresponding Buildings of the Present Day; Shewing the Present Decay of Taste*, 2nd edn (London: Charles Dolman, 1841)

——, *The True Principles of Pointed or Christian Architecture: Set Forth in Two Lectures Delivered at St. Marie's, Oscott* (London: John Weale, 1841)

Ralegh, Sir Walter, *The Poems of Walter Ralegh: A Historical Edition*, ed. by Michael Ruddick (Tempe, Arizona: Renaissance English Text Society, 1999)

Reece, Steve, *The Stranger's Welcome: Oral Theory and the Aesthetics of the Homeric Hospitality Scene* (Ann Arbor: University of Michigan Press, 1993)

Richter, Eugen, *Pictures of the Socialistic Future, Freely Adapted from Bebel*, trans. by H. Wright (London: Sonnenschein & Co, 1893)

Riddehough, Geoffrey B., 'William Morris's Translation of the *Aeneid*', *Journal of English and Germanic Philology*, XXXVI (1937), 338–46

Riede, David G., 'Morris, Modernism, and Romance', *ELH*, 51 (1984), 1, 85–106

Robinson, Duncan and Stephen Wildman, *Morris & Company in Cambridge* (Cambridge: Cambridge University Press, 1980)

Rogers, James E. Thorold, *Six Centuries of Work and Wages: The History of English Labour*, 2 vols (London: Sonnenschein & Co., 1884)

Rollins, Hyder Edward, ed., *The Letters of John Keats*, 2 vols (Cambridge, Mass.: Harvard University Press, 1980)

Ruskin, John, *The Library Edition of the Works of John Ruskin*, ed. by E. T. Cook and Alexander Wedderburn, 39 vols (London: George Allen, 1903–12)

Salmon, Nicholas, 'A Study of Victorian Historiography: William Morris's Germanic Romances', *Journal of the William Morris Society*, XIV (Spring, 2001), 2, 59–89

——, and Derek Baker, *The William Morris Chronology* (Bristol: Thoemmes Press, 1996)

Samuel, Raphael, *Theatres of Memory*, 2 vols (London: Verso, 1994)

Scott, John, *The Poetical Works of John Scott Esq.* (London: J. Buckland, 1782)

Scott, Walter, *Ivanhoe*, 3 vols (Edinburgh: Archibald Constable and Co., 1820)

——, *The Poetic Works of Walter Scott . . . Complete in One Volume* (Edinburgh: Robert Cadell, 1841)

Scott, William Bell, *Autobiographical Notes of the Life of William Bell Scott*, 2 vols (London: James R. Osgood, McIlvaine & Co, 1892)

Shakespeare, William, *The Tragedy of Macbeth*, ed. by Nicholas Brooke (Oxford: Oxford University Press, 1990)

——, *The Tragedy of King Lear*, ed. by Jay L. Halio (Cambridge: Cambridge University Press, 1992)

——, *The Winter's Tale*, ed. by Stephen Orgel (Oxford: Oxford University Press, 1996)

Shklar, Judith N., *After Utopia: The Decline of Political Faith* (Princeton, N.J.: Princeton University Press, 1957)

Silver, Carole, *The Romance of William Morris* (Athens, Ohio: Ohio University Press, 1982)

Simpson, Roger, *Camelot Regained: The Arthurian Revival and Tennyson, 1800–1849* (Cambridge: D.S. Brewer, 1990)

Skoblow, Jeffrey, *Paradise Dislocated: Morris, Politics, Art* (Charlottesville: University Press of Virginia, 1993)

Sophocles, *Sophocles*, trans. by F. Storr, 2 vols (London: William Heinemann, 1962)

Sotheby, William, *Italy and Other Poems* (London: John Murray, 1828)

Southey, Robert, *The Poetical Works of Robert Southey* (Paris: A. and W. Galignani, 1829)

Spear, Jeffrey L., *Dreams of an English Eden: Ruskin and his Tradition in Social Criticism* (New York: Columbia University Press, 1984)

Spencer, Herbert, *Social Statistics, Abridged and Revised; Together with The Man versus the State* (London: Williams and Norgate, 1892)

Stansky, Peter, *William Morris* (Oxford: Oxford University Press, 1983)

——, *Redesigning the World: William Morris, the 1880s, and the Arts and Crafts* (Princeton, N. J.: Princeton University Press, 1985)

Steiner, George, *Real Presences: Is There Anything in What We Say?* (London: Faber and Faber, 1989)

——, *After Babel: Aspects of Language and Translation*, 3rd edn (Oxford: Oxford University Press, 1998)

Stone, Lawrence, *The Family, Sex and Marriage in England 1500–1800* (London: Weidenfeld and Nicolson, 1977)

Stubbs, William, *The Constitutional History of England in its Origin and Development*, 3 vols (Oxford: Clarendon Press, 1874–78)

Sturluson, Snorri, *The Heimskringla; or, Chronicle of The Kings of Norway*, trans. by Samuel Laing, 3 vols (London: Longman, Brown, Green, and Longmans, 1844)

Swannell, J. N., *William Morris & Norse Literature* (London: William Morris Society, 1961)

Swinburne, Algernon Charles, *The Complete Works of Algernon Charles Swinburne*, ed. by Sir Edmund Gosse and Thomas James Wise, 20 vols (London: William Heinemann, 1925–27)

——, 'Charles Baudelaire: Les Fleurs du Mal', *Spectator*, 6 September 1862, 998–1000

Tacitus, Cornelius, *Tacitus in Five Volumes*, trans. by M. Hutton (London: William Heinemann, 1970)

Tanner, Tony, *Adultery in the Novel: Contract and Transgression* (Baltimore, Maryland: The Johns Hopkins University Press, 1979)

Tennyson, Alfred, *The Poems of Tennyson*, ed. by Christopher Ricks, 3 vols (London: Longman, 1987)

Thompson, E. P., *William Morris: Romantic to Revolutionary*, 2nd edn (London: Merlin Press, 1976)

Thompson, Paul, *The Work of William Morris* (London: Heinemann, 1967)

Thoreau, Henry, *Walden and Civil Disobedience*, ed. by Owen Thomas (New York: W. W. Norton & Company, 1966)

Thorpe, Benjamin, *Yule-tide Stories: A Collection of Scandinavian and North German*

Popular Tales and Traditions, from the Swedish, Danish, and German (London: Henry G. Bohn, 1853)

Tiller, P. M., 'William Morris's Translation of *Beowulf*: Studies in his Vocabulary', *Occasional Papers in Linguistics and Language Learning* (August, 1981), 8, 161–175

Tolkien, J. R. R., *The Hobbit* (London: Allen & Unwin, 1937)

Tompkins, J. M. S., *William Morris: An Approach to the Poetry* (London: C. Woolf, 1988)

Trollope, Anthony, *The Warden* (Oxford: Oxford University Press, 1990)

Tucker, Herbert F., 'All for the Tale: The Epic Macropoetics of Morris' *Sigurd the Volsung*', *Victorian Poetry*, 34 (Autumn, 1996), 3, 373–94

Turner, Sharon, *The History of the Anglo-Saxons from their First Appearance above the Elbe to the Death of Egbert*, 4 vols (London, 1799–1805)

Unwin, Raymond, *Cottage Plans and Common Sense* (London: Fabian Society, 1902)

Vallance, Aymer, *The Life and Work of William Morris* (London: George Bell & Sons, 1897)

Venuti, Lawrence, *The Translator's Invisibility: A History of Translation* (London: Routledge, 1995)

Vergo, Peter, ed., *The New Museology* (London: Reaktion Books, 1989)

Vígfússon, Gudbrand and F. York Powell, *Corpus poeticum boreale*, 2 vols (Oxford: Clarendon Press, 1883)

Waithe, Marcus, 'The Stranger at the Gate: Privacy, Property, and the Structures of Welcome at William Morris's Red House', *Victorian Studies*, 46 (Summer 2004), 4, 567–95

——, 'The Laws of Hospitality: Liberty, Generosity, and the Limits of Dissent in William Morris's *The Tables Turned* and *News from Nowhere*', *The Yearbook of English Studies*, 36 (2006), 2, 217–35

——, '*News from Nowhere*, Utopia and Bakhtin's Idyllic Chronotope', *Textual Practice*, 16 (Winter 2002), 3, 459–72

Ward, Stephen V., ed., *The Garden City: Past, Present and Future* (London: E. & F. N. Spon, 1992)

Watkinson, Raymond, *William Morris as Designer* (London: Studio Vista, 1967)

Watt, William, *Poems, on Sacred and Other Subjects; and Songs, Humorous and Sentimental*, 3rd edn (Glasgow: William Eadie & Co, 1860)

Wawn, Andrew, *The Vikings and the Victorians: Inventing the Old North in Nineteenth-Century Britain* (Cambridge: D. S. Brewer, 2000)

Weaver, Lawrence, *Small Country Houses of To-Day* (Woodbridge, Suffolk: Baron Publishing, 1983)

Weinroth, Michelle, *Reclaiming William Morris: Englishness, Sublimity and the Rhetoric of Dissent* (Montreal: McGill-Queen's University Press, 1996)

Wells, H. G., *A Modern Utopia* (London: Chapman & Hall, 1905)

——, *When the Sleeper Awakes* (Leipzig: Bernard Tauchnitz, 1899)

——, *The Door in the Wall, and other Stories* (London: Grant Richards, 1911)

——, *The Time Machine: An Invention* (London: Heinemann, 1895)

Wiener, Martin J., *English Culture and the Decline of the Industrial Spirit, 1850–1980* (Cambridge: Cambridge University Press, 1981)

Wilbrandt, Conrad, *Mr. East's Experiences in Mr. Bellamy's World* (New York: Harper & Bros, 1891)

Wilde, Oscar, *Aristotle at Afternoon Tea: The Rare Oscar Wilde*, ed. by John Wyse Jackson (London: Fourth Estate, 1991)

——, *The Artist as Critic: Critical Writings of Oscar Wilde*, ed. by Richard Ellmann (London: W. H. Allen, 1970)

[Wilde, Oscar], 'Mr. Morris's Completion of the Odyssey', *Pall Mall Gazette*, 24 November 1887, p. 3.

Wilding, Michael, *Political Fictions* (London: Routledge & Kegan Paul, 1980)

Wilmer, Clive, 'Ruskin, Morris and Medievalism' (Mikimoto Memorial Ruskin Lecture, Lancaster University, 1996)

——, 'Maundering Medievalism: Dante Gabriel Rossetti and William Morris's Poetry', *P. N. Review*, 29 (January–February 2003), 3, 69–73

——, 'The Names of the Roses: Modernity and Archaism in William Morris's *The Earthly Paradise*', *Times Literary Supplement*, 6 June 2003, pp. 3–4

Wordsworth, William, *The Poetical Works of William Wordsworth*, ed. by E. de Selincourt and Helen Darbishire, 5 vols (Oxford: Clarendon Press, 1972)

Zamyatin, Yevgeny, *We*, trans. by Clarence Brown (Harmondsworth: Penguin Books, 1993)

D. S. Brewer

P O Box 9 Woodbridge
Suffolk IP12 3DF

Telephone 01394 610600; fax 01394 610316
Bank account: sort code 12-16-39; account 00157309
Giro account: 237 6156
VAT registration no: GB 102 7864 81

Account code T70130

CHARGE TO:

Prof. Marian Shaw / Reviews
TENNYSON RESEARCH BULLETIN
11 Kingston Court
Kingston Fields
KINGSTON ON SOAR
Notts
NG11 0DL
U K

DELIVERY TO:

REVIEW COPIES

Invoice number   260752
Date   17/1/2006

Your order reference	Quantity	ISBN	Title	Price	Discount	Total

Titles to be supplied

Review   1   **18384 088X William Morris' Utopia of Strangers**
Series: English Association Studies Volume: 1

Published price: £50.00 /$85.00   Publication date 19/10/2006

This title is sent for review. We would be grateful for two copies of any review that may appear

Please quote the full title as follows:

William Morris's Utopia of Strangers
Victorian Medievalism and the Ideal of Hospitality

Siôn –
When required, cd yr pleace send yr reviews to
the Wright, ltd reviews editor;
Jane. Wright @ bristl. ac. vlc

Thanks!
[signature]

INDEX

211